D1437305

BEATRICE WEBB'S DIARIES

The Earlier Life of Beatrice Webb

My Apprenticeship, (to 1892)

Our Partnership, (1892–1911)
   Edited by Barbara Drake and Margaret I. Cole

BEATRICE WEBB'S DIARIES
1912 - 1924

Edited by
MARGARET I. COLE

With an Introduction by the
RT. HON. LORD BEVERIDGE

1724

LONGMANS, GREEN AND CO

LONDON   NEW YORK   TORONTO

LONGMANS, GREEN AND CO LTD
6 & 7 CLIFFORD STREET LONDON W1
ALSO AT MELBOURNE AND CAPE TOWN

LONGMANS, GREEN AND CO INC
55 FIFTH AVENUE NEW YORK 3

LONGMANS, GREEN AND CO
215 VICTORIA STREET TORONTO 1

ORIENT LONGMANS LTD
BOMBAY CALCUTTA MADRAS

First published 1952

PRINTED IN GREAT BRITAIN
BY WESTERN PRINTING SERVICES LTD., BRISTOL

INTRODUCTION
by Lord Beveridge

BRITAIN to-day would have been very different from what it is if there had been no Sidney and Beatrice Webb. For more than fifty years they were a ferment in society, bringing new ideas to men's minds, bringing new organisations and institutions to birth.

In the field of ideas their most important single contribution is the conception of a national minimum of income, health, housing, leisure, education and so on, below which no one should be allowed to fall. In a diary entry made in 1903 Beatrice set out this idea as follows:

> Our general social policy is to construct a base to society in the form of a legally enforced "minimum standard of life", and to develop all forms of shooting upwards—whether of individuals or of discoveries and refinements.[1]

On the side of income, the early applications of this idea were made through trade unionism and minimum wage legislation. The plan of social security embodied in the Beveridge Report is a later application of the idea of a minimum income to times of not working, though the method proposed, of contributory insurance, comes from another source—Lloyd George in 1911.

In the field of organisations and institutions their most fruitful creation is the Fabian Society; with Bernard Shaw, Graham Wallas, and Sydney Olivier, Sidney Webb was one of its effective founders and continued to be its guiding spirit for years after these other pioneers became absorbed in fresh interests; at the General Election of 1945, more than 200 of the 394 Labour members returned to Parliament were Fabians.

But the national minimum idea and the Fabian Society are two contributions only to the ordered progress for which the Webbs worked unceasingly. In the field of ideas,

[1] *Our Partnership* p. 272.

for instance, there was the conception of economics as an inductive science, with other social sciences equally to be based on collection and analysis of facts, generalisation, and verification by facts; the London School of Economics and Political Science, founded in 1895 as the largest single adventure of the Webb partnership, embodied this idea; it continued to be Sidney's favourite child. It was one only of a large and varied family of creations: the Technical Education Board of London in 1892; the new constitution, with R. B. Haldane, of the University of London in 1897; the Imperial College of Science and Technology for which, under the name of the "Charlottenburg" scheme Sidney worked with Haldane and for which he got through a large grant from the Technical Education Board in 1903, "having drafted a careful report";[1] the *New Statesman* of 1912; the effective organisation, with Arthur Henderson from 1917 onwards, of an independent Labour Party. With these practical activities, came a constant stream of books, small and large, from the *History of Trade Unionism* in 1894 to *Soviet Communism: A New Civilization* in 1935. There came recurrently the drafting of reports, sometimes Majority and more often Minority Reports, sometimes openly and more often under the counter, for Royal Commissions, official and other Committees, Conferences, Congresses and so on. Beginning with the Minority Report of the Royal Commission on Labour, advocating a legal eight-hour day in 1894 and the Minority Report of the Royal Commission on the Aged Poor in 1895, this type of activity reached its climax in the Minority Report of the Royal Commission of 1905-9 on the Poor Laws and Relief of Distress, a Report signed by Beatrice Webb and three other members of the Commission, but physically written mainly by Sidney.

The Webbs did much to make Britain as we know it to-day. It is of absorbing interest to learn how they did this, almost wholly without official position or power. Fortunately one of the partnership recorded its inner workings continually in her Diaries. She used these Diaries to make a history of the partnership till about 1910, when the

[1] *Our Partnership* p. 271.

campaign for the break-up of the Poor Law reached its height. In the present volume the story is continued in a less formal way by the Diaries themselves from 1912 to 1924.

The first entry printed in this volume deals with the Newport Trade Union Congress which the Webbs attended as one of their earliest public activities on return from their Far Eastern tour; the diarist notes acceptance by the mass of Trade Unionists of the doctrine of a National Minimum —the principal Webb contribution to social thought. The last entry deals with the formation of the first Labour Government, an achievement for which the Webb partnership had worked recurrently for thirty years. Between these two milestones of progress towards the Webb aims lie the First World War and the beginning of the dreary aftermath of desolation and defeated idealism which followed the war.

It may be that the second achievement, of establishing a Labour Government so early as 1924, was itself a product of the war; it was the war and the election that followed which destroyed the Liberal Party. The Diaries for 1919 open with an interesting comparison apposite to this point:

The British General Election of 1918 seems to be curiously analogous to the German General Election of 1871. Lloyd George, like Bismarck, appealed to an enormously enlarged electorate after a dramatic national victory for unconditional support—for a Parliament without an organised opposition. In both cases the most powerful party prior to the war had been a Liberal Party which during the war had patriotically supported the war. In both cases there had been a small Socialist minority that had opposed the war. Bismarck's election swept away the National Liberal Party and started a Social Democratic Party on a career which ended in its becoming, in the course of thirty or forty years, the most powerful political party in the German Empire. The Parliamentary revolution in Britain has been far more complete. The Liberal Party which had for years governed the Empire has been reduced to an insignificant fraction, with all its leaders without exception at the bottom of the poll. The Labour Party has doubled its numbers and polled one-fourth of the entire voting electorate. It is now "His Majesty's Opposition" or claims to be in that position.

But though world war and its aftermath may have hastened realisation of one aim of the Webbs, their other and more important aim of non-revolutionary progress suffered check. World wars have substituted revolution and counter-revolution for Fabian persuasion as the instrument of change.

In the war of 1914–18 covered by these Diaries the Webbs themselves had little influence on public affairs. Thus on June 1st 1916 the diary records:

> Except for the nightmare of the war, we have had an unusually peaceful time of leisurely but persistent work of one kind or another. Sometimes I have felt hurt that Sidney has not been called upon by the Government to do work of national importance. He has been curiously ignored by the rulers of the world, though constantly consulted by the underlings of Government Departments and the lesser lights of the Labour Movement. Within the Labour Party he has a certain influence and is allowed to draft manifestoes, bills, questions in Parliament, resolutions for conferences, and meetings for other people to gather. . . . But the inner ring of pro-war Labour men exclude him from their counsels, whilst his pro-war opinions exclude him from the pacifist movement. He has been exceptionally well and happy, directing the work of the Research Department and writing a book on *How to Pay for the War*, and helping with anything I have in hand.

Of herself at the beginning of 1917 Beatrice tells that she has bought a small typewriter and is copying out and editing MSS. diaries, so as to make a Book of her Life.

> It is no more tiring than endless reading, hardly more so than my desperate attempt at Longfords to knit soldiers' socks. And it is more interesting than either, and perhaps more useful. . . . Also I shall add notes about persons and events while I still have memory and judgment.

It was only with the second Coalition Government under Lloyd George in 1917 that the Webbs came back into the official circle—for the Reconstruction Committee and post-war problems, rather than for the war itself. "Yes, we will have one of the Webbs," said Lloyd George. "Mrs. Webb, I think. . . . Webb will be angry, Mrs. Webb won't."

But Beatrice joined the Reconstruction Committee from a sense of duty rather than of choice:

> I feel old and weak and if I had not Sidney to inspire and help me I should think I had made a mistake in joining the Committee.

The life I should enjoy, at present, would be a comfortable, small country house, noiseless, except for birds and the rustling of water and wind—with my diaries to type. Sidney meanwhile might complete those endless volumes of historical material which are almost finished, and the two of us together might write the two books we want to bring about before we die—*What is Socialism?* and *Methods of Investigation.* But the *New Statesman* and this new Reconstruction Committee are going to keep us in London, with its noise and its dirt and its constant overstrain of nervous strength and consequent sleeplessness. . . . I am in my sixtieth year—if it were not for the war I have a right to retire. Until the war is over I suppose Sidney and I ought to render national service. . . . (March 1917.)

New Statesman affairs, with the strains between the first editor Clifford Sharp and one of the co-founders Bernard Shaw, are a recurrent theme of the Diaries. The Reconstruction Committee, after two months' trial, appeared to be "not a satisfactory creation".

The essential requirement is one big brain at the top. Sidney and I think the best man available is Winston Churchill.

This is dated June 3rd. Within a few weeks Winston Churchill was called back from availability, that is, unemployment, to take charge of the Ministry of Munitions. In his own words, not being allowed to wage war he was set to making the instruments of war. He could never have been an enthusiastic Minister of Reconstruction. With other Government changes on June 18th, 1917, "Exit the Reconstruction Committee".

The Webbs in the First World War were mainly in retirement, only occasionally called to the centre of affairs. But in one way or another they met many of the decisive personalities of the day. And by making notes on persons and events, as she said, while she still had memory and judgment, Beatrice did work for posterity more important than any work of a Reconstruction Committee. It is above all her pen pictures of persons that make the Diaries so readable.

There is John Morley in 1919 "an echo from the past. The catastrophe of the Great War has compelled his pacifist soul to seek comradeship in the International Socialist movement."

There is Robert Morant, dying in March 1920, "the one man of genius in the Civil Service . . . a strange mortal, not altogether sane".

There is Oswald Mosley in 1923 "the most brilliant man in the House of Commons", but with so much apparent perfection, the question is asked, "is there some weak spot that will be revealed in a time of stress?"

There is George Lansbury in 1920 with "his strange combination of mystical love for men and an impatient iconoclastic fervour against all existing institutions".

There is Tawney, "the great success" of the Sankey Commission on Coal with "his personal charm, his quiet wisdom, and his rapier-like intellect".

There is Mary Macarthur, just told by a surgeon that she had only a few months to live, and telling Beatrice how when she and her husband, Will Anderson, had walked away from an earlier meeting with the Webbs, they had said to one another, "How dreadful it will be for whichever of the Webbs survives the other." "Now," said Mary Macarthur, "neither Will nor I are going to survive either of you."

There is a luncheon party with Rabindranath Tagore with his "quite obvious dislike for all that the Webbs stand for".

There is Graham Wallas, "an encouraging example of a markedly good man who is also according to his own desires, a markedly successful man with a fully satisfied conscience combined with a pleasing consciousness of public appreciation".

There is in April 1916 a "painful luncheon party, Mrs. Green and the Bernard Shaws to consult about the tragic plight of Roger Casement". Shaw refused to produce any money for legal defence of Casement, offering instead to write his dying speech "to thunder down the ages". "A world made up of Bernard Shaws would be a world in moral dissolution". So the diarist concludes in April. But in September, at the Fabian Summer School, "G.B.S. was at his best—witty, wise and outstandingly good-natured".

Lloyd George naturally makes many appearances, often at lunch or at dinner, as with Haldane in March 1918 to discuss with the Webbs the Machinery of Government, or in February 1919 to discuss the constitution of the proposed Commission on Coal Mines. The Webbs and Lloyd George were almost always in opposition to one another yet "he and we talked with the intimacy of old friends—it is impossible to do otherwise with Lloyd George". Perhaps the most entertaining of these meetings comes earlier (in 1912)—a picture of Lloyd George and Herbert Samuel in the foyer during an interval in *Parsifal*, heatedly discussing with the Webbs amid a growing circle of bystanders, the excessive sickness of married women under the National Insurance Act of 1911. The accessibility of Lloyd George, even as war Prime Minister, to people with whom he did not agree, was one of his greatest assets.

Arthur Henderson, too, appears often, for with him Sidney had much to do. On him, after contemporary notice of his dismissal by Lloyd George in August 1917, after the Stockholm Conference, a later footnote is added exceptionally in May 1918. "We none of us realised the enormous importance of Henderson's ejection from the Cabinet. He came out of the Cabinet with a veritable hatred of Lloyd George. . . . From that day, Henderson determined to create an independent political party, capable of becoming H.M. Government—and he turned to Sidney to help him." Two years later, in 1920, appears one secret of Henderson's achievement. He is "the only Labour man who considers the welfare of the party as a whole, and who is willing to work within any group within it without considering just who is to be leader".

There is Ramsay MacDonald in 1914 "the Parnell of the Labour Party—but a Parnell who does not believe in his cause"; there is that "lost soul" C. F. G. Masterman; there is Edward Grey "an incarnation of negative goodness"; there is R. B. Haldane, after his dismissal in May 1915; there are George Barnes, J. H. Thomas, J. R. Clynes, Robert Smillie, Litvinoff, Kameneff, Krassin, and many more all neatly characterised.

These are extracts from a few only of the portraits which Beatrice etched in, with care, often at some length. They must be read in full.

There are pen portraits also of conferences, organisations, and institutions, and many outspoken criticisms.

There is, for instance, on December 7th, 1916, "a dismal day for the Labour Party", a highly critical account of the Labour Party Executive in action dealing with Lloyd George's offer of posts in his Coalition Government. Sidney was against acceptance, but the offer was accepted by 18 votes to 12, with the miners abstaining because they had no instructions.

> It is very difficult to analyse the state of mind of these men. The prospect of six offices with an aggregate income of some £16,000 a year, to be distributed among 18 persons is a big temptation. . . . But I don't believe that this pecuniary motive was dominant in the minds of the eighteen who voted for accepting office. A thorough beating of the Germans may have passed through their minds. But their main motive—at any rate the motive of which they are individually and collectively most conscious—is the illusion that the mere presence of Labour men in the Government, apart from anything they may do or prevent being done, is in itself a sign of democratic progress. . . . "They are a hopeless lot," sighed Sidney, as he turned with a contented smile to his morning's work. "We are in for some strange events this coming year—let us get on with our work while we can."

There are numerous intriguing references to Russia. Thus in 1918 the negotiations proceeding between Germany and Russia at Brest-Litovsk produce the following comment:

> The Prussian devil believes in security at home and violence outside. The Bolshevik believes, or thinks he believes, in law between nations whilst preaching violence to bring about the state of society desired by the militant minority of the proletariat within each community.

To some observers to-day, the Bolshevik also has proved his satanic quality by readiness for violence at home as well as abroad.

In 1920, Soviet Russia has become "the Servile State in being". This is developed in the same year, in an intriguing critical account of Kameneff and Krassin at the Fabian Summer School at Godalming:

This realisation that the Soviet Government was in fact an oligarchy made up of the hired workmen of the towns governing a nation of peasant proprietors was certainly unexpected, at any rate to me. . . . Personal freedom, whether in the production or the consumption of commodities, had to be suspended until Russia had conquered her enemies and reconstructed her economic life. In the minds of many of the audience the question arose "How would it be possible to depose from power these three castes, the elders and leaders of the Communist faith, the scientific experts and the town workmen, not to mention the two castes not referred to —the Red Army and the Secret Police—when the need for this autocratic Government had disappeared with Russia's enemies? "The re-establishment of a caste system—a very natural impulse in an Asiatic race", remarked the Belgian Socialist Minister, with a grin and a shrug of his broad shoulders.

How to get rid of dictators, whether in Spain or in Russia, when the pretext for them has vanished! That is still the question to-day. Perhaps the practical answer for Russia is that Russia will not be allowed by her rulers to want for apparent enemies, so long as fear of enemies abroad can be used to support their personal power at home. The pretext will be preserved to preserve the dictators.

When the Diaries of 1918 and 1920 were being written the last great adventure of the partnership—to discover in Russia "Soviet Communism as a New Civilization"—was still ten years and more ahead. One of my later personal recollections of Beatrice was at Bournemouth after this adventure, when she dwelt on the joy of being able to accept new ideas, and abandon old views for new ones. I had to confess that in the matter of Soviet Communism I was less open-minded than she was. I still preferred the early Fabian view of Marx to the new one.

Of Trade Union leaders the joint author of the *History of Trade Unionism* has many almost savage things to say:

The Trade Union movement has become, like the hereditary peerage, an avenue to political power through which stupid untrained persons may pass up to the highest office if only they have secured the suffrages of the members of a large union. One wonders when able rascals will discover this open door to remunerative power.

This, in June 1917, is only one of several passages of like tenor.

Yet she is able also to record one delightful picture of relation with trade unionists, arising from the unanimous selection of Sidney as Parliamentary candidate by Seaham Divisional Labour Party, against the views of the Durham miners as a whole.

There is a strange irony in these simple-minded miners, living in a remote backwater seeking out and persistently pressing into their service the most astute and subtle, and be it added, the least popular leader of the Labour and Socialist movement. The explanation is that the leading men in these isolated pit villages are readers of books, and not hearers of revivalist speeches and propagandist lectures.

The bookish miners got for themselves, and were glad to get, a bookish representative in Parliament.

The miners from the first treated him as their "property"; the serious ones regarded him as their local preacher, and the younger ones as their "professional" football player whom they had acquired at a high price and had to look after. (November 1922.)

The Diaries are fascinating for their picturing of events, organisations, and persons. The core of their interest lies in their revelation of the Webb partnership—of Sidney the incurable optimist, of Beatrice with her ups and downs, her felt need for a religion, her family ties.

The achievement of the Webbs is an outstanding product of aristocratic devotion to a purpose. The scale of this achievement was made possible by the luck of their ideal companionship together. It was made possible by Beatrice Webb's possession of assured means. It was made possible by two qualities of the Webbs familiar to those who worked with them but not perhaps to outsiders—their practicality and their freedom from creators' vanity. It was made possible finally by deliberate concentration and exclusion of all things irrelevant to the purpose.

One of the earliest extracts relating to the foundation of the *New Statesman* recalls to my mind a week-end, which just at that time I spent at Beachy Head, where the Webbs were in conference on this project. The week-end included a long walk with Beatrice under Beachy Head, in which, the *New Machiavelli* having recently been published, she dwelt with perfect good humour upon what Wells had said of her, and particularly that she was "lacking in muliebrity". This brought to my mind some of the other characters who figure in the *New Machiavelli*, and I asked Beatrice whether she had recently seen anything of some of them known also to me. Her answer was, "No, I see nothing now of the T's. There is nothing at which we are working in common, and I cannot afford the time for purely social intercourse." I thought at the time that this was somewhat inhuman, that one ought not to choose one's friends for what one could get out of them, any more than one ought to read books merely for the purpose of using them as material for writing oneself. But there is a phrase in the Diaries just at this point which makes me see that my own judgment then was unduly youthful in its harshness. "It is remarkable how limited one's circle becomes when one is at once elderly and hard-working." This is the disarming explanation of what Beatrice said to me beneath Beachy Head.

The two other personal qualities of the Webbs named above, their practicality and their freedom from creators' vanity, were even more important than their concentration. Both were illustrated in the founding of the *New Statesman* and in the free hand which they left to all the successive editors. But the *New Statesman* was only one illustration of these qualities. They appeared most conspicuously in the greatest Webb creation of all, the London School of Economics and Political Science. Having founded the School they left it under successive Directors to develop as an entity in itself. And, whether it developed just as they wished or not, they remained equally ready to give any help that was wanted, on large schemes or on practical details.

Beatrice herself was fully aware of how much her and Sidney's work owed to freedom from financial cares. This awareness leads to a prophetic remark when, after an illness, she was staying in an hotel at Margate in November 1916.

One of the highest privileges of the well-to-do is to be able to live in comfort and perfect health conditions when they are ill. Shall we have the wit to communalise this advantage? It would mean not only the necessary national expenditure but also all sorts of precautions against malingering. How do I know that I am not malingering?

Have we by 1951 had the wit in the National Health Service to communalise wisely the advantage formerly limited to the well-to-do?

Beatrice, in contrast to Sidney, had a felt need for religion, though like him she was in the last resort an optimist.

As I near the end of my life (this is in September 1920 with another twenty-three years ahead of her) I become more contemptuous of cynicism, more convinced that what we know as "goodness" is in accordance with "the nature of things". Looking back on my own failures and humiliations, they nearly all arose from a strain of worldliness or cynicism, a lack of scrupulousness in my manner of life, a giving away to personal vanity and vulgar egotism and all the petty lying that this vanity and egotism entails. The great sources of my happiness, my work and my marriage to Sidney, sprang straight out of a religious purpose, an ideal end, not for myself but for the world of men.

Sidney was an optimist, without religion and without important ties other than those with Beatrice:

Life to him is not "one d—d" but one pleasant job "after another" and his attitude is one of continuous gratitude for his good luck. He is ridiculously happy.

He was an optimist about the war in 1915. "The Great War will seem to future generations a landmark of progress." He remained an optimist in 1919 even about the peace terms of Versailles which to Beatrice seemed "hard and brutal".

One could go on quoting these Diaries for ever without exhausting them. But they are for reading as a whole. They are there for constant and repeated reading and for dipping into again and again.

Those who read them will be divided by age into two main groups. There will be those old enough to have been managing their own affairs and active in public affairs before 1914. There will be those to whom all that happened before 1914 and perhaps much that has happened later is a matter of history and hearsay rather than experience.

To the first group, to have the feelings, fears, hopes, and personalities of the years from 1912 to 1924 recalled by the Diaries of Beatrice Webb is a poignant experience. Continually as one reads comes the need to remind oneself that all this relates only to the First World War, its eve and its aftermath, that since then there has been a Second World War with the same exaltations and agonies endured by man's unconquerable mind. Since then too there has been, and continues to be, over a large part of the world, a concerted totalitarian design to show that man's mind, after all, is not unconquerable, that human beings in the mass can be made to think what one man or a handful of men will for them, that if this handful want continuing power for themselves even at the cost of war a Third World War will come. All that men have suffered in the generation since 1914 may not have been enough to bring peace to the world, as it has not brought freedom.

Almost as poignant to this first group of readers will be the realisation of their own age—and of the second younger group. Half the people now alive in the world were not born or were children when the First World War began. Half the people now alive have not known by effective experience the world before 1914, a world which, with all its injustices and evils, was in two ways better than the world is to-day. It was a world of many personal liberties now denied or diminished; Britons of my own age know what so many younger people have never known—what it was to travel freely everywhere without passports or visas or restrictions on currency, to buy without coupons from any shop one preferred, to build a house or start a business or place a lorry on the road if one so desired without a permit. It was a world in which peace rather than war and preparation for war appeared the normal state; there had been no general war for a hundred years; there had never been any total war at all.

This aspect of the past is not that which stands out most clearly in the Diaries. Yet it is the aspect which makes study of the world before total war most necessary, for those who did not know it by experience. For while fear of total war remains, the reforming movement typified by the Webbs is halted.

The Diaries are to be read less for this than for their light on human nature. They are essentially personal material. They fail to mention many major events, such as the entry of the United States into the war in April 1917, or to record any reaction to this event. They are not a full picture even of Partnership activities falling within the period. The School of Economics is noticed from time to time as Sidney's dearest child, flourishing and growing and becoming independent of him. But the conversion of the School of Economics from being a small to a large institution at the end of the First World War, and the Sir Ernest Cassel Foundation in early 1919 leading to the establishment of a Commerce Faculty and Degree are not mentioned at all, though the direction of this munificence of Sir Ernest Cassel to educational purposes was unquestionably given by Sidney Webb.

The Diaries are not a complete or balanced picture of the time and were never so intended. They are, on the other hand, a contribution of outstanding value to our power of understanding ourselves and our affairs. They show in the intimate frank detail how things get done, or do not get done; how men in public life behave to one another; how they should and should not behave. They have two simple morals. The first moral is of how largely achievement in public affairs depends upon selflessness, on winning confidence of others by freedom from personal ambition. The second moral is of how much happiness depends on work in the right companionship, how easy above all it is for those to be happy whose work lies in themselves, and does not depend on the favour either of princes or of populace.

CONTENTS

PLATES

EDITORIAL NOTE

THE last Diary extract in *Our Partnership*, the second part of Beatrice Webb's autobiography, is dated June 3rd, 1911. Shortly after that, the Webbs set off on a nine-months' tour of the world, the record of which is set out in a very long typed document which from stylistic and other indications appears to have been almost entirely written by Sidney. Beatrice's personal journal begins again in September 1912, and continues until ten days before her death; the present volume covers the period from September 1912 until the formation of the first Labour Government in February 1924.

It is not, of course, in any sense *Our Partnership*, Volume II. For in that book, and still more in its predecessor, *My Apprenticeship*, Beatrice Webb used her journal as contemporary illustration to her own story of her own times, the extracts being separated—and explained—by essays upon English social history and developments of the day such as the London County Council, education in London, and the Royal Commission on the Poor Laws. It would be impossible—and impertinent to try—to produce a comparable volume after her death: this book, therefore, consists almost entirely of entries from the Diaries themselves, the brief essays prefacing the two parts being designed merely as introductory matter to recall to students the general conditions of the time in which they were written. The notes, which have been kept as brief as possible so as to produce a minimum interference with the straight reading of the absorbing text, are intended to serve the same purpose, viz. to identify the persons mentioned or to explain, in the case of the better-known, what was their contemporary position and connection with the Webbs, and to provide a sufficiency of information about movements and historical incidents which many may have forgotten after the lapse of some thirty years. A few notes added at a later stage by

Beatrice herself, are also included for interest and signed with her initials. For the rest, the Diary is obviously a document of sufficient social and historical importance to stand on its own feet unassisted.

This volume closes at the beginning of 1924. For the selection of this date there is more than one reason. The first is naturally one of length. The full text of the Diaries runs to very great length—as she grew older, Beatrice wrote more and more in her journal; and in order to produce a volume of manageable size without enormous excisions it was necessary to stop at some point or other. This particular date, however, was chosen because in fact it signifies the close of a period in Beatrice's life, that of "Our Partnership" in the strict sense. As readers of the earlier books cannot have failed to note, the Partnership in its heyday was one of work, play, and living all combined, even where the partners were engaged on different public jobs. When Sidney was on the L.C.C., for example, they would still work together in the mornings at the famous dining-table in 41 Grosvenor Road; Beatrice would rest or pursue social avocations while he attended his committees in the afternoon; and in the evening they would discuss their projects or the day's events: similarly when Beatrice was sitting on the Poor Law Commission or any of her other committees this work all fitted into the Webb Design for Living. Nor was the continuity broken, though Beatrice had feared that it would be, when Sidney was elected to Parliament, for in the comparatively leisured Parliament of 1922 a back-bencher did not have to spend his mornings in the House of Commons. But when he became a Cabinet Minister the pattern *was* broken: the mornings of quiet joint writing were gone, nor could a Cabinet Minister discuss Cabinet business, even with his wife. It is true that the first Labour Government lasted less than a year; but the date at which it was formed coincided with Beatrice's decision that she was getting too old for London life and that they must find themselves a retreat in the country. Passfield Corner had been bought in 1923 and thither Beatrice's inclination was tending more and more. Thus, though during 1924— and to a lesser extent in 1929—she dutifully fulfilled the function of a Minister's wife, her heart was less and less in it, and more and more in the writing of her memoirs and the entertainment of guests at Passfield. Only twice during the subsequent years, once for a brief while during 1927–8, when, after Sidney's resignation from the Seaham constituency, they were working on the last volume of their Local Government series, and again during their visit to the U.S.S.R. and the preparation of *Soviet Communism*, did the Partnership come back into working harness. Otherwise, as Beatrice records in the last sentence of the present work, it was a thing of the past, and she a lady in retirement.

The importance of this, from the point of view of the historian, is that from 1924 onwards the nature of the Diaries changes. They are no longer a record of contemporary history, written by one who was taking an active part in its making; they are reflections on life and on the social scene, accompanied by a good measure of personal description and narrative drawn from books and from the conversation of friends and visitors. But they are no longer first-hand evidence, and, though none the less readable and entertaining, they make a different kind of book from those which had gone before; and for this reason, besides the fact that they are naturally concerned more and more with persons who are still alive, it seemed best to stop at the date which Beatrice herself felt to be the close of an epoch.

The volume here presented does not reprint the Diary completely. Some excisions have been inevitable, though as much as possible has been retained. In the first place, as the Diary is an intimate journal, and practically unrevised by its author, certain references to living persons have necessarily been deleted. In the second place, I have tried to follow what, judging from Beatrice's own practice in *Our Partnership*, I believe would have been her own desire in giving her work to the world; that is to say, I have removed, on the one hand, some passages relating to her private feelings, particularly with regard to members of her own family, and, on the other, passages of especial frankness which, though describing persons now dead, would be liable to cause pain to others still living. Beatrice was the last person to have wished to leave behind her printed words which would seem rancorous or might hurt others. Lastly, I have taken out a certain amount of pure repetition; and a very few pieces of narrative in which, either because she was writing from hearsay or for some other reason, she had got her facts so wrong that extensive re-writing would be necessary to correct them. But what has been omitted is, save in a few instances, a whole entry at a time: I have not shortened entries, nor interfered with them; this is a Diary, not "snippets from a Diary". Where, for the reasons given above it has been necessary to omit a sentence or two from a single entry, the lacuna has been indicated; otherwise the entries are printed as they were written.

PREFACE TO PART I
1912-1917

THIS volume of Beatrice Webb's Diaries really covers two
fairly distinct phases in the life of the writer, which are
divided not, as might have been expected, by the end of the
First World War, but by the changes in the nature of the war
itself and by the feelings in people's minds about the war
and the post-war future, which were slowly gathering force
during 1917—particularly after the overthrow of the Czar.
This change in the climate of opinion coincided with a
revival of Beatrice's own health and spirits; and while,
naturally, no specific date can be assigned to it, and the
division has been made, for convenience, at the end of 1917,
the contrast in tone and content between the early entries
and those for the beginning of 1918 is very marked indeed.

The 1912 Diary began at a relatively bad period for the
Partnership. The Webbs had just returned from their
world tour, undertaken after half a dozen years of very hard
work mainly, though by no means wholly, devoted to the
Poor Law Commission and the campaign for the break-up
of the Poor Law so fully chronicled in the later chapters of
Our Partnership. They came back physically refreshed, one
assumes, but to an intellectual and political scene calculated
to depress them. On the issue of the Poor Law, they had
unmistakably failed, first to convince the majority of the
Commissioners, and subsequently, notwithstanding the re-
sounding publicity of the campaign, to force the Asquith
Cabinet to accept the proposals of the Minority Report.
Edwardian England was not ready to swallow even the very
mild dose of the Welfare State suggested in the phrase
"Prevention of Destitution"; it took eighteen years of
continuous unemployment varying only in degree and a
second world war to convince the public mind, and it was
not until 1948 that the last vestiges of the Poor Law finally
disappeared from the Statute Book. Lloyd George and his

C

Insurance Acts had "dished the Webbs" with the promise of ninepence for fourpence: they strongly disliked the Acts and the contributory principle, and were disappointed to find that the bulk of the anti-Poor Law enthusiasts appeared to be satisfied with it, that their mass-following had melted away overnight. Furthermore, the very success of the campaign up to a point had largely alienated their former friends and sympathisers in governing-class circles, as earlier the Liberal Nonconformists of London had been alienated by Sidney's support of rate-aid for denominational education. The hope of old-style "permeation", as described in the earlier chapters of *Our Partnership*, was gone for ever; the Webbs were now dangerous persons, undesirable acquaintances for rising young politicians, while at the same time, as will appear, the unrisen were not ready to trust them. As I have written elsewhere, it was then discovered, not for the first time, that qualities which are admirable in people who agree with you become vices in people who do not; their single-mindedness and steadiness of purpose were termed illiberal pigheadedness and obscurantism, and their efficient planning and grasp of detail became dirty Machiavellian tricks. The sharp and unfriendly satire of Wells's *New Machiavelli* had appeared in 1911.

Cut off by their propagandist campaign from old friends on the Right, they were no happier on the Left. Many years earlier, when they were engaged on the history of Trade Unionism, visiting the Trade Union Congress, and drafting evidence for Trade Union officials to give before the Royal Commission on Labour, Beatrice had toyed with the idea that the Partnership might become "clerks to Labour" in the medieval sense; and that hope was eventually fulfilled—but not in 1912. In 1912 the Parliamentary Labour Party was composed mainly of the stolid and sleepy Trade Unionists who excited Beatrice's intellectual contempt; it was further tied close to the Liberal coat-tails after the inconclusive elections of 1910, and in no mood to be prodded into Socialist paths. It had, it is true, under pressure set up a joint committee with the Independent Labour Party and the Fabian Society; but of that committee Beatrice, as will be seen from the text, had a very low opinion. (This was partly due to dislike of what she regarded as the woolly-minded Utopianism of the I.L.P.; a highly derogatory entry about Keir Hardie in the *Diary* was later withdrawn in her own hand.) The drive and intellectual energy in the Labour Movement in the years immediately preceding the war were to be found, for the most part, in groups which put little faith in Parliamentary debate or Fabian collectivism—Syndicalists, Industrial Unionists, Guild Socialists, militant suffragettes and ardent supporters of Home Rule for Ireland. The Webbs instinctively disliked all these movements, with their appeal to mass-emotions, as much as their promoters disliked the Webbs; but in the frustrated years 1910–14, with the cost of living slowly rising and the Liberal Government apparently unable or unwilling to carry out its promises, their influence was not in the ascendant. 1911–12 saw the Liverpool Dock Strike, the first national railway strike, and the great coal strike; the Webbs came back to find more strikes in transport and other trades, working up to the great thunderclap of the Dublin dispute of 1913.

All this industrial warfare was conducted by leaders who had no use at all for "gradualness", "Fabian intrigue", or slow process of negotiation and conciliation.[1] As a crowning blow they found the new ideas burgeoning within the Fabian Society itself. Just before leaving England, Beatrice had meditated ways and means of using the Fabian Society as a political weapon, permeation having failed and the Labour Party being too poor a thing; but the Fabian Society to which she returned was rent by violent ideological conflict. The Guild Socialists failed by a hair's-breadth to capture the Society itself, but they captured the new Research Committee and enrolled the keenest and most vigorous of the Fabian membership, the dispute being conducted with a great deal of sound and fury. "We are extraordinarily unpopular to-day", Beatrice noted; and she did not possess Sidney's gift of accepting unpopularity with unshaken calm.

On top of this came the war, which the Webbs had no

[1] "Men of tact that arbitrate—slow reform that heals—Save the stinking grease, master, save it for the wheels!" wrote Chesterton in 1911.

more anticipated than had the vast majority of the British people. Fabianism, as Shaw told the Society again and again, was a thoroughly insular movement; the Fabian Society was always glad to welcome distinguished foreigners—and Beatrice compared the intellectual level of foreign Socialists favourably with that of the I.L.P. or the Labour Party— but it took no interest in "foreign affairs"; and though Haldane was a close friend of the Webbs and Grey at least their acquaintance it does not seem that Haldane imparted to them any of his apprehensions about the future of Europe. If he did, Beatrice either did not listen or did not think them of sufficient importance to be mentioned in her Diary. They were thus completely taken by surprise; after the first shock, they accepted the war as a fact, neither "feeling warlike" nor having any sympathy with the anti-war pacifists. But Beatrice, several of whose blood-relatives were soon drawn in, was deeply distressed both by "the going-out of the lights all over Europe" and by the rapid development of mass-slaughter. In the immediate war-situation, she could find little to do, personally or politically, which she regarded as worth-while; and it is significant to note that the Diary until 1917 barely mentions Sidney's work with the War Emergency Workers' National Committee, that first gathering of *all* organisations representing the working classes, which did by 1918 result in the formation of a new Labour Party with a Socialist programme for home affairs, for the colonies, and for the international world, and also built up Sidney as its "clerk" and counsellor; she seems barely interested in it. Under all the circumstances, it is not surprising that the entries in the Diary contain so much of gloom and frustration, or that in 1916 she had a serious breakdown, from which she was only gradually recovering in the following year.

M.I.C.

PART I
1912–1917

SEPTEMBER 1912—DECEMBER 1913

September 5th, 1912. *Newport Trades Union Congress.*—It is now over three months since we got back to England and not a word have I written. It took me at least two months to get over the effect of the tropical climate and perpetual journeyings—my nerves were all to pieces, and waves of depression and panic followed each other. Now I am all right again and in good working form.

I am writing now in the early morning of my third day at the Trades Union Congress. Not substantially different from the Congresses of twenty years ago. The extreme left of those years—the State Socialists—are now on the defensive against the new left—the Syndicalists. The bulk of the delegates are the same solid stupid folk they have always been, mainly occupied with their Trade Union work, their own eating, drinking and smoking, and their family happenings: they take a placid, good-humoured and somewhat contemptuous interest in this or that "new talk"—very much as a city man discusses the new toys that are sold on the pavement, or the members of a congregation listen to the particular theological doctrines of the new preacher. But there is one change of outlook. The ordinary Trade Unionist has got the National Minimum theory well fixed in his slow solid head—it has taken twenty years to mature—but there it stands at last, the substance of his political desire. And I think the idea of nationalising the great Public Services is just emerging out of the shibboleths of a minority into the settled intention of the majority. But here the Syndicalist enters a caveat—the protest of the idealist against what actually happens when services are nationalised and worked by officials having the same assumptions as the ordinary capitalist in respect of remuneration and status of the wage-earner.

October 11th.—Since we returned to London I have been in a whirl of work—a fine mix up of activities—the winding up of the National Committee,[1] the I.L.P. and Fabian campaign on the National Minimum; our own course of lectures on the Control of Industry, and the starting of the Fabian Research Department. In all these enterprises Sidney has been helping by counsel and drafting, by writing Tracts and taking his share of public speaking. Meanwhile

[1] The National Committee for the Prevention of Destitution, which conducted the campaign for the Minority Report on the Poor Law. See *Our Partnership,* Chapter VIII.

he has been finishing, without help from me, the book on Roads,[1] one of the innumerable fragments of our unfinished work.

It is annoying not to be able to complete that big task of historical research to which we devoted so much time and money. But there seems to be a clear call to leadership in the Labour and Socialist Movement to which we feel that we must respond. For that purpose we are starting a new weekly next spring, and the planning out of this organ of Fabianism is largely devolving on Sidney. It is by far the most risky of our present enterprises—we start with a quite insufficient capital: £5,000 (Shaw, Whitley,[2] Harben[3] and Simon[4] each £1,000 and £1,000 more in small sums), without the advice of anyone who understands newspaper production. To the experienced journalist it must seem a mad adventure, and we ourselves hardly expect more than a run for other people's money and our own hard work. But then the London School of Economics did not seem much more promising, and to-day it rolls on majestically from success to success. Sidney has not even troubled to become Chairman again, realising that the School has now a life of its own. He still watches over the growing library and is always on the look-out for new endowments or new opportunities for work.

The Fabian Society, which we found in a state of disruption, has settled down with admirable good temper to the work of research and propaganda. The troublesome Reform Committee,[5] which had got absurdly on the nerves of the old gang, has formally dissolved itself and we are all the best of friends. The Standing Committee of the I.L.P. and Fabian Society is a success and is controlling the policy of the Labour and Socialist movement in this country—in so far as this movement has any policy. What annoys me is the absence of any relation, good or bad, between the Labour M.P.s and the Labour Movement in the country. The Labour M.P.s seem to me to be drifting into futility—a futility that will be presently recognised by all whom it may concern. J. R. MacDonald has ceased to be a Socialist; the Trade Union M.P.s never were Socialists; Snowden is embittered and Lansbury is wild. At present there is no co-operation among the Labour Members themselves nor between them and the Trade Union

[1] *The Story of the King's Highway*, published 1913.

[2] Edward Whitley (d. 1945) Research chemist and Fabian.

[3] Henry Devenish Harben (b. 1874), son of the Chairman of the Prudential; Secretary of a Fabian Committee on Rural Reconstruction.

[4] Lord Simon of Wythenshawe (b. 1879), Chairman of B.B.C. (1947–52), at that date Liberal member of Manchester City Council and supporter of the Webb Poor Law policy.

[5] The Fabian Reform Committee, a group within the Fabian Society led by H. H. Schloesser and Marion Phillips (see p. 85), mainly for the purpose of securing that Fabian electoral support should be confined to candidates who were members of the Labour Party. There was much dispute about this point for a year or more; but finally the broader view prevailed.

leaders. We personally have no relations either with the Parliamentary Party, or with the Trade Union or Co-operative Movements; our only connections are with the I.L.P. branches and individual Fabians throughout the country. All the Labour Members seem to me to have become cynics except Lansbury, who has become a raging revivalist preacher of general upheaval. All one can do is to go steadily forward without considering the likelihood of results.

December 1st. Clifton. St. Vincent's Hotel.—Down here for a conference and public meeting on "War against Poverty", an afternoon P.S.A.[1] on Syndicalism and a Free Church Council Meeting at Bath on the National Minimum. I came down exhausted, but the isolation from work in this pleasant and quiet hotel has counterbalanced the fatigue of speaking. The conference was successful; about 150 delegates from Trade Unions and socialist societies. The majority of these men were silent, they passed the resolutions, listening attentively to what was said: whether they understood the issues or were really in favour of the resolutions, I do not know. There are backwaters in these men's minds: fear that a particular mine or factory will be shut up by an increased wage, fear that shortening of hours will result in lessened wage, distrust in the capacity of the working man to govern anything, real admiration for the "Boss" just because he is "Boss", pious anxiety that religion and morality may be threatened, hereditary loyalty to the Tory or Liberal cause. All these doubts and hesitations may not give them sufficient conviction to speak or vote against resolutions at working-class meetings, but it prevents them from joining in any vigorous action on behalf of the policy. The majority of the Bristol delegates were, I believe, Liberals; they showed no approval of abuse of the Liberal Government and in their hearts they acquiesced in the Insurance Act, though they passed a resolution for its drastic amendment. There were a little knot of extreme Socialists and Syndicalists, who wanted to tack on or substitute the usual class-conscious revolutionary resolution. As a compromise I drafted a socialist declaration to wind up the meeting and the whole conference voted for it, after they had altered the word nationalisation to socialisation at the request of the Syndicalists.

Syndicalism has taken the place of the old-fashioned Marxism. The angry youth, with bad complexion, frowning brow and weedy figure, is now always a Syndicalist; the glib young workman whose tongue runs away with him to-day mouths the phrases of French Syndicalism instead of those of German Social Democracy. The inexperienced middle class idealist has accepted with avidity the ideal of the Syn-

[1] Pleasant Sunday Afternoon. A Nonconformist invention to describe spending Sunday in a "brief, bright, brotherly" gathering.

dicalist as a new and exciting Utopia. But to the Trade Union organiser or to the Labour Member of a municipal council, Syndicalism appears a fantastic dream barely worth considering. So far as we can foresee, Syndicalism will disrupt the B.S.P.,[1] it will detach some of the branches of the I.L.P. and some impatient Fabians; it will increase discontent with the Labour Party—but it will have no appreciable effect on the larger currents of Trade Unionism.

* * * * *

The plain fact is that Lloyd George and the Radicals have out-trumped the Labour Party. They have dealt out millions of public money, they have taken up semi-socialist devices like compulsory insurance, which cannot be easily opposed even by the Conservative Party. By no other measure could twenty-five millions have been raised and spent on sickness. The fact that it will be wastefully collected and wastefully spent may condemn it to the thoughtful Socialist or to the economical-minded citizen—but to the ordinary elector it makes no difference since he is too dull witted to understand that it will be so. And given the fact that the money could not be got otherwise there is much to be said for the acceptance of the scheme by the Labour Party, especially as they had not the wit to offer an alternative. Who cares that a large part of the Workmen's Compensation fund is wasted, that industry is heavily taxed without benefiting the injured or their dependants?

But we must make the best of the Insurance Act, and use to the full all its incidental advantages—it is something to have got the whole of the working population registered from the age of 16; it is a step forward to have some sort of machinery for paying out weekly pensions to the sick and invalided without the stigma of pauperism, and the statistics of illness automatically collected will be of great value. The big fault of the Act is the creation of huge vested interests—the Industrial Insurance Companies' method of collection and the Panel System of medical attendance. These vested interests mean not only waste of public money and financial chaos in the relative insolvency of the different societies, but wholesale demoralisation of character through the fraudulent withholding or the fraudulent getting of benefits. Trade Unions will be turned into great Insurance Societies, and their leading men, already too much distracted by politics, will be further diverted from their special work by being made responsible for the technique of insurance. It would be far better if the Co-operative

[1] British Socialist Party. Formed in 1909 by fusion of Hyndman's Social Democratic Federation with part of the I.L.P. After the outbreak of war, Hyndman's group again seceded owing to the anti-war stand of the B.S.P.; in 1920 the latter became the nucleus of the Communist Party of Great Britain.

Movement undertook all insurance and the Trade Union leaders devoted themselves to their function of securing good conditions of employment. With Trade Unions as associations of consumers (of insurance benefits) there will be some unedifying disputes with their new staffs of calculators and clerks!

Xmas 1912. *Weymouth.*—Gaining strength and energy for the next year's work, walking from ten to fifteen miles a day, with a day's rest now and again. C. M. Lloyd[1] and his young wife with us. Long days in the sea air, even if it be in wind and rain, too tired to think and not too tired to sleep, is the best of recreations.

Our plans for the coming year are already cut, I will not say dried —they are still moist with uncertainty as to detail. First there is the starting of the *New Statesman*. During the next three months we have to get, by circularisation, a large number of postal subscribers; if we can get 2,000 the success of the paper is secured; if we get only 500 it is extremely doubtful whether it can survive two years. Then Sidney and I have to contribute the long series of articles on "What is Socialism?" We have also to help Sharp[2] to get other contributors.

Secondly, we have to complete the Enquiry into the Control of Industry and draft the report, probably as a supplement to the *Statesman*. I don't feel anxious about this seemingly gigantic task—we could write the report now; and getting the new material is largely a method of educating our young people. Finally, I have to take my share in organising the next I.L.P. and Fabian campaign, a difficult business as the Labour M.P.s are stupid, suspicious and timid, and we have to work with them. There are lectures to be given at Cambridge, Edinburgh and Glasgow—the remainder from last autumn's campaign. And if there is energy left over we have to complete the eighteenth-century books on Local Government. A formidable programme.

Sanders,[3] Schloesser,[4] Anderson,[5] Johnson[6] and I had an important interview with a committee of the Labour M.P.s (Parker,[7] Snowden,

---

[1] Charles Mostyn Lloyd (1878–1946). Assistant Secretary to the National Committee for the Prevention of Destitution, later foreign editor of the *New Statesman* and head of the Ratan Tata Foundation, London School of Economics.

[2] Clifford Dyce Sharp (1883–1935). Editor of *The Crusade* and then of the *New Statesman*, 1913–31.

[3] William Stephen Sanders (1877–1942). Fabian travelling lecturer and General Secretary of the Society, 1914–20.

[4] Schloesser, Henry (Lord Slesser, b. 1883). Then member of Fabian Executive and of Fabian Reform Committee.

[5] William C. Anderson (1878–1919). I.L.P. Member of Parliament, 1914–18; husband of Mary Macarthur.

[6] Francis Johnson (b. 1878). Secretary of the I.L.P.,, 1904–23.

[7] James Parker (1863–1948). I.L.P. organiser. M.P. for Halifax, 1906; Coalition Government Whip, 1917.

Richards,[1] O'Grady[2] and Henderson[3]) about promoting bills embodying the "War against Poverty" campaign, and deciding on the subject for next autumn's propaganda. Parker is a feeble creature, acting as MacDonald's deputy during the latter's absence in India: he was much concerned lest we should "rouse expectations" which could not be fulfilled. "Surely," I suggested, "to rouse expectations is the business of Socialists, expectations which would not otherwise but ought to be fulfilled." Henderson tried to bully and talked about "irresponsible agitations". To which I had to reply that we did not want to intrude ourselves on the Labour Members, that in some ways it would be far easier and much more pleasant to hand our bills to Robert Harcourt[4] or Lord Henry Bentinck[5]; there were plenty of Tories and Liberals who would introduce our bills if the Labour M.P.s found themselves unable to make use of them. "I hope it has not come to that, Mrs. Webb," quickly replied Henderson, in quite a different tone. "I hope not, indeed; the bills are really Labour bills." "That is why we came here," I retorted pleasantly. Then we began an amicable discussion. I was surprised by a certain bitter hostility on Snowden's part—he is getting soured. O'Grady was the most cordial and remarked that it would be well to throw over their miscellaneous Trade Union bills and concentrate on a systematic programme. The interview ended by a proposal from Henderson that we should have a regular meeting for the discussion of policy between the Standing Committee, the P.C.,[6] the Labour Party and the Labour Members. In the meantime they would introduce some, if not all, of our bills. These Labour M.P.s are not a strong body of men, and they are plainly enervated by the atmosphere of the House, and MacDonald's astute but over-cautious and sceptical leadership—sceptical of all the reforms which he is supposed to believe in. If we could see into MacDonald's mind I don't believe it differs materially from John Burns's mentality. But the Labour Party exists and we have to work with it. "A poor thing, but our own."

January 1913.—For the last fortnight I have been exclusively engaged in circularising for postal subscribers to the *Statesman*. We start

[1] Tom Richards (1859–1931). Secretary, South Wales Miners' Federation. M.P. West Monmouth and Ebbw Vale, 1904–20.

[2] Sir James O'Grady (1866–1934). President, National Federation of General Workers. M.P. East Leeds, 1906.

[3] Arthur Henderson (1863–1935). "Uncle Arthur", Secretary and later Leader of the Labour Party.

[4] Robert Vernon Harcourt (b. 1878). Son of Sir William Harcourt; Liberal M.P., 1910–18.

[5] Lord Henry Cavendish Bentinck (1863–1931). Progressive Conservative. M.P. for South Nottingham for many years between 1886 and 1929.

[6] Parliamentary Committee of the Trades Union Congress—the only executive organ of the Congress until the setting-up of the General Council in 1921.

with the clientèle of the Fabian Society and the National Committee, and upon this we are building a card catalogue of 20,000 possible subscribers to the paper. To all the most promising of these we send out personal, to the less promising, manifolded, letters from me: G.B.S. and Sidney are appealing to the Fabians who are not members of the National Committee. We have secured some 150 subscribers —I doubt our getting 1,000. To make the paper pay we must get a circulation, postal or trade, of 5,000.

We heard from Colegate[1] the opinion of the *Nation* group with regard to our chance of success. They put the lowest sales at which the paper can keep going at 3,000, and the maximum that we might get at 5,000. (Something between these two figures is, we think, the circulation of the *Nation* itself.) This cannot be done, they argue, unless we attract a good many different groups of readers. G.B.S., they think, is good for 500 to 1,000, the Webbs for 200 to 300, and Squire,[2] if you please, for 100, making up 1,000 to 1,500 in all. Hence the venture is bound to fail. The paper that will be turned out will be one-idea'd: the Webbs only know the social and economic question, and they will always be hammering at it exactly like Belloc and Chesterton hammer at the one theme of political corruption in the *New Witness*. How can they get a really well-informed article on Persia, for instance? The paper will be the Webbs flavoured with a little Shaw and padded with the contributions of a few cleverish but ignorant young men. People may take it in, at first, out of curiosity, but they will soon drop it.

There is truth in this criticism. The group of men who write in the *Nation* are an able, experienced and fairly versatile lot, who have worked together for many years. Massingham[3] is an exceptionally brilliant journalist and editor. But I think that Sidney and I are not so one-sided as we look—we have never written on other questions, but Sidney has an encyclopaedic knowledge and we have seen a few things. G.B.S., if he really throws himself into it, has a far larger public than is thought by the Liberals, and I believe we can attract around us able persons of quite different interest and outlook and in harmony with our general position. And though we are wholly inexperienced on the business side we have initiative, persistency and audacity, which more conventionally experienced persons lack. So I think that our friends of the *Nation* may be unpleasantly disappointed. However, they are obviously better judges than we are and the chances are that they are right. In that case we shall have spent our money and our

[1] W. Arthur Colegate, M.P., Burton-on-Trent; till 1912 an Assistant Secretary to the National Committee for the Prevention of Destitution.
[2] Sir John Collings Squire (b. 1884). Literary Editor of the *New Statesman*, 1913–17, and acting Editor, 1917–18.
[3] Henry William Massingham (1860–1924). Editor of the *Nation*, 1907–23.

time, not exactly in vain because we shall have raised the standard of Socialist journalism. If I were forced to wager, I should not back our success.

April 8th.—Our promoting is at an end and we start with 2,300[1] postal subscribers, a notable result. We are now at work on the series of articles on "What is Socialism?"—for the first twenty numbers of the paper. S.W. is booked for a weekly article on his own range of "expertise". G.B.S. has surprised and disconcerted us by refusing to sign any articles, but sends us three for the first number, and apparently means to write regularly. The first number will be brilliant but it cannot be good.

Sidney is enjoying this work. Once again he takes the lead. He is a far more accomplished journalist than I, and he is the reputed Father of the new venture. He likes Sharp and works well with him and he enjoys expressing himself on current affairs.

Meanwhile the Report on the Control of Industry[2] oppresses me and I regret starting the idea. We shall get it done, but it will mean a horrid grind for us. I doubt whether the Committee will justify its name of Research Department—I have not the strength to run it, and there is no one in the Fabian Society capable of doing it but ourselves. What may happen is the development of a semi-Research Department in connection with the *New Statesman*.

May 25th.—I find it increasingly difficult to find time or energy to write in my diary. The *New Statesman* absorbs both. We started with 2,450 postal subscribers. How many of these we shall keep depends on the uniqueness of the paper. There are all sorts of conflicting criticism—the paper is dull: it is mere brilliant writing and there is not enough solid information; the political articles are good but the literature "rot"; the literary side is excellent but the political articles not sufficiently constructive.

Our main difficulty is with Bernard Shaw—a difficulty which we always knew would arise in one way or another. He won't write over his own signature and some of the articles and notes that he sends are hopelessly out of keeping with our tone and our methods. And in

---

[1] *Sic*; but see below and pp. 18 and 24.

[2] This Enquiry, started by the Webbs as a major task for the newly formed Fabian Research Committee, brought out into the open the ideological conflict between the Collectivists and the Guild Socialists. The non-controversial parts of the Enquiry, on Co-operation, State and Municipal Enterprise, and Professional Associations, appeared as Supplements to the *New Statesman*. But on the question of "workers' control" and the rôle of Trade Unionism no agreement was possible. The Webbs issued their version in the post-war edition of *The History of Trade Unionism*, the Guildsmen theirs in books and pamphlets by Cole, Arnot, and others. Reverberations of this battle occur in the *Diaries* for the next half-dozen years.

order to threaten us, he writes signed letters to the *Nation*, Massingham of course trying to capture him from us. However, we have, just to go on making the paper valuable.

July 5th.—Our attempt to connect up with the Labour Party in the House of Commons has failed. The Labour Members, guided by Henderson, tried to persuade the Joint Committee of the I.L.P. and Fabian Society to give up its separate propaganda and merely contribute its funds and its speakers to the Labour Party campaign. Anderson and I objected, and though we have patched some sort of consultative committee, it is clear that we are not going to work together. The Labour Members, either from stupidity or ill-will, have failed to introduce our bills, which they distinctly promised to do. The Parliamentary Labour Party is, in fact, in a bad way. The Leicester electoral fight[1] has further discredited it, and even the I.L.P. has been seriously injured by its connection with it. Within the Fabian Society there is growing up an anti-Labour Party section, in direct conflict with the late rebels who wanted the Fabian Society to bind itself to the Labour Party; the Executive holding the balance between the old faction and the new. The Parliamentary Labour Party has, in fact, not justified its existence either by character or by intelligence, and it is doubtful whether it will hold the Trade Unions. The Labour and Socialist Movement is in a state of disruption, there is more evil speaking and suspicion than there has ever been before, and there is less enthusiasm. As a matter of fact the Fabian Society is the only Socialist society that has increased its membership and income during the last year, and we should have been stronger if we had kept clear of the Labour Party. George Lansbury is preaching, alternately, universal goodwill and universal revolt, whilst the B.S.P. is rent asunder by the rival impossibilisms of the old-fashioned Marxist and the new-fashioned Syndicalist. The Trade Unions are submerged beneath the card catalogues of their respective Approved Societies.

* * * * *

July 12th.—Old friends drift apart. We sometimes see Graham Wallas[2] and I am more friendly with Audrey[2] than ever before, but there is no common work and our meetings are rare. Sydney Olivier[3]

[1] Fought in June, 1913. Leicester was a two-member constituency, held by J. R. MacDonald and a Liberal. When the second seat fell vacant, Labour headquarters were opposed to fighting it, for fear of endangering MacDonald. There was, however, strong local feeling, and eventually the B.S.P. put up a candidate, who was returned well at the bottom of the poll, after his Liberal opponent had produced an alleged repudiation of him by the Labour Party.

[2] Graham Wallas (1858–1932). The Fabian Essayist and political theorist; Audrey was his wife.

[3] Sydney Olivier, Lord Olivier (1859–1943). Fabian Essayist. Secretary for India in 1924 Labour Government.

has been in London as Permanent Head of the Board of Agriculture for eight months or more, and we have only seen him twice. We have dined twice with Haldane since we returned from India, and Herbert Samuel has dined here once—otherwise we have not even said "good-day" to a Liberal Minister. Of the smattering of "Society" I used to see, Betty Balfour alone remains with A.J.B. as an occasional guest. Sidney still keeps an eye on the School of Economics and is good friends with Reeves[1] and all the Staff. On the other hand the L.C.C. is in the far distance and we never hear of its internal doings. My sisters I often see and our relations with them are of the most affectionate. But the centre of our lives are the three offices, of the Fabian Society, the National Committee and Research Department, and the *New Statesman*; and it is with the inhabitants of these that we spend our outdoor life, whilst there streams through our little house the usual assortment of students, travellers and fellow-workers. It is remarkable how limited one's circle becomes when one is at once elderly and hardworking. Our close comradeship, our day by day joint work—the long enduring honeymoon of our holidays, in fact the ideal marriage—dwarfs all other human relationships. And as personal life draws quietly to its end, one's thought concentrates on the future of the race and the search for the Purpose of Human Life.

September 28th. Innesfail, Ropley, Hants.—We spent two exhausting weeks at the Fabian Summer School at Keswick. The large, ugly bare and somewhat dirty house, the punctually provided but scrimagy meals, the strange medley of guests—these standing features of the institution—were dignified by the atmosphere of hardheaded discussion on definite points in the theory and practice of Socialism, in the two successive conferences—that of the Research Department and that of the Joint Committee of the Fabian and the I.L.P. Perhaps the fact that, owing to these conferences, the company was three-quarters male instead of three-quarters female improved the occasion. For six days, for five hours a day, sat I in the chair, directing the various discussions on the material gathered together by the department. The conference with the N.A.C.[1] was more disjointed—the I.L.P. was absorbed in its own meetings and more inclined to holiday making than the sterner Fabians. Both conferences were voted a great success and are to be repeated. . . .

December 8th. Midland Hotel, Bradford.—On a short lecturing tour, Bradford, Liverpool and Burnley, five lectures in four days.

[1] William Pember Reeves (1857–1932). New Zealand Socialist. High Commissioner for New Zealand, 1905–8. Director of London School of Economics, 1908–19.
[2] National Advisory Committee—the governing body of the I.L.P.

S.W. and my lectures at King's Hall were a great success: we cleared £250 profit for the Fabian Society and had a regular audience of 600 to 700 persons—a sober, solid set of people, who had come to listen and to criticise, seriously but within enthusiasm. Few new members join the Society, but its tenets still permeate thought and break down resistance.

The Labour Movement, indeed the whole of the thinking British public, is to-day the arena of a battle of words, of thoughts and of temperaments. The issue is twofold: are men to be governed by emotion or by reason? Are they to be governed in harmony with the desires of the bulk of the citizens or according to the fervent aspirations of a militant minority in defiance of the will of the majority? Two quite separate questions but each of them raising the same issue: the validity of democratic government. The Webb conception of the relative spheres of intellect and emotion on the one hand, and, on the other, of the right relation of the leaders to the average sensual man, is vehemently objected to by all the "A's", by the artist, the anarchist and the aristocrat. Our answer to the first question is that the idealist chooses the purpose of life, whether of the individual or of the community, whilst the man of science thinks out the processes by which this purpose can be fulfilled; our answer to the second is that leaders, idealist or man of science, *propose but that the ordinary man* (in his collective capacity of being the mass of the people) *disposes, and that it is right that he should dispose.* We uphold the authority of the mass of the people and object to any defiance of it or any tricks of evasion. The minority must submit until they have succeeded, by the magic of their idealism, or by the verification of their reasoning, in persuading their fellow men to accept their aims or their methods of reaching those aims. This applies, of course, only to collective action. One of the ends of Political Science is to discover the laws or institutions through which we can get, not only the maximum of co-operative effort, but also the maximum of personal invention and individual divergence alike in ends and means from the common mean, so long as this divergence is not downward towards the animal in men. I admit that these formulas are often mutually contradictory, requiring adjustments and compromises between one principle of conduct and another.

This philosophy postulates deliberate division of labour; it demands patience, discipline and tolerance—characteristics which do not appeal to either the revolutionary or the reactionary. That is why the Webbs are so hated—all the more so because we seem so "damned sure" of our conclusions. We are extraordinarily unpopular to-day—more disliked, by a larger body of persons, than ever before. The propertied class look upon us as their most insidious enemies; the revolutionary

Socialist or fanatical sentimentalist see in us, and our philosophy, the main obstacle to what they call enthusiasm and we call hysteria. Our one comfort is that both sets of opponents can hardly be right.

I spent an unreasonable amount of energy on my three lectures on Equality, Science and Religion, and Woman. Hitherto I have always lectured on technical questions, I have never plunged into the general philosophy of conduct, but now that I am rapidly getting old I long to sum up my experience of life in its larger and more intimate aspects. Oddly enough I seem to have lost the art of writing, but to have gained a certain art in speaking. In writing I am parasitic on Sidney; I never write, except in this diary, in my own style, always in a hybrid of his and mine. But I *must* speak my own words and sentences.

December 6th. 54, Ullet Road, Liverpool.—At Bradford I had an I.L.P. audience—the usual Sunday evening meeting of some four hundred working men and women, and the following day a Guild of Help[1] annual meeting—mostly middle class. It is significant that Jowett,[2] the Labour Member, appeared on the Guild platform and proposed the vote of thanks to the Lady Mayoress, the wife of a leading Conservative, who took the chair. At present it is practically impossible to arouse any spontaneous class-conscious feeling in England: all the more impossible in those districts represented by Labour Members. It does not seem in the least strange to the British mind that Jowett, one of the most advanced and Socialist of the Labour Party, should approve of the Guild of Help, with its mission of individual charity from the "Haves" to the "Have Nots": any more than it seems strange that such a body should ask a leading Socialist to address it. I stayed with a family of Priestmans—Mr. Priestman was the leader of the Liberal Party, but all his children are Socialists, two or three are members of the Fabian Society. . . .

[1] The Guilds of Help were local charitable bodies founded for the purpose of individual study of cases of destitution, working on the same general principle as the Charity Organisation Society. Cf. the *Life of Canon Barnett*.

[2] Frederick William Jowett (1864–1944). I.L.P. member for various Bradford seats, and First Commissioner of Works in 1924 Labour Government; advocate of municipal enterprise, milk for school-children, the reorganisation of Parliament, etc.

JANUARY 1914—DECEMBER 1914

January 2nd. Minehead.—A fortnight's walking and motoring tour in Cornwall and Devon with G.B.S. It has been a delightful and luxurious holiday—our first intention of tramping round the coast, with knapsack and mackintosh being transformed, by the advent of G.B.S., into walking over 10 or 12 miles of picked country with the motor car in attendance to take us when tired to the most expensive hotel in the neighbourhood. Our old friend and brilliant comrade is a benevolent and entertaining companion, but his intellect is centred in the theatre and his emotion in his friendship with Mrs. Pat.[1] . . . We talked more intimately than we have done for many years. He is interested in the newer developments of Fabianism—not at all impressed with militancy or Syndicalism—a good deal less anxious to conciliate the newcomers than we are. He is in fact more rigid in his adhesion to his old doctrines. He is estranged from the *New Statesman* and Sharp, but he is not at all hostile. "It is not my Organ, but it may be none the worse for that." . . .

February 6th.—The Labour Party Conference was a personal triumph for J. R. MacDonald. The first day's criticism, in which Sanders took a leading part, was steam-rollered by the platform. There was much discontent among the I.L.P. delegates, but the solid phalanx of Miners and Textiles don't want the Labour Members to cut loose from the Liberal Party, and MacDonald knows it. The other big controversy—Proportional Representation—(what a subject for heated discussion at a Labour Party Conference!)—was also dominated by the sectional interests of industries massed in narrow areas. MacDonald, with his romantic figure, charming voice and clever dialectics, is more than a match for all those underbred and under-trained workmen who surround him on the platform and face him in the audience. So long as he chooses to remain leader of the Labour Party he will do so. In his old-fashioned Radicalism—in his friendliness to Lloyd George—he represents the views and aspirations of the bulk of Trade Unionists. Owing to his personal distinction and middle-class equipment he is superior to all his would-be competitors. The British Workman has been persuaded by the propaganda of the I.L.P. that a Labour Party is useful, that some of his class

---

[1] Mrs. Patrick Campbell (d. 1940).

17

ought to enjoy the £400 a year and the prestige of the M.P.'s position, but the closer the Labour Member sticks to the Liberal Party the better he is pleased. So far as he has any politics he still believes in the right of the middle and professional class to do the work of government. He does not believe his own mates are capable of it, and roughly speaking he is right. The landslide in England towards Social Democracy proceeds steadily, but it is the whole nation that is sliding, not the one class of manual workers.

Our present anxiety is the chance of renewal of the 2,400 postal subscribers to the *New Statesman*. We gathered these up by all sorts of understandings and misunderstandings, curiosities and expectations. We shall probably lose one half of them and start the second year of the *Statesman's* life with 1,500 or 2,000 annual subscribers. Our other sales are 2,000 or over—that would mean a circulation of 4,000 and would warrant a determined effort to keep the paper in existence. If, on the other hand, we lost 2,000 of the postal subscriptions, the position would be hopeless. In the Supplements, I think we have found quite a new and permanent attraction, but an expensive one to maintain before we have found our public.

February 12th.—Sanders, who is now on the Labour Party Executive, in succession to Pease[1], gave me a depressing account of the Labour Members. Apart from MacDonald, and with the exceptions of Snowden, who has intellect but is a lone-hander, and Keir Hardie, who is now little more than a figure-head, the Labour Members are a lot of ordinary workmen who neither know nor care about anything but the interests of their respective Trade Unions and a comfortable life for themselves. He makes an exception for Arthur Henderson, who feels that the Labour Members ought to take a more distinctive line and whose uneasiness has a bad effect on his temper. MacDonald rules absolutely and the other Labour Members stick to him as their only salvation from confusion. Whenever anyone like poor little Jowett wants to strike out in the constructive Socialist direction, MacDonald quietly proves that his proposed action is "out of order". MacDonald, himself, does not want anything done in particular; he honestly disapproves of nearly all the planks in the ostensible party programme. His political policy is to fight eternally on the "Right of Combination" and the "Right of Free Speech" and any other old Radical shibboleth. He abhors and despises the "Rebels" and dislikes and distrusts the "Reformists". He is bored with his Labour colleagues and attracted to Front Bench Liberals. But he feels it difficult to go back on his past. So he remains the

[1] Edward R. Pease (b. 1857). One of the founders of the Fabian Society and author of the only history of that body. General Secretary of the Society almost continuously from 1889 to 1914, and Honorary Secretary for many years thereafter.

Parnell of the Labour Party—but a Parnell who does not believe in his cause. His aloofness is, in fact, restricted to his own followers: with the Liberal leaders he is on terms of personal friendship, and they always address him, in the House, as "My Honorable Friend". From the standpoint of the Liberal Cabinet he has been better than Burns, as they have his steady support without giving him place or programme. The one drawback to the existence of a Labour Party are the three-cornered contests. J. R. MacDonald would like to stop them: this he cannot manage because of the genuine faith in a Labour Party instilled, by years of propaganda, into the rank and file, and reinforced by the ambition of every local Labour leader to get into the House of Commons.

The middle and working class Socialists are in a quandary. They are hopelessly outnumbered within the Labour Party, and whenever they protest they are voted down. They have pledged themselves to working-class representation as part of the process of making the manual labourer conscious of his disinherited condition, and of arousing, in the working class, faith in the class struggle. But they are by their adhesion to the present Parliamentary Party bolstering up a fraud—pretending, to the outside world, that these respectable but reactionary Trade Union officials are the leaders of the Social Revolution. Moreover, by belonging to the Labour Party they are, to some extent, hampered in the old Fabian policy of the permeation of all parties, this policy demanding that Socialists should be free to work inside all social sets and political parties. But to go back on the creation of a Labour Party would be to admit failure.

February 20th.—Our old friend Robert Morant[1] turned up again. We gave him the draft Insurance Supplement[2] to read. As a result he brought us a great scheme for taking the Birth and Pregnancy Benefit out of Insurance in order to make complete provision under the Public Health Authority at the cost of seven millions a year. Lloyd George has intimated that if that would make the Insurance scheme financially sound he would consider it. The outcome of our Enquiry is that all our prophecies of disaster have come true—only more so. The position is, in fact, so bad that something must be done and done on a big scale. The one and only advantage of this monstrosity is that the Insurance Act, being universal, will lead by its own weight to huge social readjustments—always in the direction of more State enterprise and responsibility.

[1] Sir Robert Laurie Morant (1863–1920). Educational administrator, and Chairman of the Insurance Commission, 1912–19. See also pp. 97–8 and 178.

[2] *New Statesman.* Special Supplement on "The Working of the Insurance Act"; an interim report of a committee of enquiry instituted by the Fabian Research Department, March 14th, 1914.

March 8th. Newcastle.—Here for a Socialist Unity meeting with Hyndman and Keir Hardie. The Socialist Unity Movement arose out of the direct and persistent pressure of the International Socialist Bureau, set in motion by the B.S.P. The accomplished leaders of the Continental Socialists—Vandervelde,[1] Jaurès,[2] Huysmans[3] and the German Social Democratic Party—dislike the disreputable dissensions of the British Labour and Socialist Movement as shown in the mutual abuse of the I.L.P. and the B.S.P., the "Liberalism" of the Labour Members and the absence of any concerted Socialist policy. These continental leaders are bigger men than our leaders and the continental working-men are far more thorough-going in their Socialism. The B.S.P., having failed to attract many branches or even individual members from the I.L.P., and finding itself ignored by the International as having neither numbers, prestige, nor parliamentary representation, decided to appeal to the International Socialist Bureau to bring about unity between Socialist organisations in Great Britain as has been done in France. This agitation culminated in the meeting of the International Socialist Bureau in London, to which the Executives of the I.L.P., B.S.P. and Fabian Society were summoned. The friction is between the I.L.P. and B.S.P.; the Fabians, as usual, are only anxious to oblige in any way acceptable to the other two Socialist bodies. Under this foreign pressure the three Executives came to a provisional agreement. The B.S.P. agreed to ask their members to join the Labour Party, while the I.L.P. and Fabian Society agreed to ask their members to allow them to move an amendment to the Labour Party constitution permitting members of the B.S.P. to stand as Labour and *Socialist* candidates. At present a candidate may not call himself anything more or less than "Labour candidate". When the B.S.P. has joined the Labour Party the three Executives are to form a United Socialist Council. Meanwhile a small committee of the Executives has been formed to hold meetings throughout the country in favour of Socialist unity. There is, of course, great reluctance on the part of the extremists of the B.S.P. to join the hated and despised Labour Party—and a still greater reluctance, not so openly expressed —of the more conservative members of the I.L.P. and Labour Members—to have anything to do with the B.S.P. Indeed, if it were not for the Fabian Society, the proposed reconciliation would have broken down. The peacemaking character of the Fabian Executive is proved by the unanimity with which the two other Executives chose

[1] Emile Vandervelde (1866-1938). Chairman, Belgian Parliamentary Socialist Party and Professor of Political Economy, University of Brussels.
[2] Jean Léon Jaurès (1859-1914). Leader of the French Socialist Party and editor of *L'Humanité*; assassinated at the outbreak of war.
[3] Camille Huysmans (b. 1871). Belgian Socialist. Secretary, from 1905, of the International Socialist Bureau.

Sidney as Chairman of the meeting held under the auspices of the International, and elected me as Chairman of the Standing Joint Committee of the three Executives.

*   *   *   *   *

In one direction our plans have turned out better than we expected. When I started the Fabian Research Department I did not realise that it would be extraordinarily useful in providing Supplements for the *New Statesman*. It seems that the only chance of success for the *New Statesman* lies embedded in these Supplements. If it survives it will become primarily an organ of research and secondarily a general weekly paper. Fortunately G.B.S. has taken a sudden fancy to Research as the primary purpose of the Fabian Society. At the members' meeting at which the new group of rebels—G. D. H. Cole, Mellor[1] and Gillespie[2]—tried to alter the basis and upset the policy of the Fabian Society, Shaw supported the resolution, moved by them, to limit the Society to the work of Research as against Sidney's amendment that Research was one of the principal functions of the Fabians. The situation is certainly humorous. The Webbs have not been behind in the work of Research—indeed, we have been up to now the only Fabians who have been noted for Research. Of course, what the little knot of Rebels are after is not Research at all, but a new form of propaganda and a new doctrine which they believe themselves to be elaborating with regard to the Control of Industry.

My purpose is to connect the Research Department with the International Socialist Movement and thus bring to bear, on all the problems that confront the Socialists, the finer intellects of our German, Belgian and Dutch comrades. We ought to have an International programme and an International literature, and the Fabian Research Department ought to be the centre. But who is to do the heavy and highly skilled brain work involved? The young men talk, but they do not get through much work, and they are fanatical and one idea'd. Mellor is not an ideal Secretary, and yet I see no other means of livelihood open to him. However, he is very much alive, and if he does not produce light, he produces heat.

April 22nd.—The turmoil over Ulster and the recalcitrant officers loomed large at Westminster, and in the Party papers; and among little cliques of the fashionable and the wealthy, the talk was of civil war and revolution. For about three days members of the governing class

[1] William Mellor (1888–1942). Fabian and Guild Socialist. Secretary of Fabian Research Department, 1913–15; later editor of *Daily Herald*.
[2] H. J. Gillespie. Active militant suffragist and editor of *The Smart Set*: Guild Socialist and Honorary Secretary of Fabian Research Department: afterward an official of the Mining Association.

glared at each other and social entertainments were boycotted by one of the party clans or the other. In the end Asquith came out on top by his bold bid for popular confidence as War Minister. The Hyde Park Ulster Demonstration was merely a festival day for City men and their clerks and the "hangers on" of Conservative associations. Bonar Law is proving himself a contemptible leader. If it were not for the unpopularity of the Insurance Act, the Liberal Ministry would be stronger than ever. But that is proving an even bigger blunder than we foretold.

We have resumed relations with two of the Liberal Ministers— Lloyd George and Herbert Samuel. At a performance of *Parsifal* Sidney and I ran up against them during the long interval in the outer hall and presently found ourselves heatedly discussing, surrounded by an ever-widening circle of amused and interested listeners, the excessive sickness of married women under the Insurance Act owing to the humorously ignorant omission by the Government actuaries of the "risk" of pregnancy. As we hurried back to the gloriously dramatised religious service, Lloyd George appealed to us to help him to get out of the financial hole. The result was a breakfast at 11, Downing Street, with Montagu[1] (Financial Secretary to the Treasury) and Dr. Addison[2] as fellow guests; and a dinner at Grosvenor Road to enable Lloyd George to meet Margaret Bondfield[3] and Mary Macarthur.[4] It is certainly to his credit that he bears no malice for our criticism—perhaps it is to our credit that we, also, are willing to let bygones be bygones in order to get the best out of the situation. We are anxious to make the deficit the occasion for a big scheme for maternity and infancy under the Public Health Authority. In this we have Masterman[5] as an opponent, and Herbert Samuel, now at the Local Government Board, as an ardent supporter, honestly intent on promoting a really big development of Public Health, during his term of office. He has spent two evenings with us; he is sound in his proposals and very industrious. But he is said to carry little weight with

[1] Edwin Stanley Montagu (1879-1924), of the Montagu-Chelmsford reforms in Indian affairs, in 1914-16 was Financial Secretary to the Treasury, and made Vice-Chairman of the Reconstruction Committee (see p. 80) in 1917.

[2] Christopher Addison, Lord Addison (1869-1951), Labour Party Leader in the House of Commons and Lord President of the Council, 1951. Then Liberal Parliamentary Secretary to Board of Education: Minister of Munitions, 1916-17, of Reconstruction, 1917, and of Health, 1919-21.

[3] Margaret Grace Bondfield (b. 1873). Then organiser, Shop Assistants' Union, afterwards Parliamentary Secretary to Ministry of Labour in 1924 Labour Government.

[4] Mary Reid Macarthur (1880-1921). The most brilliant woman Trade Union organiser; Secretary of Women's Trade Union League and of National Federation of Women Workers.

[5] Charles Frederick Gurney Masterman (1873-1927). Liberal M.P. Chairman, National Insurance Commission.

the Cabinet, and Lloyd George is, unfortunately, more under the influence of that "lost soul" Masterman, who seems to have some kind of spite against all Public Health Authorities. Our hope is, that this year's budget, being an election budget, must take into account the present popular sentiment for the improvement of the race. Incidentally, our conversations showed that the *New Statesman* is proving a considerable force; Ministers and permanent officials read it.

We attended the Gala days of the I.L.P. conference (the twenty-first anniversary of its existence) as fraternal delegates from the Fabian Society, and listened to endless self-congratulatory speeches from I.L.P. leaders and a fine piece of oratory from Huysmans—a man of far finer calibre than our British leaders. When the conference settled down to business the I.L.P. leaders were painfully at variance. J. R. MacDonald seems almost preparing for his exit from the I.L.P. I think he would welcome a really conclusive reason for joining the Liberal Party. Snowden is ill, some say very ill, at once bitter and apathetic; Keir Hardie "used up", with no real faith left in the Labour Movement as a revolutionary force. Jowett—that dear, modest, dull but devotedly pious Socialist—shone out among his cleverer brethren and carried his unpractical resolution that Labour Members ought, on all questions and at all times, to vote "according to the merits" of the particular issue before the House. The rank and file are puzzled and disheartened, and some of the delegates were seen to be weeping when Snowden fiercely attacked his colleagues of the Parliamentary Labour Party. The cold truth is that the Labour Members have utterly failed to impress the House of Commons and the constituencies as a live force, and have lost confidence in themselves and each other. The Labour Movement rolls on—the Trade Unions are swelling in membership and funds, more candidates are being put forward; but the faith of politically active members is becoming dim or confused whilst the rank and file become every day more restive. There is little leadership but a great deal of anti-leadership. Neither the *Daily Citizen* nor the *Daily Herald*[1] has any real influence—the first is smug, common and ultra-official, the second is iconoclastic and inconsistent in the policies it takes up and drops with fiery levity. We remain good friends with all parties: the Rebels are the more attractive but we agree, to a larger extent, with the standpoint of the I.L.P. leaders in respect to current reforms.

*   *   *   *   *

[1] The *Daily Herald*, after a brief run in 1911 as a printers' strike sheet, started life as an extreme left-wing Labour journal in April 1912: in October the Trades Union Congress sponsored a moderate rival, the *Daily Citizen*. The latter perished early in the war; the *Herald* became a weekly but revived as a daily after the war was over.

The renewals of the original subscriptions to the *New Statesman* are extremely satisfactory—some 1,800 out of the original 2,600 and others coming in day by day. We shall probably start the second year with at least 2,000 postal subscribers. What is unexpected is the trouble and cost of the renewals—due, no doubt, to lack of method in cataloguing. Now we have to make a success of the meeting of subscribers, and I have to prepare a short address on "The Contempt of Women in the Press of to-day". But oh! how tired I am: I should like, at least, a fortnight's complete rest, with nothing to do or think about.

May 3rd.—Harben and Lansbury—now respectively the proprietor and editor of the *Daily Herald*—lunched here yesterday. Harben, rich man and Rebel, excited and enthusiastic, controlling a team of clever and intellectually unscrupulous young journalists with Will Dyson,[1] the cartoonist, at their head, and Lansbury exercising an emotional paternal influence. Mellor, late Secretary of the Research Department, a very determined Rebel, has joined them, much to our relief.

* * * * *

I am anxious about the future of the Fabian Society and the Research Department. We do not seem to be securing competent successors to take over the leadership. In the School of Economics Sidney was able to gather together a body of teachers and students and to create an organisation which became self-sufficient both in brains and money. The *New Statesman* has attracted a group of able young men, and if once it can be put on a safe financial basis we shall be able to retire quietly from it. The same is true of all Sidney's work on the L.C.C.—in every case he created something that superseded him. But hitherto we have failed with the Fabian Society. The successive groups or individuals, who have aimed at taking over the leadership, have not had the combined conduct, brains and faith to enable them to do it. Each in turn—J. R. MacDonald, H. G. Wells, S. G. Hobson,[2] Schloesser and Co.—have attacked the old gang without being willing to do the work. I am wondering whether this new lot of rebellious spirits—Cole, Gillespie and Mellor—will prove any more capable. Cole is the ablest newcomer since H. G. Wells. But he is intolerant, impatient and not, at present, very practical. I am not certain whether the present rebel mood is in good faith or whether it is just experimental—seeing how it will go down. The root of the difficulty may be that the Fabian Society has very little to offer to an

[1] Will Dyson (1883–1938). Australian-born artist and Syndicalist. Cartoonist to *Sydney Bulletin* and to *Daily Herald*.
[2] Samuel George Hobson (1864–1940). Fabian and leading Guild Socialist; author of *National Guilds*, etc.

ambitious young man except unpaid work and a humble type of leadership; there is no career that would be considered a career. To the isolated lower middle-class man of humble faculties and modest needs it offers companionship and intellectual stimulus and a certain contact with men and women whose names are known. But work for it brings neither money nor fame—not even the barest livelihood. If the *New Statesman* became financially successful, this might be changed—the Fabian Research Department might be a subsidised feeder and a good jumping off place into influential journalism, and the Fabian Society might, in return, furnish an ever increasing subscription list for the *New Statesman*.

July 31st.—Barrow House, Derwentwater.—A fortnight here with two weeks' Research Department conference, the first week on the Control of Industry and the second on Insurance.

* * * * *

Meanwhile, Europe has flamed up. All the great Powers may be at war in a few days, perhaps in a few hours. A hideous business. Ulsterites, Suffragettes, Guild Socialists and Rebels of all sorts and degrees may be swept out of mind and sight in National Defence and National Subsistence.

August 5th.—It was a strange London on Sunday: crowded with excursionists to London and baulked would-be travellers to the continent, all in a state of suppressed uneasiness and excitement. We sauntered through the crowd to Trafalgar Square where Labour, Socialist, pacifist demonstrators—with a few Trade Union flags—were gesticulating from the steps of the monuments to a mixed crowd of admirers, hooligan war-mongers and merely curious holiday-makers. It was an undignified and futile exhibition, this singing of the Red Flag and passing of well-worn radical resolutions in favour of universal peace. We turned into the National Liberal Club: the lobby was crowded with men, all silent and perturbed. Sidney went up into the smoking room and brought down Massingham and Hammond.[1] Both these men were bitter and depressed. We argued with them that if Belgian neutrality was defied we had to go to war—they vehemently denied it. On Monday the public mind was cleared and solidified by Grey's speech. Even staunch Liberals agree that we had to stand by Belgium. But there is no enthusiasm about the war: at present it is, on the part of England, a passionless war; a terrible nightmare sweeping over all classes—no one able to realise how the disaster came about.

[1] John Lawrence Le Breton Hammond (1872–1949). Liberal journalist and historian; author with his wife Barbara of the *Town Labourer*, etc. etc.

The closing of the Bank for four days and the paralysis of business (no one seems to know whether the closing is limited to banks and many businesses have stopped because there is no money to pay wages) gives the business quarters of London a dispirited air. Every train that steams out of London, every cart in the street, is assumed to be commandeered by the Government for the purposes of war. Omnibuses and taxi-cabs are getting sparse. There is strained solemnity on every face—no one has the remotest idea of what is going to happen now that we are actually at war with Germany. Personally I have an uncomfortable conviction that Germany is terribly efficient—overpoweringly efficient in its army. As for its navy, who knows what will prove to be the winning factor in strategy or arms? And there is complete uncertainty as to what is the ultimate issue before the civilised world. To the Englishman of to-day it seems the survival of France, Belgium and Holland. To the Englishman of to-morrow it may seem a mistaken backing up of the Slav against the Teuton. Even if we realise that the mistake was due to the unbearable insolence of the Prussian autocracy, we may live to regret it. If we are beaten at sea as well as the French on land it will mean compulsory military service and a long submission to discipline. The "Servile State"[1] will be on us as vengeance for our past disorder—the "Webbs" won't be in it —figuratively, I mean—actually they may be helping to run it. There never has been a war in which the issues are so blurred and indistinct—we English, at any rate, are quite uncertain who ought to win from the standpoint of the world's freedom and man's spiritual development. The best result would be that every nation should be soundly beaten and no one victorious. That might bring us all to reason.

August 6th.—It is difficult not to feel distracted with depression and anxiety. There is still no enthusiasm for the war but a good deal of quiet determination: even such pacifists as the Courtneys agreeing that we had to stand by Belgium. If this little race had not been attacked the war would have been positively unpopular—it could hardly have taken place. The Government have played a bold hand, far more radically collectivist than we could have hoped for. The retirement of John Burns (no one notices Lord Morley's resignation) from the Government and of J. R. MacDonald from the Chairmanship of the Labour Party are both desirable events. Sidney is busy devising plans for increasing employment during the war. If only we could hear of a decisive naval victory, we could settle back to our work.

The *Statesman's* financial position, with no advertisements, the rising price of paper, is serious. The young men are naturally intent on keeping alive their source of livelihood, but our four available

---

[1] *The Servile State*, by Hilaire Belloc, first published in 1912.

capitalists are not likely to want to pay up. The Fabian Research Department and the new offices of the Fabian Society are commitments, and even the Shaw course of lectures are a big speculation.

August 10th.—The Government is calling to its aid innumerable Committees—everyone who has any kind of reputation as a social reformer is on some Committee or other. The Cabinet has shown remarkable energy and freedom from pedantry either financial or administrative. We all live in a state of tense anxiety for the first decisive battle by land or sea. The opening of the war has gone badly for Germany, and some are saying that her efficiency is all paper and that she has no great war leaders. Openings of campaigns are deceptive. But Germany cannot afford to wait for her victories, as we could in the Transvaal. She is too big and too isolated from supplies of food and money—relatively to her opponents—to have staying power. If she cannot win in six weeks she will have to give in, though she may delay her surrender through desperation for many months. No one knows to-day whether our troops are landed in Belgium—there is not a pennyworth of news about either our navy or our army since the declaration of war. It is a miracle of secrecy.

We shall do very little the next months but sit on Committees—Government Committees and Labour Committees. I attended one at the Local Government Board with Burns in the chair, and Sidney went off to another. Everyone is excited and perturbed; and most of us are haunted by the horrors that we know are taking place a few hundred miles away.

August 25th.—Haldane dined with us last night: serious with the first bad news of the war—the fall of Namur. He was full of his past participation in diplomacy and military organisation. He was greatly admiring of Kitchener, and anxious to tell us that it was he who insisted on "K" going to the War Office. "K" says we must prepare for a three years' war and is expecting initial disasters. The Germans expect to walk through the French Army "like butter", and our own Expeditionary Force they consider a mere "demonstration". Sidney explained to him the urgent need for the re-establishment of the remittance market and the way in which the Government had been "got at" by the Joint Stock Banks. Also the Government were holding back grants for new public works. Haldane was excited and anxious like the rest of us.

We are going away for ten days or a fortnight's holiday to walk ourselves into a quieter state of mind. Sidney has been drafting memoranda for Government Departments and resolutions for Labour meetings. I have been drifting between letter-writing and reading successive editions of papers. It is almost impossible to keep one's mind off that horrible Hell a few hundred miles away.

August 28th.—Before we left London we dined with Haldane to meet Grey, Lloyd George, Isaacs[1] and Montagu. These men are changed. Grey has lost his conventional aloofness; he was intensely "human", eager for intimate discussion of practical difficulties, and terribly concerned that he had not been able to prevent the war—suffering, I think, from an over-sensitive consciousness of personal responsibility. Haldane has lost his bland self-sufficiency. Lloyd George showed at his best in his lack of self-consciousness, his freedom from pedantry, his alert open-mindedness, and his calm cheeriness. Montagu and Isaacs were eager to be helpful. They were all working at their highest efficiency, no dinners and week-ends. At dinner we talked finance and unemployment. Lloyd George was convinced that the Germans had methodically prepared for war in the financial as well as in the military sphere and had succeeded in getting comfortably into debt for some 200 millions. Consequently her merchants were flush of money. He was equally certain that Holland was, at present, aiding and abetting Germany with all sorts of accommodations. All the Ministers grave and fully aware that we were in for the supreme struggle for the life of the British Empire, and that the war would be waged along all frontiers and in every department of life. Whatever else might be the outcome, the war would mean political ruin to one side and financial disaster to all. "We well-to-do," said Haldane, "will have in the future to live on half our incomes." Grey thought that the war would mean the advent of Labour Parties to power. Lloyd George is prepared for the boldest measures to re-establish credit and keep the population employed. There was, according to him, a great feeling of confidence in the temper of the United Kingdom and of the Empire: there was no friction, all were working with a quite amazing unanimity. Of course the Cabinet are wise to emphasise and even exaggerate the gravity of the struggle; and the Germans, by their brutalities, burnings and wanton destruction, are helping us mightily: they may cow the combatants they cannot get at—and these happen at present to be the stronger and more formidable.

Germany has been badly served by her intellectuals. Her passion for philosophising has played her false: no human being can afford to translate into general propositions the "blood and iron" theory of international relations. How far this mass of print—from Nietzsche and Treitschke to Bernhardi and other common pamphleteers—does, in fact, represent the German people is very doubtful. But England and her Allies and even America firmly believe that these writers

[1] Rufus Isaacs, Lord Reading (1860–1935). Liberal Attorney-General, 1910–13; Lord Chief Justice, 1913–21.

are typical and that the German soul has become brutal in its valour and egotistical and vain in its attitude towards other races. Also the glee with which the German press has greeted the clever dodges to deceive and forestall its elaborate spy system, its huge indebtedness and its horrible surprise armaments—demonstrate a total absence of honour in times of apparent peace and an unscrupulous use of the Will to Power. When Great Britain was building up her great Empire, she did it without any Philosophy of Power: she even invented the Philosophy of non-intervention and "The Open Door". The Germans are shockingly bad politicians: they do not understand how to get their own way without raising opposition: they apply to the whole world the bad manners and intolerable insolence which we English show only to little or weak races on the borders of our great Empire, when no one is looking.

There are two perturbing moral paradoxes in this war. There has been a disgusting misuse of religious emotion in the assumption of the Almighty's approval of the aims of each of the conflicting groups of combatants. France, it is true, has kept herself free from this loathsome cant, and our "religiosity" has been tactfully limited to formal mediaeval phrases and to an Erastian prayer for the use of the Established Church. But the Kaiser and the Czar have outdone each other in fervent appeals to their tribal Gods: the German, vulgar and familiar, the Russian dignified and barbaric. The theologians of Europe have disgraced themselves. No Eastern mystic would be guilty of such vulgar blasphemy. To those who aspire to faith and holiness and love as the end of purpose of the evolution of life—this horrible caricature of religion is depressing.

The other disturbing reflection is that war is a stimulus to service, heroism and all forms of self-devotion. Hosts of men and women are willing to serve the community under this coarse stimulus, who, in ordinary times, are dully immune to any other motive but self-interest qualified by self-indulgence. War, in fact, means an increase of corporate feeling and collective action in all directions. An unholy alliance and disconcerting to the collectivist who is also a believer in love as the bond between races as well as between individuals. I am beginning to loathe the newspapers—with their bombast and lies about atrocities, or their delighted gossip about the famine and disease in "Enemy" countries.

With one tiny exception, the whole nation is unanimous for the war. The tiny minority is the I.L.P., with its Executive, and its few admirers among disgruntled Whigs—who have quarrelled with the Government. The *Labour Leader*[1] is the only anti-war organ—but

[1] The weekly journal of the I.L.P., edited by Keir Hardie; became *The New Leader* in the twenties.

it has attracted first-rate literary talent to controvert or support the
I.L.P. manifesto. The brutal invasion of Belgium has compelled the
anti-war propagandists to come out in favour of non-resistance, pure
and undefiled: if we are not to defend Belgium why defend ourselves?
There is no morality in watching a child being murdered, refusing to
interfere until you, yourself, are attacked, and then fighting for your
own life—there may be morality in refraining from any physical
force whatsoever, whatever the provocation. I don't believe in non-
resistance. Physical force does not differ in morality from mental
force: both alike are dependent, for their rightness, on the purpose for
which they are exercised—is the purpose consistent with love or not?
The act of killing may be a manifestation of love. It is only right to
add that it usually is not.

*   *   *   *   *

November 3rd.—Work this autumn has gone badly. I have been
idle and distracted—mooning over an extravagant expenditure on
newspapers for hours during the day, trying to find my bearings in a
mass of detail, the technique of which I do not know: puzzling over
the paradoxical morality of war, and suffering from mental and
physical depression. And though Georgie's[1] death leaves no gap in my
life, it is yet another break with the past—a past which is rapidly
becoming the greater part of my personal life. One wonders which
one next? The great war will raise issues which I have no longer the
strength and elasticity to understand. The root of my trouble is, of
course, a bad conscience: I am neither doing my share of emergency
work nor yet carrying forward, with sufficient steadfastness, my own
work. Now and again I bolster up my conscience with the plea that
I am elderly and past work—the very way to become so.

The darkening of London, now the days are short, adds to the
national sobriety but also to the national gloom. It is reported that
Berlin and its suburbs are blazing with lights so as to produce optimism.
Our Government seems to think that what our people want is
increased anxiety and seriousness: they certainly have helped to create
a consciousness of personal peril by absence of light and absence of
liquor. The Germans, I believe, are far more confident than we are of
ultimate victory: they do not seem in the least conscious of the intense
and world-wide hostility that would rise up against such a victory—
unless their victory were to be so overwhelming as to transform them
into World Dictators. And that hope has been killed by the retirement
from the gates of Paris.

[1] Georgina Meinertzhagen, née Potter (1850–1914). The fourth of the Potter
sisters, married to the banker, Daniel Meinertzhagen, and author of *From Plough-
share to Parliament*, a little book on the early history of the Potter family.

JANUARY 1915—DECEMBER 1915

January 3rd.—Ten days' walking and motoring with G.B.S.
—tempestuous and heated argument. The terms of settlement [of the
war] and his proposals for bringing about equality were the subjects discussed. He has been firing off brilliant but ill-digested stuff at the newspapers and in lectures. Yet his aims are straight. He has kept the
crucial purpose of Socialism before us as distinguished from the
machinery for getting it. And his protest against the self-righteousness
of British public opinion about the causes of the war is, in my humble
opinion, justified. We were all three of us gloomy as to the results on
the Socialist and Labour Movement. It rids us of the Rebels, Feminist
and Guild Socialist. The danger ahead is that the country may slip
into a subtle form of reaction—lose faith in democracy and gain enjoyment from the mere display of Power. We shall almost certainly
have some form of conscription. Whether it be military service or
physical training, class-ridden or democratic, depends on the vitality
of the Socialist Movement. The terms of peace may be oppressive,
leading to a war of revenge, or conciliatory, leading to supernational
law. I still think that the only safeguard against future wars is a long
continued war almost equally disastrous to all the races and governments concerned. If we are triumphant we shall be demoralised.

*   *   *   *   *

February 14th.—Hard at work on Professional Organisations for
the fourth part of our report on the Control of Industry. It is most
exhilarating to get back to research, and research into a quite new
subject. In our work on Trade Unionism we omitted the professional organisation of brainworkers and only referred to it in a note
as requiring investigation. It was only when the Syndicalists and Guild
Societies claimed, for the manual working Trade Unions, complete
control over the organisation of industry, that we insisted that we must
enquire into the self-government claimed and exercised by organisations of brainworkers, such as the lawyers, the medical men, the
teachers and the civil engineers. The Guild Socialists were not
sympathetic and took no part in the enquiry. Sidney has been engaged
on Insurance, so that I have started the work alone. To some extent
the enquiry bears out the Guild ideal regarded as a trend towards
control by the producers of commodities and services. There has been

31

quite a remarkable growth of professional organisation during the last decade. It is a new element, alike in relation to the consumer and to the manual working producer. On the other hand, the long history and considerable claims made by these brainworking organisations reveal an unexpected obstacle to the realisation of the cruder forms of Syndicalism and Guild Socialism.

The Fabian Society and Research Department show signs of healthy development. This autumn I have tried to inspire new work without controlling the direction of it. Cole is now Vice-President with G.B.S. as nominal head. He and Arnot[1] and Sanders have arranged with Henderson and Middleton[2] to issue a Labour Year Book. Owing to the generosity of Joseph Rowntree[3] we have started L. S. Woolf[4] on an enquiry into possible developments of supernational law. Cole and Mellor are writing elaborate descriptions of British Trade Unionism which the Department is going to publish in a series. Sidney and I want to start the F.R.D. as we started the London School of Economics and the *New Statesman*, and then leave it in younger hands. We should be only too glad to retire into the life of research and pleasant social companionship that I, at any rate, enjoyed before I joined the Poor Law Commission. Since then I have been the servant of successive organisations.

* * * * *

April 16*th.*—For unknown reasons the governing cliques are far more hopeful than heretofore of eventual victory. We dined with Haldane alone the other day: his state of mind was one of quiet confidence more concerned to curb anti-German unreasonableness and hostility to any machinery for preventing future wars than anxious about the military situation. By next Xmas he expects to have peace. The basis of this optimism is the exhaustion of German manpower. There is still very little hatred of Germany among the people we see —far more fear of the growth of bureaucratic and militarist tendencies in our own country. On the other hand an able German-American, friendly to England, has been travelling in Germany and he reports that confidence in victory is complete and hatred of England intense. He believes in eventual stalemate as the most likely result, and as the best, from the standpoint of a permanent settlement of international

---

[1] Robert Page Arnot (b. 1890). Fabian and Guild Socialist, subsequently Communist. Became General Secretary of Fabian Research Department in 1915.

[2] James Smith Middleton (b. 1878). Assistant Secretary to Labour Party, 1903–35, and General Secretary, 1935–45.

[3] Joseph Rowntree (1836–1925), the founder of the Joseph Rowntree Trust, was a director of Rowntrees and a philanthropic and temperance reformer.

[4] The present joint editor of the *Political Quarterly* and Chairman of the Fabian International Bureau.

relations. Sidney remains stolidly patriotic; I am still a depressed agnostic. One continues one's work—and I am enjoying the enquiry into professional associations—with a background of exasperated misery. Does one over-rate the horror and insanity of the killing and maiming of millions of the best of the human race? I cannot bear to look at the fresh young faces in each week's "Roll of Honour". And yet there is moral magnificence in the unsensational dutifulness unto death of the millions now enlisting. The common youth, workman, clerk, or shop assistant, squares his shoulders, spits out his ugly joke; he is obsessed by his thoughts of food, drink and women, but dies game without any particular consciousness of being a hero or a patriot. And the young intellectual, with a privileged life before him, accepts risks and discipline with equal equanimity.

* * * * *

May 3rd.—The inner circle of the Fabian Society is distinguished for the intensity of the difference of opinion with regard to the cause of the war and the right way of ending it. Clifford Allen,[1] the youngest member of the Executive, is a fanatical anti-war pro-German advocate who distorts every fact to prove his country wrong. Ensor,[2] one of the most accomplished of the middle-aged members, is complacently convinced of the imperative need not only of beating Germany but of dismembering the German Empire, of setting up Hungary and the Slav provinces of Austria as independent states, whilst adding South Germany to a Germanised Austria! Prussian Germany is to be stripped of her colonies and compelled to disarm. Sidney is just the sane British patriot repudiating any attempt to dismember or humiliate the German people and intent on a brave attempt, engineered by Great Britain and the U.S.A., to establish a supernational control over all states alike. Sanders agrees, but is more distinctly anti-German. The bulk of the members follow Sidney, but there is a small but intense section of pacifists. The Guild Socialists would be pro-war if they were not in rebellion against the Government on principle. The Junta that control the I.L.P. are vehement pacifists, the leading men of the B.S.P. violent anti-German patriots. The ruck of the Trade Union officials are just sane and commonplace supporters of the British Government against its enemies. The war has developed the antagonism between the Parliamentary Labour Party and the I.L.P. almost to a breaking point—the latter being now in close communion

[1] Lord Allen of Hurtwood (1889–1939). Elected to Fabian Executive in 1912. Leader of the "absolutist" conscientious objectors during the war; afterwards Chairman and Treasurer of the I.L.P. G.D.H. Cole (elected 1914) was exactly the same age.
[2] Robert Charles Kirkwood Ensor (b. 1877). Historian. Journalist on *Daily Chronicle*.

E   33

with the sentimental Whigs of the Arthur Ponsonby,[1] C. P. Trevelyan,[2] Courtney[3] type, whilst there is a distinct increase of friendliness between the Front Bench of the Fabian Society and the Parliamentary Labour Party. Perhaps the most noted result is the consciousness of world failure on the part of the international Labour and Socialist Movement, a consciousness of a certain self-deception—all our fine talk, all our glowing shibboleths are proved to be mere surface froth. The I.L.P. try to prove their faith in internationalism by asserting their absence of faith in their own country as represented by the existing Government. And oddly enough there is, at present, no anger with them—there is no Jingo mob. There is a section of the working class who are slacking and drinking, who, like the army contractors, are making the country's need the opportunity for exactions, but there is no popular anti-pacifist feeling. The I.L.P. is simply ignored —it has dropped about 10,000 of its working-class membership and added as many hundreds of middle-class adherents. The criminal classes are the only ones visibly to improve in character—they have given up crime and enlisted in large numbers. The women of all classes have emerged into public life—industrial, social and militarist.

* * * * *

May 10th —Last night I lay awake thinking over the absence of any recognised ethic of friendship. To most men friendship does not entail the continuance of the feeling of friendship when the intimacy has ceased to be a pleasure to both sides. Successive friendships seem, on this assumption, to have, each one, its natural life: to be born, to grow, to decay and finally to die. Some times the friendship will die a violent death, but among well-bred persons death by senile decay is preferred. "We have ceased to be friends" is a no more tragic phrase than "we have ceased to be neighbours". There are even temperaments who would regard any more rigid view of friendship with distinct dislike and impatience. A friend is a book which you read and when you have satisfied your curiosity the thing is put on the shelf, in the waste-paper basket, or sold. This assumption of lack of permanence is, to me tragic—and the few troubles of my life have arisen from broken friendships. But if all friendships are to be permanent then it is unwise to enter into personal intimacy and mutual

1 Lord Ponsonby of Shulbrede (1871–1946). Liberal M.P. for Stirling Burghs, 1910–18; then joined Labour Party owing to pacifist convictions. Under-Secretary to Foreign Office in 1924 Labour Government.

2 Sir Charles Philips Trevelyan (b. 1870), joined Labour Party as pacifist after first world war; married Mary Katharine Bell, daughter of the ironmaster, Sir Hugh Bell.

3 Leonard Henry Courtney, Lord Courtney of Penwith (1832–1918). Liberal M.P. who just missed being Speaker. Married to Kate, the second of the Potter sisters.

affection unless you are certain of your own and the other person's faithfulness. For there is no sense of decay or death when the relation has been one of impersonal friendliness to another human being, a friendliness which terminates because the occasion for it ends. Some of the pleasantest and most hopeful of human relations are discontinuous because they have never reached that degree of mutual affection which leads to their being carried on when the occasion for personal comradeship ceases. The test of a closer relation than mere friendliness is, I think, intimate written correspondence. One does not correspond for the joy of it with a friendly acquaintance, a colleague on a committee, a neighbour, or the most faithful of servants, unless you have permitted the relationship to become a friendship with some obligation of permanence. As one gets aged one is less inclined to take this step forward from human friendliness to personal friendship. There are, indeed, some persons—some of the holiest and most loving—who preserve this equable relationship of friendship with all their fellow beings; no more and no less intimacy with a person whom they judge to be admirable than with an unfortunate whom they know to be despicable. Towards all men they are pitiful, helpful and calmly and wisely sympathetic. They are never hurt or wounded by neglect because their love transcends any personal aspect. Such are the saints of the world, and it is they who are the most beneficent travellers through life. They measure their intimacy and their warmth of expression, the carefulness of their thought, not according to the attractiveness of the person concerned, but according to the person's need. Such one was our old nurse Dada,[1] whose memory is the shining light of the childhood of the Potter girls. She had no friends because all who needed friendship were her friends, and she became unconscious of anyone who no longer desired her sympathy or help. But the saint has no need of recognised conventions, since the saint's morality absorbs and transcends these conventions. It is the fellowship of ordinary sensual men that needs an agreed mode of conduct. I know of no rule but the ungracious doctrine of restricted liabilities: do not agree to become an intimate friend unless you are prepared to carry out the obligations of friendship to the bitter end. And if others refuse to meet their liabilities, turn your thoughts away —try to forget their indebtedness—imagine that the relation has been no more than human kindliness and that it has ceased because the occasion for it has passed away. There will always be many who will gladly accept the thought and feeling set free by the dead friendship, who will accept it as they do the sun, not as a thing belonging to themselves, but as part of the divine order of living beings.

[1] Martha Jackson, under whose auspices Beatrice made her first acquaintance with the working-class movement. See *My Apprenticeship*.

May 15th.—At the annual meeting of the Fabian Society yesterday evening, the "Rebels" made their great attack on the Executive of the Fabian Society. They had started the attack by a cleverly written manifesto in the April *Fabian News*, signed by the new Guild Socialist clique and the old pro-Labour Party set (led by Schloesser) in favour of a revision of the basis restricting the Society to the work of research and ousting all Liberals or supporters of Liberals from the Society. Upon this manifesto nine of this new opposition stood for election to the Executive. Of course, they were heavily beaten—they were, in fact, at the bottom of the poll—Cole and Clifford Allen just retained their seats, whilst Mellor and Arnot found themselves last of the list of defeated candidates. But they persisted in their attempt to carry the annual meeting. . . . So there ends my amicable attempts to work peacefully with the Rebels. . . . It is all the more annoying to us, as we are honestly anxious to find successors, and if these rebellious youths and maidens had only refrained from asking for a public execution of the old people we would have gladly stepped down from our position directly they had secured some sort of respect from the members at large. But these young people delight in "frightfulness" for its own sake: they do violent and dishonourable acts just for the sake of doing them. The Labour and Socialist Movement is not a pleasant atmosphere to live in, and sometimes I think it would be well to wind up the Fabian Society and retire definitely into our researches. But that would be a mean proceeding. One ought to take one's share of the rough and tumble of life: the Labour Movement is not rich in intellect and experience. The implication is conceited, but I think true—even old folk like we would be missed.

*   *   *   *   *

May 19th.—All I have accomplished since Easter is the section on Secondary Teachers' Organisations in our monograph on Professional Associations. The atmosphere—I mean the mental atmosphere—has been suffocating. The war rages with ever-increasing fury: it seems almost like the end of civilisation. The complacent optimism of the British official world has disappeared. The sinking of the Lusitania was felt to be the "Limit", and middle-class opinion, and to a lesser extent working-class opinion, has become infuriated—a strange fact because it is not really so brutal as the devastation of Belgium. This collapse of official optimism may be "calculated". Except for the defeat of the Russians, which no one seems to understand—the position is not worse than it has been all along. What was not to be explained was the official optimism itself—the complacent assumption, in the early spring, that we were going to beat the German war machine. To-day we have a new force in Italy on our side, though we are all doubtful about the tenacity of her armies. It has even been suggested that we should send 100,000 men to "pace" the Italian army, as we did the French army in the first days of the war, during the terrible retreat from Mons. Once habituated to fighting the "Invincible German", the Latin is as good as the Teuton.

* * * * *

June 5th.—Back from a delightful holiday and a five days' conference at Barrow House on the machinery for preventing war, and an eight days' walk across the mountains with G.B.S., J. C. Squire and Guedalla.[1]

The conference was a complete success. Besides the bevy of Fabians, there came the little group of able men, who have been working, under the chairmanship of Bryce, on the same subject— J. A. Hobson,[2] Graham Wallas, R. E. Cross,[3] and Lowes Dickinson,[4] also a shrewd American lawyer and odds and ends of ex-Fabians and University men. Sidney conducted the proceedings with marked lucidity and urbanity, explaining L. S. Woolf's memorandum and the scheme worked out by the Committee of the Research Department. G.B.S. scintillated perversely brilliant criticism and paradoxical proposals, Graham Wallas enthused us with his philosophy; Hobson, Cross and Lowes Dickinson controverted details by the light of the vaguer conclusions of the Bryce Committee, and Squire, Shove[5] and Guedalla exercised their young wits at the expense of the rival contentions of their elders. The weather was glorious and the view from the terrace was melodramatic in its beauty. One result was that the Bryce group joined the Fabian Research Committee as consultative members. Moreover, we had pleasant and helpful private talks with Wallas, Hobson and Lowes Dickinson—combining the wisdom of the Fabians with that of the *Nation* group of writers. The Woolf memorandum is to be developed into a big work on International Relations, past, present and future. . . .

Meanwhile, the Coalition Government[6] threatens to break the Labour Party into warring sections. Rumours as to the meaning of

[1] Philip Guedalla (1889–1944). Liberal barrister, essayist and historical writer.
[2] John Atkinson Hobson (1858–1940). Liberal, afterwards Labour economist and sociologist. Author of *The Evolution of Modern Capitalism* and many other books, he anticipated much of the Keynesian economic theory.
[3] Richard Cross, solicitor to the Rowntree family; died shortly afterwards.
[4] Goldsworthy Lowes Dickinson (1862–1932), author and pacifist; Fellow of King's College, Cambridge, from 1887.
[5] Gerald Frank Shove (1887–1947). Socialist economist. Lecturer at King's College, Cambridge.
[6] The first wartime Coalition Cabinet was formed in May 1915. Asquith was Premier, with Lloyd George, Kitchener, Sir John Simon, McKenna, Sir Edward Grey, Bonar Law, Balfour, Austen Chamberlain and Walter Runciman as leading Ministers.

this sudden and unexpected change fly hither and thither. Some say that it has been engineered by Lloyd George and Balfour: others declare that it is the only way round the administrative incompetence of Kitchener; others again hint that the Government is expecting a big disaster at the Dardanelles and the breakdown of the Russian defence and want to silence criticism; whilst the knowing ones whisper that it means compulsory military service. The Parliamentary Labour Party eventually decided to let Henderson take Cabinet office with two Under-Secretaries—Brace[1] and Roberts[2]. Personally, I think they would have been better advised to keep out of it. But, without knowing the seriousness of the situation, one is no judge. In fact, in almost every department of war politics one can have no opinion because all the essential facts are hidden from one. The misery of acute restlessness is due to the combination of mortal concern and complete ignorance: we are a prey to rumour, both as to what is happening at the front and what the Government intends to do. Add to this that the whole range of questions raised by the war stand outside one's experience and culture, and it is easy to explain the deep depression and restlessness that has spread throughout the Labour and Socialist world. Let us hope the soldiers are enjoying it—those who are not at the front!

June 14*th*.—We had heard much gossip as to the cause of Haldane's enforced retirement. Arnold Bennett reported, on McKenna's[3] authority, that Haldane was a wreck; Vaughan Nash,[4] who is helping at 10, Downing Street, told Sidney that Asquith and other members of the Cabinet found Haldane woolly-headed and troublesome; sound Radicals regard him as sacrificed to the Northcliffe Press. Hence it was interesting to hear his own version. In response to an affectionate letter from me, he dined with us last night and seemed glad to unburden his mind. Asquith had not consulted him about the reconstruction—the first he heard of it was the statement circulated in the Cabinet box that the Government was dissolved and that all ministers were to send in their resignations. He, of course, told Asquith to feel free to dispense with his services, and his old friend accepted his

[1] William Brace (1865–1948). South Wales miners' leader; Under-Secretary to Home Office, 1916–18.

[2] George Henry Roberts (1869–1928). Secretary, Norwich Typographical Association; M.P. for Norwich. Held various offices in wartime coalitions and stayed in the Government after the Labour Party left it, ending as Food Controller in 1919–20.

[3] Reginald McKenna (1863–1943), the Liberal Home Secretary and Chancellor of the Exchequer in the Coalition, 1915–16. Later Chairman of the Midland Bank.

[4] Vaughan Nash (1861–1932). Civil Servant; private secretary to Campbell-Bannerman and then to Asquith. Secretary to Reconstruction Committee and Ministry of Reconstruction, 1917–19.

resignation with the excuse that the Unionists demanded it. Churchill fought hard and succeeded in imposing himself and is working with Balfour at the Admiralty. Haldane professed to us to be relieved: except that he regretted not being in with Grey at any peace negotiations. He is generously acquiescent and is settling down to developing the Judicial Committee. He says that he had reported to the Cabinet in 1911 that Germany was preparing for war. His advice was to prepare secretly for war whilst doing all that could be done to keep on friendly relations with Germany. He believed at that time that there was a chance of avoiding war, nor had he realised that, given the continuance of the German military caste in power, war had been inevitable. On the whole he was glad that it had come now. Looking back on the ten years of Liberal administration he thought that the Cabinet ought to have delayed old age pensions and National Insurance and pushed forward public expenditure on infants and children and on industrial and physical training. He was naturally critical of the present administration; he was regretful that on the outbreak of war the civil administration of the War Office had not been left in the hands of a strong civilian (himself or another), Kitchener being restricted to military matters. "K" was autocratic and ill-informed, and Asquith indolent, and things had been allowed to drift. He was still optimistic that the Germans would be exhausted and he was still full of admiration for their patriotism and efficiency. He did not look a physical wreck—but perpetual over-eating and over-smoking has no doubt dulled his intellect. He was far more friendly than he has been for many a long year—more friendly than he has been since he became a Cabinet Minister. He states that Grey is seriously incapacitated and very depressed: he is suffering from pigmentation of the eyes—a disease which cannot get better but may get worse. Lloyd George is the one Minister who has scored a popular success (with emphasis on "popular"). He is the "man of the hour" with the Tories, he is still trusted by large sections of the Radicals and Labour men. This was Haldane's estimate of the political situation.

There is irony in Haldane being thrown out of office by the *Times* and the City, whose approval he has always assiduously cultivated— merely because he admires German metaphysics. His deposition from the Woolsack seems mere malice, a desire to victimise someone. However, he is distinctly pacifist, anxious for International Law. Perhaps it is this kindly feeling towards many Germans and this hatred of war that has roused the fury of the Junkers of England. There is a powerful section of the governing class that sees social salvation in a victorious war and a permanently disciplined population kept ready for another war. Haldane is hostile—by temperament and by training—to a militarist state: he believes in the Reign of Law administered by an aristocracy of intellect for the good of the community: the aristocracy, be it added, receiving a big commission on account of the prosperity of the nation which they alone can secure.

June 22nd.—Jane Addams,[1] with whom we stayed at Hull House, Chicago, on our first world tour, dined with us last night. Since we knew her seventeen years ago she has become a world celebrity—the most famous woman of the U.S.A. representing the best aspects of the Feminist Movement and the most distinguished elements in the social reform movement. Some say that she has been too much in the limelight of late and that she is no longer either so sane or so subtle in her public utterances. But to us she seemed the same gentle, dignified, sympathetic woman, though like the rest of us she has lost in brilliancy and personal charm—the inevitable result of age, personal notoriety, and much business. Her late mission to the governments of the world, as the leading representative of the neutral women at the Hague Conference, has brought her into still greater prominence. She and one or two other women of neutral countries were charged with the "Peace Mission" to the Governments of Germany, Austria, Hungary, Italy, France, Belgium and England. She had found Sir Edward Grey politely encouraging, expressing his own personal pacific sentiments, but saying nothing about his Government.

The French Ministers were decidedly hostile—the most hostile of all the Governments—to any "Peace manoeuvres"; the Italians were boys with a new toy; the Hungarians were deliberately oncoming; they showed no hatred of England or Russia; disclaiming all responsibility for the treatment of Belgium, "that is Germany's affair", and suggesting that it might be quite easy for them to make a separate peace with Russia; they had beaten her, they were ready to make friends. As for the rest of the war, it did not concern them. The Hungarian Government even permitted a public meeting at which the women delegates pleaded for peace. The Austrians, on the other hand, were nervous and depressed but pretended complete confidence and refused to commit themselves. Jane Addams was most interesting in her description of Berlin. To outward seeming everything was prosperous and easy, the whole population united and confident. But there was a grimness, a restrained misery that manifested itself in bitterness against England and the U.S.A. They had thrashed Russia and if they chose to sacrifice the men they could break through in France: Italy was negligible. In spite of this appearance of brutal self-confidence

[1] The social reformer, pacifist and feminist, who founded Hull House in Chicago in 1889 at the age of 29, and in 1931 was awarded the Nobel Peace Prize. Her best-known work is *The Spirit of Youth in the City Streets* (1909).

the Chancellor and Foreign Secretary were far more willing to listen
to peace proposals and even to encourage her to promote peace than
any of the other Governments. Bethmann-Hollweg[1] was terribly distressed at the loss of life: he had lost his son: every family was in
mourning; they could win, but at what a cost! The longer the war
lasted the more difficult it would be to persuade the military party to
give up Belgium: the sooner peace came the more reasonable Germany
could afford to be. Though Jane Addams did not herself suggest it, I
should gather that Germany feels herself to be at the top of her for-
tunes and would be glad to entertain proposals before another winter
in the trenches. Bethmann-Hollweg even suggested that there might
be a conference of neutral powers with representatives of the belligerents. They would not accept the U.S.A. as arbiter and looked to
Sweden or Spain as the initiator of peace. No one in Berlin seemed in
the least concerned about the effect, on American public opinion, of
the sinking of the Lusitania. "The Americans cannot fight," remarked
Sudicum[2] [Südekum] contemptuously, "their opinion of our doings is
really of no account."

Jane Addams herself thinks it inconceivable that the U.S.A. should
come into the war, and she clearly sees little or no difference between
British and German policy, either before or during the war—at least
that is the impression she leaves on our minds. Her great thesis to us
was "the neutrality of the seas".

June 22nd.—We are perturbed about the new munitions bill.[3]
Lloyd George, with his incomparable capacity for bewildering and
coaxing people into agreement has secured the consent of a group of
Trade Union leaders to an extraordinary proposal to establish what is
practically compulsory labour, on any terms that the employers and
the Government think proper. The miners refuse to have anything
to do with it and large sections of other Trade Unionists are in revolt
against its provisions. We are afraid that Lloyd George has been "too
clever" and that if the Government persists there will be considerable
and perhaps dangerous reaction against the patriotism of some of the

[1] Chancellor of Germany in 1909—dismissed in 1917.
[2] Dr. Südekum was a German Social-Democrat of the Right, a friend of Noske
and Walter Rathenau, and member from 1914 onwards of the *Mittwochs-Gesellschaft*,
an all-party luncheon club.
[3] The first Munitions of War Act, passed in July, 1915, among other provisions
instituted compulsory arbitration and prohibited strikes in all industries concerned
with "war work"—a category which was re-defined from time to time and gave
rise, as the war went on, to a great many legal cases. It further introduced a system
of "Leaving Certificates", under which no workman employed on munitions work
could change his job without a certificate of release from his former employer, and
set up a network of local Munitions Tribunals to hear appeals from workmen who
had been refused certificates and to impose fines upon workmen who went on strike
or committed other offences.

leaders. If the men tamely submit it means another Taff Vale[1] agitation against the Government: the war is too serious.

* * * * *

July 23rd.—We dined alone with Haldane—a luxurious dinner. He had taken the pledge at the same time as the King and Kitchener: it was a consolation for loss of office that he chose to think that it was the Lord Chancellor that was bound, not Lord Haldane. So we enjoyed his dry champagne and his super-excellent liqueurs. He was very genial, anxious that we and the *New Statesman* should start a campaign for the reconstruction of our social life after the war. Sidney got angry with him because he evaded the issue of increased taxation of the rich: tried to counter Sidney's plea of immediate and drastic taxation by the stale objection of the commitments of the wealthy and the throwing out of employment of their dependants and retainers. The flare-up passed over and he subsequently agreed that the rich would have to pay more and said that he was doing his level best to prevent the Government from cutting down the grants for education. He wanted to think out the demobilisation of the army after the war and we suggested that he should engage a clever young man to work under a committee to prepare a scheme. In all this talk we could not discover what conclusion he desired except that he wanted "intelligent criticism of the Government". He seemed to be ploughing a lonely furrow. "The country is being governed by three men: Balfour, Kitchener and Lloyd George, and Balfour is the real Prime Minister." From which remark we gathered that he had broken with Asquith.

* * * * *

September 9th. Bristol. Trades Union Congress.—Sidney and I came here from Penallt on our way to London, to refresh our impression of current Trade Unionism and to ascertain the Labour feeling about conscription and the war. The Parliamentary Committee is conventionally warlike and most of the elder Trade Union officials agree with it. A tiny fraction of the Congress accept the I.L.P. and U.D.C.

[1] In 1900, the Taff Vale Railway Company sued the Amalgamated Society of Railway Servants for pecuniary damages caused to it by a railway strike, and won a sum of £23,000 by final decision of the House of Lords. This decision, which in effect hamstrung industrial action by the Trade Unions, played a great part in the Liberal landslide in the 1906 election, and was completely reversed by the Trade Disputes Act of 1906. Mrs. Webb's apprehensions, on this occasion, were not realised: later in the year the South Wales miners went on strike and successfully defied the Act, and at no time during the war did it prevent strike action where grievances were sufficiently strongly felt, though it prevented them from being led by Trade Union officials in the official capacity—hence the great burgeoning of the unofficial shop stewards' movement. It did, however, give a fillip to the extension of arbitration and regular conciliation procedure.

standpoint. Indeed, the working-class assembly showed itself this morning quite primitive in its racial emotion. Tillett,[1] Roberts, Havelock Wilson[2] and Hodge[3] made the usual patriotic speeches of the savage and uncompromising type, accusing the anti-war party of being "cowards and traitors". The bulk of the delegates were more good-tempered and tolerant: but they were out to win the war and only seven out of three hundred held up their hands against the Parliamentary Committee's patriotic resolution. Very different was the reception of the Parliamentary Committee's mild and inconclusive resolution against conscription, supported by tame front bench speeches. Smillie's[4] vigorous denunciation of "the accursed thing" and threatening words "that if the government attempted to introduce conscription it would be the duty of organised labour to prevent its enforcement" was enthusiastically cheered. This enthusiasm was so distasteful to the Parliamentary Committee that they hastily invited Lloyd George to come down from London to address the Congress (a fact they announced after he had accepted the invitation), nominally to explain his munitions programme, but really to neutralise the anti-conscription fervour. So we shall watch the brilliant Tory demagogue (reported to be madly in favour of conscription) twisting the Congress back to unconditional support of the Government.

The Congress is no better, in fact less hopeful, than in old days, if we assume it to be representative of advanced working-class opinion. The leading men have grown fatter in body and more dully complacent in mind than they were twenty years ago; the delegates have lost their keenness, the rebels of to-day don't get elected to Congress and the "old hands" know, from long experience, that it is more of an "outing" than a gathering for the transaction of working-class affairs. What the delegates enjoy is a joke, it matters not what sort of joke so long as it excites laughter. Indignation, righteous or unrighteous, is felt to be out of place. There is no anti-Government feeling, no determination to get evils righted. Perhaps the present prosperity explains this curious self-complacency. I listened to two officials talk-

[1] Benjamin Tillett (1860–1943). Founder of the Dockers' Union, one of the leaders of the 1889 Dock Strike, and General Secretary of the Union from 1887 to 1922: a member of the Social Democratic Federation.

[2] Joseph Havelock Wilson (1859–1929). President National Seamen's (originally National Sailors' and Firemen's) Union. Liberal M.P. for Middlesbrough, 1892–1900 and 1906–10; one of the few leading Trade Unionists who never joined the Labour Party.

[3] John Hodge (1855–1937). A Trade Union leader with an enormous voice, President of the British Iron and Steel Trades Confederation. Minister of Labour, 1916–17.

[4] Robert Smillie (1857–1940). I.L.P. pacifist and left-wing leader. President for years of the Scottish Miners' Federation and of the Miners' Federation of Great Britain from 1912 to 1921. Miners' representative on the Sankey Coal Commission (see pp. 147 ff.).

43

ing over their big cigars in the hotel lounge this afternoon. "The wages are cruel," said one to the other, "perfectly scandalous." It was the largeness of the earnings, it appeared, they were complaining of! There seems to be no anxiety about the condition of things after the war: no attempt to formulate any policy with regard to women's labour or the demobilisation of the army or the discharge of the munition workers. The absence of intellectual leadership or consciousness of a common policy is really deplorable. The same old hackneyed sectional resolutions are languidly discussed and mechanically passed; and, in so far as there is any feeling, it is reserved for jealousy between leaders or for the disputes between rival Unions.

The "Rebels" are not among the delegates but they are here as observers. The Guild Socialists—Cole, Mellor and Lansbury—are here, but they are studiously ignored; Trade Union officials tell you that they have never heard of these young men. A little group of pacifists are here, with J. R. MacDonald in the semi-official position of fraternal delegate from the Labour Party Executive. The I.L.P. have been badly treated, various speakers this morning denouncing in unmeasured tone the I.L.P. and U.D.C., knowing that there was no one to reply to the charges. But MacDonald will have his chance tomorrow: we shall see how courageous he will be. Last time I heard him—three years ago at the Cardiff Congress—he was defending his support of the Liberal Government and had the enthusiastic support of the Congress. Will he have the courage of his opinions now he is one of an unpopular minority?

Lloyd George appeared on Thursday afternoon: the floor, the galleries and the platform were packed and the heat was suffocating. We were close behind the great man and could watch every gesture and every expression of his mobile face. He looked exactly like a conjurer and one expected him to say "No deception, gentlemen, there is nothing up my sleeve, you can see for yourself." The audience, after giving him a great reception, settled down to be amused and flattered. But his speech left a bad impression; it lacked sincerity. He told obvious little lies, and his tale of working-class slackness and drink was much resented. There was a curious strain of contempt underlying his pleasant banter and specious statement. The Parliamentary Committee was obsequious; the delegates were flattered by his presence, and showed it. But here and there men were boiling over with anger at his prevarications. Smillie was unfortunately absent. Will this hostile ferment upset his calculations?

J. R. MacDonald spoke the next day. His speech was a far more accomplished performance than that of the Cabinet Minister. He carefully avoided the pacifist issue on the ground that he was there not to express his own views but to represent the Labour Party Executive. But he made a dignified and impassioned appeal for unity on all labour and economic questions, and hinted darkly at the evil time in store for the workers. He had a magnificent reception, warmer than that given to Lloyd George, partly due, no doubt to *John Bull's* scurrilous publication of his birth certificate showing that he was illegitimate. His oration was, perhaps, a little too clever, but it was exquisitely phrased and finely delivered, and on the whole it rang true. We were on friendly terms with J. R. MacDonald for the first time for twenty years.

* * * * *

My net impression was that the Trade Unionists, in meeting assembled, were more sophisticated but no abler than thirty years ago at Dundee. The Trade Union official of to-day has too many different jobs to be efficient at any one of them. And he is apt to be "retained" by the Government, not only by the hope of getting a highly paid post in the civil service, but by the more insidious method of fat allowances for service on Committees etc. This latter double position is a very serious matter and ought to be stopped by the rank and file. Unfortunately it all coincides with the incurable good-nature of the Englishman towards individuals of his own set—a tolerance for "vices one has a mind to" which emasculates so much English life. There is very little that is sinister or actually corrupt in the British Trade Union Movement, but there is appalling slackness, moral, intellectual and practical. The power of the Movement lies in the massive obstinacy of the rank and file, every day more representative of the working class. Whenever this massive feeling can be directed for or against some particular measure it becomes almost irresistible. Our English governing class would not dare overtly to defy it. But mass feeling is seldom constructive. Will the British Labour Movement ever succeed in making use of middle-class brains?

In spite of these cross-currents of the conventional patriotism of the older men and the class anger of the younger, there is, I think, more unity in the Labour Movement than ever before. The War Emergency Workers' Committee[1] represents the whole movement—the

[1] The War Emergency Workers' National Committee was the clumsy title of the first completely representative gathering of the British working classes, composed of delegates from the Trades Union Congress, the Labour Party, the General Federation of Trade Unions, the Textile Factory Workers, the Miners' Federation, the N.U.R., and the Transport Workers; the I.L.P., the B.S.P., and the Fabian Society; the Women's Trade Union League and the Women's Labour League; the C.W.S., Co-operative Union and Women's Co-operative Guild; the National Union of Teachers and the London Trades Council. Originally summoned at the beginning of August, 1914, as an anti-war demonstration, by the time it met it found that war was already in being and turned itself into an organisation for the protection of working-class standards in wartime. Arthur Henderson was its first Chairman, J. S.

Trades Union Congress, the Labour Party, the General Federation of Trade Unions, the Co-operative Movement, the three Socialist societies, and even the National Union of Teachers, and it is this Committee which has laid down the policy for Labour and Socialist Movements during the war. Sidney, representing the Fabian Society, has been able to make himself useful by drafting the resolutions, the pamphlets and leaflets that the Committee has issued. How long the Committee will last and how influential it will become is still in doubt. One result of its existence is that we personally have never been more intimate with all sections of the Labour Movement. All they ask is that Sidney's name should not appear. It is interesting that in the new *Labour Year book*, though Sidney has written more than anyone else, his name is nowhere mentioned. He realised that the Labour men were not keen to have it, so he avoided contributing any of the signed articles except the one that was signed by Seddon[1] on the Trades Union Congress and its Parliamentary Committee. We can still be useful as the "clerks" of the Labour Movement if we are content to take a back seat. If the young intellectuals would serve as unpaid civil servants of the labour world and consent to remain unrecognised, they could do splendid work. But young men with vigorous opinions and healthy ambitions very naturally want to hear their own voices and see their own names.

September 25th.—Finished the final revise of the supplement to the *New Statesman* on Teachers' Professional Organisations. It is an elaborate piece of research costing me, from start to finish, six solid months, with a good deal of casual help from Sidney. It ought, of course, to have been published under the joint name, as, though I got the material and drafted each part of it, he corrected it, added to it, and, in one or two of the sections, completely rewrote it. We had not realised how much work he would do on it, and, once it had been announced, he would not let me change the ostensible authorship. Sidney has no vanity or personal ambition, he never feels that he is not getting his deserts: his reward is perfect peace of mind and always-present consciousness of "good fortune"; he sits at his work, day in day out, doing every job as it comes along, leaving the result, as he often says, "on the lap of the gods". He is far more philosophical about the war than I am. "It is a sag back, but presently there will be

---

Middleton its Secretary, and Webb its chief adviser and draughtsman. Though Mrs. Webb, in this book, gives it little attention, it was an important and influential body, taking up much of Webb's time and incidentally bringing him into the close association with Henderson and the Labour Party which was of much profound importance in formulating the policy of the latter.

[1] James Andrew Seddon (1868-1939). Shop assistant; Labour M.P. for Newton, 1906-10; Chairman of Trades Union Congress, 1914-15. One of the types of "old-style", stupid Trade Unionists of whom Mrs. Webb thought little.

a sag forward, and Humanity will move forward to greater knowledge and greater goodwill: the Great War will seem to future generations a landmark of progress."

* * * * *

October 8th.—The window rattled behind me: then all the windows rattled and we became conscious of the booming of guns getting nearer. "At last the Zeppelins," Sidney said, with almost boyish glee. From the balcony we could see shrapnel bursting over the river and beyond, somewhat aimlessly. In another few minutes a long sinuous airship appeared high up in the blue black sky, lit up faintly by the searchlights. It seemed to come from over the houses just behind us— we thought along Victoria Street—but it was actually passing along the Strand. It moved slowly, seemingly across the river, the shells bursting far below it—then there were two bursts that seemed nearly to hit it and it disappeared—I imagine it bounded upwards. The show was over. It was a gruesome reflection afterwards that while we were being pleasantly excited, men, women and children were being killed and maimed. At the time it was impossible not to take it as a "Sight". Julia,[1] who was with us, suddenly remarked that she would go and get her morphine tablets in case we were wounded. But by that time the Zeppelin was just disappearing. My main desire was to see inside the Zeppelin, to see and speak with the German officers as they were sailing back from their adventure.

There was apparently no panic, even in the crowded Strand. The Londoner persists in taking Zeppelin raids as an entertainment—a risky entertainment—but no more risky than some forms of sport. "Did you see the Zeppelins?", was the first question, in the most cheerful voice, which every man, woman and child asked each other for at least four and twenty hours afterwards.

Pessimism about the war is becoming more pronounced: the optimists are silent, mere passive resisters to the panicmongers. Even Sidney is getting alarmed about the financial position, and many of us feel doubtful whether our working class would endure any considerable hardships without breaking into industrial disorder. Germany and France ruthlessly suppress their pessimists; our Government dare not do so because, like the Ulster Rebels of eighteen months ago, they are in high places. Our newspapers are amazingly free with their exasperated criticism, and certain notables like poor Haldane are pursued with venom. There is a chronic conspiracy to get rid of Asquith and Grey. There is a great deal of screaming "you see I was right": a great many cries for "Someone's head". G.B.S. is angry with the

[1] Julia Faulder, (1880–1921) daughter of the fifth of the Potter sisters, Blanche Cripps.

New Statesman because Sharp refuses to join in the abuse and the demand for resignations. Shaw's theory is that you have got to get rid of one set of ministers after another until you find a group who will "sit up". It is a foolish theory, arising from impatience and hurt egotism. He hates Grey, and has a contempt for Asquith; and a strange unfounded assumption that, somewhere or other, there is a strong man—and a strong man who will carry out G.B.S.'s policy. However, he remains friendly and good-tempered with us and shows no sign of withdrawing from the *New Statesman* his financial support —a real proof of large-minded generosity.

November 14th.—In my last lecture—on the War and the Spirit of Revolt—I had to define my position towards metaphysics. My thesis was that the Spirit of Revolt—the Revolt that looks to violence as its method—was identical with the Spirit of War. Revolutionary violence within a state and national wars on other states were both manifestations of the impulse to impose your will on other human beings. The soul of England, reflected in the rebel movements prior to the war, was not dissimilar from the soul of Germany reflected in her desire for world power. In both cases there was the excuse that the existing distribution of the good things of life was unfair, the exception being the Ulster Rebels who proposed to use violence to prevent a majority altering the existing distribution of power by constitutional means. What was the remedy for this lunatic desire to impose your polity or your culture on unwilling peoples? In halting phrases I sought to explain my faith both with regard to the purpose of human existence and the method by which this purpose ought to be fulfilled. I criticised the use of the creed of Intellectualism as suitable only to discover the right method of reaching the desired ends; I criticised the creed of Impulse, as ignoring the sphere of the Intellect and also of refusing to select any one among the emotions or impulses, regarding all as equally valid. There was only one desirable Emotion, but that one Emotion should be held to be, not the means but the one and only end of human life. That Emotion was the state of mind, which for lack of a better word, we call Love—some call it Heavenly Love, to distinguish it from animal love. To my dismay, I found myself hailed by some religious papers as a convert to religion, even to Christianity. That makes me feel a hypocrite gaining the confidence and the admiration of persons with whose metaphysic I do not agree.

What exactly is my Metaphysic? I share with other rationalists, faith in the scientific method as the only means, at present open to the human mind, of discovering the processes of the external world, including in this term the processes taking place within the human mind. But the scientific method seems to me to provide no ground for the choice of one state of mind rather than another, and therefore of one state of society rather than another. This supreme choice must rest on emotion, it may be the emotion of Fear, or Anger, or of Love. The guide to this choice of one emotion rather than another rests somewhere in the human mind; it is the conscience or Will to Believe, the religion or the metaphysic of the individual soul. The guide may reside in a Spirit outside ourselves working in the Universe, with whom we come into communion. But in this great voyage of discovery on which we all go at some time of our lives, we seem to have no one star to guide us. I read the metaphysicians: they all seem to me to argue in a circle; I read the theologians: they all seem to me to make a series of childish assertions about past history and future life which are either demonstrably untrue or unproven. I read the moralists and they seem to me to assume as premises the very conclusions they start out to prove. Hence I am thrown back on my Intuition—on my emotional Will to Believe. Why do I believe that the heart of man, if it is to remain sane, if it is to rise to higher things, must concentrate on the emotion of Love? I can give no reason for this faith—it remains an Act of Faith. Why do I believe that this concentration of the mind on Love is furthered by Prayer, by the attempt to attain the consciousness of communion with a spiritual force outside oneself? It may only be the promptings of the old habit of religious worship, taught me in my childhood and reinforced by the inherited tradition of my race. And yet this faith in Love as the one befitting purpose for the human being seems, as I go through life, observing the motives of men and the results of these motives on personal conduct and social organisation, that this End of Universal Love is constantly proved to be the only valid faith, even tested by the processes of the Intellect. To that extent I suppose I am a pragmatist. But my pragmatism is only an after-thought, a sequel to my intuition.

I deceive others unintentionally because most of the devout assume that this metaphysic must be bound up with the Christian religion. It is true that I take part, in the rites of the Christian Church, when these rites are beautifully and sympathetically rendered as in the services of St. Paul's. But exactly the same rites are repellent, even offensive to me, if they take place in an ugly building, without music, or are performed by a mediocre man. As a matter of fact, the Christian religion, as set forth in the Bible or as developed in the dogmas of the Churches, attracts neither my heart nor my intellect. The character of Jesus of Nazareth has never appealed to me. The vision of Buddha, the personality of St. Francis, the thought of Plato and of Goethe, even the writings of many minor moderns, have helped me far more to realise the purpose of Love and the way it may be fulfilled by the use of the intellect than all the books of the *New Testament*. As for the *Old Testament*, it is intellectually and ethically repulsive to me.

Sometimes I try to discover what is the Ideal that moves me. It is not a conception of a rightly organised society; it is not a vision of a perfect man—a Saviour or a Superman. It is far nearer the thought of an abstract Being divested of all human appetite but combining the quality of an always working Intellect with an impersonal Love. And when I do think of the future man as I strive to make him in myself and in others, I forecast an Impersonality—if I may so express it—perpetually disentangling the material circumstances of the universe by intellectual processes, and, by his emotional will, casting out all other feelings, all other sensations other than that of an all-embracing beneficence. Physical appetites are to me the devil: they are signs of the disease that ends in death, the root of the hatred, malice and greed that make the life of man a futility.

But it would not be true to say that this faith in love with its attendant practice of prayer is a continuous state of mind. If it were, I should be a consistently happy person, which I am not. Human nature and its problems interest me, research excites me, companionship delights me. But I am haunted with the fear that all my struggles may be in vain; that disease and death are the Ends towards which the individual, the race and the whole conceivable Universe are moving with relentless certainty. If so, my own life is not happy enough to justify human existence and that long agony of individuals and races. I don't think that even if this faithlessness were to become my dominant mood I should act differently from what I have done, because it is worth while getting for others the measure of happiness that I personally enjoy. But the difference between Faith and Faithlessness is the difference between a hopeless Purgatory and a joyful Paradise. The certainty that an abstract Being—an intellect inspired by Love—was active in the Universe and that human beings were among his agents on this Earth would transform even the life of material misery into a pilgrimage to Heaven.

December 18th.—I have been working well these last weeks, collecting material for an essay on the professional organisation of medical men. It is a long task and sometimes I get impatient. We want to come to an end of this report on the Control of Industry. When that is finished we must set to work on the book "What is Socialism?"[1] That work will be a summary of our knowledge and of our faith—our last Testament. It will follow the lines—better thought out and

[1] This book was never finished under the title here suggested, though its progress is discussed from time to time in the *Diaries*. *The Decay of Capitalist Civilisation* (1923) and *A Constitution for the Socialist Commonwealth of Great Britain* (1920) are two parts of the original project.

more comprehensively illustrated—of our articles in the *New Statesman*. Equality of circumstance, as essential to public welfare and private manners, will be the keynote of the book. A change of heart and the application of the scientific method will be the essential conditions of success in reconstruction; democracy, in all its forms, the necessary machinery—at any rate until common consent can be attained in some more perfect way. I hope we shall get this done during the next two or three years.

* * * * *

JANUARY 1916—DECEMBER 1916

January 2nd.—The year opens badly for Labour. The Munitions Act and the Defence of the Realm Act, together with the suppression of a free press, has been followed by the Cabinet's decision in favour of compulsory military service. This decision is the last of a series of cleverly devised steps—each step seeming at once harmless and inevitable, even to the opponents of compulsion, but in fact necessitating the next step forward to a system of military and industrial conscription. The Labour members were swept into the movement by the Derby recruiting campaign,[1] and were cajoled, bribed and flattered into accepting the Asquith pledge. The proposed measure seems a small one and affects exactly those persons who have the least strength to resist—the unmarried men of the unorganised industries. . . . But it is obvious that if the war continues, the married men will have to go into the trenches, and directly the Minister of Munitions *dares to do it*, industrial conscription will be introduced into the whole of industry. The Servile State will have been established.

Sidney, who is now on the Executive of the Labour Party, in place of Sanders who has taken a commission, attended the meeting of the three Executives to decide on the policy of the Labour Party and Trade Union Movement. He says that though the question of conscription was not discussed (the meeting decided to call an immediate National Conference) it was clear that nearly all the Labour M.P.s and a majority of the other leaders were converted to a minimum measure of conscription. Henderson told them that the alternative was a general election and that if that took place every Labour Member would lose his seat—certainly every member who was against military service. The extinction of the Labour Party in the House of Commons seemed to these men a catastrophe far greater than the extinction of the Labour faith in the country. They did not realise that Labour might be far stronger for the passing of its parliamentary representatives. And not one of them suggested that there ought to be some *quid pro quo* if they decided to support the Cabinet proposal.

[1] The "Derby scheme" (named after Lord Derby) was instituted in October, 1915; under it men outside the army were invited to "attest" for war service if required. This was in fact the thin edge of the conscription wedge, for the "attested" were inclined to favour all-in conscription in order to share their burden with others.

Meanwhile the rank and file, especially on the Clyde, are getting more and more discontented and revolutionary. Unfortunately, the Labour Conference that will come together on Thursday will be made up of the Executives and their nominees, not of delegates from the branches and districts. Sidney has scant hope that it will have more backbone than the Parliamentary Labour Party. The one hope is the miners, the railwaymen and the engineers. If compulsion comes and is extended, we shall witness the disruption of the Labour and Socialist movement and an era of disorder and suppression.

We are not intervening with our counsel. The workmen's organisations must decide for themselves—we can only stand by and answer such questions as are asked by those who consult us privately.

January 6th.—The Labour Conference to-day, representing about three million workers, decided by a majority of three to one against any form of compulsion and recommended the Labour Members to oppose the present bill in all its stages.

At the meeting of the three executives yesterday afternoon the sub-committee proposed a wordy resolution against the principle of compulsion, but ended in a definite acceptance of the bill on the ground of the P.M.'s pledge and "military necessity". Sidney proposed an amendment definitely declining to support the bill on the ground that the case for even limited compulsion had not been made out. Much to his surprise this was accepted, and ordered to be printed for the Conference, as the agreed resolution of the three Committees.

But the Conference would have no compromise with the accursed thing. The delegates were quite good-humoured about it, and, except for a sinister threat of industrial disturbance from the railwaymen and from the Yorkshire textiles, the speeches were as cool as they were determined. Henderson, after beginning well by asserting that he should resign from the Government if the Labour Party decided against the bill, lost his temper, owing to unmannerly interruptions, and challenged the I.L.P. M.P.s to resign their seats as he intended to do, so as to test the wishes of the constituencies. Snowden could not resist taking up the challenge, and was understood to say that he would resign his seat at Blackburn if Henderson would fight him. J. R. MacDonald swept these challenges and counter-challenges on one side as inconsistent with our parliamentary institutions, and proceeded, with eloquence, to state the case against the bill. The most weighty speeches were from Thomas[1] and Bellamy[2] of the N.U.R., who dilated

[1] James Henry Thomas (1874–1949). General Secretary, National Union of Railwaymen. M.P. for Derby, 1910–36, and Colonial Secretary in the 1924 Labour Government.

[2] Albert Bellamy (d. 1931, aet. 60). President of the National Union of Railwaymen, 1913–17; afterwards M.P. for Ashton.

on the trickery of the whole proceedings and refused to acquiesce in conscription whatever the military experts might say about the "military necessity". Bellamy threatened, if the Government carried conscription, industrial disorder on such a scale that we should lose the war, assuming that success depended on Great Britain. The dominant impression left by the Conference was one of extreme suspicion and distrust of the Government. The Munitions Act has made conscription difficult, if not impossible. How far Sir John Simon's[1] remarkable speech last night had to do with the hardening of Labour opinion against the bill is difficult to estimate.

Sidney has just returned from the meeting of the two Executives: after desultory talk they decided by 16 to 11 to ask Henderson, Roberts and Brace to retire from the Government. The Labour members decided that the Party will oppose the bill though individual members will be free to vote for it. The decision of the Conference has given the Pacifist M.P.s a mandate and it is quite clear that there will not be that "general consent" that Asquith postulated as essential to the introduction of the principle of compulsion.

January 18th.—After a meeting with the P.M. the three Executives decided to rescind the resolution withdrawing the Labour Ministers and to refer the question to the annual Conference held next week. The P.M. assured them that he would not be party to industrial conscription in any form, or to extending the Act to married men, or to continuing conscription after the war. At a further conference with Walter Long[2] some of the Labour amendments, safeguarding the future, were accepted. Sidney opposed this change of policy, but only eight out of twenty supported him and the best the minority could do was to get the final decision left to the Conference. A clear and notable victory for the patriots. The longer Henderson and Co. stay in the Government, after having accepted conscription, the more futile it will seem to the bulk of the Trade Unionists to withdraw them. Already it is being urged that their continued presence in the Government will guarantee the keeping of Asquith's pledge!

January 20th.—Again on a Government Committee, the Statutory Pensions Committee, set up to grant supplementary pensions to discharged and disabled men. The Parliamentary Labour Party asked me to be one of their three nominees and I felt obliged to accept. It is neither an agreeable nor an interesting job, and my colleagues—conservative politicians, army and navy representatives and philanthropic

[1] Sir John Simon (b. 1873) (now Viscount Simon).
[2] Walter Hume Long, Viscount Long (1854–1924). Tory politician. President of Local Government Board, 1915–16.

ladies and lawyers—are not sympathetic. The one and only advantage is that it gives me an inside position from which to watch the demobilisation of the army. My Labour colleagues are Gosling[1] and Barnes,[2] neither of them strong men. It is pathetic to watch the "Labour man" struggling with an environment that he cannot master. However, he is a portent, foreshadowing the coming of social equality—his presence compels the governing class to realise that they exist on sufferance, that they have "to make good" and that all their assumptions as to social right will be challenged.

January 31st.—The cause of national unity and the continued existence in this Parliament of a Labour Party have been furthered by the equivocal resolutions of the Bristol Conference. The 900 delegates, representing from two to three million manual workers, administered a good-tempered but effective snub to the I.L.P. pacifists. The leaders, MacDonald, Snowden and Anderson, were given warm ovations, but all their resolutions were rejected by great majorities. The resolution against the Military Service Act was nullified by the refusal to agitate for its repeal, whilst Henderson and his two attendant Ministers were authorised to remain in the Government. The plain truth is that three out of every four delegates wanted no trouble either about the Military Service Act or about the Munitions Act. They wanted to assure their pacifist leaders that they admired their pugnacious idealism, but did not want it to interfere with the winning of the war. There was no bitterness among the delegates. Even the I.L.P. leaders were glad that there was to be no split, as there undoubtedly would have been, if Henderson and Co. had been ordered out of the Government. The British workman, his wife and daughters are making good money—more than ever before—and they are working long hours and have no time to be discontented. So long as full employment and the bigger income continues, there will be nothing more serious than revolutionary talk, and occasional local outbreaks of disorder. And as no one is allowed to report either the talk or the disorder, the world will be assured that there is industrial peace in Great Britain.

* * * * *

March 9th.—The tribunals,[3] under the Military Service Act, are a scandalous example of lay prejudice—another proof that if you have

[1] Harry Gosling (1861–1930). Secretary, Watermen, Lightermen and Bargemen's Union, and President, Transport Workers' Federation. Minister of Transport in the 1924 Labour Government.

[2] George Nicoll Barnes (1859–1942). General Secretary, Amalgamated Society of Engineers from 1898 to 1908. Minister of Pensions in Coalition, 1916–18. Member of War Cabinet, 1917. An old acquaintance of Mrs. Webb's from the days of Trade Union research.

[3] The local Military Tribunals were *ad hoc* authorities, set up under the Military

a law you must have a lawyer to administer it. The most biased judge on the bench could not have equalled, in malicious bias, the old gentlemen who are now sitting on the claims for exemption. Class bias and local jobbery are rampant, and the decisions are often ludicrous in their shameless inequity.

*　　*　　*　　*　　*

March 31*st*.—Huysmans, the secretary of the International Bureau, is in London interviewing the Executives represented in the British Section—the three Socialist societies and the Parliamentary Labour Party and the Labour Party Executive. He and Vandervelde spent over an hour with the Fabian Executive on Tuesday, and he came on here to dinner and a quiet talk. He is an accomplished Belgian, belonging to the highly educated continental middle class, a fluent speaker in three or four languages and with an unrivalled knowledge of the personalities of the Socialist Movements of all countries. Since the outbreak of the war he has, at the Hague Headquarters of the International Socialist Bureau, talked with deputations of Socialists, from all the belligerent countries. The official delegates of the German Socialists, it seems, are anxious to meet the representatives of the Labour and Socialist Movements of the Allied countries; they believe that their action has been wholly misunderstood. They assert that they had as much right to support their country in its defensive war as the French, Belgian and British Socialists—that the Allied Socialists have gone further in this direction as they have been represented in Coalition Cabinets. The French Socialists, by a 60% majority, are against any meeting of the I.S.B., and Vandervelde agrees with this decision. "How could men, who were voting credits to destroy each other in the trenches, consult together: it would revolt the conscience of Europe." ("Platform oratory", whispered Huysman to us.) The French Socialists have, however, prepared resolutions embodying terms of peace to which all Socialists could agree. Huysmans pleaded for a like statement from the British Labour Party. If all the Socialist Parties were to set down what they considered a righteous peace, it might be found that there was common agreement on certain points —i.e. "no annexations, the rehabilitation of Belgium, the autonomy of Poland, arbitration and disarmament". This common measure of

---

Service Act and governed by special regulations of the Local Government Board. They had to adjudicate upon claims for exemption from service on the principal grounds of health, importance of the man's work, domestic hardship, and conscientious objection. Owing to the haste with which they were set up, and the absence of any general definition of the grounds specified, their procedure was of the most various, some granting practically no exemptions at all, and others exemptions by the dozen.

agreement might be published to the world as the "voice of Labour". We tried to convince him that, as far as Great Britain was concerned, no such statement could be hoped for. The British Trade Unions who dominate the Labour Party know nothing about foreign policy. Moreover, they dislike general propositions, and they would not desire to hamper their own Government. He suggested that, at least, the British Labour Party might denounce economic war after peace. All this discussion took place at the meeting with the Fabian Executive.

Alone with us he reported that he heard from neutrals that the Germans have sufficient men and munitions, but that their financial position is very bad. He did not believe that either side would win hands down: he thought war weariness would set in among all the peoples next winter and compel the Governments to come to terms. He was despairing about Belgium; she would not recover either her skilled mechanics or her markets, even if she got an indemnity to re-build her factories. He was pessimistic about the future of the Socialist Movement: the bubble of "Workers of the World Unite" was smashed for the next generation. Personally, he was most concerned to prevent the rise of a new International of the extreme pacifist revolutionary type, made up of "*Emigré*" Socialists from all countries, as the rival of the officially recognised body. It was for this purpose that he wanted some sort of declaration, whether or not this declaration had any influence on the terms of peace, for the express object of making it appear that there was some solidarity among Socialists of all countries. He did not convince us. It was the old game of shibboleths, acclaimed by all with fervour, without making the remotest difference to men's real thoughts or feelings, inside or outside the Socialist Movement. Confronted with millions killed and maimed on the battlefields, women and children massacred and whole countries devastated, International Socialist Brotherhood has a hollow sound, like a mocking laugh at a funeral. The revulsion of feeling may become so strong that co-operation will be possible. But at present the drift is in the other direction. And the nearer the official Socialist party is to representing the manual workers in each country the less it will incline to international pacifism. The Australian Labour leaders, for instance, are being hailed as comrades in virile national faith (or hatred) by the Junkers of our own country.

* * * * *

April 4th.—The state of my own and other people's mind surprises me. We are becoming callous to the horrors of the war. At first it was a continuous waking nightmare. But with a few months of it one ceases to feel about it. To-day one goes on with one's researches, enjoys one's comforts and pleasures and even reads the daily war news with mild interest, exactly as if slaughter and devastation, on a colossal scale, were part of the expected routine of life. This callousness to the horrors of war explains the way in which the wealthy governing class have tolerated the horrors of peace due to the existing social order. Is there no depth of misery and degradation, endured by other persons, which will not be accepted as normal and inevitable? The horrors of peace are as dependent for their existence on the human will, are as much the deliberate choice of those who govern as the horrors of war. Both are the result of lack of imagination, moral as well as intellectual imagination. We don't believe in Love, we believe in force: we insist on knocking the weakest down, if they stand in our way, we refuse to share what nature gives to man, we rob and murder in order to get more than our share. In war the murder and robbery is conscious and deliberate so that all may see. In peace it is subconscious and secret; when the facts are forced on our attention we try to look the other way. War has the great and outstanding quality of personal risk; you face death and disease, at least the soldiers do, officers as well as men: you do not merely order other men to suffer and to die through over-work or under-feeding. The horrors of war are more brutal, but more heroic than the horrors of peace; they are, in a sense, sacramental. The horrors of peace are soulless cruelties.

* * * * *

Three of the Clyde Workers' Committee[1] came down to London about the strike. They were "rebels" holding fast to the illusion of revolution. But they felt that on this occasion they were beaten. The young men of the Fabian Research Department arranged a meeting between them and the A.S.E. Executive, and persuaded them to put themselves in the hands of the District Committee of the A.S.E. What with the apathy of the governing cliques and the revolutionary myths of little knots of local leaders, the influence of Trade Unionism has, for the time being, almost ceased to exist. One wonders when the National Guildsmen will realise the weakness of their chosen instrument. The creed is still the moving force among the young generation of intellectuals; it occupies, in fact, much the same position as municipal socialism did with the Fabians and their followers in the nineties. The new generation dreams on and works as hard for the organisation of the manual workers as the Fabians did for that of the citizen consumer.

[1] The Clyde Workers' Committee, formed in 1915, was the chief unofficial executive of the engineering workers on Clydeside. The Government's Dilution Commission, established in January 1916 to speed up the substitution of skilled workers by less-skilled and by women, refused to recognise or negotiate with the Committee, with the result that a strike broke out at Parkhead Forge and spread rapidly to other factories. In March a number of the most prominent of the strike leaders were arrested and deported from the Clyde.

April 8th.—The Friends' Meeting House in Devonshire House Hotel—a large ugly circular hall with a big gallery running round it —was packed with some 2,000 young men—the National Convention of the No-Conscription Fellowship. The entries to the meeting were discreetly held by stalwart policemen of the City Division. The assembly, presided over by Clifford Allen, was good-tempered and orderly. The Chairman was a monument of Christian patience and lucid speech—his spiritual countenance, fine gentle voice and quiet manner serving him well as the President of a gathering of would-be martyrs for the sacred cause of Peace. For it became clear in the course of the meeting, that what the Fellowship is standing for, is not the right to refuse military service, but the inauguration, first in England and then in the world, of a strike against war by the armies—actual and potential—of all warring peoples. This was brought out by the enthusiastic denunciation of any alternative service, however free from military considerations. They wanted to smash militarism; they intended, in fact, to use the conscience clause to nullify the Conscription Act. "The only alternative service which we will accept, as work of national importance, is the energetic continuance of our agitation for peace"—summed up Clifford Allen, in defiant tones amid deafening applause.

Among the 2,000 were many diverse types. The intellectual pietist, slender in figure, delicate in feature and complexion, benevolent in expression, was the dominant type. These youths were saliently conscious of their own righteousness. That they are superior alike in heart and intelligence to the "average sensual man" is an undoubted fact: ought one to quarrel with them for being aware of it? And yet the constant expression, in word and manner, of the sentiment avowed by one of them—"We are the people whose eyes are open"—was unpleasing. There were not a few professional rebels, out to smash the Military Service Act, because it was the latest and biggest embodiment of authority hostile to the conduct of their own lives according to their own desires. Here and there were misguided youths who had been swept into the movement because "conscientious objection" had served to excuse their refusal to enlist and possibly might save them from the terrors and discomforts of fighting—pasty-faced, furtive boys, who looked dazed at the amount of heroism that was being expected from them. They were obviously scared by the unanimity with which it was decided "to refuse alternative service"; and they will certainly take advantage of the resolution declaring that every member of the Fellowship must follow his own conscience in this matter. On the platform were the sympathisers with the movement— exactly the persons you would expect to find at such a meeting—older pacifists and older rebels—Bertrand Russell, Robert Trevelyan,[1] George Lansbury, Olive Schreiner,[2] Lupton,[3] Stephen and Rosa Hobhouse[4], Dr. Clifford[5], C. H. Norman[6], Miss Llewelyn Davies[7] and the Snowdens: the pacifist predominating over the rebel element. The speeches in the afternoon might have been delivered at any gathering of persons dissenting from the verdict of the bulk of their fellow-citizens because they felt themselves possessed of a higher standard of morality. "You are made of the stuff of Prophets", testified Philip Snowden.

The muddled mixture of motives—the claim to be exempt from a given legal obligation, and the use of this privilege as a weapon against the carrying out of the will of the majority—marred the persuasive effect of this demonstration of the No-Conscription Fellowship. The first argument advanced by all the speakers was, "I believe war to be an evil thing; killing our fellow men is expressly forbidden by my religion, and by the religion, by law established, of my country. Under the Military Service Act *bona fide* conscientious objectors are granted unconditional exemption: I claim this exemption." But this plea did not satisfy the militant majority. They declared their intention to defy the Act, so that the Act should become inoperative, even if all the conscientious objectors, on religious grounds, should be relieved from service. They *want* to be martyrs, so as to bring about a revulsion of feeling against any prosecution of the war. They are as hostile to voluntary recruiting as they are to conscription. If the Government decided to rely on the recruiting sergeant, they would send a missionary down to oppose him. These men are not so much conscientious objectors as a militant minority of elects, intent on thwarting the will of the majority of ordinary citizens expressed in a national policy.

Now it seems clear that organised society could not continue to be

[1] Robert Calverley Trevelyan (1872–1951). The poet, brother of Sir Charles Trevelyan. First associated with the Webbs in the Poor Law campaign.
[2] Olive Schreiner (1862–1920). The author of *The Story of An African Farm* (1883). Sister of W. P. Schreiner, the Prime Minister of Cape Colony, who from 1914 to 1919 was South African High Commissioner in London.
[3] Arnold Lupton (d. 1930). Professor of Mining, University of Leeds; Liberal M.P. for Sleaford, 1906–10.
[4] Son and daughter-in-law of Margaret Hobhouse, the seventh of the Potter sisters, who married Henry Hobhouse. Stephen Hobhouse was a C.O. during the war, and author of the Fabian study, *English Prisons To-day* (1923).
[5] Dr. John Clifford (1836-1921). The Nonconformist preacher and "passive resister"; Baptist minister at Praed Street Chapel, Westbourne Grove.
[6] Clarence Henry Norman (b. 1886). Shorthand-writer. Honorary Treasurer to Stop-the-War Committee.
[7] Margaret Llewelyn Davies (1861–1944). The Secretary and leading woman in the Woman's Co-operative Guild, which did so much to educate working women on social reform and pacifist lines. She was the daughter of a Christian Socialist minister.

organised, if every citizen had the right to be a conscientious objector to some part of our social order, and insisted that he should be permitted not only to break the law himself but to persuade other citizens to break it. Moreover, when the conscientious objection is to carrying out an unpleasant social obligation like defending your country or paying taxes, conscience may become the cover for cowardice, greed or any other form of selfishness. Hence the State, in defence, must make the alternative to fulfilling the common obligation sufficiently irksome to test the consciences of the objectors. A wise statesman will make the test sufficiently severe to turn back the slackers without inflicting too great a punishment on the genuine dissenters. If the test is administered with kindliness and equity, public opinion will uphold both the law and the exemptions granted on grounds of conscience. But the public will not tolerate any use of a conscience clause for the express purpose of defeating the law.

Has this movement a future? Will it be a ferment, or one of the ferments, which will bring about a revulsion of feeling, here and on the Continent, against compulsory service? Or will it peter out like the passive resistance to the education rate, or the still feebler refusal to conform to the Insurance Act? It has the great quality of youthfulness. Personally, I think it is doomed to failure, assuming that the Act is administered with any degree of equity and good nature. (A big assumption!) The majority of conscientious objectors will not survive the test of alternative employment even if they survive the mingled coaxing and duress that will be attempted in a barrack yard to get them into uniform. . . .

May 1st.—A series of political crises: the newspapers excited, everyone else indifferent. Ten days ago it looked as if the Government would break up on compulsion, and the withdrawal of more men from the army. Asquith was confronted with the pledge he gave to the Labour Party that, if the House of Commons determined on extending the principle of conscription to married men, "someone else would have to take my place". But as one might have expected, he has broken his pledge. The actual proposal eventually agreed to was the silly and dishonest one of pretending to try voluntary recruiting again for married men, with the proviso that if they did not come in within a month they were to be conscripted, whilst extending compulsion immediately to all youths reaching 18 years of age and also to time-expired men. This compromise was accepted by the Labour Party, in spite of Sidney's appeal to stand firm. When the bill was introduced, everyone saw the absurdity and unfairness of it: so now we have compulsion, *sans phrase*. What with irritation and boredom with pledges which are always broken, and anxiety about the military position, nearly everyone was glad to have the controversy closed. The Northcliffe Press has won hands down. It is humiliating that the Labour Party has shown, if anything, less resistance than the Liberal Party. On the top of this defeat we have the criminal lunacy of the Irish Rebellion—playing into the hands of the reactionaries.

May 21*st*. A painful luncheon party: Mrs. Green[1] and the Bernard Shaws to consult about the tragic plight of Roger Casement. Alice Green has made herself responsible for the defence of her old friend. He has no money and only two relatives in England—cousins who are school teachers. On reaching London, with his Scotland Yard escort, he appealed to the only solicitor he knew—Charles Russell[2] (the son of the late Lord Russell of Killowen) who has a large Irish Catholic connection. Russell refused to defend him and sent his clerk to the Tower to tell him so. Meanwhile Mrs. Green had got Gavan Duffy[3] to write and offer to conduct the defence. The letter was not delivered for a fortnight—the unhappy rebel being in solitary confinement with the consciousness of being deserted. Alice declares that throughout this time he was harassed by visits from detectives, examining and cross-examining him. At last Gavan Duffy was permitted to see him and counsel was briefed only four and twenty hours before he had to be defended in the Police Court. To enable this to be done Mrs. Green had to put down £200. But where is the money to come from for the trial in the High Court? Gavan Duffy has already injured himself by taking up the Rebels' cause: his partners are said to have repudiated him. It is difficult to get a first-rate lawyer to look at the case, even with a fee. Healy[4] has refused, Simon will not touch it: the best that his friends can do is to offer a big fee to a second-rate K.C., who might hope to make a name for himself. But where was the money to come from?

So I asked the Bernard Shaws to meet her. Charlotte is a wealthy Irish Rebel, and I had noticed that when Casement's "treason" was mentioned her eyes had flashed defiance and she had defended his action. But G.B.S. had publicly urged clemency and had also defended Casement's action. But G.B.S. as usual had his own plan. Casement was to defend his own case; he was to make a great oration of defiance which would "bring down the house". To this Mrs. Green retorted tearfully that the man was desperately ill; that he was quite incapable

[1] Alice Stopford Green (d. 1929). Wife of the historian, J. R. Green; herself a historian and member of the Senate of the Irish Free State.
[2] Sir Charles Russell (1863–1928). Solicitor; held several Government appointments.
[3] George Gavan Duffy (b. 1882). Judge; President of High Court of Ireland since 1946; M.P. for Dublin, 1918–23.
[4] Timothy Michael Healy (1855–1931). The vehement Nationalist; Governor-General of the Irish Free State, 1922–8.

of handling a court full of lawyers; that the most he could do was the final speech after the verdict. "Then we had better get our suit of mourning", Shaw remarked with an almost gay laugh. "I will write him a speech which will thunder down the ages." "But his friends want to get him reprieved," indignantly replied the distracted woman friend.

The meeting turned out to be a useless and painful proceeding. The Shaws were determined not to pay up—not "to waste our money on lawyers". G.B.S. went off to write the speech which was "to thunder down the ages". Alice Green retired in dismay, and I felt a fool for having intervened to bring Irish together in a common cause. Alice has been heroic; her house has been searched; she herself has been up before Scotland Yard; she is spending her strength and her means in trying to save the life of her unfortunate friend. The Shaws don't care enough about it to spend money; and Shaw wants to compel Casement and Casement's friends to "produce" the defence as a national dramatic event. "I know how to do it", was G.B.S.'s one contribution to the tragedy-laden dispute between the weeping woman friend and the intellectual sprite at play with the life and death of a poor human. And yet the man is both kindly and tolerant, but his conceit is monstrous, and he is wholly unaware of the pain he gives by his jeering words and laughing gestures—especially to romantics like Alice Green. He never hurts my feelings because I am as intellectually detached as he is. He sometimes irritates Sidney with his argumentative perversities, but there is an old comradeship between them, and G.B.S.'s admiration for Sidney's ability has become part of his own *amour propre*. And there is this to be said: if everyone were as intellectual and unemotional as he is—as free from conventions in thought and feeling—his flashes might alter the direction of opinion. There would remain his instability of purpose. He is himself always in a state of reaction from his last state of mind or generalising from his most recent experience. A world made up of Bernard Shaws would be a world in moral dissolution.

June 1st.—We leave to-morrow for our summer recess, having exchanged houses with a lady, whom we do not know, with no financial obligations on either side, for a period of six weeks—an instance of mutual trust between two strangers brought about by war economy. As we have had an uninterrupted spell of London from the middle of September, broken only by the few days at the Bristol Labour Party Conference, followed by a week-end at Longfords, I am longing for the rest and beauty of the countryside. Like most persons with a small fixed income, we have economised, in food, in outings, in any but the simplest entertainments of those who are poorer than ourselves (mostly young Fabians and odds and ends of foreigners). Except for the nightmare of the war, which faded with familiarity, we have had an unusually peaceful time of leisurely but persistent work of one kind or another. Sometimes I have felt hurt that Sidney has not been called upon by the Government to do work of national importance. He has been curiously ignored by the rulers of the world, though constantly consulted by the underlings of Government Departments and the lesser lights of the Labour Movement. Within the Labour Party he has a certain influence and is allowed to draft manifestoes, bills, questions in Parliament, resolutions for conferences and meetings for other people to gather—like Anderson's Conscription of Wealth Bill, and all the reports and circulars of the war Emergency Committee. But the inner ring of pro-war Labour men exclude him from their counsels, whilst his pro-war opinions exclude him from the pacifist movement. He has been exceptionally well and happy directing the work of the Research Department and writing a book on *How to Pay for the War*, and helping with anything I have in hand.

I have been at work on three different jobs. Research for the monograph on the professional organisations of medical men has been my main occupation; but I have attended twice a week at the Organising Committee of the Statutory Pensions Committee, and I have been laying the foundation of a new organisation, developed out of the Fabian Research Department—the proposed Labour Research Society.[1] The first and principal task has meant long and interested hours at the libraries of the B.M.A. and College of Surgeons, and the drafting of the historical sections of the Report for submission to various medical men. This is work I delight in: I feel that I am a competent craftsman; I do it with the ease of an experienced professional. All the time that I am disentangling the facts and building up the narrative I am also at work coming to conclusions as to the defect and virtues of vocational organisations and as to the sphere of their rightful activities. During our six weeks in the country, S. and I are going to write the main Report on Vocational Organisations for the Research Department.

Attendance at the meetings of the Statutory Committee and its Organising Committee has been less agreeable. My old friend Samuel

---

[1] The Trade Union Survey, mentioned on a later page, was set up, with Mrs. Webb as Chairman, and brought a number of Unions into contact with the Fabian Research Department. But the ideological difference between the Guild Socialists who ran the F.R.D. and the Webbs was still too wide to make a Society uniting both a possibility; and the F.R.D. changed its name to Labour Research Department and drew steadily further away from Fabian connections. For details of the whole story see the chapter on "Labour Research" in *The Webbs and Their Work* (ed. Margaret Cole).

Beatrice Webb

Sidney Webb

Provis,[1] with whom I used to quarrel on the Royal Commission on the Poor Law, has been Chairman of the Organising Committee and we have been the best of friends. The half-dozen other elderly gentlemen on the Committee began by being hostile to me—but two months' constant meeting has produced an atmosphere of friendliness. On the whole the Labour representatives on the Statutory Committee have done well: we have secured the direct representation of the Trade Unions on the Local Pensions Committees, instead of the usual method of nomination by the Local Authorities. Whether the Labour men will be much use when they are there is another matter. Incidentally, this has helped forward my third job—the building up of the Labour Research Society. This proposed organisation is a device to connect in one working fellowship the Fabian Society, the National Guildsmen and the Trade Union Movement. Cole and Mellor stuck to the Research Department in spite of their break with the Fabian Society. These young men were, it was clear, real enthusiasts, inspired by the ideal of Industrial Democracy, and intent on getting it translated into fact by persistent work.

I still think that their plan of carrying on the nation's industries by huge associations of producers an impossible one and undesirable if it were possible. But the trend of events is so unfavourable to freedom for the producer that their ideal is valuable as a corrective. The Political State is getting far too much power and this power is far too much in the hands of the capitalist brainworker—any addition to the efficiency and influence of the manual workers' organisations, any increase of the workman's collective control over the conditions of employment, any raising of his status and standard of life—is all to the good. On the other hand, Cole and Mellor have realised some of the immediate difficulties of their task, the colossal stupidity of the Trade Union rank and file and the timidity and "smugness" of the Trade Union leaders. So our points of view are slowly converging. We let them make every possible use of the Fabian Research Department, and they cease to attack us. And as they dislike the predominance of the Fabian Society in the Department and as I want an organisation on a more catholic basis, I have proposed gradually to alter both the name and the constitution of the Department into a Labour Research Society, to include members of all recognised Socialist and Labour organisations so long as they are in favour of research for the advancement of the manual workers. A technical or scientific society for the Labour Movement as a whole is what we are after. The first step is to be a joint Committee of the Parliamentary Committee of the

---

[1] Sir Samuel Butler Provis (1845–1926). Permanent Secretary to Local Government Board, 1898–1910, and a member of the 1905 Poor Law Commission. See *Our Partnership*, Chapter VII.

Trades Union Congress and the Department, to survey Trade Unionism, so as to get better representation on such bodies as the Local
Pensions Committee. Cole, Mellor, Arnot and Middleton and I have,
with Sidney's approval, formed ourselves into an informal Committee
to bring this about. If the Parliamentary Committee (with whom I
am just now good friends owing to my association with their representatives on the Statutory Committee) fails to come in, we shall try to
get the larger unions to send representatives. This body, it is suggested,
should form the nucleus of the Executive of the new organisation.

*   *   *   *   *

July 6th.—Graham Wallas has been staying here. The oddly
slovenly young man of a quarter of a century ago, who stayed with
me—before my marriage at Box House and after my marriage at The
Argoed—with his incapacity for steady work, his large appetite and
delightful but alarming disinterested devotion to unpaying and unpopular causes, is now a leader of thought, with a settled and sufficient livelihood and a body of devoted disciples. He is an encouraging
example of the markedly good man who is also, according to his own
desires, a markedly successful man, with a fully satisfied conscience
combined with a pleasant consciousness of public appreciation. His
books are widely read in the U.S.A., his lectures are well attended, he
sits on Royal Commissions, and is often referred to and consulted. He
has many friends among leading publicists and minor Cabinet ministers.
He, Audrey, and a learned and dutiful daughter are all devoted to one
another, and they are surrounded by students and other persons to
whom they are generous and helpful. He has no use for the Fabian
Society or the Labour Party or the Trade Union Movement: he dislikes all vocational organisations: they are all conspiracies against the
public. He is a convinced cosmopolitan; an accomplished critic of
democracy, a good hater of all forms of supernaturalism: his fear of
the Church really amounts to an obsession. He is in favour of most
of our proposals but is too sceptical about popular government to want
democratic government generally extended to industry. He bores
Sidney; he interests me passably. His wide and conversational specula-
tions about man in society do not impress us; our concrete studies do
not interest him. His sympathies lie, I think, more with the young
men of the *Round Table* than with any of the Socialist and radical
groups who are in revolt against the existing governing class. One
thing is clear. Graham Wallas has a greater consciousness of success
than we have. He does not feel, as I certainly do, beaten by events.
The war is a world catastrophe beyond the control of my philosophy.
Such social philosophy as I possess does not provide any remedies for
racial wars. To-day I feel like the fly, not on but under the wheel.

Graham Wallas is working at a new book with the enthusiasm of a man in his prime: he feels he is doing his bit, and that it is a good deal bigger than some of his old friends think. He and we enjoyed a good wrangle together.

June 8th.—Vaughan Nash came down yesterday for the afternoon to consult Sidney about his Reconstruction Committee. This Committee has been set up by the Prime Minister with Vaughan Nash as trusted organiser and conciliator between the several Government Departments. He is perhaps the best person for the task; he is not only a Democratic Collectivist but also a charming personality, without conceit or personal ambition. As the Prime Minister's ex-private secretary, he is personally acquainted with all the leading ministers, officials and M.P.s. No one is jealous of him, as the office he holds—the paid Development Commissioner—is not a step to higher things. His defect is lack of intellectual grip; he is not a master-mind; nor has he any capacity for sorting questions out and dealing with them methodically one after another: he is journalistic and literary in his treatment of current problems. He and we have had a long continued relationship of mutual respect and liking without any personal intimacy or working comradeship.

* * * * *

July 15th.—Our six weeks in the country has been a good time for Sidney and a bad time for me.[1] A delightful countryside, comfortable house, lovely garden with wide views towards the sea, absolute quiet and bracing air—it might well have been a perfect holiday. But I have been sick in body and mind. Constant discomfort, sleeplessness, incapacity either to walk or to work, culminating in the panic about an internal growth, that nightmare of the middle-aged. No progress with the report on Professional Organisations, not more than a week's work in the six spent here. I have read three volumes of Treitschke's and one volume of Disraeli's life with interest, and made extracts. But the worst is that I do not know whether I shall be fit for work when I get back to London—I had hoped to come back completely rested. I do not know whether I ought to eat less or more, whether I ought to force myself to exercise my body and mind or to take a rest cure. No medical man seems able to tell you what to do; his advice is guesswork: the best he can do is to test certain organs for organic disease. We have no science of health; no one is observed unless he is diseased or under the fear of disease. We ought to be examined once a year by

[1] This was the opening of a period of bad health for Mrs. Webb. The strains of the previous four years produced a kind of war-neurasthenia which affected her seriously for some months and intermittently for some time thereafter. The *Diaries* record fears of cancer and general breakdown.

a health expert who knows us and who would warn us about un-hygienic habits or mind or body and watch the result of the regimen he recommended. For Sidney the time has been healthy and happy. He has taken long walks with the friends who have visited us: he has enjoyed the comfort and beauty of the place and the talks with G.B.S., Sharp, Squire and Graham Wallas. He has done a lot of miscellaneous work for the School of Economics, for the Research Department, for Vaughan Nash's Committee, for the W.E.A. *Handbook* that he and Arnold Freeman[1] are preparing. He has written, with some help from me, the opening pages of the Report on Professional Organisations, and he has finished the separate section on the Legal Profession. In the intervals he has read some twenty or thirty books. It has set him up in health and he goes back to London completely rested and refreshed.

* * * * *

July 27th.—Started work again though still sleepless and below par, dividing my attention between catching up the threads of the work on the Statutory Committee and continuing the Report on Vocational Organisations.

In connection with this Report it is interesting to watch the fer-ment of ideas and proposals going on in Government Departments and social reform circles, and even among employers, with regard to the Conduct of Industry. There is the able but pessimistic Report (privately circulated) of the Garton Foundation,[2] setting out in detail all the facts that will tend to a state of disorder, chaos and strife, destructive of national prosperity, but making no suggestions except joint committees between organised capital and organised labour. There are a series of articles in the *Times* on the same lines; there are the private memoranda of the Board of Trade proposing profit-making arrangements, ostensibly with the Trade Unions, but really with the employees of different establishments. There are the young men of the *Round Table*, who have been working with the Garton Founda-tion, and the Fabian Research young men, linked together by such in and out runners as Zimmern[3] and Arthur Greenwood[4]. Presumably the employers' associations are also preparing for the fray. Finally,

1 Arnold Freeman (b. 1886). At this time Warden of Sheffield Educational Settle-ment; wrote some books in collaboration with Webb.

2 Founded originally by Lord Esher and Sir Richard Garton the brewer, in order to promote the ideas of Norman Angell; thereafter became a centre of social enquiry. Its first secretary was Maurice Brett, who was succeeded by John Hilton.

3 Sir Alfred Zimmern (b. 1879), the political scientist, joined the Political Intelli-gence Department of the Foreign Office during the war.

4 Arthur Greenwood (b. 1880), the Labour Cabinet Minister, in 1917–19 was Assistant Secretary to the Reconstruction Committee and the Ministry of Recon-struction and Secretary to the Labour Party's Advisory Committees from 1920 to 1921.

there is the disorganised Labour Movement with its various Federal Committees, all in a state of exasperated jealousy of each other. Over the whole of this intellectual ferment broods the spirit of secrecy and suspicion—Government Departments refusing to publish the Reports of their Advisory Committees, employers concerting in private, rival groups of reformers and rebels scheming this way or that. But in spite of all this muddle and cross purpose there is a steady drift towards Government control and responsibility, on the one hand, and, on the other, towards the full recognition of the producers' organisations as junior partners in this control. All this means that our Report on the Control of Industry, giving the facts and discussing rival theories, ought to be as useful as the Minority Report of the Poor Law Commission.

* * * * *

August 3rd.—With growing faith in victory over the Central Powers comes a renewed interest in reconstruction after the war. We gather that the Government is contemplating a completely new departure, based on some sort of compulsory association of all the employers in each industry for the purpose of export, scientific research, limitation of profits and the better organisation and remuneration of labour. It is clear that any such scheme will either strengthen or smash the Trade Unions, according to the principle upon which it is based. And yet there is no sign that organised labour has any policy. Cole and Mellor may get National Guilds, but they may well be Guilds dominated by Capitalists, very similar to the National Companies of the seventeenth century.

September 13th.—A fortnight away from London to give our two servants the necessary holidays—a week at the Fabian School and a week with G.B.S. at the hotel near by. The time has been painful for me, because I have suffered from perpetual head trouble—throbbing and dizziness during the night destroying sleep, and dizziness and pain during the day—a nervous breakdown as disheartening as it has been disagreeable. Clearly, I am in a rotten state—and something must be done before I can get to work again.

The week at the School was otherwise successful. The company was especially interesting—the Simons, Charles Renold[1] (the scientific management employer), Zimmern, another Manchester employer, and some nine or ten other employers, either staying at the School or at the hotel in order to discuss "Labour after the War". "We did not feel justified in taking a complete holiday this year", one of them told

---

[1] Sir Charles Renold (b. 1883) engineer. Managing Director of Hans Renold Ltd., later Managing Director of Renold and Coventry Chain Co., Ltd., and now its Chairman. First Chairman of the British Institute of Management.

us, "so we came here to inform ourselves of what we had to expect."
(They were all readers and admirers of the *New Statesman* and had
been attracted by the advertisement of the School programme.)
Among the guests were the Bygotts[1] (M.O.H. of Suffolk), Lyon,
Head Master of Hawarden County School, a Commissioner for
Mental Deficiency, an Inspector under the Insurance Act, three or
four journalists, and Arnot, Gillies[2] and the Bulleys.[3] They all
enjoyed themselves, being provided not only with lectures from S. and
B.W. but with unexpected readings by G.B.S. of his two unpublished
plays as well as his lecture on equality. Charles Renold contributed a
first-hand description of scientific management as the careful "study
of jobs" and the standardisation of motions and machines—in fact
the professionalising of management. G.B.S. was at his best—witty,
wise and outstandingly good-natured. He is remarkably virile just now
—bathes or works all day, and he is really stupendous in the output of
letters and articles. *O'Flaherty V.C.* is a brilliant but serious piece of
work—a jewel of a one-act play. *The Inca of Perusalem* is poor in
comparison.

*   *   *   *   *

November 3rd. Fort Paragon Hotel, Margate.—One of the highest
privileges of the well-to-do is to be able to live in comfort and perfect
health conditions when they are ill. Shall we have the wit to communalise this advantage? It would mean not only the necessary national
expenditure but also all sorts of precautions against malingering. How
do I know that I am not malingering?

G.B.S. has definitely severed his connection with the *New Statesman*. The immediate and real reason—not mentioned to the Press—
is an adequate one—Sharp's refusal to insert his articles, signed or unsigned. Clifford is a hard-minded conservative collectivist, who obstinately refuses to condemn either measures or men unless he has an
alternative plan or an alternative Government to propose. He is also
a materialist, a despiser of all ideals which cannot be embodied, in the
near future, in social machinery to improve the conditions of life.
Sentimentality is said to be the Emotion of the Unimaginative—but
Sharp has neither imagination nor emotion. Unless he can see through
a question and all round it with his intellect he refuses to admit that
the question exists. Above all, he loathes the professional rebel. When
he does not see the collectivist solution he remains stolidly conservative. Possibly Shaw's prophecy that Sharp will presently dispense with

[1] Dr. A. Bygott (d. 1931), M.O.H. Bury St. Edmunds, and member of the Labour
Party Advisory Committee on Public Health.
[2] William Gillies. Became Secretary in 1915 to the Labour Party's Information
Bureau; and subsequently Secretary to its International Department.
[3] A. K. Bulley (d. 1942). Merchant, of Liverpool; for many years organised
Northern Fabian summer school.

Sidney may be fulfilled. Arnold Bennett is the one Director with whom he seems in complete sympathy, and A.B. is just starting a weekly article of the hard pro-liberal-minister type. But if the paper succeeds we do not grudge Sharp his independence.[1] The new generation must take its own line—it is useless for the older generation "to cut up rough". We shall watch the *New Statesman* cutting itself loose from us as we watched the London School of Economics going its own way—with placid content.

* * * * *

December 7th.—The turmoil of the political world of the last few days has been brought about by a series of disasters—the collapse of Rumania, the trouble in Greece, the cessation of the Somme offensive, and the revival of the submarine menace and, more important of all, the prospect of an actual shortage of food in the United Kingdom. But this turmoil has been sedulously fostered by the Tory Press, restive under the presumed pacific tendencies of Grey and the incapacity of the other ministers to take energetic action. We have expressed our view of the cleavage of policy in an article in the coming issue of the *New Statesman*. Asquith and his lieutenants are mildly against any interference with anyone or anything: the Lloyd George—Curzon group want to mobilize labour whilst retaining for the ruling class property intact and the control of trade and industry. Lloyd George is indifferent rather than hostile to democracy—he wants to win the war and as he finds more effective resistance to any interference from the capitalists than he does from the ranks of Labour, he limits his demands to the enslavement of the working class. A servile state, as Germany has proved recently, is an efficient instrument for waging war: an equalitarian democratic state might be more efficient, but it would entail upsetting the existing social order—at any rate for the period of the war. A Lloyd George—Curzon—Carson administration will not promote an equalitarian régime! The conclusion is obvious. As we personally belong to the ruling class the outlook is not detrimental to the comfort and freedom of our lives. But it is ruinous to the cause that we have at heart: it means death and disease to millions of our fellow citizens, a balking among four-fifths of the population of all impulse towards a freer and more responsible life. It means the continual suppression by an Imperialist Government of Ireland and India and other subject races. And it means a continuance, to the bitter end, not only of the present war, but of faith in war as the universal solvent. It means the supremacy of all I think evil and the suppression of all I think good. Lloyd George would represent Mammon, though

---

[1] The letters from Shaw and Sharp on this crisis, which throw considerable light on G.B.S. as a contributor, are printed at the end of the 1916 *Diary*.

Heaven knows that Asquith and Co. do not represent God. God is unrepresented in the effective political world of to-day.

December 8th.—A dismal day—December 7, 1916—for the Labour Party. The minor fiasco was the much advertised Conference of Trade Union, Co-operative and Socialist delegates—over 800, half the delegates being from the Co-operative Movement—to pass portentous protesting resolutions about the rise in food prices. Owing to other events the members of the Joint Board, which had called the Conference, were absent—the platform being empty except for casual visitors like myself. The Chairman, John Hill[1] of the Boilermakers, was quite incapable either of inspiring the Conference with faith in its own activities or of keeping order when the Conference, in sheer boredom, began to howl down speakers whom it did not happen to like. As this was the first general Labour Conference to which the Co-operative Movement has sent delegates on a large scale, the result was disheartening.

Meantime more sinister events were taking place. There had been a joint meeting of the Executive of the Labour Party and the Labour M.P.s to discuss Lloyd George's offer of places in the Government— a meeting which came to no decision. Unfortunately the meeting decided to hear Lloyd George, and Henderson arranged that they should meet him immediately (12 o'clock) at the War Office. Thither they went—a private gathering not supposed to be reported. Sidney states that Lloyd George was at his worst—evasive in his statement of policy and cynical in his offer of places in the Government. The pro-war Labour members drank in his sweet words; the pacifists maintained a stony silence whilst Sidney and one or two of the waverers asked questions to which Lloyd George gave non-committal answers. All he definitely promised was a Ministry of Labour and a Food Controller— whilst he clearly intimated compulsory mobilisation of labour. The joint meeting discussed these proposals at 2.30 at the House of Commons. The pacifists again lay low—Sidney thought they were playing for the disgracing of the pro-war Labour members by acceptance of Lloyd George's bait of office. The six[2] office-holders in the Asquith administration, together with Barnes and Clynes,[3] all of whom had been against joining Lloyd George, veered round. The miners' members, true to their idiotic rule of never voting without instructions, expressed no opinion and took no part in the decision. After speeches

---

[1] John Hill (1865–1945). General Secretary of the Boilermakers' Society.

[2] This figure seems to be an error. Only Henderson, Brace, and G. H. Roberts held office in the Asquith Coalition.

[3] John Robert Clynes (1869–1949). President of the Gasworkers' Union and M.P., for Platting from 1910 onwards. In 1917 became Parliamentary Secretary to Ministry of Food and Food Controller in 1918.

against taking office, from Sidney, Tyson Wilson[1] and Walsh[2] the meeting decided by eighteen votes to twelve in favour of accepting office. There was no display of temper—the most fervent objectors voting silently against it—not really wishing to prevent it. From the narrow standpoint of the pacifist movement, as a sect, the inclusion of pro-war Labour members in the Lloyd George Government may be a fortunate circumstance—a discredit to their warlike opinions. Sidney came back glad that he has done his best to prevent a decision disastrous to the Labour Party but inclined to be philosophical. He has long ceased to care about getting his own way, and he is always interested, as a student, in watching these breakdowns in Labour Democracy.

It is very difficult to analyse the state of mind of these men. The prospect of six offices with an aggregate income of some £16,000 a year, to be distributed among 18 persons, is a big temptation. To enjoy an income of £4,000 a year, or even of £1,600, for a year or two means to any Trade Union official personal independence for the rest of his life. But I don't believe that this pecuniary motive was dominant in the minds of the eighteen who voted for accepting office. A thorough beating of the Germans may have passed through their minds. But their main motive—at any rate the motive of which they are individually and collectively most conscious—is the illusion that the mere presence of Labour men in the Government, apart from anything they may do or prevent being done, is in itself a sign of democratic progress. It was this illusion that was responsible for the fanatical fervour with which the I.L.P. started some twenty years ago to get Labour representatives, whatever their personal character or capacity, on to representative authorities, central or local, from a parish council to the House of Commons. And naturally enough each individual Labour man thinks that he, at any rate, knows his own mind and will get his own way. Neither as individuals nor as a class do Labour men realise that they are mere office-mongers when they serve with men of trained intelligence or even with experienced middle-class administrators. It was this illusion that brought Clynes round; he argued that Labour must have some say in the terms of peace. Poor Labour men, they will not get much say in the terms of industrial peace at home, leave alone those of the peace of the world! And cementing pecuniary interest and class illusion there is a maddening muddle-headedness which makes them quite incapable of asking for terms for their own class before they consent to take office, and wholly blind to the distinction between supporting the government on conditions and accepting

[1] William Tyson Wilson (1855–1921). An official of the Amalgamated Society of Carpenters and Joiners. M.P. for Westhoughton: first elected in 1906.
[2] Stephen Walsh (1859–1929). Lancashire miner. M.P. for Ince. Parliamentary Secretary to the Ministry of National Service, 1917, and then to the Local Government Board.

the responsibility in advance for every plan which a majority of reactionaries may adopt. Moreover, the ordinary "rank and filer" is as muddle-headed as the ordinary Trade Union official. "We have our men in the Government," they argue, "and one of them is in the innermost Cabinet, that must be an advantage to us." And they are genuinely elated by this fact—they enjoy the vicarious glory of the Labour Cabinet Minister being among the rulers of the earth— a man whom they address by his Christian name and who sits and smokes with them. They cannot see that their representative may be a mere tool in the hands of men who have been hardened oppressors of their class. "They are a hopeless lot," sighed Sidney as he turned with a contented smile to his morning's work. "We are in for some strange events this coming year—let us get on with our work while we can."

*   *   *   *   *

December 12th.—The Lloyd George government, announced to-day, is a brilliant improvisation—reactionary in composition and undemocratic in form. For the first time (since Cromwell) we have a dictatorship by one, or possibly by three, men: for the first time we see called to high office distinguished experts not in Parliament; for the first time we behold Labour leaders in open alliance with Tory chieftains; for the first time a Cabinet has been created, not by a party political organisation or by any combination of party organisations, nor by the will of the House of Commons, but by a powerful combination of newspaper proprietors. The House of Commons, in fact, almost disappears as the originator and controller of the Cabinet. All these several momentous changes may be war measures, or they may have come to stay, or they may bring about some unexpected reaction. The fate of these new devices depends whether this new kind of government wins the war—if it does, so much of it will survive the war. If the Government fails—there will be disgust with the innovations. Whatever happens the shake-up is bound to lead to more deliberate organisation—either for the purpose of enslavement or for the purpose of enforced equality.

There are some counterbalancing advantages in the fall of the Asquith government. It was an intensely Whig government. Asquith and his favourite colleagues hated state intervention either in its regulative or its administrative aspect. This Government will be boldly and even brutally interventionist—it will break all conventions and even control inconvenient vested interests. The British ruling class is really far more concerned for their prestige as the leading members of a ruling race than for their interests as property owners within their own country.

*   *   *   *   *

APPENDIX

Letter written by Mr. Bernard Shaw in connection with his resignation from the *New Statesman*.

13th October 1916

MY DEAR BEATRICE,

It cannot be helped: it was bound to be, in the nature of things. My working relations with Sidney have always been those of a ticket-of-leave man who has forced himself on a benevolent employer by making himself useful. The benevolent employer appreciates the usefulness; but he can never trust the ticket-of-leave man, and is always surprised when his accounts turn out correct after all. This didn't matter in our Fabian work, because he never had to trust me: he had only to accept the finished work from me and wonder at its being so sensible instead of being what he expected. But a paper cannot be run on those lines. I might have wrecked the *New Statesman*: and it was psychologically impossible for Sidney to conceive that a man with my sort of mind and character, and an Irishman to boot, could do anything else. If he, as Chairman, felt this after nearly forty years' experience of me, how could novices like Simon and Bennett have any confidence in me?

A mere disagreement would not have mattered in the least: it would have been all the better, as we should have argued our policies out, and have thereby greatly improved them and arrived at a committee policy which would have strengthened and enlightened Sharp. But this would have involved our throwing aside all our work for three months after the declaration of war, and concentrating ourselves on the very knotty problem of how to encourage recruiting, give the war the character of a democratic crusade, rally even the sporting Jingoes to our side if they had any popular sympathies, and yet make the war achieve the political destruction of the worthless people who have been blocking us for the last ten years, and have at last, by a sort of judgment of God, brought the avalanche down on their own wretched heads. Well, I did that. I threw everything aside to sweat at this job for three months, almost in despair all the time because it urgently needed doing in three weeks. I solved the problem. I not only produced *Common Sense about the War*, but gave Sharp a model, in the *Lion* article, of the way to rally Old England in the interests of New England: a model which delighted the Jingo in him,

75

though he could not work up to it. For a time my stuff went into the paper because Nature abhors a vacuum; and as nobody else had put in the work and solved the problem my solution had to be accepted without understanding or sympathy. But in the end the Reign of Terror became so formidable that my line could not be taken without the conviction that only a hard stretch of work and a winning through to daylight can produce. This being lacking, the alternative was to trust me. And that alternative was, as aforesaid, psychologically impossible. I have therefore to take my solution and my policy elsewhere. And there is no elsewhere except in a book doing at long range what should be done by a journal at short range. My articles in the American papers are doing something; but there are disadvantages in attacks coming from America.

When I tell Sidney that the sword we forged has broken in my hand, he says in effect "So much the better: you are not to be trusted with a sword; and the broken-off point will come in handy for me as an oyster knife." I can only reply that he will not be allowed to open oysters with it. Northcliffe, who, after seven months' hesitation, followed my example by going for Kitchener and bringing down his man, besides achieving one of the great historic triumphs of the Thunderer in the matter of ammunition, will not let him. The *New Statesman*, after its little Shavian spurt, has come to heel; and that is the end of our influence on Cabinets.

As to Sharp, you must bear in mind that this conscription business is exceedingly trying to the nerves. Men of military age have to pretend to take it nonchalantly; but I have observed it pretty closely for some months and found that the suspense of playing for exemption is far worse than actual service. Sharp is a man of late hours and plenty of strong coffee; and he is ten times a better man in peace than in war. He is not very good at the technical business of literature: that is, he cannot bring all his personal qualities to literary expression: for instance, nobody who knows him personally would say that he is destitute of humour and generosity; but he cannot get those qualities into the paper, though he may later on, when the strain of the war is over. Meanwhile, he is a shaken man; and it was really this that determined me not to sit at the Board as a deadhead and make the nervous strain worse for him. His fundamental opposition to you will develop *unless you exercise his support of you strenuously*.

As to the financial position of the paper, you may leave that confidently to Providence. Like the old Thames Steamboat Company or the *Westminster Review*, it will struggle on long after all creation shrieks for its interment. But if you and Sidney put a violent end to it I shall not be greatly grieved. The longer I live, the more I perceive that Napoleon's rule of six years as the effective lifetime of a general applies to all public bodies and all papers. Three years ago the *N.S.* was young; to-day it is about eighty: a comfortable age for the directors, but not a promising one for the paper. A paper, unless it is to be frankly a dull paper for dull people, like *The Spectator* (which now suits my elderly taste remarkably well) or an ungenerous paper for ungenerous people like the *Saturday*, must live by adventures. The amazing journalistic feat of sacking Bernard Shaw does not indicate much taste for that sort of thing in Great Queen Street.

I could write you a great deal more on the subject: in fact, I actually have, in my laborious, intellectually conscientious way, written you a great deal more in order to find out what I ought to write and what there may be some use in writing; but I tear it all up and send you this instead.

I perceive that Stephen Hobhouse has fallen into the hands of the tormentors. I am very sorry, as in his case persecution is obviously cruel and useless. My only hope is that Maggie will get at the Commander-in-Chief, in which case Stephen will be hastily released with apologies and exempted for ever and a day. . . .

My letter to you and Sidney about my resignation crossed Sidney's letter to me, which began with a speech from the chair about my magnanimous behaviour and his regret that my disagreement with the overwhelming majority of the directors etc. etc. He is a daisy of the first flower when he obeys the call of his conscience to utter nonsense; but bless you! it doesn't make any difference to me, though it tickles the comedy writer in me. He presentedly dropped it and became human.

$$* \quad * \quad * \quad * \quad *$$

Letter written by Mr. Clifford Sharp in connection with Mr. G. B. Shaw's resignation from *The New Statesman*.

(? *October* 13*th*, 1916.)

DEAR MRS. WEBB,

Your letter rather demands an answer. It is one thing to be criticised by Shaw, another to have *you* supporting him. I don't think I have failed to do justice to Shaw's "lack of practical egotism" (as you call it—though *I* shouldn't). I have always been amazed by his willingness to go on supporting a paper which obviously represented his views in scarcely a single particular, and, of course, he has always been extraordinarily nice to me personally—so much so that I have never felt inclined to resent in the least the good-humoured contempt which he never concealed. I think he is much the most generous and sweetest-tempered person I ever came across.

But that does not affect the fact that he is intellectually the most grossly egotistical and unreasonable of beings. I cannot imagine anyone

more perverse than he has been in his dealings with the editor of the
N.S. He has never shown the smallest sympathy or understanding of
the difficulties of the job of maintaining a coherent line in the paper,
but, on the contrary, has always apparently made it a point of honour
or dignity not to compromise on the smallest point. A tentative
criticism of mine on a particular sentence of his, for example, has
always meant that the sentence would be underlined and strengthened
in the proof. His appreciative article on Moral owed its existence, I
believe, mainly to the fact that he knew from a conversation of a few
weeks before that the personal value of Moral was a point on which
he and I differed strongly.

And when a man solemnly writes that he does not of course expect
anyone else to see as far as he does—egotism has surely become a
disease. However, that's all done with now. I only refer to it because
I gather from your letter that, owing to your own relations with Shaw
being of such a special character, you may not quite have realised the
extent to which his practical generosity has always been accompanied
by the most utter and discouraging intolerance in other directions. His
money leaves one liberty, but his personal attitude refuses one not
merely the liberty of criticism but the right even to possess any view
of one's own at all. I believe that you and Mr. Webb are probably the
only people in the world towards whom his intolerance is modified—
by, as it were, a long inbred habit of affection and respect.

But what I really wanted to take this opportunity of saying was
this: you speak of not having protested, because the paper is more my
affair than yours. I think you've really gone farther than "not protesting" and let me suppose that you *actively* agreed with me in most of
my dealings with Shaw. But it's the latter part of the sentence I'm particularly concerned to reply to. *I* do *not* consider that the paper is
more my affair than yours (meaning you and Webb of course). I have
always looked on it as a co-operative concern in which the policy is
decided by common agreement. In the event of disagreement I should
expect my policy (i.e. my interpretation of the "entity" referred to
just below) to prevail in some matters, yours in others. I do not
regard the paper as representing my personal views, but rather the
views of an indefinable composite Fabian entity which it is my business to interpret. It often happens that a matter presents itself thus:
"I think so and so, but *The Statesman* ought to think so and so." Of
course such differences of opinion (or more probably feeling) between
C.S. and the editor of the *N.S.* are comparatively rare and small, but
they are not altogether unimportant. And the point is this: that it is
very difficult for me at times to discover, as it were, what the opinion
of the *N.S.*—that is the "common" opinion—really is without discussion. And if you are silent about differences of opinion because the

paper is more my affair than yours—well, it *will* become more my affair than I think it ought to be. I've no desire at all to have a *personal* organ, my whole object has always been to express a policy which shall command the widest possible measure of agreement amongst our supporters (the Board on the one hand and the readers on the other) —and, as a matter of fact, I should have been very glad to have incorporated in the policy and personality of the paper a dash of Shaw— such as has run through so much Fabian work. But it has not been practicable because he would not co-operate. I daresay it would have been possible if we had met every week, because then he might have been induced to meet one half-way. But as it was, his stuff has always been quite incompatible with the rest of the paper—and all the more troublesome because it attracted so much attention.

By the way, re your reference to the Bertrand Russell case, it was by a mere accident of convenience on press-day that the protest of four or five weeks ago appeared as a letter from MacCarthy instead of as an editorial note. All the same I think you are quite right in saying that I am not very sensitive as regards individual hardships and injustices. I strongly believe in economising as it were one's capacity to protest and never using it except when an important principle (as distinguished from a person) is involved and *where protest has a reasonable chance of producing concrete results*. If we had a protest or two every week—as we might easily do if I listened to half the requests I get—we should, I believe, lose to a large extent our power of producing an effect when it is really important to do so.

January 3rd.—I have bought a small cheap typewriter and I am using up some of my spare hours in the afternoon in copying out and editing my MSS. diaries so as to make a "Book of my Life". It is not more tiring than endless reading, hardly more so than my desperate attempt at Longfords to knit soldiers' socks. And it is more interesting to me than either, and perhaps more useful. Why should I burden a Literary Executor with this task of selection? Also I shall add notes about persons and events whilst I have still memory and judgment.

The year opens more hopefully. Peace must come this year. As Lloyd George said to Robertson,[1] "We must have a victory in three months. I am your last War Government." If there is not the Peace of Victory, there will be the Peace of Negotiation.

I have recovered my health except that I am no longer able to walk long distances. We lead a secluded life. We are both too indolent to see anyone who does not insist on seeing us. . . . We have our work, a few friends, a few strangers in search of information, my sisters and our deep and enduring comradeship to keep us occupied, interested and happy as one can be in these times.

Graham Wallas called on Sharp the other day with a message from Herbert Samuel and Montagu: would the *New Statesman* become the organ of H.M. Opposition? The younger liberal leaders were anxious to formulate a constructive policy and they liked the tone of the *New Statesman*. Sharp dined with Samuel and discussed matters with him. The *New Statesman* must remain independent, but he—Sharp—had no objection to consultations or to receiving "communications". *We* have kept in the background: the young men of the *New Statesman* had better make their own connections with the political world. Sidney continues to write weekly articles.

February 19th. Enter the Reconstruction Committee.—Routed out of my secret and pleasurable occupation of typing and editing the "Book of my Life" by an invitation to join the new Reconstruction Committee[2] set up by the Prime Minister. I had successfully reduced

[1] The Chief of the Imperial General Staff, Field-Marshal Sir William Robertson (1860–1933).

[2] The first Reconstruction Committee was set up by the Asquith Government in 1916. This Lloyd George one, under the Chairmanship of Edwin Montagu, deputising for the Prime Minister, was formed on much the same lines; it lasted until August 1917, when it was replaced by the Ministry of Reconstruction under Dr. Addison.

my work on the Statutory Pensions Committee to a perfunctory attendance—having finished my self-appointed task, as a representative of the Labour Party, of getting Labour representatives on all the local pension committees. I am not interested in the pensioning of soldiers and their dependants. Except for the relation of the treatment of disabled soldiers to a reorganised medical service, all the details of the work bored me. I don't want the ex-soldier to be treated better than the civilian population; and the function of the Statutory Committee seemed to be just this differentiation. Petting the ex-soldier on the cheap is the note of all its activities. But this new task—the task of surveying and unravelling the whole tangle of governmental activities introduced by the war, of reconsidering the relation of the state to industry, of central to local government—relations disordered by war activities—all with a view to practical schemes of reform—is an attractive one. It means the sort of work that S. and I are skilled in—if only I have the strength to perform it. Moreover, the Reconstruction Committee is not made up—like the Statutory Committee—of retired officials, retired admirals and generals with a couple of Countesses and a few philanthropists thrown in—but of young and vigorous persons with the Prime Minister as Chairman and the youngest and ablest of the ex-Cabinet Ministers as Vice-Chairman. Out of the fifteen members there are three Fabians, as well as two Labour men, and one of the two Assistant Secretaries—Arthur Greenwood—is a Fabian. The Conservative M.P.s are progressives (Hills[1] and Leslie Scott),[2] and there is the attractive young leader of the *Round Table* group—Philip Kerr[3]—one of the Prime Minister's secretaries. Altogether, if I keep my health and mind my manners, I shall find the work far more stimulating than that of the two government committees I have served on since the war. It may also turn out to be an opportunity for pulling together the Labour representatives on all the sub-committees of the Reconstruction Committee, if Clynes and Thomas are agreeable, and linking them up with the Parliamentary Committee of the Trades Union Congress (I doubt this possibility).

February 22nd.—Tom Jones,[4] one of my fellow Fabians on the Committee and a member of the new secretariat of the War Cabinet,

[1] John Waller Hills (1867–1938). Conservative M.P. allied with the Webbs in their Poor Law campaign. Financial Secretary to the Treasury, 1922–3.
[2] Sir Leslie Scott, Lord Justice Scott (1869–1950). The Conservative M.P. for Liverpool, Exchange, who was Chairman of the Acquisition of Land Committee, 1919.
[3] Philip Henry Kerr (1882–1940), afterwards Marquess of Lothian and Ambassador at Washington, was editor of the *Round Table* from 1910 to 1916 and Secretary to Lloyd George from 1916 to 1921.
[4] Dr. Thomas Jones (b. 1870). Civil servant; Deputy-Secretary to War Cabinet in first world war.

H

came to lunch here to-day to talk over the work of the Committee. He gave a most amusing account of the improvisation of the Committee by the Prime Minister. The Reconstruction Committee of the Asquith Government had consisted of Cabinet Ministers, with an ex-private secretary and an acting private secretary of Asquith's as joint secretaries. The present Prime Minister had asked one of the retiring Cabinet Ministers—Montagu—to undertake the Vice-Chairmanship and reorganise the Reconstruction Committee for the new Government. Montagu proposed a central committee of three—himself with Vaughan Nash and Bonham-Carter[1] (the secretaries of the late Reconstruction Committee) as assistants. This Junta was to revise the reports of the litter of sub-committees and advise the War Cabinet as to their value. But this was too much for the Prime Minister. "This is a mere shadow of Asquith," he remarked to the young men of his secretariat. "Bring me a list of persons with ideas": such a list being hastily furnished, he spent a spare ten minutes in considering it. He struck out some of the names—H. G. Wells and G.B.S. for instance, and added some others—among them Jack Hills and Seebohm Rowntree.[2] Then he proceeded to pick out fourteen. He came to the Webbs and pondered: "Yes, we will have one of the Webbs . . . Mrs. Webb, I think . . . Webb will be angry, Mrs. Webb won't." Then, apparently without consulting Montagu or Vaughan Nash, he ordered a letter to be written to each of the selected ones inviting them, in the name of the War Cabinet, to serve on the new Reconstruction Committee. Tom Jones tells us that Lloyd George talks about the committee as "a committee at large to advise about everything"—even India. He is going to give two hours a week to it. Meanwhile his Ministers are to go on administering their Departments without being consulted about the programmes to be submitted to the War Cabinet by this informal and "viewy" body. It is the maddest bit of machinery, and if there be neither open revolt nor silent obstruction in Whitehall, I shall be agreeably surprised. If Montagu accepts the Vice-Chairmanship, it will be because he wants to keep in with the Prime Minister. Did the Prime Minister submit the names to the War Cabinet? The membership of the Committee is so extraordinary—considering the importance of its work—that the whole business might come to grief pretty soon. The chance of the Committee surviving long enough to accomplish anything seems remote. We shall be marooned in one way or another by an enraged Whitehall.

[1] Sir Maurice Bonham-Carter (b. 1880). Financier and stockbroker; from 1910–16 was private secretary to Asquith, whose daughter he married.

[2] B. Seebohm Rowntree (b. 1871). Philanthropist and sociologist, son of Joseph Rowntree and Chairman of Rowntrees, 1925–41. Author of *The Human Needs of Labour*, etc.

The swollen world of Whitehall is seething—conflicting elements warring against each other. The permanent officials, who in pre-war times lived demure and dignified lives, mildly excited here and there by inter-departmental jealousies, are now fighting desperately for the control of their departments, against invading "interests" and interloping amateurs. Under the Lloyd George régime, each department has been handed over to the "interest" with which it is concerned. In that way, our little Welsh attorney thinks, you combine the least political opposition with the maximum technical knowledge. The Insurance Commission is controlled by the great Industrial Companies; the Board of Trade is controlled by the Shipowners, the Food Controller is a wholesale Grocer;[1] the Ministry of Munitions is largely managed by the representatives of the manufacturers of munitions, whilst a Duke's land-agent[2] has been placed at the head of the Board of Agriculture. Finally, a Trade Union official is Minister of Labour[3] and has been given, as the permanent head of his Department, an ex-Trade Union official[4]. The one shining example of this "vested interest *cum* expert" government is the distinguished University Professor—H. A. L. Fisher[5]—now President of the Board of Education. And round about, and in and out, of this government by "interested parties" there are streams of amateurs as private secretaries to Ministers or grouped in advisory committees. All this is hugely disturbing to the old-style civil servant—who has always held himself above the "interests" and aloof from the amateurs. In some cases he has retired to his tent and merely sulks; in other cases he counters intrigue by intrigue, whilst one or two brave ones defy the new Ministers and ignore the interloping amateur, refusing to submit the daily work to the new authority. Thus Sir George Askwith,[6] when he was asked to let Mr. Hodge know what his Department was doing, sent back a message to the Minister of Labour that "it was not customary to submit business unless the permanent secretary considered a ministerial decision necessary". The egregious Devon-

[1] i.e. Lord Devonport (1856–1934). Food Controller from 1916–17. Of the firm of Kearley and Tonge, grocers. Chairman, Port of London Authority, 1909–25.

[2] i.e. Rowland Edmund Prothero (1851–1937), afterwards Lord Ernle. He was Minister of Agriculture from 1916 to 1919. His "land-agency" connection was with the Duke of Bedford.

[3] i.e. John Hodge.

[4] i.e. Sir David James Shackleton (1863–1938). President of the Weavers' Amalgamation; afterwards Labour Adviser to the Home Office, and Permanent Secretary to the Ministry of Labour.

[5] Herbert Albert Laurens Fisher (1865–1940), the historian and author of the abortive Fisher Education Act, was President of the Board of Education from 1916 to 1922. Mrs. Fisher (p. 156) was Lettice Ilbert, daughter of the lawyer, Sir Courtenay Ilbert.

[6] Sir George Askwith, Lord Askwith (1861–1942). Chief Industrial Commissioner, 1911–19. Chairman from 1915 to 1917 of the Government Arbitration Committee under the Munition of War Acts.

port got so suspicious of his leading official (our old friend Beveridge) that he entered his room in his absence and seized the morning's correspondence, destroying some of it and answering other letters himself. In this welter of official life it is doubtful how far our committee will be permitted to function. The ferment may produce new ideas but the prospect is not encouraging. . . .

March 18*th.*—I was not able to attend the first meeting of the Reconstruction Committee, addressed by the Prime Minister. The summons came after we had left London for the week-end. I feel old and weak, and if I had not Sidney to inspire and help me I should think I had made a mistake in joining the Committee. The life I should enjoy, at present, would be a comfortable small country house, noiseless, except for birds and the rustling of water and wind—with my diaries to type. Sidney meanwhile might complete those endless volumes of historical material which are almost finished, and the two of us together might write the two books we want to bring out before we die—*What is Socialism?* and *Methods of Investigation.*[1] But the *New Statesman* and this new Reconstruction Committee are going to keep us in London, with its noise and its dirt and its constant overstrain of nervous strength and consequent sleeplessness. What troubles me is the doubt whether my feelings of old age and weariness are justified physiologically, or whether I am giving way to an obsession. I am in my sixtieth year—if it were not for the war I have a right to retire. Until the war is over I suppose that Sidney and I ought to render national service. . . .

June 3*rd.*—A delightful holiday at Logan Smith's[2] Elizabethan manor house set in cornfields, five minutes from the sea—with G.B.S. as companion and our host as week-end guest. I was much exhausted with two months' hard work on the Reconstruction Committee—suffering again from dizziness and general incapacity, especially for physical exercise. I feel too old and frail for the work of the Committee—though it interests and amuses me and I do it with zest and even with unnecessary energy.

The Committee is not a satisfactory creation and I think it is bound to be superseded. The Vice-Chairman, Edwin Montagu, is a great disappointment. We had always heard that he was one of the best informed and hard working of the Asquith crew. As acting Chairman of our Committee he has been, during the first months, a dead failure. He is a large-limbed, heavy-featured Jew—moody in temper, with little power of language and apparently without capacity for work, hating the mental effort of mastering the technical detail of successive

[1] Finally published as *Methods of Social Study* (1932). [2] See page 159.

questions. He is wholly inexperienced in committee work, and incapable of formulating a consistent procedure. Unfortunately, he has an incompetent staff. Vaughan Nash, the chief official, a gentle refined man of the "domestic-secretary" type, is woolly-headed, easily frightened off any decisive step and, like most weak men in responsible positions, suspicious and secretive. He has accreted, as staff, a set of dreamy cultivated amateurs, preachers of ideals rather than practical administrators or trained secretarial officers. Montagu, in the few hours he gives to the Committee, sits smoking a huge cigar, with Vaughan Nash talking to him. Indeed, the whole of the staff seem to spend most of a very short working day talking together, over cigarettes or tea—or listening to committees talking. No one seems to read the papers that pour into the office from Government Departments and from the litter of sub-committees of the late Reconstruction Committee. When the Vice-Chairman or the Secretary submit memoranda to the Reconstruction Committee it is quite evident that they have not taken the trouble to read even the official papers relating to the subject matter.

The Committee itself is not promising. Leslie Scott is the keenest-witted and the most knowledgeable member, but he is coining money at the Bar and gives us merely the leavings of a lawyer's brain. My old friend Jack Hills—the other Conservative M.P.—has moral charm and noble intentions, but he is a big baby on technical questions and without any special reasoning capacity. The Labour members seldom attend. Lord Salisbury[1] takes himself seriously as a great personage; he talks incessantly; he is obstinate in asserting himself, though he rarely sticks to his opinion if he is steadily opposed. Professor Adams[2] (one of the Prime Minister's secretaries) is a high-browed idealist, who wants to change the "world spirit" rather than alter social machinery —about which he knows little. Tom Jones is far too busy with the War Cabinet to do more than hold a watching brief for the Prime Minister. Philip Kerr, an ultra-refined aristocratic dreamer, with sentimentally revolutionary views, spends what little time and thought he has over from secretarial work for the Prime Minister in devising phrases and formulas to express standards of perfection. Marion Phillips[3] is shrewd and capable but contentious, and she tries to oppose anything I propose, out of some vague desire not to be considered a Webb disciple. There remain the three employers. Seebohm Rowntree,

[1] The fourth Marquis of Salisbury (1861–1947). President of the Board of Trade in 1905; Lord President of the Council, 1923.

[2] William George Stewart Adams (b. 1874). Warden of All Souls College, Oxford, from 1933–45. From 1916–19 private secretary to Lloyd George and editor of War Cabinet Reports.

[3] Marion Phillips (1881–1932). Investigator for Mrs. Webb in connection with the Poor Law Commission; became Chief Woman Officer to the Labour Party in 1918.

more a philanthropist than a capitalist, is an invaluable individual member of a Committee, eager to spend his time and money in working up special subjects, but too modest and hesitating in opinion to lead a committee. The two masterful representatives of the Ministry of Munitions—Sir James Stevenson[1] (Johnnie Walker) and Sir Arthur Duckham[2] are interesting examples of a new type created by the war—pioneer entrepreneurs turned bureaucrats and taking their new-found officialdom without the qualifications accepted by the highly trained civil servant. Moreover, they have no experience of committee procedure and they know nothing outside their own departments of work. They had, for instance, never heard of Gattie[3] and the New Transport Company. Duckham—a Gas Plant specialist —who had undertaken to report on the Haldane Report on Super-Power stations, was ignorant of the Lancashire and Cheshire scheme for a federated authority for Electricity and was quite grateful to me for supplying him with the confidential report of the Manchester Corporation sent me by E. D. Simon. For such able men, these big employers are singularly ignorant of the world they live in.

For the first two months Montagu and Vaughan Nash succeeded in holding up the Reconstruction Committee—their intention being to use it as a mere panel from which they might select advisers on this or that question. But after the Easter recess there was a concerted revolt among the members in favour of orthodox committee procedure for the carrying on of business as a self-governing body. Four panels acting as Sub-Committees of the Reconstruction Committee began to function: Education, Chairman Professor Adams, Secretary Arthur Greenwood; Local Government, Chairman Lord Salisbury, Secretary Bonham-Carter; Labour, Chairman Jack Hills, Secretary Greenwood; Control of Industry, Chairman, Sir James Stevenson, Secretary Bonham-Carter. I am a member of the last three panels. The Education Panel started off on idealist schemes—their special enthusiasm being adult education (W.E.A.). The Committee is, in fact, planning to do the work of the Consultative Committee of the Board of Education. This Panel was, at first, favoured by the Reconstruction Committee and the secretariat—the subjects selected for consideration being "safe subjects"—warranted not to excite criticism. But it presently launched out into a detailed criticism of the Education

[1] James Stevenson, Lord Stevenson (1873–1926). Managing Director, John Walker and Co. In Ministry of Munitions, 1915–18.
[2] Sir Arthur McDougall Duckham (1879–1932). Consulting engineer. Member of the Council of the Ministry of Munitions and Director-General of Aircraft Production during the first world war. Member of the Sankey Coal Commission.
[3] Alfred Warwick Gattie (1856–1925). Engineer and inventor. Chairman of Gattie Springs and author of the Gattie System of Goods Clearing Houses, which was taken up by Bernard Shaw.

Bill as a most imperfect measure, which brought it into disfavour with the Board of Education. The Local Government Panel was started off by Montagu asking for a memorandum on Housing from Rowntree, and one from me on Poor Law Reform. Rowntree prepared a most useful document which will be forwarded to the Local Government Board in due course. I seized my opportunity to get on with the Minority Report. Instead of preparing a memorandum I offered to get some sort of agreement between the Majority and Minority of the late Poor Law Committee and the Local Government Board—an enterprise which I think will be successful. But I doubt whether this Panel will do more than this. The Labour Panel has been held up by the litter of Sub-Committees appointed by the first Reconstruction Committee—covering nearly all the subjects in a chaotic way. These Committees have either not yet reported or are sending up reports which seem to have little bearing on immediate problems. One such report is the report of the Whitley Committee on the relations of capital and labour, which recommends setting up, in each industry, National Committees representing employers and employed—a report which resulted in an animated debate in the Reconstruction Committee, I being in a minority of one in opposing it. Eventually it was sent on to the War Cabinet with amendments. The Control of Industry Panel has been likewise held up by the dilatory proceedings of the Board of Trade Committees and of the Balfour of Burleigh Committee.[1]

The most successful bit of work hitherto done by the Reconstruction Committee was, in effect, *ultra vires*. Lord Rhondda failed to get his proposal for a Ministry of Health through the Cabinet so the matter was referred to the Reconstruction Committee. Montagu, without consulting the Reconstruction Committee, appointed a Sub-Committee—a Committee of five persons—Hills and I representing the Reconstruction Committee with Addison as Chairman and a brilliant young civil servant—Heseltine[2]—as Secretary. In three or four meetings we completed a report merging the Local Government Board and the Insurance Commission in a new Ministry of Health—a report which seems to have been accepted by the Cabinet. If the Insurance Companies don't defeat it, we shall have a Ministry of Health in a few weeks. The Reconstruction Committee was somewhat surprised that the job had been done without its knowledge between two of its meetings—a sad lack of procedure, rendered worse by Montagu's lack of tact in announcing it.

[1] The Government Committee on Commercial and Industrial Policy, set up in 1916 under the Chairmanship of the Conservative politician, Lord Balfour of Burleigh. It produced a number of massive reports.

[2] Michael Heseltine (b. 1886). Civil servant, mainly in Ministry of Health; in 1933 became Registrar of the General Medical Council.

If I had to prophesy I should say that the present Reconstruction Committee will not survive the summer. It is at once too pretentious and too powerless. If the acting Chairman and the Secretaries had been able and energetic men, determined to use the members of the Committee, each for what he or she was worth—the Committee might have won for itself a useful position. But the office-holders have a contempt for the Committee and the Committee have a contempt for the officers. The majority of the Committee do not intend to work: they are not representative of varied interests nor do they make a homogeneous body of counsellors. What is needed for the task of reconstruction is a powerful brain as Minister of Reconstruction with a first-rate staff of civil servants and an advisory Committee of picked amateurs to start ideas and represent the ministers on Sub-Committees. The present Sub-Committees should be required to report or should be superseded by others. The essential requirement is one big brain at the top. Sidney and I think the best man available is Winston Churchill. . . .

June 7th.—The Leeds Conference,[1] welcomed by Massingham in the *Nation*, as the "Birth of a new party" is significant as proving the existence of a powerful ferment in the Labour Movement which may either lead to new growth or to progressive disintegration. We fear that it is only one among many signs that the Labour Movement after the war will break into internecine struggles which will eliminate it as a force in national politics. The thousand or more delegates to the Leeds Conference were—so one of them declared—"mentally drunk"—and quite incapable of coherent thinking. They were swayed by emotions: an emotion towards peace and an emotion towards workers' control. It is an odd irony that the concrete example of "workers' control" arising out of the Leeds Conference was the seamen's refusal to permit MacDonald and Roberts to proceed to Petrograd to forward the propaganda for a negotiated peace! The very "bourgeois" leaders on the platform talked grandiloquently about "Revolution". To read the speeches one would think that they shared the thoughts and feelings of the Petrograd extremists. But who can imagine MacDonald or the Andersons, or even the Snowdens, leading a revolution of the Russian type—even if there existed the material for such a revolution in the British working class.

Meanwhile the official Labour Party and the majority of leading

---

[1] The Leeds Conference of June, 1917 was the direct outcome of the first Russian Revolution; it was a large, somewhat heterogeneous and enthusiastic gathering which passed, among others, a resolution calling for the immediate creation in Britain of Councils of Workers and Soldiers on the Russian model. It produced little concrete result, but was a clear indication of the mood of the articulate among the working classes.

Trade Union officials are becoming more and more "suspect" owing to their acceptance of places and honours from the Government—honours and places given "with no damned nonsense about merit". It is a travesty on political democracy that George Barnes should be in the War Cabinet from which Secretaries of State like Arthur Balfour are excluded. . . . The Trade Union Movement has become, like the hereditary peerage, an avenue to political power through which stupid untrained persons may pass up to the highest office if only they have secured the suffrages of the members of a large union. One wonders when able rascals will discover this open door to remunerative power.

*   *   *   *   *

May 15*th.*—We dined with Montagu last Saturday and I had a long talk with him in his study afterwards. I have also had Sir Arthur Duckham to dine to meet the chief engineer of the Manchester Corporation and Sir Harry Haward[1]—the financial controller of the L.C.C.—to discuss Duckham's proposal for state power stations. From Montagu and Duckham I gathered that there were storms brewing in Downing Street over the mishandling of the Ministry of Munitions by Addison and the unsatisfactory state of "Reconstruction after the war". The Prime Minister intervenes suddenly when matters become critical, peremptorily reorganises some department or starts a new one in a few hours, and leaves the new organisation to find its own level in a hostile world of old-established government offices. I told Montagu that I thought that the staff of the Reconstruction Committee was hopelessly insufficient for its work: that neither Vaughan Nash nor Bonham-Carter could grasp the whole range of necessary reconstruction. Montagu told me that he had been offered the Ministry of Munitions but had refused it unless he could take the Reconstruction Committee with him. He asked me to serve on a Sub-Committee to reorganise Government departments with Haldane as Chairman and Morant as Secretary, and he also asked Sidney to serve on a Sub-Committee to consider the fate of the railways after the war. Clearly the Reconstruction Committee and much else is in the melting pot. Fortunately I am quite willing to go on or go out. I enjoy the work on balance, and I welcome the opportunity of getting close to the facts of Government action, and of watching the machinations of the capitalist interests at work inside the governmental machine. But I am not vigorous enough to do well by the work; I don't like personal friction, and S. and I long to get back to our books —to bring to fruition all those years of research. We could easily spend another ten years in merely completing half-finished work. . . .

[1] Sir Harry Edwin Haward (b. 1863). Comptroller of the L.C.C. 1893–1920; author of *The London County Council From Within* (1932).

"Society" is in strange condition to-day. In spite of the deep cleavages of opinion on crucial issues—militarist autocracy *v.* revolutionary democracy, "the knock-out blow" *v.* "peace at any price" —there is no cessation of social intercourse or even of co-operation between persons holding conflicting views. We, for instance, find ourselves one day planning reconstruction with Lord Salisbury, another day with the Glasgow deportee MacManus.[1] Cole meets Huth Jackson[2] at dinner. . . . The Fabian Society and the Fabian Research Department are peculiarly middle ground—the Society being predominantly pro-war but including among its members "absolutist C.O.s". Among the curious episodes of this chaos of opinion is the use made of Clifford Sharp by a Government to which he has been hostile. Called up from the editorship of the *New Statesman*, against our pleading, he was, within a few weeks, withdrawn from his training as an artillery officer and sent by the W.O. to Stockholm— nominally as an independent journalist, but really as the agent of the Ministry of Intelligence to fathom Swedish opinion and to pick up information from foreign socialists. Meanwhile the F.R.D. has been "sheltering and sustaining" C.O.s for the last year. Cole and Kaye[3] have been exempted on condition that they continue to work for the A.S.E. and F.R.D. respectively; but Arnot and Holmes,[4] who have both been in the pay of the F.R.D., have been absentees for a year. Last week Holmes was fetched and this week Arnot will probably be arrested. The comic part of the business is that no one—not even the W.O.—would think worse of us for committing this breach of the Military Service Act. If it were brought to their notice they would try to look the other way—exactly as they tolerate the revolutionary activities of Cole—realising his influence with the A.S.E. The good temper of the English people, their readiness to tolerate and work with one another, whatever their opinions, is amazing. Whether it comes from wise philosophy or from mere bluntness of purpose and incapacity to distinguish between one thing and another— I do not know. But undoubtedly this universal good temper is an asset in times of severe strain. Will it continue after the war? Some observers think not. The nation is now enjoying the life of a spendthrift. When all classes have to go short the good temper may fail.

[1] Arthur MacManus (1889–1927). Clydeside engineer and member of Socialist Labour Party (Marxist); later General Secretary of Communist Party of Great Britain.
[2] Frederick Huth [Jackson] (1863–1921). Banker, partner in Frederick Huth and Co.; a supporter of many progressive causes.
[3] Joseph Alan Kaye (1895–1919). Socialist and pacifist; Assistant Secretary, Fabian Research Department.
[4] Walter Milton Holmes. Conscientious objector and worker in Fabian Research Department; afterwards member of Communist Party and on staff of *Daily Worker*.

July 14th.—I am enjoying my work in connection with the Reconstruction Committee. The Committee itself is most unsatisfactory: we meet casually and both the Vice-Chairman and the two Secretaries treat us with virtual contempt—the business for which we are responsible being brought before us in the most careless and uninformed way. But the Sub-Committees and panels upon which I sit give plenty of occasion for investigation and thought. There is the Employment Panel—we are considering an elaborate memorandum by Rowntree on the provision for unemployment after the war: the Local Government Panel, now engaged in a long-drawn-out discussion of another memorandum by Rowntree on Housing after the war. The Control of Industry Panel is chiefly interesting as an opportunity of studying the mind of the "two capitalist turned bureaucrats" —Sir James Stevenson and Sir Arthur Duckham. They assure us that they are preparing a lot of material for our consideration, through the Reconstruction Committee of the Ministry of Munitions, but it never comes. Besides these panels, I am on the National Register Committee of the Local Government Board, for elaborating a plan for a complete Register of inhabitants in each locality for all purposes. Recently I have been put on two Sub-Committees of the Reconstruction Committee—practically independent bodies—one for dealing with the Poor Law first and with other problems of Local Government afterwards, and the other the Machinery of Government Committee, which has for its task the reorganisation of the central government.

July 18th. Exit the Reconstruction Committee.—The last meeting of the autonomous Reconstruction Committee with Montagu in the Chair. As I predicted, the machine was too rickety to survive. This morning's papers tell us that Montagu has been appointed Secretary for India; Winston Churchill Minister of Munitions, and Addison (who failed at Munitions) Minister of Reconstruction. Carson's inclusion in the Cabinet and the translation of Geddes[1]—one of the temporary bureaucrats—to be First Lord of the Admiralty, are the most sensational of the changes, but they do not affect my world of internal affairs. A Minister of Reconstruction clearly means that the Reconstruction Committee either ceases to exist or becomes a mere advisory Committee or panel of advisors to the Minister of Reconstruction. The specially appointed Sub-Committees will, I assume, continue to function, and I shall have enough to do on the Local Government Committee and the Machinery of Government Committee.

[1] Sir Eric Campbell Geddes (1875–1937). First Lord of the Admiralty, 1917–18; Minister of Transport, 1919–21; wielder of the Geddes Economy Axe which, between 1921 and 1922, drastically reduced expenditure on social services.

The meeting was a cordial one—Montagu very gracious and pleased with himself—Vaughan Nash in good spirits—and all of us anxious to be pleasant on the final occasion. There has been singularly little friction between the various members of the Committee—the trouble has been between the old office holders—Montagu and Vaughan Nash and, to a lesser extent, Bonham-Carter—and the new Committee of outsiders. The only regret I have in parting from the general work of the Committee is that I shall not get all the reports of the Sub-Committees—I shall especially regret those dealing with industry and labour. One wonders when the whirl-a-gig of change in the personnel of the Government is going to stop—to the old inhabitants of Whitehall it must be like a perpetual shooting the rapids.

August 5th.—Sidney has been unusually busy with the Labour Party, owing to the crisis over the Stockholm meeting[1] of the International, and he spent yesterday drafting the resolutions for the Labour Party Conference on the 10th and the Allied Conference on the 28th and 29th. Whether the Labour Party will accept his draft we doubt: it is an anti-German but not a British Imperialist peace that he suggests—couched in the phraseology of International Socialism. No one knows whether the British Government desires the Stockholm Conference or not—we believe that the German Government does and that the French and Italian Governments are against it. The pacifist M.P.s believe that it will happen; we think it will not happen. But if it does take place we two go to Stockholm, if a British delegation representing all parties is decided on by the Labour Party Executive and is permitted by the British Government and the Seamen's Union. The Labour Party Conference will show us what are the sentiments of the world of Labour after three years' war. The Andersons, who were dining here on Friday, believe that the revolutionary pacifist movement is the coming force—but the sect to which they belong lives in a state of exalted optimism which may be a little "previous".

* * * * *

August 12th.—The Labour Party Conference surprised itself, the Labour Party Executive and the political world, by deciding by a three to one majority in favour of going to Stockholm. This decision,

[1] The Socialist Parties of the neutral countries such as Holland and Scandinavia, under the leadership of Hjalmar Branting, earlier in the year had proposed a Conference of Socialists of all countries, including the belligerents, to discuss terms of post-war settlement; this suggestion was eagerly taken up by the Russians. Arthur Henderson, sent by the Cabinet on an exploratory mission to Petrograd, returned convinced that this Conference ought to be held, and the Government was at first prepared to issue passports to the Labour Party delegates. The violent opposition, however, of the Sailors' and Firemen's Union—whose members had the most direct experience of U-boat warfare—and the *volte-face* of the miners' representatives, described in the text, enabled Lloyd George to go back on his previous decision.

which depended on the vote of the miners and the railwaymen, given *en bloc* after hearing Henderson's speech, has led to a Cabinet crisis. Henderson has been dismissed by the Prime Minister—not only dismissed but dismissed with a public charge of having deceived the War Cabinet and misled his own party. But all the evidence, documentary and circumstantial, which is before us points to the fact that it is the Prime Minister and War Cabinet who have been caught out in an unsuccessful gamble. All published documents prove that Henderson, since his return from Petrograd via Stockholm, has been consistently in favour of the British Labour Party being represented at the Stockholm International Conference: all published documents show that he was left a free hand by the War Cabinet to recommend this course to the Labour Party. And so far as his colleagues on the Labour Party Executive know, he has been equally straight in his private utterances. His counsel and his votes in committee have all been in strict accordance with his public words. Moreover, all the Labour Ministers—all of whom were against going to Stockholm—*knew that he was privately advising the Labour Party to go to Stockholm.* Now Lloyd George declares that Henderson, in spite of his public utterances, assured the War Cabinet that he was going to recommend the Labour Party Conference not to send delegates to Stockholm. How he could take this course, even if he agreed to do so, it is difficult to understand, since he was party to the resolution of the Executive in favour of Stockholm and as Secretary of the party he was obliged to carry it out or to resign his office.

The plain truth is that the War Cabinet, on the information given them by their tame Labour men, believed that the Labour Conference would either negative the Stockholm delegation or would agree to it by so small a vote that it would be easy for the Cabinet to arrange with the French Government to veto it or with the seamen to make it impossible. Henderson himself thought that he would be defeated and that Stockholm would be rejected—he signified as much to Sidney on Thursday—he may have said as much to one or other of his Cabinet colleagues. The War Cabinet counted on this rejection—they wanted to appear ready to leave Labour freedom to decide while secretly intending to stop any International gathering. It was only another gamble made safer by duplicity—a way of behaving for which the Prime Minister has become notorious. It is, of course, possible that the terms of peace[1]—Sidney's memorandum—published on Friday and telegraphed to all corners of the earth—may have compelled the War Cabinet to reverse their decision to permit Stockholm—if the

---

[1] *Labour's War Aims*, published unsigned and finally approved by the Party's Conference in December, 1917. It had a remarkable reception, in the United States in particular.

Labour Conference should so decide. The "Terms of Peace" would create a veritable panic among the Milner and Curzon crew—not only hostile tariffs barred but the African Empire and Mesopotamia handed over to a Supernational Authority. So Henderson has been made the scapegoat.[1]

August 22nd.—Owing to the stampede of the miners . . . the majority in favour of going to Stockholm sank to a nominal figure. But we expected the vote to be reversed. Henderson distinguished himself by a lucid and eloquent defence of his action—by far the best speech he has delivered. But the atmosphere of the Conference was confused and disorderly. The pro-war party were somewhat shamefaced about Henderson's rude dismissal and the Labour ministers sat uncomfortably on the back benches. There were cries of "blackleg" when Barnes rose to defend himself for accepting Henderson's position. The pacifist minority were silent, acutely conscious that the reverse had been brought about by Snowden's acid speech at the last Conference and their own unpopularity as a group. Everyone was crestfallen and somewhat ashamed of the Labour Movement.

The net result of the episode is that Henderson emerges as the one and only leader to the exclusion of the Labour ministers, on the one hand, and, on the other, of MacDonald and the pacifists. . . .

September 1st.—The Inter-Allied Socialist Conference was a fiasco. The French delegation was made up of equal numbers of the "majority pro-war" and "minority", "stop-the-war" parties. The "majority" led by Thomas[2] and Renaudel,[3] had come to obstruct and prevent a pro-Stockholm decision—and they used every device of

[1] May, 1918. We none of us realised the enormous importance of Henderson's ejection from the Cabinet. We gathered afterwards that it was not so sudden as it appeared. He had apparently become aware, for some time, that he was a mere hostage for the good behaviour of Labour and that he had no say in policy. At Petrograd he took himself seriously—at Stockholm he came under the influence of Branting and Huysmans and was converted to International Socialism as a way of ending the war. Hence he expected his colleagues, on his return to London, to treat his opinions with respect: instead of which they kept him "on the doormat" while, with the help of George Barnes, they discussed his conduct. He went to Paris to arrange for the Inter-Allied Conference after a threat of resignation. He came out of the Cabinet with a veritable hatred of Lloyd George, who insulted him at their last interview immediately after the Labour Conference, and whose letter, published the next day, was the sort of communication which would not have been made to any one recognised to be a social equal. From that day, Henderson determined to create an Independent political party, capable of becoming H.M. Government—and he turned to Sidney to help him. B.W.

[2] Albert Thomas (1878–1932). French Socialist. Friend of Jaurès; later moved rightwards and became Minister of Munitions, 1916–18. Secretary of the International Labour Organisation, 1920–32.

[3] Pierre Renaudel (1871–1934). Leader of the French right-wing Socialists; editor and manager of *L'Humanité* from 1906 to 1918.

delay and denial they could invent. The Russian delegates were tire-some and childish in their insistence on their own importance and their long-winded revolutionary pedantry; the Italians were "impossibilist"; the Belgians were hostile in a dignified and eloquent manner; the Greeks were represented by an absurd and fussy little English spinster; the Portuguese, thanks to the fact that they could speak neither French nor English, were silent. The British, made up of four mutually contemptuous sections—all alike contemptuous of the foreigners—were well-behaved but divided in opinion. The foreigners wrangled for two days with each other and the Conference finally broke up into two separate and informal meetings—the British and French majority parties and the Belgian delegation at the Waldorf Hotel, and the British and French minorities and the Russian and Italian delegations at the Fabian Hall. From these meetings will issue, I assume, separate reports. One wonders what Stockholm would have been like! The British and Germans might have found themselves trying to do business together with the Latins and Slavs storming around them. There is a real cleavage of temperament between the British and the French and one wonders whether it does not show itself at the front. One notable distinction is the British dislike of rhetoric and delight in a joke—the worse joke the better. Any attempt to relieve the tension by a joke gives dire offence to the French, and when G.B.S., impatient at Renaudel's blatant use of rhetoric to obstruct progress, asked what was the French word for "obstruction" and Longuet[1] shouted back "Majorité" Renaudel threatened to leave the Conference. Not being allowed to laugh, the British delegation settled down to a grim silence.

Result—Nil.

*   *   *   *   *

October 3rd.—J. H. Thomas, the General Secretary of the Railwaymen, dined here last night to talk over the policy to be pursued on the Local Government Committee of the Ministry of Reconstruction. He is one of the ablest of the Trade Union leaders and one of the most statesmanlike of their parliamentary representatives. He and Henderson are running the new party. It is interesting to note that, for the first time, he told Sidney that the responsible Trade Union officials would like him to stand for Parliament, and Henderson repeated this request yesterday. But I gather that this desire is due, in the main, to their feeling that the Labour Party ought not to continue to make use of Sidney without giving him the opportunity of making use of the Labour Party! As Sidney has not the remotest wish

[1] Jean Longuet (1876–1938). Grandson of Karl Marx and leader of the minority in the French Socialist Party.

to go into Parliament, and much prefers to remain in the background, I hardly think the request will be pressed. We should hate to be forced into political life in our old age. Sidney would not refuse if the Labour Party appealed to him—he is strong enough for it, but he personally feels he can be more use as a confidential counsellor than as a competitor for ostensible leadership. The position of Parliamentary leadership is so little coveted! And in the Labour Party the majority of the leaders are conscious of their incapacity for constructive thought—Sidney delights in it—it is his peculiar craft.

October 5th.—Six successive air raids have wrecked the nerves of Londoners with the result of a good deal of discreditable panic—even among the well-to-do and the educated. The first two nights I felt myself under the sway of foolish fear—my feet were cold and my heart pattered its protest against physical danger. But the fear wore off, and by Monday night's raid—the nearest to us—I had recovered self-possession and read through the noise of the barrage with the help of an additional cigarette. If the raids continued for a year on end I suppose we should hardly notice them except to be more sparing of evening engagements. But it would mean an effort of will and intelligence which might prove impossible to the neurotic elements in the population.

I am perpetually asking myself how the war is affecting the mind of the Englishman. The sustained horror of it is depressing. Friends lose husbands and sons: promising men, on whose careers one had counted, are swept away. One realises that an indescribable torrent of misery and bestiality has overwhelmed millions of men on the battlefields and desolated cities and countrysides in the occupied districts. This war seems a universal bankruptcy of human intelligence and human goodwill. It adds to my depression that the problems involved in its settlement are wholly outside my grasp—I have come to no conclusions as to the fundamental cause of it, or as to the right end of it. But there is one consolation. The catastrophe is so huge and so discreditable to the Governments of the world that it must lead to big changes. Never again will the manual workers accept the position of outcasts from all that makes for civilisation: never again will they agree to a position of social servility: never again will they trust the representatives of the ruling class to dictate foreign and colonial policy without even deigning to discuss it. Their leaders will fall into all sorts of traps, but the great multitude behind will press forward, stumbling slowly over innumerable obstacles to a world based on social equality.

Tom Jones lunched here yesterday. The War Cabinet is much perturbed at the rumours of revolutionary feeling among the working class. A certain Professor Arnold[1] (the presumed author of *Times* articles on the ferment of Revolution) sent in the most alarmist memorandum to some members of the Cabinet—a document which was solemnly discussed. Not only the Central Labour College[2] was denounced, but also the Workers' Educational Association cited as spreading revolutionary ideas in the guise of University education for the working class. The Secretary of the W.E.A.—MacTavish[3]—was called upon to answer this accusation—and both the accusation and the defence were despatched to Buckingham Palace. Forthwith a royal summons was issued to MacTavish (a blunt, energetic and somewhat commonplace Scot). . . . Milner is said to be the most alarmed and to be hankering after peace by agreement with the Hohenzollerns lest worse befall the British and German Junker class alike.

Meanwhile revolutionary ideas, more especially of the syndicalist type, are being discredited by the collapse of Russia. The folly of the I.L.P. in acclaiming the Russian Soviet Government of "Workmen and Soldiers' representatives" as the "new model' is becoming every day more obvious. The success of the Labour Party depends largely on how far its leaders can free themselves of the old assumptions of the capitalist State whilst keeping themselves free from the cant of anarchic rebellion against any form of deliberately ordered social action.

November 14th.—I am working steadily at my Committees— Local Government and Central Government—Sidney helping me to prepare memoranda for their instruction and guidance. The Local Government Committee is accepting the Minority Report—piece by piece, with very little amendment. The Central Government Committee is less familiar ground and far more instructive to me. Haldane, George Murray,[4] Schuster[5] and Morant[6] know far more

[1] Edward Vernon Arnold (1857-1926). Professor of Latin, University College, Bangor, 1884–1924.

[2] Founded in London in 1909 as a Marxist breakaway from Ruskin College, Oxford; though failing to survive as a residential institution it gave birth to the "Plebs League" and the present National Council of Labour Colleges.

[3] John Mackenzie MacTavish (1872–1938). General Secretary, Workers' Educational Associations from 1916.

[4] Sir George Evelyn Pemberton Murray (1880–1947). Civil Servant; secretary to the Post Office, 1914–34.

[5] Claud Schuster, Lord Schuster (b. 1869). Civil Servant. Permanent Secretary to the Lord Chancellor, 1915–44.

[6] We have known and liked Morant since he appeared as a student in the early days of the London School of Economics—an abnormally tall and loosely knit figure, handsome in feature, shy in manner and enigmatical in expression. At that time he was a little over thirty and at a loose end, having failed to keep an official position at the court of Siam. I think, in some part of my diary, I have told the story of his engagement by Michael Sadler, as private secretary, and his rapid rise, some-

about the working of Cabinets and Government Departments than I
do, but I try to make them face the newer problems of combining
bureaucratic efficiency with democratic control—they are for ever
insisting that the working of Parliament makes sensible, leave alone
scientific administration, impracticable. It is a pleasant sport. We sit
twice a week over tea and muffins in Haldane's comfortable dining
room discussing the theory and practice of government. I tell them
that I am discovering the land of Whitehall for the future Labour
Cabinet. Heseltine and I prepare memoranda raising questions and
have at length persuaded Haldane to call leading officials to give informal evidence, besides supplying us with all their office papers. One
afternoon last week George Murray came here to tea and I tried to
explain to him what we mean by an "efficiency audit". It is clear
that these Committees will take up all my time for the next year. I
wish I were stronger-brained—the subject matter of the Machinery
of Government Committee is immense and the importance of the
questions raised vital to the success of the Equalitarian state.

*   *   *   *   *

December 11th.—This autumn's work has been exhilarating. I
have piloted the Minority Report proposals through the Local
Government Committee, and unless some unforeseen obstacle arises

what at Sadler's expense, to be Permanent Head of the Board of Education, his
brilliant career there, his quarrel with the N.U.T., and his eventual compulsory
transfer, by the Asquith Cabinet, to the sterile office of the Insurance Commission.
Morant is the one man of genius in the civil service: but he excites violent dislike
in some men and much suspicion in many men. He is public-spirited in his ends but
devious in his methods. Since he has been in the Insurance Committee his life has
been poisoned by trying to work a system which he knows to be rotten through
men he knows to be corrupt. Throughout the 1902-3 Education legislation Sidney
and he worked confidentially and cordially together, and he was most helpful with
the Minority Report. Then when we failed to bring off the Minority Report and he
became the official head of a system which he had opposed, but failed to stop,
Morant, perhaps quite naturally, no longer cared to consort with us. I think he felt
that while we could not help we might easily injure him. We had no influence over
the Liberal Cabinet; we had not even any influence with what there was in the way
of a Labour Party; we had lost any footing we had among a certain class of Tories.
Hence, for some half-dozen years, we saw little or nothing of Morant. The Reconstruction Committees brought me again into connection with him. But our relations
though friendly had not been quite those of working comradeship. Robert Morant
and the Webbs have different ends and they suspect each other's methods. He certainly does not want social democracy—he is an aristocrat by instinct and conviction. And his immediate personal end is to be Permanent Head of the new Ministry
of Health, and he is not sure that we are not interfering with this by hammering
at the abolition of the Poor Law. So Morant and I meet week by week at Committees
and often collogue together—but with many reservations, especially on his side.
He is a strange mortal, not altogether sane, but in spite of his malicious tongue and
somewhat tortuous ways, he has done more to improve English administration
than any other man. And he is always interesting to watch, with his rapidly
working intellect and self-consciousness, deep-seated prejudice and, be it added,
indifference to conventional standards of honour between men of "equal stations."

B.W.

we shall get a unanimous report before Xmas. This is the crown of those three years' hard propaganda after the three years' hard grind on the Poor Law Commission.[1] My success was mainly due to Lord George Hamilton's generous help, coupled with innumerable argumentative memoranda with which I plied both the members of the Committee and persons having influence with one or other of them. Also I have learnt committee manners—an art in itself.

Meanwhile Sidney has become the intellectual leader of the Labour Party and he is also happy and contented with his work. The time is ripe for bold constructive leadership. It may be that this last decade of our working life is to prove the most operative.

Anyway, I have put my diaries away again—partly because I felt my attempt to compose "The Book of my Life" was not successful— but mainly because there is sterner work to do and work for which I am peculiarly fitted by long experience and training.

[1] Note, 1918.

The inception of the Local Government Committee and the pressing through it of a unanimous report within three months embodying all the conclusions of the Minority Report of the Poor Law Commission was, I think, my masterpiece. With Montagu's permission I set out to get agreement between the representatives of the majority and minority of the Poor Law Commission and the Local Government Board. I first approached the Local Government Board through Sir Samuel Provis, with whom I had worked with great cordiality on the Statutory Pension Committee. I pointed out to him that since the issue of the two reports the status of the L.G.B. had gone from bad to worse. The Insurance Commission had been set up and now claimed to be the main department concerned with Health; the new Ministry of Labour had taken over the function of dealing with the destitution due to unemployment; and within the last month yet another department had been set up—the Ministry of Pensions which, after the war, would be controlling the treatment, training and maintenance of millions of persons—and controlling these services through a series of Local Authorities excluded from the jurisdiction of the L.G.B. His old department was, in fact, being throttled by its connection with an obsolete and emasculated Poor Law. No Government dared give any function to a Poor Law authority—central or local. This argument seems to have convinced the L.G.B. and they consented to the appointment of the committee and nominated Symonds— the Head of the Poor Law division—to represent them. My task with Lord George promised to be a more difficult and delicate one. An affecting interview at his house and we were reconciled. He walked all the way to Hyde Park Corner with me, chatting about the war and the Report of the Mesopotamia Enquiry of which he had been Chairman. "You want me to serve on this Committee, Mrs. Webb? Very well, I will," were his parting words. I gathered that he had been converted to the break up of the Poor Law by service on the Venereal Disease Commission. But he acted with great generosity, and backed me up nobly in my duel with the wily Symonds who did not want to abolish the Poor Law but merely to change its name. The Report was published soon after Xmas and, except for the protests of Boards of Guardians, was received as an overdue reform. But the Local Government Committee was squashed by Vaughan Nash as a dangerously effective body. The question of areas and powers remains still to be dealt with before a really radical reform of the tangle of local authorities can be brought about. ·B.W.

PREFACE TO PART II

1918–1924

DURING the period which stretches from the winter of 1916 to the beginning of 1918 a slow change took place in the general attitude of the British people, which manifested itself in three ways—"war-weariness", interest in the possibility of a negotiated peace, and "post-war reconstruction". These, like any other movements of the mind, cannot be isolated or precisely dated; but they seem to have arisen more or less in the order listed. By late 1916 the original impulse of 1914 which sent hordes to the recruiting offices had almost died away; no more was heard of Belgium or of Nurse Cavell; the realities were the Conscription Acts, the fearful slaughter on the Somme (and later at Passchendaele), arguments about exemptions, dilution of labour, "starred men", Leaving Certificates, etc.—all against the sombre background of a war which appeared, as far as anyone could see, to be going on for ever, conducted by national governments which also were going on for ever.

Under these circumstances men's minds began to question whether the struggle must be fought to a finish, and whether anything would really be gained thereby. The winter of 1916–17 saw the letter of Lord Lansdowne to the *Daily Telegraph*, President's Wilson's Peace Note addressed to all the belligerents, and the "peace resolution" passed in the Reichstag; later in the year, after the first Russian revolution, came the abortive "Stockholm Conference", which was to have been attended by the Socialists of all countries. Nothing happened directly as a result of all this, though early in 1918 the reconstructed British Labour Party summoned an Inter-Allied Labour Conference and put through it a document on Labour war aims which made nearly as much stir as the famous Fourteen Points; the Governments on both sides were determined to see the war through to the end.

Nevertheless, the effect in Britain was manifest in the attitude towards "Reconstruction" and to the Trade Unions. Both these were, of course, in part the result of the first dose of total war and of war shortages. Labour became comparatively scarce and valuable; Labour leaders had to be courted and mild concessions made to them and to their followers; some measures towards limitation of profits and equality of sacrifice had to be put into force—though nothing, of course, resembling the severe controls of 1939–1945. Above all, it became necessary to persuade the people who were being ordered to fight and to make munitions that if they held on until final victory they would gain something worth having. Accordingly the Reconstruction Committee was stiffened up into a Ministry; reports of all kinds were produced; forward-looking legislation such as the 1918 Education Act was passed; and all these bright hopes worked up to a crescendo of promises culminating in the 1918 general election.

In this atmosphere the Webb Partnership again began to flourish. Beatrice, her health now much improved, entered the Reconstruction Committee and found herself very happily working in a number of groups on particular subjects, all of which were looking forward to a brave new efficient world and were much more disposed to be sympathetic to Webb suggestions than before the war. Sidney collaborating with the Labour Party and Trade Union chiefs, and after Stockholm a close advisor of Arthur Henderson, Secretary of the Party, was laying the foundations and shaping the structure, not merely of a Party organisation more flexible and more suited to modern conditions, but of a Socialist statement of policy which it could adopt for the nation. Between them, it seemed, they were helping to fashion a collectivist post-war programme and the instrument wherewith to carry it out; and the increasing buoyancy of Beatrice's writing in the Diary (notwithstanding her still poor opinion of the human material available for Labour leadership) reflects her feeling that the world was on the upgrade and the Partnership again doing a worthwhile job.

Nor was that feeling seriously affected either by the

electoral débâcle of 1918, or by the post-war depression. The first she regarded (rightly, so far as the home front was was concerned) as a trifling and transient political set-back; the correct counter was to continue to push the reconstruction projects, to help the Labour Party steadily to improve its own organisation and practical proposals, to write books to convert the still-unconverted—and incidentally to instruct the newly-enlisted Liberal pacifists in the principles of Socialism—and to bring the Sankey Coal Commission, appointed in 1919 to stave off a national mining strike, to a successful and successfully propagandist conclusion. Right through the post-war boom, up to the beginning of 1921, Labour continued to gain in strength and the Webbs in energy. And though they recognised the disaster of Black Friday, when two great Unions of railwaymen and transport workers called off their promises to the striking miners and sent them down to defeat, they were less depressed by it than others of their contemporaries, partly because their studies in Trade Union history had shown them many previous instances of decline and revival, so that they could apply a sense of proportion to one particular defeat, but more because their attention was soon redirected to politics. Very soon afterwards Sidney, who had for long been running a campaign to induce local Labour Parties and their Trade Union supporters to adopt Parliamentary candidates of better calibre, was himself asked by the Durham Miners to stand for Seaham. He accepted; the Partnership set itself the task of providing a thorough political education for a single community, and produced the triumphant results of the 1922 election. Thereafter, Sidney was learning his new trade, and before them both was the possibility, achieved at the beginning of 1924, of a Labour Government in Britain.

With that event this volume closes. It marks the end of the second period, the period during which, recovering from pre-war turmoil and war-time shock, both the Labour Movement and the Webbs went ahead to what seemed at the time to be a great triumph, for though the first Labour Government was heavily in a minority and came to an ignominious end, it is too often forgotten how much longer Labour supporters had believed they would have to wait for any Labour Government at all. It might well have marked also the end of Beatrice's active life; she was sixty-four, suffering as always from insomnia, and the passages in the Diaries which refer to Passfield Corner indicate that rest and retirement were much in her mind. But, as everyone knows, there was a great deal more to come.

M.I.C.

PART II
1918–1924

JANUARY 1918—DECEMBER 1918

January 10th.—Five days of complete rest at Longfords. Arthur and Mary Playne and their companion Bichy Ross[1] lead a sheltered and secluded life, in two or three rooms of their charming home in the midst of delightful gardens and grounds. Arthur is a lithe and happy old man, doing little or nothing of any importance, but occupying himself with mechanical magistrate's work and silent attendance on County Council committees—he having been made an Alderman, as he himself delights to tell you, "in respect of the services of his wife". Mary is a benign old woman, somewhat restless in body and forgetful in mind—she knits endlessly and smokes at intervals. Bichy Ross, a buxom middle-aged woman—energetic and amazingly pleasant tempered and dutiful—superintends the communal kitchen and working parties. Bill and his wife live 1½ miles away from the family home—we never see them, as he apparently dislikes Sidney and loathes me. The mill at the bottom of the garden grinds out cloth: there is no connection at all between the house of the leading capitalist and the hands who toil a few yards off—neither good feeling nor bad —mere indifference. . . .

Sidney and I have plenty of work before us—Sidney in the Labour Party and I on Government Committees. The Labour Party is bounding forward into public notice and Henderson becomes every day more audacious in his programme. How far this new reputation is fictitious, I do not know. We do all we can to stimulate both Henderson's audacity and to advertise the reality of the movement. The party itself is tumultuous in its cross-currents. Its apparent unanimity arose from its being, for the first time, in open opposition to the Government on all economic issues and insisting on independence in the statement of war aims. It is the "new thing" round which all who are discontented with the old order foregather. . . .

Litvinoff[2]—the Bolshevik "Ambassador"—lunched with us on Wednesday; he had written asking whether he could call. He is an anglicised Russian Jew of unprepossessing appearance—but with a

[1] Arthur Playne (1845–1923) was a country squire and owner of cloth mills, husband of Beatrice's third sister, Mary. Bill Playne was their son. "Bichy" (sometime spelt "Bice") was Beatrice Ross, secretary-companion and intimate friend of Mary Playne.
[2] Maxim Maximovitch Litvinoff (1876–1952). In 1918 U.S.S.R. plenipotentiary to Great Britain. Foreign Secretary, 1927–39. His wife was the novelist, Ivy Low.

certain honest sturdiness. He has lived nine years in London, married an English wife and earned a humble livelihood as clerk in a publisher's office. He is not a bad sort—a crude Marxist in his views, without experience of administration or knowledge of political or economic facts. He believes in Government by the "Proletariat", and he does not believe the English race capable of it. He is pessimistic about the Russian Revolution. Unless capitalism is overthrown in other countries the Russian Revolution will not survive. If Europe militarism does not destroy it, economic pressure will. The catastrophe must be universal, or the superior efficiency of "Bourgeois" Government will make the "Proletarian" Government appear a failure! When we asked him what was the alternative to the success of the Bolshevik Revolution he replied "We shall become a colony of the German Empire".

January 21st, Nottingham.—Two days awaiting the Labour Party Conference and chatting with the members of the L.P. Executive. There are about forty of the leading Labour men in this hotel. But this crowd is sharply divided into members of the Executive of the Labour Party and those who are primarily members of the N.A.C. of the I.L.P.—each section having its own private sitting room. There is not overt hostility, they all greet each other with good-mannered intimacy—cloaking their differences in banter and chaff. There are some who belong to both camps. Sidney and I are on friendly terms with all, though we belong to the Labour Party group. We have had much talk with Henderson and Purdy,[1] and other Trade Unionists who are on the L.P. Executive. Henderson is nervous about the rejection of his new constitution by the block vote of the big Unions. Cotton has a majority against, and the miners, who decide to-day, are still uncertain on which side they will cast their vote. The opposition of the cotton delegates is led by Tom Shaw,[2] a pro-war Socialist. He wants the Labour Party to remain a close preserve of the officials of the great Unions, acting as a select group in the House making terms with either of the principal parties and securing places for leading Trade Union officials either as ministers or as permanent officials. He dislikes the advent of the ambitious middle-class politician and the intrusion of the missionary Intellectual. This conservative section is, to some extent, backed up by the revolutionary Syndicalist who is against "Parliamentarianism". But Shaw's main strength lies in the jealous exclusiveness of the Trade Union Bureaucracy—the same element that ousted the Trades Councils from the Trades Union

---

[1] William Frank Purdy (1872–1929), an official of the Shipwrights' Union.
[2] Tom Shaw (1872–1938). Cotton textile official. Secretary, International Federation of Textile Workers, 1911–29. M.P. for Preston; Minister of Labour in 1924 Labour Government.

Congress.[1] The I.L.P. opposition to the new constitution is from an exactly contrary standpoint. The leaders of the I.L.P. want to construct a "People's Party" in which the Trade Unions would take their place in the constituency organisation either as local bodies, or as individuals. Henderson wants to make the best of both worlds. By the new constitution he aims at combining the mass vote and financial support of the big battalions incorporated in the National Unions with the initiative and enthusiasm of the brain-working individual members of the Local Labour Parties. He is ambitious: he sees a chance of a Labour Party Government—or a predominantly Labour Government, with himself as Premier. I was amused to find that he looks forward to having Sidney either as Secretary to the Labour Premier or to the Labour Cabinet.

Meanwhile the leaders of the Labour Movement are distinctly uneasy about the spirit of revolt among the rank and file, which openly proclaims its sympathy with the lurid doings in Petrograd. At the Labour Party Executive on Saturday they decided to send a private telegram to the P.M. begging him to put off the Man-Power Bill Committee stage until after the Conference. They believe that there may be an epidemic of "down-tools", disastrous equally to the conduct of the war and to the reputation of the Labour Movement. The I.L.P. leaders do not know whether they want a revolutionary movement or not. Mary Macarthur told me, with a measure of satisfaction in her voice, that there would be famine in six weeks' time. She and some others are playing with Bolshevik ideas—they enjoy the reckless defiant attitude and they have various scores to pay off. J. R. MacDonald tries hard to sit on the fence and bewilders his admirers by his agility in saving himself from tumbling over on one side or the other. He is playing a waiting game—helping neither side—doing nothing either to foment or to prevent trouble.

January 24th.—The usual good-humoured tone in the Conference, in spite of contentious business and underlying unrest: the usual unpunctuality in starting and extreme punctuality in adjourning for the midday meal and at tea-time. The British Trade Union representative will, on no account, be late for his meals or early for his meetings. The new constitution was adjourned for one month for consideration by the affiliated bodies. It would have been rejected altogether if it had not been for a powerful speech by Henderson, appealing to the great working-class organisations not to miss becoming a great National Party through petty jealousy of Trades Councils and outside middle-class members. The Labour Movement

[1] In 1895; the Trades Councils were then believed to be too much under the influence of the S.D.F. and the newly formed I.L.P.

is a great lumbering mass moving forward towards the equalitarian state, slowly and irregularly, lurching now on one side, now on the other. At the evening meeting for the reception of the fraternal delegates, the Bolshevik "Ambassador" was enthusiastically received by the militant minority in the gallery. But his contemptuous reference to the "forms of democracy" (in defending the dismissal of the Constituent Assembly) was listened to in cold silence by the somewhat scanty audience of delegates on the floor of the hall. The other foreign comrades were listened to attentively—especially the pacifists Longuet and Huysmans—but only about one half of the delegates had taken the trouble to attend this extra sitting—the public gallery being crowded. At the business meetings of the Conference there was no sign of the coming Revolution—the delegates were the usual well-fed placid type—the atmosphere was distinctly not electric and the tame Government Labour men were allowed their say. The Labour ministers were severely snubbed but were not withdrawn from the Government. The British Trade Unionist is not yet in a revolutionary humour—the wife standing in the queue is his most solid grievance. But the whole body of delegates seemed determined that the social order shall be different after the war and for the first time they are keen on the International. The *réclame* of the International was the outstanding feature of the Conference.

* * * * *

February 14th.—Saw Sidney off to Paris with the rest of the Labour delegation. S. is very happy in his new rôle of adviser in chief to the Labour Party, and Henderson, Middleton and the Trade Union leaders quite clearly are grateful to him. His old enemy, MacDonald, is friendly in manner to him—and if he is not liked by the I.L.P. they have confidence in his essential friendliness. And he is too old to excite jealousy in the young men.

February 19th.—Sidney back from Paris reports that the unpunctuality and indecision of the French Socialists in all arrangements was distracting—the British delegation spent most of its time running after meetings adjourned from place to place or beginning some hours after the agreed time. But a fair measure of unanimity was reached which it is to be hoped will be further defined and affirmed at the London Conference. Henderson and MacDonald were the only operative members of the British delegation—both of them made admirable speeches. But not even MacDonald could talk French and Henderson could not even understand it. Sidney had not only to act as one of the responsible delegates but also as interpreter and general courier to the whole party. Huysmans was invaluable. The three

Trade Unionists—Thorne,[1] McGurk[2] and Bowerman[3]—were "cripples" and spent most of their time in eating and drinking, enjoying the luxurious plenty of Paris. The position of privilege, irrespective of capacity—a position occupied by many Trade Union officials —is becoming the most scandalous circumstance of the Labour Movement. It makes one despair of the Labour Party as an organ of Government. These men are not only incapable of doing the work themselves; they are not fit judges of other men's capacity. It is a mere lucky chance that they have Sidney at their disposal, and it is only his long service to Labour and Socialism that makes them trust him sufficiently to enable him to do their work. The cleavage between the somewhat neurotic intellectuals of the I.L.P. and the Trade Union leaders is becoming more marked.

The rout of the Bolsheviks clears the air. The Bolshevik creed was the latest edition of the philosophy represented in Western Europe by Syndicalism and Guild Socialism—a philosophy which had its foundation in a contempt for intellect and an almost equal contempt for "conduct". It relied on impulse, more especially the impulse to violence. It is a strange irony that this faith in violence has been, in nearly all countries, intertwined with Tolstoyan cosmopolitan pacifism —this unnatural alliance being due to the possession of a common enemy—the Law-and-Order Imperialistic Capitalism. The German Junker believes in order, security and, he would add, material prosperity, within the state, together with the use of physical force towards other states. The Bolshevik believes, or thinks he believes, in law between nations, whilst preaching violence to bring about the state of society desired by the militant minority of the proletariat within each community. The tragic-comic struggle that is now taking place at Brest is between these two evil forces.[4] There is little doubt which evil one will win. The Prussian devil, making use of intellect, will show itself a devil in successful doing; the other devil will prove its satanic quality by being undone.

February 27th.—Litvinoff brought to see us, yesterday evening, Kameneff,[5] who, with another comrade, has come to enlighten the western democracies on Bolshevik foreign and home policy. These

[1] Will Thorne (1857–1946). Gasworker. Founder and General Secretary, National Union of General and Municipal Workers. M.P. for Plaistow from 1906.

[2] John McGurk (1874–1944). Agent, Lancashire and Cheshire Miners' Federation; on Executive of Labour Party.

[3] Charles William Bowerman (1851–1947). Secretary to Trades Union Congress, 1911–23, and M.P. for Deptford.

[4] i.e. over the Treaty of Brest-Litovsk, when Germany imposed such harsh terms on the defeated Russians.

[5] Leo Borissovich Kameneff (1883–1936). Russian revolutionary. Lived in Paris 1908–14. Exiled as Trotskyist, 1927; executed.

two have been accredited as "ambassadors" to the French and Swiss people respectively. Litvinoff who, a month ago, was feeling himself a great personage, is now quivering with mortified racial and personal vanity. He has not only been ignored by the British Government, but he has been referred to contemptuously, in the House of Commons, as a man of many aliases and even as an undesirable, if not criminal, alien. The "Ambassadors" to France and Switzerland, when they landed at Aberdeen, were searched and all their belongings, including a cheque for five thousand pounds and their "diplomatic valise", taken from them and sent to Scotland Yard to be examined—they being instructed to call there on their arrival in London. Our Russian comrade threatened us with reprisals on the English in Petrograd. Litvinoff said that he had, some days ago, wired to Trotsky that he would prefer to return to Russia as his position was humiliating and that he had only delayed his departure in order to help the Bolshevik emissaries to bring their case before the democracies of England and France. He bitterly complained that one or two East-End Russians had been arrested (apparently for sedition). His companion was a commonplace elderly man of German Jew physiognomy—looked a superior clerk—with no experience in politics except in repeating shibboleths. He asserted and reasserted that the Bolsheviks were in power with the assent of the great bulk of Russians. He made a halting apology for their failure at Brest—the munitions had fallen into the hands of the advancing Germans because these wicked ones had not respected the armistice. Hate of Germany was for the first time springing up in the hearts of the Russian people; but unless the Allies recognised the Bolshevik Government, hate for the Allies would be equally intense. I asked them whether the Bolshevik Government wished us to accept the terms of their peace with Germany as a settled fact. They both replied that we should be compelled to do so because we could not beat Germany. They did not seem to care for the lost provinces—nor did the Russian proletariat—they said. All they wanted was to be let alone to complete the social transformation they had begun. "We have given the factories to the workers and the land to the peasants: was that not a sufficiently glorious achievement to make up for all their other failures?" I asked whether the Germans might not establish themselves in Petrograd and disestablish the revolutionary Government. "Take a city with three million starving inhabitants mostly with rifles," they jeeringly replied, "what good to them?"

We were courteous to them, but so far as we could make out they did not want us to help them in any way but only to listen to their story. They were clearly conscious that the Bolsheviks were discredited and the only answer they had to make was threats of reprisals on the British in Petrograd. "I have means of letting Trotsky know, and he will be without conventional scruples," asserted Litvinoff. It did not seem to occur to these simple-minded advocates of physical force that being without scruples was hardly a recommendation for supreme power in Russia, from the standpoint of the Allies. Poor fools!

The Inter-Allied London Conference was an outstanding success. Sidney spent an agitating three days as Chairman of the commission on territorial adjustments, but in the end he got all the nationalities to agree. The Labour Memorandum [on *War Aims*] is now acclaimed by the *Times* as a model document, and the prestige of the Labour Party has been enormously enhanced. This reputation has been further extended by the acceptance by the adjourned Conference of the new constitution after a short morning session. Henderson's star is rising in the political firmament. Let us hope that it won't set at the General Election.

March 1st.—We dined yesterday with Haldane to meet one other guest, at his own request—the Prime Minister. Haldane asked me some weeks ago whether we would spend an evening alone with him and the P.M. to discuss the memorandum which I had circulated to the Machinery of Government Committee on the reorganisation of Government Departments. It is needless to say that there was no such discussion, neither the P.M. nor our host showing any inclination for it.

Prime Ministers usually excite, in all but the most sophisticated minds, a measure of awe and instinctive deference. No such feeling is possible with Lloyd George. The low standard of intellect and conduct of the little Welsh conjurer is so obvious and withal he is so pleasant and lively that official deference and personal respect fade into an atmosphere of agreeable low company—but low company of a most stimulating kind—intimate camaraderie with a fellow adventurer. We talked about reconstruction, current politics, the late crisis, the personal traits of Generals and Ministers, the Russian Revolution, the terms of peace, and the prospects of the next Election. His object in meeting us was, I think, to find out whether any co-operation with the Labour Party was practicable—or at any rate how the land lay with regard to the L.P. and the Asquithian Liberals. It was, in fact, a counter-thrust to the Asquith touting for coalition with the Labour Party. He could not approach Henderson, so he approached Sidney. Like many other persons, who have known Henderson as a Cabinet Minister, he thinks that all the recent success of the Labour Party must be due to someone else—who else is there but Webb? "I know Henderson," he laughingly remarked; "it is not Henderson who has made the *réclame*—all the distinction comes from . . ." and he waved his hand towards Sidney. He made distinct advances—pressed us repeatedly to come and dine with him and meet Milner—apparently to discuss the terms of peace. But I was not responsive: I don't want to go to Downing Street—in fact I had told Haldane when I accepted the invitation to meet the P.M. that we would not go to 10 Downing Street. But we parted with cordiality.

The P.M. re-seen (we have not met him for three or four years) did not impress me favourably in spite of his flattering friendliness. He is a blatant intriguer—and every word he says is of the nature of an offer "to do a deal". He neither likes nor dislikes you; you are a mere instrument, one among many—sometimes of value, sometimes not worth picking up. He bears no malice for past opposition; he has no gratitude for past services. He is no doubt genuinely patriotic and public-spirited, but all his ways are crooked and he is obsessed by the craving for power. His one serviceable gift is executive energy—he sees that things are done and not merely talked about. Unfortunately, he does not care whether or not they are thought about. He is the best of boon companions: witty, sympathetic, capable of superficial argument and quick retort, and brilliant in his observations on men and things.

What was clear from our talk is that the P.M. and Milner are thinking of a peace at the expense of Russia. He repeated with more frankness and emphasis what he has said publicly, that the Russians must lie in the bed made by the Bolsheviks, that neither France nor England would fight on to restore Courland and Lithuania, leave alone to restore the lost Poland. I interposed "Would Wilson and U.S.A. agree?" "The U.S.A." he almost snapped out "could not go on with the war if England and France refused to do so." I am not at all sure whether his desire to meet us and his desire that we should meet Milner is not connected with this possible sacrifice of Russia and her Revolution. He wants to know how the Labour Party would take such a peace—whether it would be considered a betrayal of the course of democracy. I gather that Haldane is also looking forward to a reconciliation between the Junkers of Germany and those of England over an agreed extension of both Empires. With Russia to cut up, the map of the world is capable of all sorts of rearrangements which would give all the more powerful and ambitious belligerents an opportunity to expand their jurisdiction over the more helpless races—not only the German Empire but the Empires of Great Britain, of France, of Italy and of Japan. But would the one disinterested Power—the U.S.A.—agree to such a peace and would the democracies of the Powers look benignantly on the victory of the Junkers of all countries?

March 3rd.—The surmise that Haldane is at heart an aristocrat and an imperialist and is working with Milner and Lloyd George was yesterday verified. Camille Huysmans, Haldane and Frankfurter[1] (a clever American lawyer and sympathiser with Labour) met here at tea. I opened the discussion by explaining to Huysmans, in impartial and even favourable terms, the feasibility of a speedy peace at the expense of Russia. Supposing we had our International Socialist Conference and that by that time Germany had made peace with the Bolsheviks on the basis of extensive annexations and indemnities in the form of financial concessions, and supposing Scheidemann[2] were, in committee with Henderson, Vandervelde and Renaudel, to offer a favourable peace to the other Allies—not only the evacuation of Belgium and France, but also "accommodation" with regard to Alsace-Lorraine, the German colonies and the Trentino—what would our representatives answer? Haldane seconded me enthusiastically before Huysmans had time to reply. "On these lines", he said, in tones of emotion, "the International might solve the problem. The Russians dragged us into the war and then betrayed us. The Socialists would bring fresh minds to bear on the question—they would bring a new authority direct from the people—they could settle the war in a new way that would be resisted, if it came from Governments, but which would be accepted if it came from the democracies of the world."

"Would the International agree to these terms, M. Huysmans?" I pressed for an answer. There was a pause . . . Huysmans seemed taken aback, while Haldane bent forward eagerly with his most engagingly beneficent expression. "I cannot imagine Scheidemann making such a disgraceful proposal—Scheidemann is a good Socialist; your press is quite mistaken in thinking that he is a mere representative of the German government." "But if Scheidemann did make such a proposal," I persisted, "would Henderson, Renaudel and Vandervelde accept?" "Certainly not," replied Huysmans, "it is inconceivable". "Would the pacifists and I.L.P. . . . would MacDonald accept it?" I continued. "Ah, your I.L.P. . . . they might . . . they are peace-at-any-price—but not MacDonald—he is not a pacifist. It would be inconceivable," repeated Huysmans slowly, "such a peace would destroy Socialism." Haldane looked disappointed, but began, in his inimitable way, to cover up the question since it had proved so unpromising a quest. At that moment Frankfurter joined us. After compliments between him and Haldane I returned to the charge: I explained to Frankfurter, somewhat elaborately, the issue and asked

[1] Felix Frankfurter, (b. 1882) the Supreme Court Judge; Professor at Harvard Law School, 1914–39.
[2] Philipp Scheidemann (b. 1865). Leader of German Social Democratic Party Secretary of State 1918, and President till 1919 of first Republican Government.

him "What would Wilson say?—would your country agree?"
Frankfurter with modest manner and in polished words was not less
emphatic than Huysmans. "We are a naïve people, Mrs. Webb," he
concluded, "we really do believe in what we call Democracy—we are
in this war quite honestly—though the Germans don't believe it—
for a clean peace. Such a peace as you suggest would mean the defeat
of America and the triumph of German militarism. The worst thing
that has been said in the war was Lloyd George's suggestion that such
a peace would be possible. It gave Americans a cold shudder."

From this clear and distinct issue the conversation wandered to a
possible compromise. Haldane presently began to reminisce—he
charmed the two foreigners by an account of his visits to Berlin—1906
and 1912. He gave a vivid description of Bethmann-Hollweg as a
wise and pacific statesman fighting against the German General Staff,
and he intimated that he had had messages from Bethmann during the
war, through neutrals, reminding him of their common attempts to
secure peaceful relations between two great countries. But after this
interesting diversion he returned to the question of the participation
of the International in a peace by agreement with the German Government. "I know these men," he said, "the wise brains of Germany—
the financial and political statesmen—they might be ready to have
independent states made up of the present occupied territories of
Russia—they might feel confident that being their neighbours they
could get all they wanted without annexation—would the International Socialists accept?" Huysmans remained silent for an appreciable time. "It would depend entirely on the wishes of the populations
concerned and on the reality of their independence when they expressed
these wishes. Some of these people hate Germany, and if left to themselves would refuse to be penetrated by her." There was no more to
be got out of the conversation and presently Haldane departed.

Then Huysmans, Frankfurter and we two resumed the discussion
of a peace at the expense of Russia and decided that this would mean
the defeat of all that Wilson and the International Socialists desired.
What could be done to prevent it? If only Wilson would join hands
with the British Labour Party; if only he would instruct Gompers[1]
to link up with the International, we should have a lever against the
imperialists of the world coming to a bargain over the corpse of an
independent Russia and the rout of democratic forces. To bring about
this it was necessary that the Labour deputation to the U.S.A. should
be of influential men—Thomas ought to go. Sidney clinched the
conversation by writing Frankfurter a long letter, which could be

[1] Samuel Gompers (1850–1924). Leader of American Trade Unionism. President
of American Federation of Labor, 1882–4 and 1886–1924.

forwarded to Colonel House, summing up the dangers of a cynical peace at the cost of democracy, and urging that the U.S.A. Government should back up the demand for an International congress. The British Labour Party was Wilson's one supporter in Europe. . . .

March 7th.—On reflection, I think it is unfair to blame Milner and Haldane for wishing to make peace with the German Junkers. Haldane has always believed in the German governing class—or rather in the financial and industrial and professional sections of it. He has always been an admirer of the Prussian state and of German mentality. Milner too, by birth, by training, and by temperament has an almost identical "make up" with that of the German imperialist— he admires and hates the same characteristics in men and states. It is the same reason that makes Parmoor[1] a pacifist—and it is a rare joke to see our dear brother-in-law posing to himself and to the revolutionaries of the Labour Movement as a believer in democratic liberties. All these public-spirited and highly gifted men honestly believe in German civilisation. And obviously there are magnificent elements in the German state, and in many Germans it is these elements that are predominant. But neither Haldane nor Milner have the moral fastidiousness necessary to realise the sheer brutal devilry of the German world purpose. With the P.M. it is different. By birth and training he is a pacifist rebel against authority, and he is totally unaware of and unsympathetic to the finer elements in the German character. If he desires peace at the expense of democracy to the glorification of German autocratic efficiency and militarism throughout the world, it is mere cynical opportunism.

What will the professional pacifists say to a cynical peace? All the pacifists who are pacifists on account of the injury to property by war —and every day the number of these increases—the Lansdownes[2], Parmoors, Hirsts[3] and Dick Holts,[4] will be made keener in their demand for peace by immediate negotiation with Germany—the consequent defeat of the Russian Revolution adding an agreeable zest to the endeavour to come to terms. The Tolstoyans will blindly and

[1] Charles Alfred Cripps, Lord Parmoor (1856–1941). Barrister, married Theresa, sixth of the Potter sisters (d. 1893): father of Sir Stafford Cripps. Originally a Tory, he became a strong supporter of the League of Nations and Lord President of the Council in the 1924 Government.
[2] Henry William Edmund Petty-Fitzmaurice, 5th Marquess of Lansdowne (1845–1927): Leader of the Tory Opposition in the House of Lords from 1906: Minister without Portfolio in the Asquith Coalition. His famous letter to the *Daily Telegraph* urging the conclusion of a negotiated peace which he had previously proposed in a private memorandum to Asquith, appeared in January 1917.
[3] Francis W. Hirst (b. 1873). Liberal economist and Free Trader. Editor of the *Economist*, 1907–16; governor of the London School of Economics.
[4] Richard Durning Holt, of Alfred Holt & Co., Liverpool shipowners; son of Lawrencina, the eldest of the Potter sisters.

fanatically continue their cry for peace at any price. But the men and women who are believers in democratic equality between man and man and race and race will become more in favour of continuing the war. This is largely the state of mind of Huysmans, Henderson and ourselves. The *Nation* will not know its own mind—it will denounce with equal vehemence the British Government for failing to take any grounds for negotiations or any minister who suggests the possibility of accepting the only conceivable grounds the Germans would agree to. The attitude of the Courtneys is peace, peace, and again peace: the terms will come right on the day that peace is signed or the day after. Let everyone stew in his own juice.

It is, of course, conceivable that we may be forced to accept a German peace. But for the first time during the war I feel warlike.

March 20th.—The Labour Party is the most ramshackle institution in its topmost story. Henderson sits alone in the untidy office at 1 Victoria Street: no member of the Executive or of the Parliamentary Party ever comes near him except Sidney. J. R. MacDonald, the Treasurer, supposed to be his fellow Executive officer, is conspicuous by his absence. Neither the pacifist nor the pro-war M.P.s trouble him with their advice or take counsel with him as to their own action. Snowden, the Chairman of the I.L.P.—the leading Socialist organisation within the Labour Party—never loses an opportunity of sneering at Henderson or denouncing the "official Labour Party". The fair-minded and gentle-natured Middleton, the Assistant Secretary, sits in another tiny room and supervises two seedy male clerks—ex-trade union workmen—and as many somewhat inferior female typists. There is the little dwarflike Gillies—an honest over-sensitive and obstinate minded but well-informed little Glasgow Fabian—as intelligence officer, and a certain journalist—Tracey[1]—a pleasant and, I think, competent young man as publicity officer. Upstairs, superintending the women's section, sits the redoubtable Marion Phillips—hardly an element of solidarity in an office. There are some one hundred Parliamentary agents, most of whom I saw yesterday at a Fabian Research Department reception—old men, unkempt men, half-educated men—an inferior brand of the Trade Union branch official—with no alertness and little organising capacity. The chief Parliamentary agent—Peters[2]—is of the Sunday School type, who trudges through his work with a sort of mechanical persistence, carrying out Henderson's orders. And added to this decrepit staff is the circle of

[1] Herbert Trevor Tracey (b. 1884). Journalist; joined Labour Party headquarters staff, 1917, and became its chief publicity officer.
[2] Arthur Peters. A hairdresser by trade; National Agent for the Labour Party, 1908–19.

rebellious spirits and idealist intellectuals who have gathered round G. D. H. Cole and ourselves—Tawney, J. J. Mallon[1], Delisle Burns,[2] Arthur Greenwood, Arnold Toynbee, and H. J. Gillespie. These young men have formed themselves into a sort of informal advisory committee, sometimes presided over by Sidney as Henderson's representative, sometimes left to their own devices. This morning I found them foregathered in the Fabian Common Room engaged in constituting a series of Advisory Committees to the Labour Party on some half a dozen subjects, whilst two of them—Tawney and Arnold Toynbee—were drafting a leaflet against the intervention of Japan in Russia. Cole, in fact, regards himself as Sidney's successor, if not his supersessor, as chief intellectual adviser to Henderson. The I.L.P. leaders seem altogether out of it. I suggested, when called in to advise as to the membership of the Advisory Committees, that J. R. Mac-Donald and W. C. Anderson should be asked to be Chairmen of the two principal committees. The suggestion was accepted, but without enthusiasm. Unless the two old parties have completely lost their cunning, it is difficult to imagine that such a crazy piece of machinery as the existing Labour Party will play a big part in the reconstruction of the U.K. and the British Empire after the war. All one can say is that the very formation of such a party, and the gathering round it of distinguished intellectuals, represents a sort of sub-conscious determination of the politically conscious minority of the working class and its intellectual adherents, to get a radically different state of society after the war. Always the old, old question repeats itself—is there sufficient public spirit and sufficient knowledge and reasoning power to make the change from the capitalist to the equalitarian state practicable?

German culture is to-day in the ascendant because its governing class has both public spirit and intelligence to a far greater degree than the governing classes of Russia, Italy, France, England, and, maybe, of America. The fact that this public spirit and this scientific intelligence are directed to a brutish end—from the standpoint of the world at large—does not destroy the immediate effectiveness of these national characteristics: it does not even rob them of their inherent greatness. The nemesis of the evil purpose will come—the Germans will suffer for their sins. But this suffering will not diminish the suffering of the Russians for their lack of conduct and capacity, nor will it prevent the French and the English from being battered on account of their relative inferiority in skill and orderliness. What distresses me is that

[1] James Joseph Mallon, (b. 1875). The Warden of Toynbee Hall: at that time Secretary to the Anti-Sweating League and member of many Trade Boards and Government Committees.

[2] Cecil Delisle Burns (1879-1942). The lecturer and historian; between 1917 and 1919 a civil servant in the Ministry of Reconstruction.

public opinion refuses to recognise the distinction between purpose on the one hand, and method or process on the other: refuses to see that a nation or an individual may excel in one and not in the other, and that excellence in both are needed. If science and self-control are practised by persons of evil purpose, science and self-control are damned as the attributes of the devil: if wilfulness and incompetence are usually connected with a glowing idealism, then the other school of thought holds cynical motive to be a sign of grace. We please no one with our gospel of the use of scientific method in social service. That "Law is the Mother of Freedom", that science should be the parent of law, and that love should be the director of science, is the most unpopular of creeds.

March 31*st.*—A week of miserable anxiety. We first realised the seriousness of the German onslaught last Sunday—a realisation further intensified by Tom Jones who came straight from the Cabinet to supper with us. Not one minute did I sleep that night, and even Sidney has been disturbed in his usual equanimity, though he does not let his anxiety have any influence on his output of work. The success of the Germans when all the authorities thought the Western Front secure is only another instance of their superiority in forethought, in technique and in concentration of purpose.

What is the explanation of the paralysis of British brains which shows itself in the W.O., in the Admiralty, in Parliament, and in private enterprise?

The answer is a complicated one. The British governing class, whether aristocrat or bourgeois, has no abiding faith in the concentrated and disinterested intellectual toil involved in the scientific method. Science, to them, is a sort of intellectual adventure to be undertaken by a rare type of man. The adventure may or may not turn out worth while, but, in any case, it is silly to expect this adventurous spirit from ordinary men in the conduct of daily life. Indeed, applied to social, economic and political questions the scientific method is to be shunned as likely to lead to experiments dangerous to liberty and property and the existing order of society. Also science means measurement; it means the objective testing of persons and policies and this measurement and testing is against all good comradeship in common undertakings. For the Englishman of all classes—peer, shopkeeper and workman—is a kindly creature who hates the thought that anyone who is related to him, who belongs to his own set or class, or with whom he usually consorts, should be made uncomfortable or dispossessed of that to which he is accustomed, however inefficient he may be. The perpetual emphasis on rights as against obligations is part of this preference for the comfort of the individual over the welfare of the whole community. The Englishman, though he has a talent for impromptu organisation—for the organisation that introduces order or good manners into a meeting or a society—dislikes and suspects any more deliberation and self-control than is necessary for this imperfect purpose. Finally, he is a protestant and delights in sectarianism —in little cliques of fellow thinkers who regard their thoughts as religious exercises. The Englishman hates the impersonality of science.

* * * * *

April 20th.—We dined the other night with Haldane to meet Sir William Tyrrell, the head of the Foreign Office Intelligence Department. He has apparently been commissioned by Lord Robert Cecil to open up communications with Sidney as director of the foreign policy of the Labour Party. He told us that a very private Committee was sitting to consider alternative ways of dealing with the German colonies and Mesopotamia—how to avoid either giving them back to Germany and Turkey respectively or keeping this territory ourselves. The difficulty of placing all these lands under an international authority was the intense possessive feeling of France and Italy and Portugal, who cling to their colonies far more than Germany does. We and Germany might agree on some neutral Government—the Latin countries would not. He professed to be sympathetic to the advanced Labour programme and even to be inclined to the Bolsheviks—talked about "the tragedy of Stockholm", and intimated that Lord Robert Cecil had been in favour of permitting Stockholm. His Intelligence Department has in it young men of Bolshevik leanings—the Leepers[1] and Arnold Toynbee—who prepare revolutionary memoranda which are apparently read by A.J.B. To listen to Tyrrell one would imagine that the F.O. was pacifist, not to say pro-German.

April 25th.—We had the first of a series of meetings of Labour leaders at dinner last night to discuss some kind of common policy. The loneliness of Henderson in his tiny office, and his consciousness of isolation, led me to suggest that our house might be used as a meeting place. He responded gladly, and at his request I asked him to meet the Andersons, J. H. Thomas, George Lansbury—the latter regarded as important as editor of the *Herald*. The meeting went off unexpectedly well and they all agreed to meet here again at lunch on Monday. Sidney and I did little more than promote an exchange of views. The main questions raised was what should the Labour Party do if the Lloyd George combination collapsed over Ireland or over the

[1] Sir Reginald Wildig Allen Leeper (b. 1888), the Ambassador, entered the Foreign Office in 1918. His brother, Alexander Wigram Allen Leeper (1887–1935) took up a post in the British Museum.

ill success of the war. Henderson put forward the view that if Asquith were asked to form a Government and stated that he could not do so without the participation of the Labour Party the leaders would be obliged to take office "on terms". Henderson declared that he would ask that the Liberal leaders accept the "War Aims" of the Labour Party and give a guarantee of good faith by offering a sufficient number of places to the Labour Party to be filled by the Party itself. He intimated that leaders not in Parliament would have to be taken in— Webb and Lansbury he suggested, half jocularly. Thomas supported him. Lansbury said he would support any Government prepared to end the war, and would judge any offer from the Liberals exclusively from that standpoint. Sidney laid down quite other conditions—half the candidatures for the General Election and the acceptance of the Reconstruction proposals. I insisted on Anderson expressing his opinion. Anderson, with unusual seriousness and deliberation, stated that he was against any participation in an Asquith Government— and, when asked explicitly by Henderson, said that he, at any rate, would not take office. He would advise the Party to support, without taking office, any anti-Lloyd George—Milner Government that would end the war on any terms; but he distrusted the Front Bench Liberals. Accepting office in another coalition would finally ruin the Labour Party. The discussion was on a high level of ability and the temper was admirable. . . .

Bryan's Ground: Radnorshire.—Leonard Courtney passed away, after a short illness, the day after we left London for our Whitsun holiday. I saw him on Wednesday, weak from one of his recurring attacks of internal haemorrhage, but still vigorous in intellect and emotion. He denounced Wilson, his eyes flashing under his heavy eyebrows as he beat the bed with his closed fist. He had just dictated a letter and sent Kate off with it to the *Times*—(the *Times* refused it, and it appeared the next day in the *Manchester Guardian*)—the plea of a noble old man for readiness to negotiate with the Germans when they were so minded.

He and Kate had become not only the central figures of two families to the third generation, but also of a distinguished group of Liberal journalists and publicists. He was one of those rare natures that grow in breadth of vision and warmth of sympathy with old age. He was a noble man. When I first remember him, as Kate's fiancé, he was distinctly unpleasing—at any rate to his lively sister-in-law. He wore his personal distinction badly. Our family life did not suit him. He and father disliked each other. Father thought him an intolerable doctrinaire prig with little knowledge of human nature or of practical affairs; he thought father a somewhat loose commercial man of limited

culture and reactionary views. As years went on father became proud
of his son-in-law, and when Leonard refused to support Gladstonian
Home Rule in 1886 father's respect became admiration. During
father's long illness Leonard became tenderly appreciative of the
mutual devotion of the father and the nine daughters.

Leonard combined moral genius, and a good mechanical intellect
with considerable artistic faculties. He was an artist—or, at any rate, a
true lover of art. He was a man of exquisite tastes in literature, in
nature, in music, in art—even in wines and food. But all this highly
developed sensuous nature was under moral control. I cannot conceive
Leonard telling a lie, or being lewd or cruel, or refusing to sacrifice
his comfort or prestige to a public end. What he lacked was any
distinction in the quality of his intellect. He had no subtlety, no
originality—he thought in grooves made by other minds and by
minds of the plainer sort. He kept to the well-worn tracks of conventional reasoning and conventional observation and resented any intellectual adventure. This mediocrity of intellect accounted for his one
moral failure: he was an ungenerous critic of contemporary talent;
he regarded new schools of thought with an almost insolent contempt.
He was, to all who disagreed with him, an impossible person to talk
to except on the trivialities of daily life. Unless you agreed, he refused
to discuss for the sufficient reason that he had not the mental equipment to carry on an argument on any other premises but his own.
Sidney and I, for instance, in spite of our affection and admiration for
him, never succeeded in doing more than "make conversation"—
never once did we find ourselves in communion with him on an
intellectual issue, even where our views did not clash. And all who
belonged to other schools of thought had a like experience. He selected
his conclusions according to his emotional sympathies, using his fine
mechanical memory and his power of incisive and picturesque speech
to explain, illustrate, and emphasise his views. His marriage to Kate
reached an ideal happiness. The bond of sympathy between the
Courtneys and the Webbs was, in fact, this rare experience on both
sides of a perfect married comradeship, together with the fact that
both couples were childless and absorbed in public affairs. Kate has
lost her other and most loved self: but her devotion to his memory
and her amazing kindliness will cover her loneliness, and her old age
will, I think, be a happy one.

May 31st.—Back in London after seventeen days' delightful holiday in a garden cottage belonging to the Russell-Holt[1] nieces. Time

[1] Daughters of Robert Durning and Lawrencina Holt: one, Elizabeth, married
Edward Stanley Russell, a Unitarian minister, who was killed in 1917; the other,
Mary, married John Harold Russell, a sheep-farmer in Montana.

was spent in long walks—sometimes whole days in Radnor forest, I
having recovered my walking power up to eight or nine miles. Sidney
wrote articles and revised drafts, whilst I amused myself typing out
and adding notes to the current diary book. . . .

June 16*th*.—I note with interest that not once in this diary have I
mentioned the outstanding event of the year's home affairs—the pas-
sage of the Representation of the People Act, extending the suffrage
from eight to about eighteen millions and admitting women to citizenship. This revolution has been in my consciousness the whole time,
but it has not risen into expression because I have been a mere spectator
—not in the least a participator. It is only the events that are vital to
one's own life that get into so personal a record. I have always assumed
political democracy as a necessary part of the machinery of government. I have never exerted myself to get it. It has no glamour for me
—I have been, for instance, wholly indifferent to my own political
disfranchisement. But I do not ignore the fact that the coming of the
Labour Party as a political force has been largely occasioned by this
year's extension of the franchise.

Almost accidentally this great revolution has forced Sidney to enter
the electoral arena, for a few months, as part of the stage army of the
Labour Party. Sidney from the first decided that the Labour Party
must contest the University seats as part of its pretensions to be a
national party, and if these seats were to be contested he had to stand
for London. We are spending money and time on the election—more
as a great propagandist attack on the conscience and intelligence of
10,000 graduates than as a serious attempt to win a seat. Sidney does
not want to be in Parliament unless there proves to be a real "change
of heart"—and a change of heart common to brainworkers as well as
manual workers. If there is not this revolution in public purpose we
are better outside trying to make it by writing and speaking and re-
searching. The only compensation for the disturbance of our settled
occupation and personal comfort entailed by S. being in Parliament
would be the opportunity of actively guiding a real political force
within Parliament—say 200 Labour members. So we remain largely
indifferent to the results of our electioneering. My daily work is
divided into three parts: Government Committees, Labour Advisory
Committees, and London University election. About once a week we
have some Labour men to meet Henderson. We had all the Chairmen
of the Advisory Committees—MacDonald, Anderson, Jowett,
Tawney and J. A. Hobson—to meet Henderson, and all the Secretaries came in afterwards. I get on very well with MacDonald, and
he and I generally find ourselves in agreement against the wilder
spirits.

June 23rd.—We spent an evening at Haldane's with one of Lloyd George's "business ministers"—Sir Albert Stanley[1]—to talk over the Board of Trade's Committee Report on the electricity scheme of the Haldane Committee, a "wicked report," Sidney says, as it cloaks recommendations in favour of profiteering under sham Government ownership of the new Super Power-stations. Sir Albert Stanley is a plain man of the professional manager type, wholly uninterested and uninformed in political questions. As the notorious capitalist Perks[2] said, "he is good at management and bad at profit-making"—a valuable testimony to character. He is certainly no genius, but competent and disinterested, with the bias towards collectivism characteristic of the professional manager. One wonders what that accomplished bureaucrat Llewellyn Smith[3] thinks of this manager person as his parliamentary chief! Stanley seemed sympathetic to Sidney's criticism of the report—S. tactfully alluding to the double-dealing of the report as "bad editing", but intimating that the Labour Party would not condone the undertone of commercialism and that unless the scheme was altered it would not be accepted. Haldane as usual showed his faith in the ubiquitous need for the money-making motive as the only source of efficient management. It is odd that he should believe in us!

Another type of the governing class—Lord Eustace Percy of the F.O.—dined here last night, brought here by Alfred Zimmern. A delicate-featured, thoughtful aristocrat—anxious to discuss with us the League of Nations. Really against it, feared its interference with the British Empire and its subject races. But like so many English aristocrats he is, in outward attitude, sympathetic to advanced thought, and in talking to us he was modest and even deferential. Also he said that Frankfurter, the democratic little Jew, was one of his greatest friends in the U.S.A.

Our old friends, the Talbots,[4] and our new friends, the William Temples,[5] dined here last night to meet Henderson and discuss the future of the Church. Willie Temple was a Fabian for many years, and he has recently joined the Labour Party. He is the leader of the "Life and Liberty" movement, a movement for the self-determina-

---

[1] Albert Henry Stanley, Lord Ashfield (1874–1948). The American-born General Manager of the London Underground Group, 1912, and of the London Passenger Transport Board, 1933–47; President of the Board of Trade from 1916–19.

[2] Sir Robert William Perks (1849–1934). President of the Wesleyan Conference; leader of the Nonconformists on the London County Council and much disliked by the Webbs. See *Our Partnership*.

[3] Sir Hubert Llewellyn Smith (1864–1945). Civil servant and investigator; worked many years in the Board of Trade.

[4] Edward Stuart Talbot (1844–1934), Bishop of Southwark, 1905–11, and of Winchester, 1911–13, married to the Hon. Lavinia Lyttelton. In his early days something of a Socialist and a supporter of the Webbs' social policy.

[5] William Temple (1881–1944), the Archbishop of Canterbury, in 1918 was Rector of St. James's, Piccadilly. His wife was Frances Gertrude Acland Anson.

tion of the Anglican Church—even at the cost of disestablishment. The Bishop of Winchester was not so light-hearted about disestablishment; he wanted to be quite clear about the terms. Henderson was, of course, for disestablishment, but inclined to be generous about endowments. What he was keen about was the union of the Christian Churches. He sat and listened to Temple, Talbot and ourselves: he shows to much better advantage with outsiders than with his Labour colleagues, with whom he lacks graciousness and is apt to be sullen and rude. I rather like Henderson; he has sterling qualities, a veritable rock of bourgeois respectability and self-control. But he is personally most unattractive. I have never known a man of undoubted power with so little personal charm or magnetism. In general society he has the one redeeming characteristic of a "listening" silence. Temple is a vigorous democratic priest. He is too fat and too exuberant a talker for an ideal Man of God—his phrases run away with him—but he is sincere, courageous and disinterested.

June 30th.—The Labour Conference[1] has come and gone in the full limelight. It must be an odd sensation for the wirepullers of the two old parties to watch this young rival take the platform with self-assurance, not only in social reconstruction but also in world politics. It is the only national non-governmental gathering the incidents of which are flashed to the Foreign Offices of the world. The dramatic appearance of Kerensky[2]—the noisy protest of the little knot of British Bolsheviks, the overwhelming reception accorded to him, the great oration in Russian watched and heard in dead silence, the kiss on the cheek of the blushing Henderson—the whole scene a magnificent staging of the new people's party claiming its right to control international affairs. Instead of the split in the Labour Party prophesied by the Tory Press, the leaders stood solidly together and, whilst Henderson carried the breaking of the party truce, Clynes, the minister, was elected at the head of the poll for the Executive. It is not logical, but it is war on the old social order. The three great successes of the Conference were Henderson's management of the Kerensky episode, which really amounted to genius, the Clynes speech justifying acceptance of office, and, I venture to add, the Webb programme. It is true that the heat of the Conference was evoked, not about the *New Social Order*, but by the clash between the Labour ministers and the Labour Party in the country, and still more by the fight over Kerensky. But there was solid satisfaction among the delegates that they had a pro-

[1] The special Labour Party Conference held to give approval to the reconstruction policy of the Party as drawn up by Webb in the report published under the title *Labour and the New Social Order*. Kerensky's appearance there was unexpected.

[2] Alexander Feodorovich Kerensky (b. 1881). Russian Prime Minister from July 1917 to the Bolshevik Revolution.

gramme, more complete than that of either of the two great parties, and that the Labour Movement was sweeping forward to national leadership. No doubt there is a good deal of nasty suspicion abroad; a certain growling of the revolutionary elements on being headed off rebellion into a network of detailed and measured reform. They don't like the way but they have no other way to propose. The Bolshevik policy of violence at home and meekness abroad does not look sufficiently successful in Russia to be good propaganda. Henderson and Clynes carried off the honours of the Conference.

I watched and talked to Kerensky in the ante-chamber while he was awaiting the decision of the Conference. He is singularly like Massingham in appearance and expression, only that he has the flash of genius in eye and gesture. He is a great orator, that fact shone through the strange but musical language which not a single man among the delegates understood. But he seems, as one watches his expression, to lack executive will and intellectual stability—he gave you no confidence that he knew what he wanted done. One can see him dominating masses of Russians by the nervous magnetism of his personality and then, when they crowd behind him, hesitating which way to lead them. He is a creature and a creator of impulse: is he not an originator and executor of a possible plan of campaign? He appealed passionately for help, but he gave no indication as to the character of the help he demanded. There was, at the end, a disappointing sense of vagueness and futility.

It is noteworthy that Huysmans, Branting[1] and the Belgian and French Socialists (except Longuet) are even more anti-Bolshevik than the Front Bench of the British Labour Movement. Men like Thomas and Henderson show the same sort of good-natured tolerance to the Bolsheviks that they give to their own rebels. But the Continental leaders are bitter—almost as bitterly contemptuous as the *Morning Post*. And Longuet is the only exception, because he is set on peace and he does not want any diversion or delay in order to save Russia either from the Bolsheviks or from the Germans. He has no sympathy with small or weak nations—except for Belgium, mainly because France is responsible for her invasion—and for Ireland, because he wants some accusation to fling at England. In the conflict between the British and the German Empire, I think his sympathies are with the Teuton. He is pro-German as well as pacifist—always assuming the integrity of France as she existed before August 1914. Branting is solidly pro-Anglo-American democracy, Huysmans anti-German, and the French and Belgian Socialists eager for the consciousness of victory to redeem them from the shame and loss they have suffered during the German occupation of their countries.

[1] Karl Hjalmar Branting (1860–1925). Leader of the Social-Democratic Federation of Sweden and Prime Minister in the Coalition Government of 1920.

July 1st.—Branting, who lunched here yesterday, is a big heavy man, physically and mentally: he might have been a great man if he had been healthier in his habits. But he eats, drinks and smokes too much—the result being mental slowness and inertia except when he is stimulated by some big occasion. Massive judgment is his outstanding characteristic. He dislikes and despises the Bolsheviks; they are unscrupulous and ignorant fanatics—a diseased and poisonous product. He has no sympathy with rebels within the democratic Government or even within a political democracy. . . .

July 13th.—There is great unrest in the civil service. On the two committees enquiring into the machinery of Government—one governmental and the other Labour Advisory—I have an opportunity of studying its various aspects. On Mondays and Fridays I sit with Haldane, Murray, Morant and Heseltine—sometimes Montagu or Allan Sykes[1]—discussing with the powerful chiefs of the civil service the constitution of the Cabinet and its secretariat, the relation of the Treasury to the other departments and of all departments to Parliament. On Thursdays I sit, in a committee room of the House of Commons, as Secretary of the Labour Advisory Committee of which MacDonald is Chairman, listening to the revolutionary claims of the younger men or subordinate classes in the civil service—voiced by the Secretaries of the new associations.

The permanent heads are sore about the intrusion of the "business" man and scornfully sarcastic of his ignorance of the larger responsibilities of government and of his casual and disorderly habits of work. It is comic to hear old-fashioned individualists like George Murray vehemently asserting that the salaried civil servant has nothing to learn and everything to teach the typical profitmaker—professional pride overcoming class economics! But their greatest contempt is reserved for Parliamentary institutions to which they attribute every folly or weakness of their chiefs, or to the stunt Press with its ignorant clamour against "bureaucracy". I get tired of the reiterated excuse for all shortcomings—"You have to play down to Parliament". John Anderson,[2] the able Secretary of the Ministry of Shipping, declared that the perpetual sniping at Government officials in Parliament and in the Press bred a wrong sort of civil servant—it developed the critical faculty instead of the constructive. The man who was prized in a department was he who kept his minister out of trouble and had

[1] Colonel Sir Alan John Sykes (1868–1950). Tory M.P. for Knutsford 1910–22. Subsequently Chairman of the Bleachers' Association. Member of the Haldane Committee on the Machinery of Government but signed Part I only, as he was out of the country during the later discussions.

[2] Sir John Anderson, Lord Waverley (b. 1882) was Secretary to the Ministry of Shipping from 1917 to 1919.

a smart answer to an awkward question. His remedy was significant. He advised the setting up of Parliamentary committees on the various subjects of government, similar to the standing committees suggested by Sidney in the memorandum circulated to the Samuel Committee.[1] By this machinery civil servants would have a responsible and well-informed body before whom they could not only defend their past actions but explain their constructive proposals. To these committees would automatically go all stray accusations either in or out of Parliament.

The unrest of the younger men and of the subordinate classes takes other forms. They are not over-sensitive to external criticism, which they often think is justified. What worries them is the lack of prospect either of responsible work inside the office or of free and vigorous citizenship in the outer world. During the war the abler or more fortunate of these men have found themselves suddenly promoted to big affairs, in close co-operation with young business men or young aristocrats "doing war work" with incomes and standards of expenditure that make the civil servant feel himself existing on the margin of decent livelihood. There will be, we are told, a great exodus after the war of these younger men tempted by offers, from their quondam colleagues, of far higher salaries and more interesting work than what may be hoped for in the civil service. Men of the lower grades, who see neither the way to escape out of the civil service nor the opportunity to rise within it, have been attracted by the vision of vocational control through Whitley Councils or it may even be through the civil service "guilds", suggested by Cole and his friends. Anyway, they mean to insist on complete freedom to take part in the political life of their locality or their creed or their class. Some of the more revolutionary spirits are asking for greater privileges in this direction than those enjoyed by the ordinary man, claiming that the civil servant should not only be permitted "reasonable facilities" for pursuing a parliamentary candidature without resigning his office, but that he should have the right of reinstatement if he or his constituency got tired of one another. But this claim was negatived by our Labour Advisory Committee, and the bold ones had to content themselves with the Australian clause exempting a ci-devant civil servant from the examination enforced on all other candidates for state employment.

*   *   *   *   *

July 29th.—A sallow-faced dark-haired, unhealthy Russian[2] called on us yesterday afternoon, with an introduction from Litvinoff. Like the other Bolshevik emissaries he was an unattractive mortal—more

[1] The House of Commons Select Committee on National Expenditure, 1916–17, of which Sir Herbert Samuel was Chairman.
[2] There is some confusion here. The editor of *Pravda*, at the time was Kameneff himself.

unattractive than former ones because he had not the redeeming quality of fanatical faith in his cause—he seemed to have a detached view of the creed he was serving. He was the editor of the official organ of the Bolshevik Government, *Pravda*, at Moscow, and has been sent over here by Lenin, ostensibly as an official courier to Litvinoff, but mainly, we think, to ascertain the condition of Great Britain and the prospect of world famine. He had seen no one but George Lansbury. We gave him an introduction to Camille Huysmans. He spoke fluent but ugly French and, as we talk French with difficulty and were more anxious to listen than to inform, he spent an hour or so explaining to us, with considerable lucidity, the constitution of the Bolshevik Government and its relation to industrial enterprise. As a preliminary he was anxious to impress on us the wickedness of the bourgeois intellectuals in refusing to serve the Bolsheviks: he, an engineer by profession (he added that he disliked his profession), and one or two lawyers, had put their services at the disposal of the Bolsheviks—but they were the exceptions. The other intellectuals were attempting to gain a miserable livelihood by petty trading or menial labour rather than help the Revolution.

The electoral units of the Soviet Government were an odd combination of geographical and vocational delimitation. "The industrials" voted by factories or groups of factories, provision being made for the inclusion of individual producers and for separate constituencies of unemployed persons. The peasants formed another series of electoral units and the soldiers yet another. But all these vocational units were delimitated by the boundaries of village, district and province—the two latter authorities being indirectly elected by the village councils. The central or national assembly sitting at Moscow was similarly elected —and it was to this supreme assembly that the National Executive was responsible.

All factories and other industrial enterprises were managed by committees of the workers of the separate establishments. This primitive organisation was applied to the railways—the Moscow "station operatives" managing the Moscow railways—by which, I imagine, he meant the railways having termini at Moscow. But all these workers' committees acted under the direct and explicit orders of the central or provincial Soviets. The Trade Unions had no kind of control—not even over the conditions of employment. Having no power they were ceasing to function and threatened to disappear. So the new constitution provided that membership should be compulsory, no non-unionist being admitted to citizenship. What the Unions did, or were expected to do, we could not exactly make out—he suggested propaganda, technical education and acting as advisers on technical matters to the National Executive. The Co-operative Movement had also been affected adversely by the Bolshevik industrial organisation—

and here again compulsory membership was being suggested as the only remedy. He emphatically denied that the Bolshevik Government was Syndicalist any more than it was Collectivist—it was Communist. But its essential feature was the dictatorship of the proletariat: no person living on rent, interest or profit being accepted as a citizen. In practice, no one not included in one of the vocational groups described above would exercise the suffrage.

This emissary of the Bolsheviks professed the same fatalism as Litvinoff and Kameneff. Unless the Russian Revolution spread to other countries it would collapse. All the evils of the Bolshevik régime —the disorder tempered by despotism, the idleness of the workers (which he admitted), the mass of worthless currency, the hunger and pestilence—all were the heritage of the old order. If left to itself the Russian Revolution would take twenty years to work out into an efficient Government, capable of holding its own in a world of bourgeois Governments. But whether it lived or died, it was the only form of self-government that the Russian people would or could practise. The only alternative was for Russia to become a colony of her most powerful neighbour—the German Empire. He leered at us as he said this—a sardonically complacent emphasis on the word "colony". Whether our visitor believed what he said or was telling the tale he had been instructed to tell we do not know. He spoke without enthusiasm or conviction. "Will you not return with me to Russia and see for yourself what is happening." "No thank you," I replied with a pleasant laugh: "we remember that there are such things as hostages and their usual fate in revolutions."

September 1st. Grosvenor Road.—A month's holiday at Presteign, with G.B.S. and Maggie Hobhouse as successive visitors. . . . The day before I left I had a telegram from the P.M. asking me, in no uncertain language, to be Chairman of a Committee on the relation of men's and women's wages. The subject did not attract me, but I was flattered and excited at being offered the Chairmanship and forthwith wired a gracious acceptance. Great was my discountenance when the following day I received an apologetic telegram announcing that Mr. Justice Aikin [Atkin][1] was to be Chairman and that I had only been invited to be a common or garden member of yet another Committee. It appears that an incompetent typist had repeated the message to the selected Chairman to all the members of the Committee, and that they each and all accepted the Chairmanship. It remains to be added that we all accepted the position with dignified good humour.

* * * * *

[1] Sir James Richard Atkin, Lord Atkin (1867–1944). The distinguished judge.

September 26th.—The fourth Inter-Allied Labour and Socialist Conference went off with an unusual amount of orderliness and to the satisfaction of the Centre Party in the world of Labour, and to the capitalist Press outside. Three resolutions on the Austrian peace note, the Inter-Allied intervention in Russia, and the war aims were passed by large majorities. These three resolutions were all in support of the Inter-Allied Governments with reservations in favour of political democracy and against Imperialist aims. But the main interest of the Conference was one of racial psychology. The professional pacifists of Great Britain and France have always prided themselves on being the high moral element in the Labour Movement as distinguished from the opportunism of Henderson and Renaudel and the bourgeois patriotism of Albert Thomas, Vandervelde and our own fire-eaters. But the Americans, headed by Gompers, altogether outshone the I.L.P. in sanctimonious self-righteousness, and highsounding declaration of ultra-democratic principles. They asserted and re-asserted that the war—at any rate since they entered it—has been a war between Democracy and Disinterestedness, on the one hand, and Autocracy and Lust of Power on the other. Whenever this thesis was controverted the Americans repeated their credo—more slowly, more loudly, and alas at greater length. "Are you stupid, criminal, or merely deaf?" was implied in their intonation, whenever the I.L.P. delegates expressed their pacifist sentiments. Result: the pacifists denounce the Conference as a hideous failure which they will not allow to be repeated. And it is not the pacifists alone who are disgruntled. Camille Huysmans, who is not an admirer of the I.L.P. or of Longuet, still less of the Bolsheviks, bitterly remarked that this Conference was the final act of the parody of Internationalism that has been played during the last three years.

I had a long talk with Huysmans yesterday in his little room at the office of the Labour Party. He hotly resents the ignorant presumptions of the American delegates and the sliding scale terms of the British Trade Unionists with regard to an International Congress—terms which vary according to the state of the Western Front. He believes in the *bona fides* of the German Majority Socialists, and he regards the present attitude of the British Labour Party as a betrayal of the claim of the International Labour Movement to settle their own terms of peace according to their conception of the welfare of the peoples. He foresees two Internationals: a Continental International, including German, French, Italian, Belgian and Russian, to which the British Socialist societies would come, and an American and British International made up of Trade Union representatives with a few satellites from the Continent—so-called "nationalist" socialist societies. He is specially bitter against Vandervelde, who, he declares, has become a "King's minister" in spirit as well as form, and is no longer the representative of the Belgian workmen.

Kerensky dined with us the other night and is lunching with us on Wednesday to meet Sir William Tyrrell. He has lost the nervous tension so noticeable in his appearance two months ago. He has an impressive personality, a broad and cultured outlook on men and affairs, a fine and fastidious political morality. Clearly he has neither experience nor knowledge of administration; the technical problems of democratic government do not interest him. But compared to the American or British Trade Unionists, he belongs to the aristocracy of intellect in an old civilisation and regards, with dreamy philosophy, the social organisation of the European Continent in dissolution. He has [not], and has never had, any sympathy with the "Dictatorship of the Proletariat". He is trying to engineer, from his position of an *émigré*, a reconciliation of classes in Russia. His speech in favour of the Inter-Allied Intervention, with its fiery peroration against any attempt to set up the old régime in Russia, was the one distinguished note of the fourth Inter-Allied Socialist Conference. Sir Esmé Howard,[1] the British Minister at Stockholm, who spent Sunday evening with us (on an introduction from Clifford Sharp) declares that the Social Revolutionaries no longer accept Kerensky as a leader. Meanwhile the British Government has refused him a passport for Murmansk, offering him instead a passport for Stockholm, from which place he cannot enter Russia except through Bolshevist territory.

* * * * *

October 11th.—Our own pre-occupations have been broken into by the arrival of AE.[2] and his colleagues to address a joint meeting of the Labour Party Executive and the Parliamentary Committee of the Trades Union Congress. (AE. is staying with us, Johnson[3] and Douglas[4] come in to consult with him.) Poet, artist, saint, and propagandist, George Russell is a sensationally delightful person and many are those who glow about his personal charm. He bores Sidney: I enjoy his wonderful talk. He is vain but modest: somewhat too concerned with his own intervention and with the effect of his own personality in the troublous Irish world; yet fully, almost self-consciously, aware of the limitations in his mental life; believes in the undifferen-

---

[1] Esmé William Howard, Lord Howard of Penrith (1863–1939). From 1913 to 1919 Minister to Sweden, afterwards to Spain and to U.S.A.
[2] George William Russell, the Irish poet (1867–1935).
[3] Thomas Johnson (b. 1872). Secretary of Irish Trades Union Congress, 1914–29. Became Senator in 1928.
[4] James G. Douglas (b. 1887). Irish haberdasher from Rathmines, Senator and friend of Sir Horace Plunkett, and member of the Constitution Committee.

tiated man, doing some simple individual job with dutiful care, but with his heart in pleasant comely things, and developing, here and there, into the mystic and the saint. The less organisation and government the better; and only just enough science to add intellectual curiosity in the processes of nature to the life of the agriculturist. He hates cities, railways, machinery, division of labour, rule, method and specialised science or logical reasoning. The expert out for intellectual adventure, the organiser of complicated human relationships, are types he dislikes. He never tires of abusing, with rash ignorance, the politician and the official. After listening to one of his tirades I fired up, "So far as Anglo-Saxons are concerned, you are stabbing democracy in the back by your perpetual derision of Parliamentary institutions and all that these involve. You are not only mischievous, you are grossly ignorant." He laughed at my railing and reverted to Ireland. He is passionately attached to Ireland. His ambition has been to be the Great Liberator of Irish thought from superstition, of Irish character from irresponsibility, of Irish converse from derision of all men and all things. "Then why," I nagged, "do you indulge in so much derision yourself—and derision of men and affairs which you admit you do not understand?" All the same, AE. is one of the most winning of the modern preachers of the Kingdom of God.

He and his fellows give a tragic account of the condition of the Irish mind. They foresee, if conscription be enforced, bloodshed and wholesale imprisonments, with an aftermath of bitterness which will last for generations. Johnson, like other Irish Labour men, has convinced himself that the Irish people will secure representation at the Peace Conference and that this feat will be all the easier if the British Government is, at the time, engaged in a murderous suppression of a subject race whilst claiming self-determination for the races of the Austrian Empire. They told the Labour meeting that the only reason for conscripting Ireland was to maintain conscription in Great Britain —they had proof of this in a letter from one General (Wilson,[1] I think) to another—so as to "put down strikes". This threat was not taken seriously by the British Trade Unionists. But the Labour men were touched by AE.'s eloquence and their pride aroused by the faith of the Irishmen in the power of the British Labour Movement to prevent disaster. There remains the uncomfortable fact that many of the Labour Party candidates, even pacifist candidates, believe that the cry of "conscript Ireland" will be popular with the electorate. That is also Herbert Samuel's opinion. George Barnes, whom I happened to meet at the War Cabinet offices on his way to a Cabinet said that he intended to stand by his principle of "No Home Rule, no Con-

---

[1] Probably Field-Marshal Sir Henry Hughes Wilson (1864–1922), who was Chief of the Imperial General Staff in 1918.

scription". It is reported that Northcliffe is determined to push conscription through at all costs. Sidney has always refused to believe that such madness is possible and maintains that the nearness of peace with victory, and the presence of American soldiers in France tumbling over each other to get to the fighting line, makes the mere consideration of it an absurdity. . . .

October 13*th.*—The acceptance by Germany of President Wilson's terms will be welcomed by all the good and cursed by all the bad men among the Allies. The struggle of the next few days will test the relative power of the saints and the sinners among the Allied nations. The fact that the U.S.A. controls the situation is some guarantee of the victory of the saints. If it were not for that supremely important fact, I should fear the defeat of virtue. Revenge and greed die hard when satisfaction seems at hand. . . .

October 28*th.*—Apparently the sinners have prevailed—even over President Wilson. There is an unnecessary hardness in his subsequent communication. It may be that the German Government will surrender unconditionally: but, in that case, the terms Germany will have to accept will be past endurance: they will break her or turn her into a secret rebel against the world.

* * * * *

November 4*th.*—There is little or no elation among the general body of citizens about the coming peace. We are magnificently successful in the completeness of our victory over the Central Powers, a miracle when we remember the spring German offensive. But are we confronted with another Russia in Austria, possibly even in Germany —a Continent in rampant revolution, over which there will be no Government to which we can dictate our terms? Great Britain and France are themselves exhausted, living on their own vitals, whilst they smash German civilisation. For whose benefit? Will Wilson be able to resist the brutality of his own philistines flushed with victory?

The absence of public rejoicing, and sombre looks of private persons arises, I think, from preoccupation as to the kind of world we shall all live in when peace has come. Burdened with a huge public debt, living under the shadow of swollen Government departments, with a working class seething with discontent, and a ruling class with all its traditions and standards topsy-turvy, with civil servants suspecting business men and business men conspiring to protect their profits, and all alike abusing the politician, no citizen knows what is going to happen to himself or his children, or to his own social circle, or to the state or to the Empire. All that he does know is that the old order is seriously threatened with dissolution without any new order being in sight. What are the social ideals germinating in the minds of the five millions who will presently return from the battlefields and battle seas? What is the outlook of the millions of men and women who have been earning high wages and working long hours at the war trades, and will presently find themselves seeking work? What are the sympathies of the eight millions of new women voters? What has happened to the churches and the ten commandments? The Bolsheviks grin at us from a ruined Russia and their creed, like the plague of influenza, seems to be spreading westwards from one country to another. Will famine become chronic over whole stretches of Europe, and will some deadly pestilence be generated out of famine to scourge even those races who have a sufficiency of food? Will western civilisation flare up in the flames of anarchic revolution? Individuals brood over these questions and wonder what will have happened this time next year. Hence the depressed and distracted air of the strange medley of soldiers and civilians who throng the thoroughfares of the capital of a victorious Empire.

Sidney reports that Henderson is in the depths of depression, doubtful whether he will win his seat or, if he does so, whether he will have any Party to lead. The P.M. is said to be assured that an election on December 7 will return him to power as "the man who won the war" and who alone can be trusted with reconstruction. The Labour ministers, including Clynes, are pressing the L.P. executive for a continuance of the Coalition during the period of reconstruction, and it is quite uncertain whether the Labour Movement, as a whole, will be prepared to assert itself at the polls in opposition to the present Government. Most of the glamour around the Labour Party during the spring, due to its international and national programme, has faded away; personal jealousies and internecine strife having dissipated it from below, whilst the near prospect of a brilliant peace has dissolved it from above. Sidney, of course, remains unmoved in his determination that the Labour Party shall become H.M. Opposition, but his expectation of being elected by the London graduates has considerably lessened. We are not personally depressed because we have the patience of life-long propagandists, who have watched their ideas taking root in the minds of their former opponents. But we are contemplating retirement from active political life after the election, to finish our books and watch the young folk work for the success of social-democracy at some future election.

November 7th.—Sidney reports a vehement discussion at the L.P. Executive as to whether they should recommend the Conference on Thursday to decide to break away from the Coalition and call upon the Labour ministers either to leave the Government or leave the Labour Party. The Parliamentary Labour Party, under pressure from the Labour ministers, decided to wait until peace was actually signed between all the belligerents. That would mean accepting office in the new Government and continuing in office, at any rate for the many months that will elapse prior to signing the Treaty of Peace. If this policy be pursued, it seems extremely unlikely that the Labour ministers would carry out their present intention (which could always be reversed) of resigning from the Government on the formal conclusion of peace. Clynes came to the Executive determined to induce his colleagues to recommend this compromise to the Conference. Even Henderson wavered. Clynes threatened that all candidates who did not get the "Lloyd George letter" would be swept into oblivion and that the Labour Party would be finally smashed. By twelve to four the Executive insisted on its former policy, that at this election they must be in opposition to the present Government whatever fate were in store for them in the ballot boxes. The Labour members have no nerve: or perhaps they lack personal disinterestedness; they hate being out of Parliament, still more [the prospect] of losing office. What with placemen on the one hand, the professional rebels on the other, the Labour Party goes into the electoral battle a distracted, divided and depressed rabble of some three hundred nondescript candidates. Sidney thinks that the Party will be fortunate if it comes back sixty strong, and all the successful ones will be for massed Trade Union constituencies. He has now no hope of winning London University or any other middle-class constituency.

We visited the G.D.H. Coles this afternoon in the first abode of their married life. I forget whether I have before described this promising union of two devoted fellow workers. Margaret Postgate, familiarly known as "Mop" because of the mop of short thick black wavy hair in which is set swarthy complexion, mobile mouth, sharp nose and chin and most brilliantly defiant eyes, is the daughter of a Professor of Classics, one of a typical university family. She is herself a distinguished Cambridge graduate. She succeeded Arnot as paid Secretary to the Research Department, and shocked us old folk with her daringly unconventional ways and rebellious attitude. She kept what hours she chose, smoked the most masculine pipe, was on affectionate terms, first with Arnot then with Cole, receiving meanwhile the adoration of Kaye—the obedient servitor of the group. But though her manners have been disorderly, her ways have been straight: she has wit and reasoning power of an unusual quality, and she is fundamentally sweet-tempered and kind. Courtship and marriage have increased her womanliness and self-restraint. She and Cole seem perfect intellectual comrades. On both sides the marriage is an unworldly one.

The little house in a by-street of Chelsea is the interior of choice spirits, comfortable, even luxurious in lounges, restful in colouring, furniture solid and old, with a plenitude of books. These two are now friendly with us, convinced that, however we may differ from their vision of the future, we mean to help, not to hinder, their careers in the Labour Movement. Cole is preparing himself for political leadership. But he has a hard way to go. He is marked for life as a C.O.; how soon will the man in the street forget this bad mark? The new shop steward movement is not only indifferent but hostile to his elaborate proposals of centralised national Guilds, whilst there is appearing among the general body of citizens a dislike of the selfish and conservative spirit of many Trade Unions. "We are, after all, the paymasters," say the representatives of the consumers, "and we are going to choose what we are to pay for and who is going to be paid." Moreover, the demobilised soldiers and their organisations are going to cut into Trade Union solidarity. Meanwhile, Cole, who is from the intricate convolutions of his subtle brain to the tips of his long fingers an intellectual and an aristocrat, is becoming disillusioned about the Labour leaders, far more than we are. All the same, I believe he will win through. But it will not be the old folk and the old movements that he will have to overcome; it will be the surge of the new interests and the demagogie of the new leaders, more extreme than himself.

November 11th.—Peace! London to-day is a pandemonium of noise and revelry, soldiers and flappers being most in evidence. Multitudes are making all the row they can, and in spite of depressing fog and steady rain, discords of sound and struggling, rushing beings and vehicles fill the streets. Paris, I imagine, will be more spontaneous and magnificent in its rejoicing. Berlin, also, is reported to be elated, having got rid not only of the war but also of its oppressors. The peoples are everywhere rejoicing. Thrones are everywhere crashing and the men of property are everywhere secretly trembling. "A biting wind is blowing for the cause of property", writes an Austrian journalist. How soon will the tide of revolution catch up the tide of victory? That is a question which is exercising Whitehall and Buckingham Palace and which is causing anxiety even among the more thoughtful democrats. Will it be six months or a year?

November 17th.—The Emergency Labour Conference yesterday decided, by a large majority, to withdraw its representatives from the Coalition, the miners, the railwaymen and the engineers carrying it against the cotton weavers and labourers and sundry smaller unions. Clynes was the protagonist of the Labour ministers; Smillie, Thomas and Henderson, with G.B.S. (as Fabian delegate) intervening, brilliantly championing what was a foregone conclusion. . . .

The two great parties are gathering up their forces, coalescing on the Boom of Victory and the Fear of Revolution—the two most potent emotions of to-day. Clynes openly threatens every Labour member who refuses the coalition ticket with annihilation, and every Labour candidate who refuses his allegiance with the loss of the £150 deposit dependent on polling one-eighth of the votes. Whatever remote chance Sidney may have had of being the elect of London graduates has faded away. I begin to doubt whether he will poll more than 1,000 or 1,500 votes, though if the three other candidates go to the poll he may be second. All that can be said is that the governing class is willing to promise anything that is unanimously demanded by the Labour Movement rather than endanger their hold on the seat of power. Whether after they have won the election they will be equally complacent is not so certain. Germany really holds the fate of nations in her hands. If the German Social-Democrats succeed in establishing a successful Socialist Republic, or even a successful Political Democracy, there will be no holding back the British and American Democracies. If she sinks into chaos, still more if she develops the disease of terrorism, we are back in triumphant Capitalism for another two decades. The next few years are going to test the validity of the Socialist faith in the present stage of human development.

The toll of the war for our family is three killed and four others wounded, two seriously injured, out of a total of seventeen nephews and nephews-in-law in khaki. Betty Russell has lost her husband, Maggie Hobhouse has lost her Paul,[1] and now, three weeks before the signing of the armistice, the dead body of Noel Williams[2] is reported found. Paul and Noel were among our favourite nephews, clean living gallant youths of intellectual promise. . . . Every day one meets saddened women, with haggard faces and lethargic movements, and one dare not ask after husband or son. The revelry of the streets and the flying flags seem a flippant mockery of the desolation caused by the slaughter of tens of millions of the best of the white race.

*　　　*　　　*　　　*　　　*

December 8th.—The final meeting of the Haldane Committee. Result, a unanimous Report, with slight demurrers from Murray and Sykes. The Report embodies all the right ideas and follows closely the lines laid down in the Webb document. But these ideas appear in nebulously-phrased hesitating propositions: a concession to Murray's

---

[1] Youngest son of Margaret and Henry Hobhouse.
[2] Son of Mrs. Rosalind Dobbs, the youngest of the Potter sisters, by her first usband, Arthur Williams.

vested prejudices and Sykes's vested interests and Haldane's incurable delight in mental mistiness. It has been a pleasant interesting experience examining, over tea and cigarettes, in Haldane's comfortable dining-room, a succession of the chiefs of the civil service and gossiping with them, Haldane, Murray, Montagu and Morant, about different Cabinets and Cabinet ministers. This informal review of our bureaucracy leaves an impression of good temper and good manners, of native capacity and no systematic training, of philosophical indifference to ends, tempered by a moderately felt loyalty to the ideals of the British ruling class. Contempt for Parliament and a disdainful dislike for the newly imported "business man", a steady depreciation of Parliamentary chiefs, are almost universal in the higher ranks of the civil service. There is no contemporary statesmen for whom Murray, Morant and their fellows have any considerable admiration, and many for whom they have contempt frequently expressed in unparliamentary language. Murray is a simple-minded reactionary, but with a certain engaging modesty as to his fitness to judge the new developments. He has even shown curiosity about them and would ask me to explain exactly what was meant or intended. "There seems to have grown up an entirely new phraseology round all these new proposals which I don't understand," he remarked one afternoon; "the world is becoming foreign to me." And he is reported to have told another high official that there were a lot of new ideas about and that they were "damned interesting". He and I liked each other, and we parted good comrades.

The War Cabinet Committee on Women in Industry bores me. I am not in the least interested in the relation of men's and women's wages. My colleagues do not attract me. And it looks like my being forced to have a minority report, all by my little self. Hammond having resigned (to go off to Paris as *Manchester Guardian* correspondent) I am left alone as the only representative of advanced thought. This means that on the War Pledges, the Judge and the two K.C.s[1] examine on behalf of the Government, whilst I cross-examine on behalf of Labour. Hence there arises an inevitable antagonism. Moreover, we all feel that the Committee's Report will be still-born: the War Pledges are ancient history and any conclusions we come to about the future relation between men's and women's wages will have little or no effect on what actually happens. Alterations of the wage system will depend on the relative political and industrial forces and neither the Government nor the Trade Unions, certainly not the employers, will proceed on the lines of ideal principle. . . .

[1] The Judge was Sir J. R. Atkin. The two K.C.s were Sir William Warrender Mackenzie, later Lord Amulree (1860–1942), who was Chairman of several tribunals, of the Industrial Court and of the 1929 Royal Commission on the Licensing Laws; and Sir Lynden Livingstone Macassey, engineer, barrister, and authority on transport, who also headed many Government Committees and Tribunals.

December 12th.—I feel physically sick when I read the frenzied appeals of the Coalition leaders—the Prime Minister, Winston Churchill and Geddes—to hang the Kaiser, ruin and humiliate the German people—even to deprive Germany of her art treasures and libraries. These preliminaries of peace have become almost as disgusting as the war itself. It may be all election talk, but it is mean and brutal talk degrading to the electorate. It is the nemesis of having, as Premier, a man of low moral and intellectual values. The one outstanding virtue of the Labour Party, a virtue which is its very own, not imposed upon it by its intellectuals, is its high sense of international morality. Alone among British politicians the leaders of the Labour Party do honestly believe in the brotherhood of man.

December 16th.—Sidney has left for the first day's count of the University Poll. I have to go to the War Cabinet Committee to cross-examine important witnesses. He has hopes of success, largely, I think, because he desires it: I hold to my opinion that Magnus[1] will keep the seat, but then I am not keen that he should be in Parliament, and also I am afraid that he may be disappointed, so I deprecate optimism. When peace came we were certain, he, as well as I, that he could not win. Since then the streams of satisfactory letters and postcards have revived his faith in his own star.

The predominance of women at Saturday's polls has its serious aspect. Parliament will become the organ of the feminine, or be thought to be so. Soldiers' and workers' councils will seem not only the alternative to communal representative assemblies, but also the alternative to the rule of women.

December 22nd.—We leave to-morrow for a fortnight's country holiday. It is the end of a period. For the last three years, such energies as I have had, poor in quantity and quality, have been absorbed in Government Committees. Our own work has been in abeyance: and we have published no book since the war began except Sidney's *Works Manager.* The *History of Trade Unionism* has gone out of print awaiting cheaper paper and time to bring it up to date in a final chapter. Hence I have decided to refuse service on any other Government Committees. It is too great a strain on me and not fair to Sidney who has to do the drafting of the memoranda and reports upon which my usefulness on these Committees depends. This coming year I shall devote myself to three tasks: getting our own publications forward, helping with the Advisory Committees of the Labour Party, and, in holiday intervals, typing out the back volumes of my diary. This latter occupation, I can hardly call it work, pleases me most. I am tired of investigating new subjects. I want to brood over the past and reflect

[1] Sir Philip Magnus (1842–1933) was M.P. for London University from 1906 to 1922.

on men and their affairs. It amuses me to watch, in these jottings of my diary, the development of my own thought and of Sidney's activities. I want to summarise my life and see what it all amounts to. For long years I have constrained my intellect, forced it to concentrate on one subject matter after another; on some of the dullest and least illuminating details of social organisation. I recall, for instance, the weeks of grinding toil spent on disentangling the various methods of recovering the cost of public maintenance from different classes of recipients of relief and their relatives. I vividly remember the nausea with which, day after day, I went on with this task. But I accomplished it. I think I am losing this power of grappling with new material; in any case, I have lost all inclination to do it. And I want, before I cease to have any faculty of expressing myself, to add to my past diaries, in the form of notes, descriptions of persons and reflections arising from being "wise after the event".

Sidney is disappointed that he has not won the University seat.[1] I think he had been looking forward to a spell in Parliament—wanted to test his powers as a Parliamentarian. And yet he does not want it sufficiently to get himself adopted for a constituency which he could win; he wants to be pushed into Parliament; he does not want to push himself in. Once he is engaged in a fight he fights hard and leaves nothing undone. But he hates taking the plunge from the dignified and detached position of a disinterested helper into rivalry with colleagues for prized positions. He fought the University seat because no other member of the Labour Party would dream of doing so. He cannot bring himself even to hint that he has a claim to a winnable constituency. . . .

[1] The 1918 election result was: Magnus (Unionist), 2,810; Webb (Labour), 2,141; Somerville (National Union of Teachers), 885; Herringham (Ind.), 715; Nordon (Ind.), 210.

JANUARY 1919—DECEMBER 1919

January 10th. Grosvenor Road.—The British general election of 1918 seems to be curiously analogous to the German general election of 1871. Lloyd George, like Bismarck, appealed to an enormously enlarged electorate, after a dramatic national victory, for unconditional support—for a Parliament without an organised opposition. In both cases the most powerful party prior to the war had been a Liberal Party which during the war had patriotically supported the war. In both cases there had been a small Socialist minority that had opposed the war. Bismarck's election swept away the national Liberal Party and started a Social-Democratic Party on a career which ended in its becoming, in the course of thirty or forty years, the most powerful political party in the German Empire. The Parliamentary revolution in Great Britain has been far more complete. The Liberal Party which had for years governed the Empire has been reduced to an insignificant fraction with all its leaders without exception at the bottom of the poll. The Labour Party has doubled its numbers and polled one-fourth of the entire voting electorate. It is now "His Majesty's Opposition", or claims to be in that position. Lloyd George with his conservative phalanx is apparently in complete command of the situation; as the only alternative Government there stands the Labour Party with its completely Socialist programme and its utopia of the equalitarian state. But the Parliamentary Labour Party is a very sham lion. All the militants—because they happen to be also pacifists—have been ousted from Parliament. Out of the fifty-nine Labour members twenty-five are miners—for general political purposes dead stuff. The Party is led by the respectable but dull-witted Adamson,[1] elected Chairman because he is a miner. Clynes and Thomas are the only good speakers, and such intellectuals as have survived the election are very inferior. Sidney reports that at the joint meeting of the Labour Party and the Parliamentary Party it was decided with only one dissentient—O'Grady—to claim the position of His Majesty's Opposition. Whereupon Sidney, in the absence of Henderson (laid up with influenza) offered the services of the Labour Party staff as well as his own to help the Parliamentary Party to carry

---

[1] William Adamson (1863–1936). Scottish Miners' official: Chairman of Parliamentary Labour Party, 1917–21, and Secretary of State for Scotland in the first two Labour Governments.

out its new and difficult duties. The offer was received with friendly appreciation: but no suggestions were made by the M.P.s of how it could be carried out. . . .

January 14th.—I had never seen Adamson, the Chairman of the Parliamentary Labour Party, before he lunched with us yesterday, except as a squat figure on the platform of the Albert Hall mass meeting just prior to the election. He was then declaiming, in high singsong voice, pompous platitudes—the terms "statesmanship" and "statesmanlike" constantly recurring—words that roused the Bolsheviks in the audience to howl him down. All I knew about him was that in the last Parliament he had been on the side of the Coalition Government and against Henderson's policy of independence.

He is a middle-aged Scottish miner, typical British proletarian in body and mind, with an instinctive suspicion of all intellectuals or enthusiasts: a thick, broad-shouldered and relatively short man, clumsy in movement, with straight sandy hair cropped close round a low forehead, big jaw and mouth, formless but slightly upward-tending nose, and lifeless blue eyes. In private conversation he is painfully slow in speech, every word seems to need deliberate effort. He is a total abstainer and is, I am told, domesticated and pious. He has neither wit, fervour nor intellect; he is most decidedly not a leader, not even, like Henderson, a manager of men. He has pushed his way up from hewer to checkweighman, from checkweighman to district agent, from miners' agent to miners' M.P., by industry and trustworthiness and the habit of keeping himself to himself, making no enemies and never giving himself away.

He came to us straight from his interview with the Speaker on the all-important question of the claim of the Parliamentary Labour Party to be His Majesty's Opposition. I think he had hesitated before accepting our invitation, and he was more at home with me than with Sidney. But we soon got on friendly terms and a good lunch relaxed his cautious temperament. He repeated slowly and mechanically the Speaker's evasive answer to his claim to be the leader of His Majesty's Opposition: he was clearly pleased and self-complacent with the vision of himself as the principal figure on the Front Opposition Bench, and only dimly conscious that he would need help to fill the position. He had brought with him a typewritten paper and read from it the requirements which he and his pals among the Labour members had decided were necessary to enable the fifty-eight to tackle Lloyd George and his immense following. "Two clerks, three typists—we cannot do with less", he deprecatingly insisted. But what exercised his mind most were the messengers. The Liberals in the last Parliament, he said, had had three messengers; *he thought*, and it was clear from his wrinkled forehead and slowly emphatic tone that he had thought strenuously on this question—*he thought* that the Parliamentary Labour Party might take over one of these messengers to fetch members to important divisions. He waited anxiously for Sidney's reply. "There is always the telephone," I said, to relieve the intense gravity of his suggestion—but he shook his head: no, the messenger was all important. Sidney cheerfully agreed, but gently implied that the Parliamentary Labour Party would require something more than three clerks, two typists and one messenger. Could not the Labour Party Executive, advisory committees and staff supply them with information on foreign affairs, finance and other technical questions not connected with trade unionism? Sidney asked. "Ye-es" (this dubiously)—"concise notes, statistics, facts, that is what we want." But he would be frank with us, he added with some energy. At their meeting yesterday they had discussed their relation with the Labour Party at Eccleston Square—in the past it had not been satisfactory. The Labour Party Executive, he complained, had during the last two years taken the initiative in deciding policy without consulting the Labour M.P.s—the Labour members had found themselves committed to programmes (Sidney looked like a guilty little boy) with which they might not agree. This must be remedied by joint meetings (Sidney looked relieved) of the M.P.s and the Labour Party Executive—a sort of joint committee. They were willing to co-opt experts from the Executive to sit on their standing committees. After this Sidney discussed with sympathetic attention all his requirements, made a few additional notes, and took him off to Eccleston Square to the meeting which had already been arranged. "You must make use of my husband for all that he is worth," I laughingly said as I stood in the hall. "We mean to make use of your husband," he retorted with a broad indulgent smile and beneficent wink at the fond woman; but the singsong voice was decidedly non-committal as regards the man. "Poor old Sidney," I said to myself as the front door slammed, "trying to direct political affairs with that bent stick." Adamson fumbles in political life as we should fumble with a pickaxe in the dark recesses of a mine, and gets about the same output as we should do. The thought of him as the leader of His Majesty's Opposition is even more strangely absurd than Barnes in the War Cabinet or at the Peace Conference.

Sidney reports that the result of the lunch was excellent. The meeting of the joint committee of the Parliamentary Labour Party and the Labour Party Executive went off most amicably. Whether the Labour M.P.s understand the conditions of successful co-operation remains to be seen.

The impression created by the reports of the Paris Conference is that if great words count the saints are winning. Wilson apparently

dominates the impressionable Lloyd George and the sanity and moderation of the Anglo-American diplomats appear to curb the demands of
the greedy and glory-loving Latins. Probably the most telling argument in favour of goodwill and reason is the incipient revolt of the
armies. The practical pacifism of the common soldier, intent on getting
home, is counteracting the "Power Policy" of the General Staffs.
One can almost hear our little Welshman clapping the old Tiger on
the back and explaining: "My dear friend, our soldiers won't go to
Russia, not even to Berlin: that is the plain fact. And don't rely on
Wilson. He himself is obsessed by his great dream of self-determination: his people have only one settled intention—to get back to
lucrative business. Unless your armies are ready to conquer Russia
and police the world we must have a peace which will be in fact a
peace of consent. And you see that we are already spending millions in
feeding Germany. Not much indemnity in that."

I find myself wholly uninterested in France. My thought and
feeling goes out to Germany in her heroic struggle to reconstruct her
political and social machinery. The future of the civilised world
depends on her success. Will she, cast down by defeat, weakened by
famine, threatened by physical and mental pestilence from Russia,
pull through into a well ordered socialist state? Can the present
Government call out from the depths of the German character a Will
to Order as her militarist rulers called out her Will to Power?
Will her science and her public spirit be sufficiently supreme
to carry her through the transition from the capitalist to the socialist
state? . . .

February 10th.—As an experiment in helpfulness to the Labour
Party in Parliament we had the first of a series of little dinners of
Labour M.P.s. Seven accepted, including Adamson; but he, Sitch[1]
and Davison[2] could not get here owing to strike distractions. There
remained Ben Spoor,[3] William Graham,[4] Lunn[5] and Neil Maclean.[6]
The Coles joined us at dinner and one or two others afterwards,
members of the advisory committees of the Labour Party. All the
M.P.s were new to their job and belonged to the left of the Labour

[1] Charles Henry Sitch (b. 1887). Secretary, Chain-makers' Union; M.P. for
Kingswinford.
[2] John E. Davison (1870–1927). Foundry Workers' Union official; M.P. for
Smethwick; Labour Whip, 1924–7.
[3] Benjamin Charles Spoor (1878–1928). Auctioneer; M.P. for Bishop Auckland.
Chief Whip in 1924 Labour Government.
[4] William Graham (1887–1932). M.P. for Central Edinburgh. Financial Secretary
to Treasury in 1924 Labour Government, and President of Board of Trade, 1929–31.
[5] William Lunn (1872–1942). Yorkshire miner. M.P. for Rothwell. Parliamentary
Secretary to Department of Overseas Trade in 1924 Labour Government.
[6] I.L.P. Member for Govan, 1922–50.

M.P.s. Of these four Ben Spoor impressed us as the most promising. This fair-haired, full-eyed, high-browed, sanguine man of pleasant appearance, strong self-controlled character and alert intelligence, of lower middle-class origin, who during the war was one of the organisers of the Y.M.C.A., has a clearly defined but not fanatically held social purpose and the gift of easy and unself-conscious manners. Lunn is a middle-aged miner, a well-known Poor Law Guardian, and, unlike most miners' representatives, sympathetic to and experienced in Labour politics unconnected with mining. William Graham—a graduate of Edinburgh University and member of Edinburgh Town Council—looks like an industrious and highly respectable clerk and seems at first sight insignificant and unattractive; but he is said to be a good administrator, a lucid speaker with considerable capacity for facts and arguments. He has the Fabian opinions of the late nineties, he dislikes big words and revolutionary sentiments: he prides himself on knowing more than the other Labour members—he is in fact a bit of a prig, but an honest and warmhearted prig. Neil Maclean is the exactly opposite type of Scot. With curly fair hair, markedly blue eyes, set close together, small and delicately shaped features, narrow forehead—all his face wrinkled with exasperation—an exasperation expressed also in his voice—he seems to be the incarnation of rebellious feeling—an extremist openly defiant of existing institutions, just because they are existing institutions. All four were detached from the trade union centre of the Labour members without being attached to the defeated Independent Labour Party members. All alike were disheartened by the state of mind of the Parliamentary Labour Party. They reported that the dominating note at all the private meetings was suspicion and hostility to all other Labour men. The little gang of pro-war trade unionists were jealous of the Labour Party Executive, determined not to be bossed by Henderson and wholly neglectful of the new members. They were not going to be helped by outsiders—all they would accept from Eccleston Square was clerkship and typing. . . .

We warned our guests against following the example of the pacifist leaders in the last Parliament, i.e. withdrawing themselves from the uncongenial atmosphere of the Parliamentary Labour Party in order to co-operate with advanced Liberals—and Cole reinforced our plea. The Labour Party, we suggested, had to pretend to solidarity until it attained it, and it was the business of the Left to resist, with all their might, disintegration. We had all to play for the next election and the return of convinced Socialists to Parliament. We discussed the strikes. Maclean hailed the electricians' strike as the first stroke towards the Dictatorship of the Proletariat; the other three condemned it. Cole supported the shop stewards' strike in defiance of the A.S.E.

Executive as the first step to an industrial union of engineering operatives. Graham was wholly unsympathetic to all this revolutionary talk.

February 11*th.*—The War Cabinet Committee on the relation of men's and women's wages ambles along quite amicably. I have presented a memorandum on the war pledges—a verdict against the Government on all counts. S. and I have prepared a treatise on wages, giving the Socialist interpretation of the trade union theory and practice of the standard rate and all its derivatives. My colleagues are fully aware that I intend a minority report. I tell them that it will really suit them that I should produce an extremist manifesto: "it will be a foil to your statesmanlike document." The Judge is, at heart, a reactionary about wages; the two K.C.s want everything referred to legal arbitration (they are both professional government arbitrators); Nathan[1] and Janet Campbell[2] want a philanthropic settlement of women's wages, based largely on the function of motherhood but preserving for the woman the right to undercut the man. I have announced my intention not to amend the majority report and the Judge has relieved me, with some alacrity, of attendance at the meetings to discuss it, though politely inviting me to do so if I feel inclined to come. Which means that I shall occasionally put in an appearance for politeness' sake. We are all most friendly and courteous to each other. We are unanimous in wishing to end the task as quickly as possible. . . .

February 22*nd.*—A curious episode and difficult to explain. A week to-day Haldane called here: he had been summoned to Downing Street the evening before and asked by the P.M. to arrange "another dinner with the Webbs." He had given a noncommittal answer—would we come? "Certainly we will meet the P.M. at your house; we should not care to go to Downing Street—but we have not the remotest objection to being his fellow guests. In fact we should enjoy it," I answered. "We are quite ready to discuss any subject with Mr. Lloyd George and to give him our most considered advice if he wants it," said Sidney. "At any rate, he always entertains us," I added. Haldane and we agreed on a date ten days off, but next morning Haldane's butler telephoned that the P.M. had fixed the coming Thursday and that "his Lordship had put off an engagement and hoped we should do likewise." So we went.

1 Sir Matthew Nathan, Lord Nathan of Churt (1862–1939). Civil servant; Secretary to Ministry of Pensions, 1916–19.
2 Dame Janet Mary Campbell, Senior Medical Officer for Maternity and Child Welfare, Ministry of Health; later Chief Woman Medical Adviser to Ministry of Education.

Three and a half solid hours of lively and interesting talk with the
P.M., with Haldane occasionally intervening, left us completely
puzzled. Why was it worth while for a great man, burdened with the
world's destiny at the Paris Conference and coming straight from an
exhausting Conference with the miners that very afternoon, to spend
a long evening alone with us? As it afterwards turned out we learnt a
good deal from this meeting and made ample use of it. But what did
he get or expect to get from it? He and we talked with the freedom
and intimacy of old friends—it is impossible to do otherwise with
Lloyd George. He is so easy in manner, so amusing, so direct and
apparently spontaneous in his observations and retorts, and he enjoys
like qualities in others. He opened the evening by telling us about the
Paris Conference—the antagonistic temperaments of Wilson and
Clemenceau—how he interpreted the doctrinaire puritan to the autocratic and emotional Celt: he scoffed at Hughes[1] of Australia and at
Clemenceau's admiration for this blatant British Imperialist. But
directly we sat down to Haldane's excellent dinner he begged permission to "talk shop". He wanted to consult us about the personnel of
the Royal Commission on the miners' claims and on the larger question of nationalisation. He explained that he had offered this Commission to the miners, and gave us the gist of his address that afternoon.
He felt in his coat pocket: "I meant to have brought the list of
names that has been suggested to me, but I find I have not. Perhaps
your butler would telephone to Downing Street—ask my secretary
(he spoke directly to Haldane's discreet body servant) for the list of
names of the Royal Commission on the Mines." (There proved to be
no response to the telephone at Downing Street—an odd incident in
a Prime Minister's abode.) He expected, he continued to explain, that
the miners would refuse to be represented, might even refuse to give
evidence. But the Commission would be set up, whether they agreed
to it or not, and would report on wages and hours by the 30th: and
on nationalisation later on. If the miners carried out their threat of a
strike, the Government would fight. "We shall beat them—we
control the food." But he wanted our advice as to the personnel of the
Commission. He must have trade unionists: Clynes had been suggested as the obvious person and a man named Cross[2] connected with
the textiles. Sidney acclaimed Clynes, but if it was Cross of the cotton
weavers he was an unfit man; he mentioned instead Purdy and
Stuart-Bunning.[3] The P.M. mentioned other names as the repre-

[1] William Morris Hughes (b. 1864). Prime Minister of Australia, 1915–23;
Australian representative at Versailles Conference.

[2] Joseph Cross (d. 1925 aet. 55.) Secretary of the Amalgamated Weavers' Association.

[3] George Harold Stuart-Bunning (1870–1951). General Secretary, Postmen's
Federation. Chairman of Trades Union Congress, 1919.

sentatives of the community—Redmayne[1] of the H.O. "A paid official," retorted Sidney; "he could hardly be considered impartial." And then Sidney explained with decisive firmness and lucidity that if such a Commission were set up there would have to be four sets of representatives—trade unionists, employers, and two kinds of outsiders holding the rival assumptions of the parties concerned. This seemed a novel idea to Lloyd George; he insisted that he wanted "impartial persons". No such persons exist, we assured him, and in this assertion Haldane supported us. "Who would you suggest as outsiders?" he asked. Here we were in a difficulty, as we could hardly give Sidney's name. We proposed Cole: the P.M. had never heard of him.[2] We described him, but the P.M. was not convinced. Other names were mentioned, among them Tawney and Greenwood: all through this drawn-out conversation we were wondering, since he wanted to see us, why he did not ask Sidney to serve. Haldane intervened: "Appoint Webb and Cole as the miners' experts." Still the P.M. did not respond. "Who wants the Commission and what is the conclusion you want it to come out at?" I asked innocently. "The membership must depend on the report you wish it to make," Sidney said with impatient bluntness. More fencing. "I have no prejudices against nationalisation"—suavely intoned the P.M.—then, with a burst of confidence—"this morning I persuaded the Cabinet, but with difficulty, to accept a bill for the nationalisation of the railways and power stations." From this and other calculated indiscretions we gathered that the P.M. meant the Commission to report in favour of nationalising the mines—though the omission from the proposed membership of any convinced nationalisers roused my suspicion. "Tom Jones, you know Tom Jones—he has the matter in hand—see Tom Jones about it—tell him I told you to see him." "I will telephone him to-morrow to come to lunch," I agreed, and the discussion on the proposed Commission petered out. After dinner the P.M. and Haldane settled down to their luxurious cigars and we to our cigarettes, chatting over many things with no apparent intent on his side. I told him about the minority report of the War Cabinet Committee against the Government,[3] and reminded him of his letter

[1] Sir Richard Augustus Studdert Redmayne (b. 1865). Colliery manager and civil servant. Chief Inspector of Mines under the Home Office, 1908-20. Assistant Coal Controller, 1916-20.

[2] This can hardly have been the case. As Minister of Munitions, Lloyd George could not have failed to know the man who was research officer to the Amalgamated Society of Engineers, whom, also, he was almost immediately to appoint as Secretary to the National Industrial Conference (see p. 151). But Lloyd George took an impish pleasure in baiting Webb.

[3] Mrs. Webb's own Minority Report, subsequently published by the Fabian Society under the title *The Wages of Men and Women—Should They Be Equal?* It remains one of the best statements of the case for equal pay.

to Sylvia[1] Pankhurst, defining the meaning of the clause affecting women's wages; he seemed wholly oblivious—(I did not remark to him that I gathered from the effusive tone of his letter that he had mistaken his enemy Sylvia for his friend Christabel).[1] We talked about Berne, Henderson, the condition of Russia and of Germany. Haldane and we pressed upon him the bad condition of Germany and its need for food and raw materials. "If Germany goes over the precipice as Russia has done, Heaven help France and Italy in spite of their victories at the expense of other peoples," I exclaimed. Sidney brought forward the question of the indemnities payable by Germany. "The Allies may ask for two thousand millions: they will be lucky if they get one thousand—not enough to restore the devastated territories of Belgium and France." The P.M. looked meditative as he lay back in his armchair smoking his big cigar: "That stunt about indemnities from Germany that *they* started during the election"—with an emphasis on *they*—he said slowly as if thinking aloud, "was a very foolish business." This left us gasping, but being fellow guests we agreed cordially with him and turned the conversation on to Russia, about which he did not differ from our view. The prestige of a lonely dinner with the P.M., at his own request, is considerable, and the amusement of watching this remarkable political performer is great. But as we walked away at midnight, through the drifting rain, we felt that the evening had been empty of meaning. The credit account of the transaction is an interesting entry in my diary, I reflected. But it proved otherwise.

I telephoned the next morning to Tom Jones to lunch with us "at the request of the P.M." Tom Jones, who is now Acting Secretary of the War Cabinet in the absence of Hankey,[2] is a simple-minded, true-hearted man whose peace of mind is perpetually destroyed by the conflict of his personal devotion to Lloyd George with his sense of truth and fair play between individuals and loyalty to the principles of democracy. He let the cat out of the bag and a very ugly cat it was. The persons in the list of names which could not be got from Downing Street were all hostile to nationalisation. The mysterious Shaw was not the egregious Tom of the cotton weavers but a far abler man—the Trade Union Secretary of the Woollen Trade Board,[3] known to the Research Department as the most astute of the supporters of joint control with a capitalist trust. The "impartial persons" designated

[1] Christabel Pankhurst (b.1880), was the militant suffragette daughter of Mrs. Pankhurst, who became a strong Government supporter during the war. Sylvia Pankhurst (b. 1882) was both militant suffragette and Socialist; during the war she organised the left-wing Workers' Socialist Federation in the East End of London.
[2] Maurice Pascal Alers Hankey, Lord Hankey (b. 1877). Secretary to Committee of Imperial Defence, 1911–38, and to Cabinet, 1919–38.
[3] i.e. Arthur Shaw (1880–1939). General Secretary, National Union of Bleachers, Dyers and Textile Workers; served on many Government Commissions.

were of the capitalist-cum-Guild-Socialist school who dislike the least Government control leave alone Government ownership and management. Jones felt compelled to consult us about the membership—but he would not hear of Cole or Chiozza Money[1] and he sat glum when I suggested, in friendly intimacy, that he might consider Sidney. And from other things he said or did not say we gathered that Lloyd George had been converted, possibly in the last few days or hours before he met us, to the plan of the coal owners published this morning. . . . That little game of appointing a Committee to report against nationalisation must be stopped, we said, directly the door closed on him.

Sidney thereupon sat down and wrote a long letter to Smillie explaining the exact meaning of the coal owners' proposals and telling him what he believed were the Government intentions with regard to the membership and, therefore, the report of the Coal Commission. This morning he wrote off to Cole and Chiozza Money, and Money arranged by telephone a meeting between him and Sidney and Smillie and Hodges[2] at the Russell Hotel, for this very afternoon.

Sidney found Smillie depressed with a cold and the feeling of responsibility. The four sat for a couple of hours discussing every aspect of the question. Money was boiling over with lively wrath, said the coal owners' proposals were infamous; he wanted the miners to go straight into the fight and win. Sidney reasoned in favour of accepting the Commission on terms: it must be a court to investigate, not a tribunal to determine; it must report by the 14th; it must be composed of equal numbers—employers and their outside experts and the miners and their outside experts, and the outsiders on the men's side must be selected by the miners. If the Government refused this offer the miners would have put themselves right with public opinion in refusing to take part in a Commission packed against them, and would go into a pitched battle with a better chance of success. (Sidney believes that they would be badly beaten if they held out for nationalisation, the bulk of the miners caring for nothing but hours and earnings.) If the Government accepted, there could not be a unanimous report against them—they would either get a majority report in favour of their claims or two reports of equal authority. The miners must have as their representatives two of the only three men who could argue their case—Cole, Chiozza Money, and himself. He thinks he persuaded the other three as to the wisdom of accepting the Commission

[1] Sir Leo Chiozza Money (1870-1944). Journalist, Fabian, and Liberal M.P. Author of *Riches and Poverty,* one of the more influential social studies of the Edwardian age. Parliamentary Private Secretary to Lloyd George, and Parliamentary Secretary to Ministry of Shipping, 1916-18.

[2] Frank Hodges (1887-1947). Became Secretary to Miners' Federation of Great Britain in 1918. Civil Lord of the Admiralty in 1924 Labour Government. He married Henrietta Carter of Abertillery.

on these terms, but Smillie doubted whether he could get his delegate meeting to go that far in meeting the Government. The miners were out for a fight.

We await the events with some anxiety. We believe that such a Commission would mean substantial victory for the miners' case. If the Government, confident of their power to beat the miners, go into battle—theirs is the responsibility. And it is a heavy responsibility. "Blockading the miners" will be a difficult and dangerous task: the railwaymen and the transport workers might be drawn in, the army might refuse to act. And then?

February 28th.—I attended the afternoon session of the Industrial Conference.[1] . . . The Minister of Labour was in the chair and the P.M. was at his side listening patiently to the tirades of the Labour delegates and the laboured commonplaces of the employers' representatives. A mild sensation was created by the defiantly boisterous speech of the official of the Police and Prison Union.[2] "Never again will the police allow themselves to be used to suppress the liberty of their fellow workers," he shouted, shaking his fist at the chair and incidentally at the P.M. Henderson delivered a sonorous and somewhat pompous oration about the reconciliation of capital and labour and carried his resolution for a joint committee of thirty employers and thirty trade unionists to deliberate on labour unrest, conditions of employment, unemployment and the setting up of a permanent national council. Then came the turn of the P.M. He was looking more than ever the actor-conjurer—only instead of the malicious sly look he had when I watched him at the Bristol Trade Union Congress he had assumed the most beneficent air; he might have been the Heavenly Father of the World of Labour. With a combination of pleasant persiflage and emotional sympathy with the monotony and sordidness of wage-earning life, he ended in a somewhat forced rhetorical peroration—a stale refrain of the song of victory. The Conference laughed and cheered but were not convinced. Then occurred an incident which excited me. Adamson came on to the platform and took his seat behind Lloyd George, evidently waiting till he had finished. "He has come from the Miners' Conference," a friendly

[1] A Conference of employers' associations, Trade Unions, Whitley Councils, etc., called for the promotion of industrial peace. The Unions of miners, railwaymen, transport workers and engineers did not accept the invitation. Arthur Henderson was Chairman of the Labour side, G. D. H. Cole its Secretary and Allan Smith Chairman of the employers' side. The Conference discussed many questions, including a proposal for a standing National Industrial Council, an Eight Hours' Bill, and a Minimum Wage Bill; but in the event nothing came of any of them.

[2] John Henry Hayes (1887–1941). General Secretary, Police and Prison Officers' Union. M.P. for Edgehill, and for Dartford. Parliamentary Secretary to Ministry of Pensions in 1924 Labour Government.

official of the Ministry of Labour whispered to me, "to tell him the result." The P.M. left the platform with Adamson. In half an hour's time he returned, looking extremely angry, almost dignified in his anger. He was evidently explaining to Horne[1] what had happened; he frowned, threw back his head of hair like a lion shaking his mane, and shook his head and spoke with evident vehemence. Tom Jones also looked depressed. "The miners are going to strike," I whispered to the friendly official. "Yes," he agreed, "look how glum our chief looks." When I heard at the Research Department, whither I went at the close of the meeting, what had actually happened I smiled. The miners had told the P.M. their terms: the Conference had decided that morning to postpone the strike until the 22nd and to accept service on the Commission provided they nominated half the Commission, and they had on the spot nominated Chiozza Money, Tawney and Sidney as their outsiders. They had given the P.M. ten minutes to decide whether he would accept their terms or have a strike. "The delegates must catch the five o'clock train," Smillie had stated. The P.M. had felt he had to accept the terms and this explains his anger.

This Commission of eleven or thirteen persons, appointed in such a strange and unconsidered way, is to decide not only the wages and hours of the miners but also whether or not the mines are to be nationalised. But where is parliamentary government? If the miners accept the findings of the Commission, the Government will be compelled by its promise to do likewise and Parliament will have to endorse the verdict or turn out the Government.

March 12*th.*—I looked in at the Coal Commission this afternoon. It was a scene of strange contrasts. The robing room of the House of Lords is appropriately decorated with highly ornate frescoes of faded and sentimental pomp. But to-day it is serving as the crowded stage —crowded by an audience of all the interests in a mood of exasperated anxiety—for a body calling itself a Royal Commission on the Mining Industry, but in its proceedings far more like a revolutionary tribunal, sitting in judgment on the capitalist owners and organisers of the nation's industries until the 20th of March.

The ostensible business of the Commission is to examine and report on the miners' claim for a rise in wages and a reduction of hours; but owing to the superior skill of the miners' representatives it has become a state trial of the coal owners and royalty owners conducted on behalf of the producers and consumers of the product, culminating in the question "Why not nationalise the industry?" Mr. Justice Sankey[2] is

[1] Robert Stevenson Horne, Viscount Horne (1871–1940). Conservative politician. Minister of Labour, 1919.

[2] John Sankey, Viscount Sankey (1866–1948). Became a Judge in 1914: later joined the Labour Party. Lord Chancellor, 1929–35.

an urbane lawyer, who treats every Commissioner, in turn, as the most distinguished of the lot and gives almost unlimited licence to questions and answers, interruptions and retorts. On his right sit the representatives of capital: three inferior business men who are coal owners[1] and three superior business men representing other interests. On his left sit Smillie, Hodges and Smith, three miners' officials, then Sidney, Tawney and Chiozza Money—typical intellectuals of the Labour Party. Smillie is the protagonist of the miners' cause, Chiozza Money is the most aggressive and self-assertive of the miners' advocates, Sidney draws out damaging admissions and claps on the right conclusion to every line of argument, whilst Tawney raises the whole discussion to the highest planes of moral rectitude and sweet reasonableness. The other side are absurdly outclassed: the three mine-owners are narrow-minded profit-makers with less technical knowledge than the miners' officials, or, at any rate, less power of displaying it, with not the remotest inkling of the wider political and economic issues which are always being raised by the miners' advocates. Balfour of Sheffield is a heavy reactionary with a quite undeserved reputation—Sidney thinks. My old friend of the Reconstruction Committee, Arthur Duckham, is undoubtedly able and he gives the impression of being indifferent to the result, or uncertain as to what he wants it to be; he sits mostly silent, holding a watching brief not for the employers but for the present Government. Royden, M.P., a wellbred and accomplished capitalist at large, is looking to politics as a career and is not over-anxious to offend the coming democracy. The official evidence against the coal owners' administration of the mines has been overwhelming, and the public opinion which was hostile a week ago to the miners is now indignant with the coal owners' profits at the consumers' expense. But the significance of the proceedings is the precedent set for similar state trials of the organisation of each industry by a court made up, half of the prosecuting proletariat, half of the capitalist defendants, with power to call for all accounts and all documents and to search out the most secret ways of the profitmaking craft. Sidney is enjoying himself hugely: I have never seen him so keen on any task since the halcyon days of the L.C.C.

In our personal life we are happy, interested and fully occupied. But when one looks out on the world one passes through a succession of nightmares. The clouds in the east grow steadily darker and the

1 The coal owners referred to were R. W. Cooper, J. T. Forgie, and Sir Evan Williams (b.1871), who was Chairman of the Mining Association of Great Britain from 1919–44. The "superior business men" were (1) Sir Arthur Balfour, afterwards Lord Riverdale (b. 1873), a steelmaker who was Chairman of the 1924 Balfour Committee on Trade and Industry; (2) Sir Arthur Duckham (see p. 86); (3) Sir Thomas Royden, Lord Royden (1871–1950), M.P. for Bootle, who was President of the Liverpool Chamber of Shipping. Subsequently Cooper and Royden resigned, and were replaced by Sir Adam Nimmo and Sir Allan Smith (see p. 160).

flood of anarchy and barbarism seems to get steadily nearer. One is conscious of great waves of agony, mental and physical, traversing continents to break on one's imagination, stunning hope and faith in the white race. Even fear for England's future points the pain. With national indebtedness mounting up, the birth rate at its lowest, the death rate at its highest, unemployment increasing day by day, one wonders when the crash will come. Will the western world ever right itself and produce sufficient for its annual consumption plus the tribute exacted by the holders of the war loan at home and abroad? If not, we must have equality in subsistence or drift into chaos: no section of the people will stand being destitute through lack of work or half destitute through sweating whilst other sections have enough to live in luxury without work. And when the propertied classes realise that it is surrender or war will they fight for their privileges? And if class war—in its literal and not its metaphorical sense—begins in countries exhausted and demoralised, how will it end?

Meanwhile, knowing that our unearned income is at great risk and our working days numbered, we are going full steam ahead with expenditure of money and energy on finishing tasks we set ourselves years ago. I am scheming out our book on British socialism: its past achievements, present policy, and immediate controversies—designed to be a summary of the Wisdom of the Webbs—a sort of "last will and testament" to all whom it may concern. I sit down every morning and scribble paragraphs, forthwith dictated to Miss Schmidt[1] and re-dictated, withholding this first draft from Sidney until I can submit it to him as a chapter of the book. I brood day and night, in the old way, over the links in my argument and the phrasing of my descriptions of the facts as I see them. Felix Crosse[2] has begun his researches at the Record Office. We can offer him only £200 a year to supplement his small private means, but we hold out to him the prospect of using our accumulated material for future books of his own. Possibly also we may be helpful in teaching him our methods of research and suggesting hypotheses and new categories.

March 20th.—Sidney has been working at high pressure for the last fortnight—attending nine hours or more at the Commission; in the intervals drafting the miners' report. On Sunday Smillie, Chiozza Money, Smith and Tawney came here to discuss and amend it; on Tuesday Sidney gave it to the Chairman; yesterday it was circulated to the six other members of the Commission. The Chairman told Sidney that "the die was cast," he could not recommend nationalisa-

[1] Ivy M. Schmidt, later Mrs. Bolton, L.C.C. Sometime personal secretary to Mrs. Webb.
[2] Felix Warren Crosse (b. 1892). Civil servant; in Ministry of Munitions, 1915; War Office Intelligence, 1918; Foreign Office, 1919-23.

tion. . . . But he had prepared no alternative report: he assumed the coal owners would have their own experts' report, and the other capitalists a more conciliatory one. Sidney suggested that the Chairman should not sign any of the reports but should send them with a covering letter to the Cabinet stating his personal views. Meanwhile the coal owners handed in a half sheet of paper: 15% rise, one hour less and no state interference. The Chairman asked whether this was all, at which they seemed perturbed—they had prepared nothing else. But they would have something ready to-morrow. "It will have to be in to-night, gentlemen, or it can't be printed." Duckham has persuaded Royden and Balfour to join with him in proposing 20% rise, two hours' reduction in two stages, unification but not state management, and he is drafting a document to that effect. It is possible that the Judge will sign it. All indications point to a general strike of miners and transport workers.

Lloyd George has, of course, done the unexpected thing to better the situation from his own standpoint. A letter appeared in the press this morning by Wilson, Clemenceau and Orlando begging him to stay in Paris and appealing to the patriotism of the British people to make it possible. We do not see, as yet, the inwardness of the move to the rear. It may be that the War Cabinet has refused to permit him to say the blessed word "nationalisation" (they are said to be raging against Geddes' speech in favour of railway nationalisation) or to give way to the miners on wages and hours. There is a section of Tories and capitalists, led by Curzon and Churchill, who think that war must come and that it had better come at once—during mobilisation. It may be that the P.M. thinks he can play the old game of patriotism and the supremacy of foreign affairs. But probably he has decided to remain away at the critical time so that he may appear suddenly next week as a detached autocrat, to arbitrate between the Cabinet and the miners and close the strike in favour of the men. Or he may think that the War Cabinet had better try its hand at intimidating the men: if they succeed so much the better; if they fail "Why was I not told?"

Evening of the same day.—This afternoon while Sidney, Tawney and I were having a cup of tea Tom Jones broke in upon us in a great state of excitement. He had seen the three reports. The War Cabinet was meeting at six o'clock to consider what they would do. They were determined not to be bullied into conceding the miners' demands—especially nationalisation. He was hot about the miners' representatives having included nationalisation as one of their recommendations. "The Commission had been instructed to report on wages and hours only." "Not in the reference," interrupted Sidney. "And Smillie at the recent conference with the P.M. did not take up the attitude that nationalisation was a *sine qua non*; he had implied that if the wages and hours were granted nationalisation could wait." Sidney explained that the wages and hours could not be granted without raising the price of coal, unless unification were carried out, and unification meant nationalisation. Jones agreed and admitted that nationalisation was implied in the Chairman's report. But the Cabinet was obdurate. "What could be done?" asked Jones in genuine concern. I suggested that an article in the *Times* was the most effective pressure—Sidney might go and see the editor tonight. Sidney protested that he did not know the editor, but agreed to do so, also to advise Gardiner[1] of the *Daily News* to take a quiet line about it and to assume that nationalisation had been agreed to by the majority of the Commission. Could we bring any other pressure to bear—on Fisher or Addison? We promised to see Fisher. "The Government is prepared to give away the whole annual product of the nation in advance and more than the whole annual product rather than tamper with property," I interjected. "The Exchequer could subsidise the bad mines so that the price of coal should not be raised—the Cabinet would be willing to do that," Jones answered.

10 *o'clock.*—I have just been into Dr. Fisher—three doors off. He told me that Bonar Law announces to-night in the House of Commons that the Cabinet accepts the Sankey Report as the limit of what they could grant. He expressed himself quite satisfied with this decision and not in the least anxious about the result. This was the best time for a strike: business had not begun, orders were not coming in, they had better settle with the miners or any other recalcitrant body of men now rather than later on when the national industry had got fairly started. "You don't know how the miners are hated up and down the country," snapped out Mrs. Fisher. "We could not agree to nationalisation at a week's notice; a strike will be regrettable," remarked Fisher, "but we must just go through with it"—he smiled and suppressed a yawn. Directly I heard that Bonar Law had an-

---

[1] Alfred George Gardiner (1865–1946). Editor of the *Daily News* from 1902–1919. It was generally assumed that, if the Commission's report recommended nationalisation, the Government would accept it. Bonar Law, as Acting Prime Minister, had written a letter to Frank Hodges in which he said: "*I have pleasure in confirming, as I understand you wish me to do, my statement that the Government are prepared to carry out in the spirit and in the letter the recommendations of Sir John Sankey's report*". When, however, Sir John Sankey's second report in favour of nationalisation proved to be a majority report and not a unanimous one (see p. 161), the Government rejected it, and adopted a modification of the report produced by Sir Arthur Duckham. As that appeared to appeal to nobody, the Government, possibly feeling that the danger-point was passed, abandoned it in October. The whole sequence of events goes far too explain the bitterness of the miners and the emotions roused by "Black Friday" (p. 201).

nounced the acceptance of the Sankey Report I knew that it was useless to argue. "I hope that there will not be any violence on either side," I said. Fisher smiled and said nothing.

March 27th.—Contrary to our expectations Bonar Law's speech and Sankey's Report won the day. The miners' delegate meeting, after considering the concessions granted by the Sankey Report and Bonar Law's promise that the Coal Commission should report on nationalisation by the 20th of May, agreed to recommend their members to cancel the strike notices. The National Union of Railwaymen and the Transport Workers also accept the better terms offered them and the acute crisis in the world of labour seems at present safely past. The credit of the peace is divided between Smillie and Thomas who emerge from the crisis great personages.

The report of the Industrial Conference and the memorandum of the Trade Union members, both written by Cole, taken with the proceedings of the Coal Commission, have made a great impression. Henderson is quite "bucked up" by his success and has again put himself at the head of the Labour Movement, this time on the industrial side. "I have done better work in the last three weeks," he told me yesterday, "than I did in fifteen years in the House of Commons." The proposed industrial council on the basis of trade unionism and employers' associations altogether gives the go-by to the Trades Union Congress and its parliamentary committee. It is a remarkable development due to Cole's ability and Henderson's wisdom in making use of him. Henderson is the only working-class leader who understands making use of the brains of Socialist intellectuals. It was a stroke of genius to make Cole the Secretary on the workmen's side of the Conference. If it survives as a permanent institution it will become the central authority of the Labour Movement on its industrial side, and Henderson will be its Chairman. But will the Trade Union movement accept this new body—the Triple Alliance has already refused to join it—and what will the House of Commons say to his new style of legislature on an industrial basis? Soviet Government peacefully incorporated in the British Constitution; a revolution in a fit of absentmindedness, without machine guns or barricades—without even waving the red flag.

April 6th.—Two echoes from the past, the near past and the remote past. H. J. Mackinder[1] lunched with us: we had not seen him since the outbreak of war. He is still a stalwart imperialist and

[1] Sir Halford John Mackinder (1861–1947). Professor of Geography in the University of London until 1925; Director of London School of Economics, 1903–8. A strong Protectionist in politics.

tariff reformer—a survival of the faithful few who believe in triumphant capitalism dominating the world. He still talks in continents and waterways, in mass movements and momentums—great races emerging from plains or descending from mountain heights to conquer coastlines and cross oceans. But he has become uncomfortably aware of another kind of mass movement, of another type of momentum—the uprising of the manual workers, within each modern state, organised as political and industrial democracies, to oust those who own the instruments of production from their property and their power. He refuses to believe that this drive towards the equalitarian state is a permanent factor: sooner or later it will be brought to a standstill, long before it has reached its goal, by the superior organisation of the brain-working capitalist, stimulated by the love of riches and the delight in adventure. All the same, it is an uncomfortable shadow falling across his admirable maps of the rise and fall of empires.

In the afternoon we journeyed down with Haldane to see Lord Morley, who for some unexplained reason desired to see us. We have never been on terms of friendship with John Morley. We have neither liked nor disliked him; and we have always assumed a similar attitude on his part. But it seems that in his political prime he was acutely aware of the socialist criticism of Gladstonian politics and deeply resented it. To-day he is a dignified, benevolent and infirm old man, pathetically anxious to make his peace with the new world of social democracy. In his old age he is more open-minded to the new thought than he was when he had the vigour to grasp its meaning. The catastrophe of the great war has compelled his pacifist soul to seek comradeship in the international socialist movement. We talked all about the place of the past, the present, and the future, doing our best to interest him. As Sidney said goodbye he said wistfully "There is no malice between us?"—as if our visit had been one of reconciliation after personal estrangement. We have been quite unconscious of any relationship—good or bad—between us and him. Once or twice we have met him at dinner at the Courtneys, a few more times at the Haldanes, but he has never been at our house nor we at his. We have respected John Morley as a man of distinguished manners and tone, with a fine literary intelligence. But we have never taken him seriously as a political thinker and he has certainly not distinguished himself in administration or in the rough and tumble of politics. Our dominant impression, in fact, has been that he was a singularly over-rated man: there has been a conspiracy among his friends, and they have been the most devoted of friends, to impose him as a great man on public opinion—a conspiracy that largely succeeded. Possibly we under-rated him. All the more touching was his graciousness to us on Sunday afternoon.

April 29th.—A delightful twelve days with Logan Pearsall Smith[1] and Alys Russell at Big Chilling. During the eight days that Sidney was there—he had to go up for three days to the Coal Commission— we wrote Part I (five chapters) of our new book on British Socialism from the draft that I had prepared in the last two months. The walks by the sea in mid springtide in brilliant sunshine—waves, birds and buds—were healthful and happy. We enjoyed the companionship of our hosts: Logan spent his time in cross-examining us about our experience, thoughts and feelings. He is an observant and subtle psychologist. The publication of his "Trivia" has brought him literary fame through his invention of a novel literary form. His particular speciality is to represent, with scientific accuracy and literary charm the actual content of his own mind as an example of the mind of most intellectuals. He exercises this new craft with consummate skill and with ruthless and cynical frankness, revealing how much of the stream of thoughts and feelings, even of the enlightened and moral man, are pathologically trivial in their vanity and egotism. The evenings of Sidney's absence he read us extracts from his selections from Santayana's works—an author who, he thinks, combines the most perfect style with the truest philosophy of life. Anyway this poetical prose, intoned in Logan's pleasant voice, was a recreation after the day's work on the prosaic facts of British Socialism.

*   *   *   *   *

May 10th.—A hard and brutal peace, made more intolerable by the contumely of circumstances deliberately devised, in the method of its delivery to the representatives of the German people. What digusts me most is the fact that Great Britain gets the cleanest cut of all out of the possessions of the fallen enemy. France has hurt Germany most; Italy has been the most unreasonable. But it is Great Britain who adds most to her territory, prestige and power. The German colonies, Mesopotamia, the acknowledgment of Egyptian sovereignty, the destruction of the German navy and mercantile marine, the undisputed dominion over the ocean highways—all this without further effort or risk—are a greater and better secured asset than extensions of frontiers which have to be fortified, huge indemnities which cannot be paid, and the right to continue in costly and hazardous occupation of enemy country. Moreover, France has suffered, relatively to her strength, incomparably more than Great Britain alike in men and material. Meanwhile Germany has gained little or nothing from her abandonment of autocracy and militarism; and Wilson's fourteen points, upon

---

[1] Logan Pearsall Smith (1865–1946). The American-born essayist, brother of Alys Russell, first wife of Bertrand Russell; she broadcast, when eighty years old, reminiscences of early Fabians.

which Germany surrendered, have been, in the spirit and in the letter, repudiated.

That is my verdict. Sidney says that the terms are better than might have been expected when you examine each one in detail. He maintains that there is not much to object to except the large and uncertain indemnities and the project of "trying the Kaiser". These two clauses are, he thinks, a way of climbing down for Clemenceau and Lloyd George, confronted with the demand, by powerful sections of their own people, for financial relief and vengeance. These impossible claims will be thrown over when they have served their purpose and are seen, by everyone, to be impracticable. But Sidney is an optimist.

*   *   *   *   *

May 22nd.—I have had to break off my work on our book to prepare an address on local government for the Research Department Conference and also another on prison administration (resulting in a twenty pounds subscription to the prison committee). The latter address enabled me to go through all the material collected by Felix Crosse for our book on prisons. I have also had to supervise Miss Schmidt's researches at the Record Office and the B.M. for the new edition of our *History of Trade Unionism.* And there is always the distraction of the steady stream of persons who want either to consult us or to impress us—from the representatives of some obscure race in the Near East struggling to be free to the young women in search of a delectable career; sometimes a bevy of men or women from the other side of the Atlantic on one of the innumerable government commissions in which our cousins delight. Sidney is absorbed in the daily sittings of the Coal Commission and is showing slight signs of fag. It is a happy and interested life, but I sometimes long for the leisure to concentrate on our own job and get it done.

*   *   *   *   *

June 23rd.—The second and final stage of the Coal Commission has not been so exciting as the first, but it has been an equally strenuous time for the Commissioners. One of the coal owners and the agreeable but futile Royden retired in favour of Nimmo[1] (the ablest of the coal owners) and Allan Smith[2] (the official of the engineering employers) who is considered the star among the professional representatives of capitalism. These two militants carried the war into the enemies' camp, but in such an objectionable way that at the end of the sittings they were no longer on speaking terms with the Chairman and

[1] Sir Adam Nimmo (d. 1939). President, and later Vice-President of Mining Association of Great Britain; director of many companies.

[2] Sir Alan Macgregor Smith. Solicitor; Chairman for many years of the Management Board of the Engineering and Allied Employers' National Federation.

did not appear themselves or permit the other two coal owners to appear at the final meeting for signing the four reports. Sankey's temper gave way at the end—he became intolerant of Nimmo and Allan Smith, neglectful of Chiozza Money, relying exclusively on Tawney and Sidney as counsellors and also as intermediaries with the miners' three officials; Smillie's melodramatic obstinacy about "no compensation" to the royalty owners "injured the miners' case" in the country. But after wrestling with Smillie and co-operating with the Judge, Sidney and Tawney, supported by Chiozza Money, Smith and Hodges, brought about a satisfactory conclusion to the whole business—a Chairman's report in favour of nationalisation and a separate but short endorsement of this report, with one or two demurrers on particular proposals, by the six miners' representatives, thus securing a majority of the Commission for nationalisation. Sidney gathered from Sankey that in reporting in favour of nationalisation he had the P.M.'s approval. Sankey added that there would be a general election—not before July and not later than November and that nationalisation of the coal mines would be in the Lloyd George programme. What is abundantly clear is that Lloyd George is busily putting about that a general election is imminent and that it will be precipitated by a breach between him and the reactionaries of his Cabinet. Whether this is merely part of the process of bluffing the Conservatives into accepting his policy or whether it is a feeler for radical and labour support, none of us know—perhaps he does not know himself; if the first policy fails, he may fall back on the second.

Sidney has come out of the Commission with a great admiration for Tawney, for his personal charm, his quiet wisdom, and his rapier-like intellect. Tawney has, in fact, been the great success of the Commission. For Chiozza Money, Sidney has a somewhat contemptuous liking—contemptuous is too strong a word—for his cleverness and untiring industry he certainly respects him. Smillie, the protagonist of revolutionary labour, the outstanding personality of the Commission from the standpoint of the newspapers, has been a trying colleague, with his fanatical unreason, always acting and speaking as if the day of judgment on capitalism was coming within a week. Smith and Hodges in their different ways have been ideal representatives of the old and the new school of trade union officials. With all the employers Sidney has been on excellent terms. Allan Smith, who refused to shake hands with the Chairman at the last meeting, went out of his way to be civil to Sidney and was always eager to talk to him. Cooper was the "gentleman" of that side and acted in the last stages as "go-between" of the two parties. Arthur Duckham, who took his own line and had his own report, was furious with Nimmo and Allan Smith, disliked Chiozza Money, and was friendly with all the others. It remains to be said that Sidney has thoroughly enjoyed service on the Commission and says that he has had a rollicking good time. He believes that the Coal Commission will be the beginning of a landslide into the communal control of industries and services.

* * * * *

June 24th.—We are all so disgusted with the peace that we have ceased to discuss it—one tries to banish it from one's mind as an unclean thing that will be swept away by common consent when the world is once again sane. Two years ago I was angry with G.B.S. when he said that if the Allies won "they would skin Germany alive" —he made of course a small verbal error— he ought to have said "they would *try* to skin Germany alive." As it is necessary that Germany should keep alive, if only in order to fulfil the right conditions of the peace, and as, in any case, 60,000,000 persons cannot be compelled to die, the Allies will fail. The dramatic sinking of the German fleet by the German sailors in British waters is to my mind the most fitting celebration of this peace by violence. The Germans will sink other things besides their fleet before the Allies repent this use of victory: the capitalist system for instance. The Germans have a great game to play with western civilisation if they choose to play it, if they have the originality and the collective determination to carry it through. They can compel their victors to accept the new order which they devise to heal the sorrow and the misery of their own people.

July 1st. Grosvenor Road.—Sidney was considerably gratified by the Poll for the Labour Party Executive—his name heading the list. This is a testimony of respect and appreciation of his silent work for the Labour Movement.

He reports that there was the usual atmosphere of good nature; rather more than the usual discontent with the Labour M.P.s and their bad attendance at the H. of C. and their complete failure to live up to the position of H.M. Opposition.

Hodges of the miners made the best speech, and Clynes the best impression—relatively to his reputation. In friendly talk Spoor was acclaimed as the only success among the Labour M.P.s, with William Graham following. But most of Sidney's time was spent in committee with the delegates explaining to them that the Labour Party Executive had no jurisdiction in the matter of strikes and could only promote peaceful *demonstrations* against the invasion of Russia, etc. The leaders of the Triple Alliance—especially the miners—declare that they will change the face of the T.U. Congress and its Parliamentary Committee. But I doubt their success. The rank and file of trade unionists are no more idealist about international affairs than the ordinary middle- or upper-class man. In this lies the weakness of the Labour Party. In its ideals and its programme it represents the better spirit of the most moral and intelligent men and women of all classes —though possibly most of all the idealists among the manual workers: in its constitution it assumes itself to be representative of the special interests of the disinherited and propertyless men and women of all races. And disinherited and propertyless men and women are not specially moral and intelligent persons—not even the majority of them—they are just the lowest strata of average sensual men. The creed of the Labour Party is too good for its ostensible constituents. "Not one million out of the five million trade unionists voted Labour at the last election," said Henderson to us the other day: "we had, as supporters, a larger fraction of the ministers of religion—at any rate, of those outside the Church of England."

July 5th.—Completed Part I of our new book on Socialism—the indictment of profit-making Capitalism. I started at the end of February after finishing the Minority Report on Women in Industry. It has entailed a lot of reading and considerable toil of thought. But I have worked well at it and we are back in our old style of partnership: I designing the separate chapters and dictating a rough draft, and re-dictating until it expresses my mind, and then Sidney correcting all of it and re-writing and adding sections to it after discussion with me— the finished product representing the combined thought of "the Webbs". In the end we never disagree!

Now I am preparing the material for Part II—the achievements of British Socialism—attempting to get together sufficient stuff for work on it during our recess at Bryan's Ground. But as Sidney has to write that new chapter for *The History of Trade Unionism* and also make use of Felix Crosse's new material for our book on prisons, and I shall be without my secretary, I doubt whether we shall make much positive progress with it before our return to London in the middle of September.

July 14th.—The three old wives—Kate, Mary and Beatrice— watched this morning with gladness, tinged with sorrowful memories of our sister Theresa, our dear brother-in-law Alfred married to Marion Ellis, daughter of the late Liberal statesman John Ellis.[1] Alfred has excellent taste in women. He chose the most charming of the Potter sisters; he wanted, as a widower, to marry the saint-like Beatrice Creighton,[2] and he has now won an exceptionally attractive

[1] John Edward Ellis (1841–1910). Quaker, colliery owner and banker, Nottinghamshire; Liberal M.P. for Rushcliffe from 1885.
[2] Daughter of Mandell Creighton, Bishop of London, and a close friend of Mrs. Webb's. Later became a deaconess at Ootacamund.

woman, good as gold, able, and most pleasant to look at. All his children and their mates were there beaming their goodwill. The two were reverently ecstatic: Southwark Cathedral and Bishop Burge[1] added a gracious solemnity to the marriage of the Vicar-General of York and Canterbury.

During the war Parmoor has developed into a political idealist. Whatever may have been his reasons for being against the war at the beginning, the horrors of it, and the revengeful spirit of the peace, have turned him into something very like an international Socialist. So does evil company corrupt good manners! All the men who held fast by the capitalist creed that he used to believe in have been eager to crush Germany and impose their countries' material power on the world; all those who have believed in the coming of a brotherhood of individuals and races, based on equality in material circumstances, have hated the rule of force and "spoils to the victors". The Church has bitterly disappointed him in its casuistical support of the powers that be. "I really do not know where I stand in all economic questions," he said to me the other day; "all I know is that I disagree fundamentally with all those with whom I used to act in the House of Commons."

We spent the week-end at Lion Phillimore's[2] with Edward Grey —whom we had not seen since August 1914 when he told us, at a dinner at Haldane's, that this war would bring into being Labour Governments all over the world. When I reminded him of his prophecy he said: "I thought that the crust of the present social order had worn very thin and that a great war would break it down. I did not believe that the war could last for more than a year. But now after four years I believe that we shall see a world revolution comparable to the break-up of the Roman Empire." He is far more convinced of the imminence of revolution here in England than we are. "Any day Downing Street may find that they have behind them neither the police nor the army, and that some other body, not sitting at Westminster, is exercising the Executive authority based on the people's will." He awaits calmly, through his physical blindness and curious intellectual aloofness and personal disinterestedness, the coming changes—it is difficult to discover whether his attitude is one of hope and faith or lack of hope and faith in the new social order—he is uncertain whether it will be order or anarchy. For the rest, he is the same true-hearted, public-spirited and fair-minded English gentleman that he has always been; without originality, without any specific intellectual gifts, without the desire for social change, and without any

[1] Herbert Murray Burge (1862–1925). Bishop of Southwark, 1911–19, and of Oxford, 1919–25.
[2] Mrs. Lucy Phillimore (née Fitzpatrick). Fabian enthusiast, wife of R. C. Phillimore.

prejudice against it, without evil instincts and without heroic passion
—an incarnation of negative goodness. He and we have known each
other slightly for at least thirty years: we have always respected and
mildly liked him, never been intimate with him, never sought him out.
I imagine his attitude towards us has been very similar: possibly there
has been less personal liking; I think we may have offended his "good
taste": our aims are too defined and too hardly pressed on the rest of
the world. But both he and we were glad to spend a week-end talking
to each other, and our mutual "good-bye" was many degrees more
cordial than our opening greeting.

July 15*th.*—The political world awaits the emergence of Lloyd
George with a new programme from his Welsh retreat with anxiety;
and he doubtless awaits the result of the two by-elections to be
declared next week after the soldiers' votes have been counted. He
permitted his Cabinet to throw the bomb of the 6/- increase on coal
into the Swansea contest[1] a day before the election. "There were all
the motor-cars in Wales and a lot from London turning inside out the
Swansea slums in search of voters against the miners' candidate,"
reported Egerton Wake,[2] the Labour election agent, innumerable
"bringers up" telling the women that the 6/- was put on "by the
miners who are earning £5 to £10 a week." "We had won the election on the eve: then lost it on the day of the Poll," he added sorrow-
fully. Meanwhile the sinister reactionary, Winston Churchill, had
been down to Criccieth colloguing with his chief, and he tells everyone that he is going "to root out Bolshevism" at home and abroad.
On all sides we hear of consolidation of the forces of Capitalism and
a readiness to bring about *The Day* when Labour is to be routed.
The extravagant claims, made by the miners, to control not only their
own industry but foreign affairs by "direct action" has injured the
Labour Party in the eyes of the community, and the Coalition Government has made clever use of this "headiness" of the extremists. I am
inclined to think that the P.M. will come down on the right and
remain head of a National Party intent on maintaining the dictatorship of the property owners. It will be the capitalist press which will
enable him to keep his hold on a chaotic democracy. at the mercy
of suggestion—combined with the incapacity of the Labour
members, whom no one believes could form a Government that could
govern.

[1] East Swansea, now a safe Labour seat, returned a Coalition Liberal in the khaki
election. When the sitting member died, a Labour victory was confidently expected;
but Labour was defeated by 1,000 in an 18,000 poll.
[2] Egerton Percival Wake (1871-1929). Accountant; National Agent to Labour
Party from 1919.

July 23rd.—The Cabinet seem bent on provoking a big strike so as to avoid the issue of nationalisation and clear up on the relations between Capital and Labour. This is the meaning of the trouble in Yorkshire. The Yorkshire Miners' Association had agreed with the Yorkshire Employers' Association for a certain rise in piece work rates. The Coal Controller,[1] having left the matter to collective bargaining, suddenly forbade the increase and laid down a lower rate. This policy of pinpricks and of deliberate falsification of news, taken together with the refusal of the Government to declare itself on nationalisation, has inflamed the already irritated state of mind of the miners, who feel that they gave up the General Strike on the understanding that the Sankey Commission was going to settle the question and that its majority verdict would be accepted by the Government. Meantime trouble is brewing in other industries—both the reactionary employers and the militant trade unionists are just spoiling for a fight. I saw G. D. H. Cole to-day. He remarked that we were in for something like civil war: the men will be beaten but they will revenge themselves by a wholesale policy of "ca' canny".

*   *   *   *   *

September 24th.—Henderson dined with us yesterday evening and reported progress. He is naturally enough self-complacent about his great victory at Widnes, but considerably disconcerted at being asked by the L.P. Executive (at which Sidney was not present) to go down and speak for Dunstan at Rusholme[2] so soon after he had received the active support of the Liberals at Widnes. Sidney was in favour of fighting Rusholme—partly because the L.P. Executive could not have prevented it, and partly because he thinks it is better to sacrifice some seats now and build up a Labour Party rather than split the Labour Party by an alliance with Asquithian Liberalism. The Labour Party has to go through much tribulation before it is sufficiently sound to exercise any real influence: with its present leaderlessness it can exercise no effective control over the Government. Henderson is inclined to shirk H. of C. work—hating to find himself subordinate to Adamson and in competition with Clynes and Thomas for the chairmanship of the Party, if the Party succeeds in displacing Adamson—which I rather doubt if Henderson sulks. We begged him not to go off to the U.S.A. either during the autumn or the spring session, but just to stick to his H. of C. work, seeing as much of the Labour

---

[1] Sir Andrew Duncan (b. 1884). Coal Controller, 1919–20. Chairman, Executive Committee of British Iron and Steel Federation.

[2] There was a by-election in the Rusholme Division of Manchester in October. Dr. R. Dunstan stood as Socialist and Labour against W. M. R. Pringle, a left-wing Liberal; and the Tory was returned. This contest raised the question of Liberal-Labour relations in an acute form.

M.P.s as possible—without thinking too much whether or not he was proposed and elected to the chairmanship. He wanted Sidney to draft a complete scheme for "Socialising Industry"—the whole of industry —said that "we must come down to bedrock and show that the principle of socialisation was applicable to-day to all industries": why should the miners and the railwaymen have the privilege of being socialised?—the engineers and other operatives resented this partiality: it would be far better electioneering to have a complete scheme for all industry and get it accepted by the L.P. Conference. We pointed out the difficulties—the demarcation between one industry and another, the absence of brain power and goodwill in the government service, the peculiar technical requirements in each industry, the universal alarm that any such scheme would arouse—and rightly arouse—considering the incapacity of the Labour Party for the everyday work of their own organisations. At the same time, he had a vague idea of making each industry bear the whole cost of its unemployment by a reserve fund from the profits of good years.

September 28th.—The Great Strike—which has been brewing since the close of the war—has happened. Not of the engineers as was expected, nor of the miners as the public has long expected—but the railwaymen.[1] Never has there been a strike of anything like this in magnitude or social significance which has burst on the world so suddenly; the Parliamentary Committee, of which Thomas is Chairman, knew nothing about it; the Labour Party Office and Labour Research Department were equally ignorant—even the Triple Alliance to which the railwaymen belong was uninformed. As for the general public, they knew nothing of it before the day when all the trains stopped running.

In our view it has been desired, if not engineered, by the Government—engineered by the Geddes brothers,[2] and subconsciously desired by the P.M. The Geddes brothers represent the universal determination of the capitalists to reduce wages to pre-war level, if possible, pre-war money level, but in any case pre-war commodity

[1] The railways, still under Government control, had been negotiating a new wage agreement for months past. Sir Eric Geddes, the Minister of Transport, made a "definitive offer" for a cost-of-living sliding scale, with a very low minimum. This was indignantly rejected, and the men came out on strike. They were strongly supported by other sections of the movement, particularly the printers, who threatened a strike if the railwaymen were not allowed to state their case in the Press; and the case was so effectively stated that the Government greatly improved its offer. The first attempt to take back the wage gains of the war years thus met with defeat; subsequent ones, made after prices had broken and unemployment begun, were more successful.

[2] Sir Eric's brother was Auckland Campbell Geddes, later Lord Geddes (b. 1879), Director-General of Recruiting and Minister of National Service during the war. In 1919 he was Minister of Reconstruction.

value level. The P.M. has let the strike happen because he sees in it a good stunt for the next election—he may even think of an immediate election on the issue of Bolshevism and the dictatorship of the extremists of the manual working-class. Such an issue would effectively submerge the failure in Russia and all the scandals of his Government. It would strike a big blow at the Labour Party and side-track the Asquithian Liberals; it might be the making of a centre party publicly pledged to uphold the traditions of political democracy and secretly intent on fastening profit-making capitalism more firmly on the community. We think that the railwaymen were justified in making the continuance of the war wage a test question—though the manner of the strike is not easy to justify. It is exactly one of those occasions when "Direct Action" is justified by its success, and condemned by its failure. The purpose of the strike, to stop a reduction of the wages of the lowest grade of labour, is the most commendable of all strikes. Whether the means taken are right depends on the event.

We are all at sea as to what will happen in the next few days. There are rumours that the Government are preparing heroic measures—for confiscating the railwaymen's funds, for starving the railwaymen's families, for running the railways with soldiers: there are equally rumours that the T.U. are preparing for Soviets to take over the Government of the country. We tend to believe that these suppositions are baseless and that in a week or so there will be a compromise arranged between Thomas and Downing Street—the difference between the terms offered by the Government and those stated to be acceptable to the men is really very small—much smaller than seemed to be the case when Geddes hurled his ultimatum at the N.U.R. Executive and the N.U.R. Executive hurled back its proclamation for a strike. . . .

October 2nd.—The Labour Research Department at Eccleston Square have taken over the whole organisation of the Parliamentary publicity campaign for the N.U.R. and are running it with great ability under Arnot's direction—Cole being ill. There have come day after day Mallon, Lloyd, Tawney, Greenwood, Bacharach[1] and Clifford Allen and Harben; Sidney has joined them off and on, whilst I have contributed my secretary and the typewriter. They are setting themselves to state the facts against the Government propaganda, and the result of their work is seen in the altered attitude of the Press. In fact, considering the weakness of the men's case and the gross ignorance and bias of the public, the capitalist press has been unusually fair—partly the result, by the way, of pressure of the compositors, who have

[1] Alfred Louis Bacharach (b. 1891). Research chemist; at this date on the Executive Committee of the Labour Research Department.

threatened to bring out the whole printing trade unless the N.U.R. case is given equal publicity with that of the Government. The one good feature in this strike has been the imposing status of the "neutral" Unions led by Henderson and Gosling as official intermediaries, accepted alike by the Government and the N.U.R. The leaders of trade unionism in this instance have acted with good sense and with an excellent temper: reasonable towards the Government and loyal towards the railwaymen. . . .

October 6th.—The settlement is satisfactory and neither party has "scored" a victory, and the Government extremists and the direct action extremists are equally disillusioned. The net result is: the capitalist conspiracy, backed up by one section of the Government, to reduce the slightly enhanced standard of life arising out of the war is completely checkmated; the status of trade unionism—especially of the leaders of the T.U. world—has been greatly improved—the "fourteen" have emerged as national statesmen as well as the authorised representatives of the working-class. The "Direct-Actionists", especially the revolutionary "Direct-Actionists", have been severely disillusioned—the lightning strike has failed to paralyse the community, and the railwaymen have actually got very little by it—they could have got more by negotiations backed up by the whole T.U. Movement. It is clear that the unorganised working-class, not to mention all the other sections of the community, will not tolerate the dictatorship of the organised minority, and the manual workers will not permit the dictatorship of the Government. Both sides have learnt to respect each other's defensive powers.

Further, the strike has revealed to the T.U. world the imperfection of their national organisation and the weakness of their leadership. Whether this revelation will lead to any improvements is questionable. And there are rumours that the Government could not rely on the army and the police. Both the Government and the N.U.R. felt the odds against complete victory, and, being British, they compromised.

* * * * *

November 18th.—For the last six weeks I have been helping Sidney with the three final chapters of the *History of Trade Unionism*—adding sections to each—more especially to the second one on the status of Trade Unions within the state. This entailed some research into the genesis of the new ideas—Syndicalism, Industrial Unionism and the Shop Stewards' Movement—from original documents. The whole work is now going rapidly through the press and will be published in the New Year. We have arranged to print off a special edition at the low price of 5/- for the Trade Unions and other working-class organisations, and have sent out in conjunction with the L.R.D. 60,000 circulars asking for orders prior to December 13th, and for new affiliations to the Department. I am now back at work on my own special task. Sidney spends most afternoons on the Government Profiteering Committees and in helping Beveridge to organise new developments of the London School of Economics. He is in fact acting very much as if he was Chairman of the School and has secured from the Fisher Unwins[1] the gift of a country hostel for students and professors—the old home of Cobden.

Meanwhile the Labour Party has had two notable successes: great victories in the municipal elections throughout the country, especially in London, and the adoption by the Cabinet of the non-interventionist policy towards Russia. The disasters to the anti-Bolshevik forces are doubtless the immediate cause of the Cabinet's somewhat ignominious confession of the failure of its policy of subsidising civil war in Russia. But the excellent news service of the *Daily Herald* and the repeated and angry protests from the Labour and Socialist world has made it impossible for the Government to hide its head in the sand. Even the middle class would not stand further expenditure in Russia, with prices steadily rising and the National Debt increasing—a debt which sooner or later must be paid by the property owners.

* * * * *

December 1st.—Again distracted from work on the book by a small but difficult task. The twenty or thirty delegates from the British section of the International Congress met the other day at the House of Commons preparatory to the meeting at Geneva in February or July and appointed a committee of eight to draw up memoranda on the political system of Socialism and on socialisation respectively.

This committee consisted of two each from the four constituent bodies—the Labour Party Executive, the Parliamentary Committee of the T.U.C., the N.A.C. of the I.L.P., and the Executive of the Fabian Society. Sidney is on it as representing the L.P., I (and Sanders) as representing the Fabian Society. Each section is to draw up its own memorandum to be considered in Committee. So that Sidney will draft the scheme for the Labour Party Executive, and I shall draft that for the Fabian Society, whilst Bramley[2], representing the Trades Union Congress, asked me to help him with his proposals.

[1] Thomas Fisher Unwin (1848–1935), the Liberal founder of the publishing firm, married Jane Cobden, Richard Cobden's daughter. The house mentioned, Dunford House at Midhurst in Sussex, was used by the School for a brief while only.

[2] Fred Bramley (1874–1925). Organising Secretary, Furnishing Trades Association. Assistant Secretary to the Trades Union Congress; became its General Secretary in 1923.

As Sidney is completely absorbed in all sorts of work, plus the heavy task of seeing the *History of Trade Unionism* through the press, I have had to set to and write a tract on socialisation which will serve as a tract for the Fabian Society—a tract long overdue. I am getting deadly tired of this question of the control of industry!

The meeting of these twenty delegates was significant as typical of the different elements in the fast developing Labour Party. Henderson was there dominating the gathering with his ponderous and somewhat pompous common sense, Hutchinson[1] of the Parliamentary Committee acting as a mild-mannered Chairman. The I.L.P. contingent was the strongest faction, among them J.R.M. and both the Snowdens, Ben Spoor and Neil Maclean (I.L.P. M.P.s) and C. P. Trevelyan and Arthur Ponsonby—typical aristocratic recruits to the most popular of the Socialist societies. . . . Such discussion as took place over the proposed adjournment of the International Conference from February to July and the election of Committees to prepare memoranda was exclusively carried on by Henderson, J.R.M., Snowden and Sidney—with Bramley intervening to represent the views of the absent Parliamentary Committee members. The only subject of interest was the question of the adjournment asked for by the Austrian, Hungarian and Dutch Socialists—ostensibly because of their coming Parliamentary elections, but—so J.R.M. stated from "private information"—because of a divided opinion as to the relative merits of the Second and Third International. The I.L.P. are apparently unanimous for the Second (the B.S.P.—or the remnant of it—having decided to join the Third International)—but they are decidedly uncomfortable at being on the less "advanced" body and one hostile to the Russian Bolsheviks—just now in the ascendant owing to their military successes. But what amused me was to see those ultra Whigs—by tradition and temperament—Trevelyan and Ponsonby—sitting among the left wing of the Labour Party, whilst Sidney and I sat as supporters of Henderson and the Trade Union Movement. I was put on the only other committee appointed—the committee on labour laws—as representative, not of the Fabian Society but of the Labour Party Executive.

December 22nd.—Huysmans, Renaudel and Longuet came into lunch yesterday after their conference with Henderson and Stuart-Bunning (J.R.M., the other member of the Acting Committee, having discreetly gone off to Scotland) to decide whether the International should be put off from February to July. "We have adjourned it,"

---

[1] William Harold Hutchinson (b. 1878). Patternmaker, member of the Executive Committee of the Amalgamated Society of Engineers. Here and elsewhere, Mrs. Webb's remarks show that she was unaware of Hutchinson's close connection with the Guild Socialist Movement.

they told us, "all were in favour of the adjournment, even Branting had signified his approval." "We must wait for things to settle down on the Continent," added Huysmans. Longuet was doubtful whether his "Majority" will stand being associated with the Second International: "MacDonald," said Huysmans, "is quite capable of voting for the holding of the Second International in February and then refusing to go himself." "Not one of the Continental Socialist parties likes to be connected with an International Socialist organisation hostile to Lenin and repudiated by the Independents of Germany." "Surely," I suggested, "there is not much chance of our ever again having a united International? Apart from the present cleavage, there is the future cleavage between Socialist parties controlling or providing Governments and Socialist parties in opposition." "That would be humorous," retorted Huysmans—"Lenin and Vandervelde and Scheidemann in our camp, Henderson, Longuet and all the other insurgent nationalities in the other!" I tried to turn the conversation on to the cleavage as to the basis of representation and the many-sidedness of democracy, but they were not interested. The two Frenchmen were depressed—continually sparring with each other as to the reason of the débâcle at the recent French elections. Huysmans was enigmatic about Belgium. Renaudel was bitter about Great Britain's acquisition of the German colonies. Apparently exactly as we blame France for the wicked treaty, the French blame us; we are each of us vividly conscious of the other one's "imperialistic greed" at the expense of the fallen enemies. They don't love us, these foreign allies. Our prosperity and prestige relatively to all the Continental countries annoys them intensely. They are angry, too, with the United States of America. Will there gradually arise an anti-Anglo-Saxon bloc in Europe, Africa and Asia?

Meanwhile the mysterious Bolsheviks stride on from success to success with their new and little understood conception of social order.

* * * * *

December 25th.—A great bookselling adventure—selling nineteen thousand copies of the new edition of the *History of Trade Unionism* to the Trade Unions prior to publication at the absurdly low price of five shillings post free with one in thirteen copies thrown in. We expect to take in sufficient money to pay our whole printer's bill for the three thousand public edition at £1-1-0 as well as the nineteen thousand cheap edition. But even if we do not quite manage this we shall be rewarded by being read by the right people.

We submitted the new part to Arnot and Cole for their criticisms —they gave us many useful suggestions, but they were very angry with some parts of it and wrote contemptuous little remarks on the margin which amused us greatly. . . . But the L.R.D. insisted on sharing the circular to the fifty thousand branches and were on the whole quite helpful. We are on excellent terms with these young folk —there is the most friendly difference of outlook between us. But they were annoyed at our bringing the *History* up to date. "Why not leave it for your successors to finish—you have ploughed the furrow up to a certain point; leave it to us to complete it," said Arnot naïvely when I told him a few months' ago our intentions. However, they ought to be satisfied with the way we have advertised all their opinions. The book will not make us more popular with the governing class. It will be amusing to see whether we shall be ignored or abused in the capitalist newspapers. I should not be altogether surprised if the thousand copies we have sold to the United States of America are refused mail rights—assuming that the post office censor is sufficiently acute to discover the gist of the final section of the book.

JANUARY 1920—DECEMBER 1920

January 30th.—There is one remarkable characteristic which has been barely noticed in the Press about the Labour Party as a political organisation. The representatives in Parliament may be inefficient, its Parliamentary leader may be "pour rire": but the Party as a force outside Parliament is quietly asserting itself as having a right to settle imperial and foreign affairs here and now without becoming H.M. Government. Thus we see a deputation of Labour leaders going over to Ireland to take evidence as to the condition of that unhappy country and to formulate their own plans of Home Rule. First Henderson, as Secretary of the Labour Party, and then a group of leading trade unionists representing the T.U. Movement, issues elaborate manifestoes warning the Government about its policy towards Russia: calmly insinuating that the Labour Party will not, if they come into power, recognise the validity of any treaty or promise entailing hostility to the Bolshevik Government of Russia, and suggesting that meanwhile British soldiers will refuse to fight the Russian Revolution. These Labour leaders, stupid though they may be, feel far more responsibility for the administration of subject races and foreign affairs generally than any former H.M.O. And the activities of the dozen or so Advisory Committees of the Labour Party, with their determination to discover facts and formulate policy on all sorts of technical questions, is only another sign of a new type of politics—the initiation of social change from outside the recognised machinery of government.

February 5th.—Tom Jones sent a note yesterday, saying that political affairs were critical, might he come to lunch the following day. "By all means," I replied; and he came. He wanted to tell us that the P.M. was in trouble about his Cabinet and about his seat—immediately about the miners' demand for nationalisation, and generally because he had not made up his mind whether he would continue to manipulate the Coalition or come out into opposition. The P.M. feels there is a set against him in the Labour Movement; Jones told us with a note of interrogation in his voice. . . . The P.M. had tried to come to some sort of understanding about the mines—had had interviews with the coal owners and tried to drag them along to accept continued Government control, and joint management with the men. . . . Smillie and Hodges and Hartshorn[1] had declined to discuss matters with the P.M. without the other twenty-five of the Federation Executive. "If only Smillie were like Thomas we could arrange matters," wistfully remarked Jones. "The P.M., Thomas and I settled it all up together over the heads of the Geddes brothers and the N.U.R.," he added with a chuckle. "Three Welshmen intriguing against the self-determination of the English race," I observed. "You can't get our old covenanter Bob Smillie into your toils. He regards the miners' proposals as a part of the Shorter Catechism." And so the plaint and counter-plaint went on over a lot of details. We told Jones that whether Lloyd George would be accepted by the Labour Party in the House of Commons *after the next election* we did not know: the "Bolshevik" speech before the last election stuck in the throat of every Labour man. But one thing was clear: if he wanted the chance of leading or even of co-operating with the Labour Party at some future time, *he had to take his decision now.* The parting of the ways had come, and no one who was not prepared to go the whole way towards the Socialist equalitarian state *as his goal* would be accepted even as a colleague. Either you wanted Capitalism to continue or you did not. Lloyd George's present colleagues had not the remotest intention of changing the existing order. Some of them would fight to the last to defend it. Lloyd George had to come out now and defy them. It was his last chance. Or he had to make the best bargain he could with them by threats of something worse. "Oh! he is always threatening them," said Jones.

* * * * *

February 18th.—In the last few months Sidney had been the central figure in an internal struggle among the miners in the Seaham Division of Durham. In August he had pathetic requests from various miners' Lodges and I.L.P. branches within this Division that he should allow himself to be nominated as candidate for adoption by the Divisional Labour Party, made up almost exclusively of miners' Lodges. He wanted to refuse straightaway, but I begged him to pause because I thought he ought to respond to any request by organised labour to have him as their parliamentary candidate in the coming crucial contest. So he temporised and tried meanwhile to find out what were the wishes of the Central Executive of the Durham Miners' Association. For five months they maintained dead silence on the matter. At last—about a week ago—he provisionally accepted nomination. Yesterday he got a courteously but formally worded letter from the political secretary of the Durham Miners' Association to say that the matter had been

---

[1] Vernon Hartshorn (1872–1931). President of the South Wales Miners' Federation. M.P. for Ogmore and Postmaster-General in 1924 Labour Government.

considered by the Executive and that they had decided that as Seaham had been "endorsed as a mining constituency" and as they had candidates who had been selected by ballot as Parliamentary candidates and who had not yet been placed, they had informed the Seaham Labour Party that they ought to select a miner to fight the seat. Sidney wrote immediately to all his supporters withdrawing his name and sent a copy of his letter to the political secretary with the assurance that he only desired to be of service to the Association and would abide by the decision.

Now this dispute raises in an acute form the question whether or not the Trade Unions are going to limit the candidates to members of their respective organisations. Sidney stated that he would be financially responsible for the election and would neither ask nor accept trade union funds in payment of his expenses. Further, the Durham miners have excluded their officials from being M.P.s, so that the miners are limited to checkweighmen and working miners who would in any case have to give up their work and their pay if elected. What is interesting is that, according to some Durham miners who came up to London, Sidney's selection by some of the Lodges was only a sign of a growing distrust of the competence of the present miners' members for parliamentary careers and a desire to make use of sympathetic intellectuals. So far as Sidney is concerned, the matter is closed: but it may lead to a reversal of the present rule or custom of limiting the choice of trade unionists to their own membership. If so, it will be immensely significant.

February 25th.—I have been working in the mornings at the Report on Socialisation and the constitution of the State of to-morrow, and spending spare hours in the late afternoon and evening typing out my diary—a task which amuses and interests me vastly. I find all sorts of interesting facts and impressions—not to mention the development of my own inner emotional and intellectual life—which I had completely forgotten. I am, in fact, on one of the watersheds of life. Behind me is the long record of each stage of my journey—a record which excites my curiosity—in piecing it together into a connected whole and describing the successive environments of men and things that I have passed through: in front of me, the last stage of our working comradeship—and probably a short stage—completing as far as strength permits all our unfinished work. The Report we are now writing is one part of this completion—an early draft of our conclusions, to be incorporated in a future book. When the report is finished we shall bring out the first part of our big work on Socialism —the part giving our indictment of capitalism—and probably finish up our historical work on prisons. If we can get this done before the summer recess, or even before Xmas, I shall be more than satisfied.

Meanwhile the big public event is the victory of Soviet Russia over all her enemies and the transformation of the Bolshevik Government into a bureaucratic administration exercising far-reaching coercive power over the life and liberty of the individual citizen. George Lansbury's spectacular visit to Russia and his wireless message to the *Daily Herald* have certainly raised his prestige and that of his paper. Lansbury has, in fact, become the "chartered revolutionary of the world"—he has achieved a position from which he can collogue with the Coalition Government and get all sorts of permits denied to the authorised representatives of organised labour, and yet preach revolution from the platform of the Albert Hall, and be accepted as a leader by the most *enragés* of British Bolshevists. He has gained this position not only because of his many talents, but also because he is known to be a fervent and pious Christian and a model domestic man. He is one of the most significant men of to-day—ranking in his unique position above either the leading trade unionists or the leaders of the I.L.P. He has no constructive capacity—he cannot, in fact, distinguish between one type of society and another. But as a ferment for dissolving the present order of things by a strange combination of mystical love for men and an impatient iconoclastic fervour against all existing institutions—he is certainly most uniquely effective.

One of the exciting issues of the immediate future is how long will the rebels admire Bolshevik Russia. At present the swing of the Socialist movement throughout the world into the Third International seems irresistible, and Lenin's and Trotsky's military and administrative and diplomatic successes and the humiliation of the capitalist governments in having to recognise them as the rulers of Russia have undoubtedly intensified the movement towards what is thought to be the Left. But it is clear, even from Lansbury's rose-coloured message, that Bolshevism is "government from above" with a vengeance—and will be presently making use of the capitalist in the reorganisation of Russian industries.

March 18th.—Robert Morant gone—died suddenly of septic pneumonia—at the zenith of his powers and in the place in which his talent was of most service. With all his faults—and he had some grave ones—he remains one of the biggest minds and one of the most attractive personalities I have known. Looking over five and twenty years of friendship and common work, he has been a stalwart—alike as a brilliant and devoted public servant and also as a true friend. His loss is like the loss of Creighton[1] or of W. C. Anderson—irreparable

---

[1] Mandell Creighton (1843–1901). Bishop of London and first President of the London School of Economics.

—he will not be replaced by some other man. He had not finished his work—in fact, he had just attained to the position, as head of the new Ministry of Health, in which his best work would be done. He had some of the enigmatical quality of Creighton; a strange complex of mysticism and cynicism, of principle and opportunism, of quixotic affection and swift calculation. I doubt whether he ever "found himself" completely in life. . . . Though we admired him and liked him, though his strange personality half fascinated, half repelled us—we never understood the settled purpose of all his activities—did he understand it himself?

The last incident that dwells in my memory is Mary Macarthur's account of Morant, hearing that her husband's life might be saved by oxygen—arriving with the oxygen and a medical man at her house, having ransacked London to get it, and overbearing all the *amour propre* of Anderson's medical attendant over the telephone and seeing himself that the distinguished practitioner was permitted to administer it. A year afterwards he was to die of much the same complaint coming on the top of a nervous breakdown from overwork.

There must be something radically wrong in the organisation of the civil service that resulted in the waste of so much of Morant's genius in overcoming friction and in the day to day detail of an office. He gave me always the impression of a man who worked far too intensely and far too long hours to be free to do all that he could have done in the finest part of administration. He was bitterly contemptuous of the parliamentary machine and of nearly all of his parliamentary chiefs. He seemed continuously hampered by a network of interdepartmental intrigues and by the absence of competent lieutenants. Part of the tremendous strain which brought about his last illness was due to the fact that all the competent men he had trained in the National Insurance Commission were taken from him for service in other departments and he was left to grapple with the tremendous task of organising the Ministry of Health with one or two younger men and with the old reactionary officials of the Local Government Board. . . . At the service this afternoon there was a great gathering of civil servants—a fine body of men—I think the most upright and intelligent class in the community. Far from the civil service being over-staffed, it is under-staffed and underpaid. The silly cry of a "swollen bureaucracy" is perhaps the meanest ingratitude of political parties and of the political press.

May 11th.—The last six weeks has been strenuous work, day after day, finishing our book on *A Constitution for the Socialist Commonwealth of Great Britain*. It has been a great lark writing it—I have never enjoyed writing a book so much—it has been real sport thinking out each separate part and making each part fit the others. But it has also been a "tour de force", and when we sent Part IV to the printer on Saturday I was completely exhausted—suffered that curious physical nausea without sickness which is a sure sign with me of bad brain fag. I have still the last chapter to devise and Sidney has the summary to prepare and all the proof corrections. Neither of us could have written the book alone—it is the jointest of our joint efforts. No one will like our constitution; we shall offend all sides and sections with some of our proposals. But someone must begin to think things out, and our task in life is to be pioneers in social engineering.

June 8th. Roker Hotel, Sunderland.—On the 18th February I entered in this Diary the first act of our connection with the Seaham division of Durham. The Seaham miners persisted in their demand for Sidney as candidate in spite of the opposition of the Executive of the Durham Miners' Association, who had scheduled the seat for a miner and had some half a dozen official candidates to provide for. So Sidney consented to come here for a fortnight's tour of the constituency and then to abide by the decision—of the Local Labour Party; and promised to stand if the selection conferences were practically unanimous. So here we are, speaking in all the miners' villages "on approval". There seems little doubt that he will be selected as their candidate, so we are in for the job of winning the constituency.

The division is a long, narrow belt of coast with some eighteen pit villages at about two mile intervals, and the Port of Seaham as the centre. The miners themselves are a mixed lot drawn to new mines from all parts of the United Kingdom—Staffordshire, Lancashire, Scotland and Ireland. They are very well off in the way of wages; their houses are substantially built but terribly overcrowded; their hours short, and they enjoy the priceless advantage of field and wood and coast wherein to roam about in their spare time and as a playground for their children. But there is no centre of intellectual or spiritual life; a mechanically blackleg-proof union as the only corporate life, a dingy and commercialised co-operation, a vigorous club movement for the purpose of drinking "out of hours", little or no social life—nothing but the "pictures" in the larger villages or the same pictures on a more sumptuous scale in Sunderland. The women have no leisure and not much sleep with the three, sometimes four, shift system and the perpetual coal dust to grapple with. Consequence, every woman is short and pale. There is a lot of money flying about and much spent in alcohol and betting. The life seems, in fact, to be completely materialist, though fairly respectable. There are groups of fervent chapel folk. Here and there is a bookish miner, usually a secularist, with quite a large bookcase filled with the well known poets and classics—a little philosophy and more economics. It is to these "bookish miners" that is due the pertinacity with which Sidney's candidature has been pursued. How far they represent their rough and stupid fellow miners is doubtful: though probably these will vote in herds when the day comes. But the present member[1] is a Liberal who stood with uncertain colours as regards the Coalition. . . . He was returned with a 3,000 majority over the miners' candidate at the last election. There is little or no organisation in the constituency and a quarrel with the Executive at Durham over the prospective candidate. The bookish miners are not good organisers or leaders, and there is no one of light and leading in the constituency. Against this is the fact that it is virgin soil: these miners are not blasés; they are children in politics; they are not critical and they are solid trade unionists. And the climate is invigorating and the coast beautiful, and we have discovered a pleasant little hotel to live at with a private sitting room at 7/6 a day, overlooking the sea. So, on the whole, we are content to proceed with this adventure. But it will mean six weeks' work in the year, organising and lecturing—£300 a year expenditure or more prior to the election, and probably £800 or a £1,000 for the election whenever it comes. And we are both over sixty! And it is I who am responsible for persuading Sidney to undertake it with the risk, if not the certainty, of getting into Parliament and all the disturbance of our daily life that this would involve.

Just before we left London we had a farewell dinner to W. Sanders who has become an official of the League of Nations. Our old secretary and friend, F. W. Galton,[2] has been elected General Secretary of the Fabian Society. It is pleasant to see and work with him again. He is now a middle-aged man but exactly like his old self: strong, cynical and full of cheerful energy: he drops his h's as vigorously and defiantly as of old: he dismisses ideas and sentiments with the same good-natured tolerance to weaker brethren, and he is still a faithful friend and admirer of the Webbs except that he regards them as very distinctly "Old Folk" who may be a little past their work. He has plans for the Fabian Society and declares that it still has life left in it: but his mind runs on somewhat commercial lines. He scans the new movements and wonders whether they have anything in them: "I have seen four and twenty leaders of revolt" is his attitude towards Cole and Co. "You won't get the better of the Webbs, I think." He is disgusted with the old political parties; and does not much believe in the Labour Party. "There are too many genuine Labour men in it —they're no match for the old gangers in Parliamentary life!" But

---

[1] Major Evan Hayward (b. 1876). Solicitor and insurance agent: elected for Seaham as Coalition Liberal in 1918.

[2] Frank Wallis Galton (b. 1869). Private secretary to the Webbs from 1892 to 1898, and General Secretary of the Fabian Society until 1939.

with all these shortcomings for the Secretaryship of a Socialist society, he has remained a clean-minded, clear-headed man—good to look at and good to work with.

June 18–25th. Scarborough Labour Party Conference.—An unpleasant episode for MacDonald! About three weeks ago "pars" appeared in the Press stating that J.R.M. had been asked by the Parliamentary Labour Party to come down to the House every morning to advise the Parliamentary Labour Party as to policy. Quickly following on this inspired news, there appeared in the *Times* and other Tory organs maliciously worded statements that the Parliamentary Party had met and considered the proposal and turned it down —"not needing to be taught their business by an ex-M.P. who had been rejected by a working class constituency exactly because of his outrageous pacifism—not to say treachery to this country—during the war".

The truth seems to have been that a sub-committee of the Parliamentary Labour Party with Clynes in the chair had actually agreed on Thomas's suggestion to the proposal that J.R.M. should be invited to attend the House every day with a view to consultation—the Committee being made up largely of "Mac's" friends. Clynes had not objected. But at the full meeting of the Party, Clynes, who was in the chair as vice-chairman during Adamson's absence, had been against it, and the proposal was rejected. It is an episode typical of the Labour Party as at present constituted. The I.L.P. members tried to rush the position and published what they thought to be a victory over the trade union M.P.s on the platform and in the press before the event. There was an immediate "ruck-up" of the trade union M.P.s —especially the miners, who regarded it as a vote of censure on Adamson. Clynes, instead of doing the frank and friendly thing by advising MacDonald not to accept the invitation and telling him he (Clynes) would oppose it at the full meeting, allowed MacDonald and his friends to think that he was favourably inclined. And so this ugly, published snub to MacDonald became inevitable.

I came upon J.R.M. yesterday morning, and after some talk about his boy at Bedales, whom I had seen and liked when staying at Rosie Dobbs'[1] the other day—I asked whether he (the son) was going in for politics. "He is very much against the Labour Party," volunteered MacDonald, "and I don't wonder at it." And then he burst out into angry contempt—he thought it might be better to make a new combination and "smash" the present Labour Party, he said defiantly. "We could do it if we liked: we made Clynes, and we could unmake him." "They call the Parliamentary Labour Party the party of

---

[1] The youngest of the Potter sisters.

checkweighmen," he added somewhat indiscreetly; and you could see the festering wound in his expression. He is more than ever dis-gruntled with the Labour Party. Meanwhile Henderson's dangerous illness and doubtful recovery have made one realise his relative superi-ority to all the other men. He is really the only Labour man who considers the welfare of the Party as a whole and who is willing to work with any group within it without considering who is to be the leader.

* * * * *

July 1st. Grosvenor Road.—We were well satisfied with the Labour Party Conference. Hutchinson of the A.S.E. (a quiet, pro-gressive-minded trade unionist) made an admirable Chairman. Over the great assembly of twelve hundred delegates (including many extremists, with a crowded strangers' gallery) he kept perfect order by tapping the glass of water in front of him with his pencil. The Conference discussed with admirable temper and intelligence foreign and imperial affairs—Russia, Hungary, India, Ireland—together with the internal organisation of the Labour Party and its relation to the Parliamentary Labour Party. The speaking was excellent and there was a unity of sentiment and a considerateness of statement that was beyond praise. The weak side of the Labour Movement showed itself behind the scenes—i.e. the utter lack of any desire for mutual consulta-tion among the leading men. We were staying in the big hotel at which the Labour Party Executive, the principal miners' delegates and the leading men of the other unions, as well as practically all the intellectuals, were quartered. Never once did I see MacDonald, Thomas, Clynes, Smillie, Hodges, Shaw, talk to one another. Middle-ton, Egerton Wake, Gillies, Tracey, Marion Phillips and Sidney would be consulting together about staff matters; and with Thomas, Clynes and Shaw, Sidney and I had some confidential talk whilst we chatted with the miners' officials exclusive of Smillie—and with Bevin and Bromley [? Bramley].[1] For the rest, each leader, whilst scrupulously polite to all the others, sat apart with his wife and admirers—or fellow delegates of the same industry. MacDonald wandered about—a restless and uneasy spirit—generally in company with the ex-Liberal M.P.s who have joined the Labour Party and who are now posing as Left Wing. The undercurrent of mutual antipathy between the leading trade unionists and the leading I.L.P.ers ran strong, and Jowett, the I.L.P. member, was last but one on the list. Sidney did not keep his high place of last year and came eighth

---

[1] John Bromley (1876–1945) was General Secretary of the Associated Society of Locomotive Engineers and Firemen. But Mrs. Webb was almost certainly referring to Fred Bramley (see p. 170).

among the thirteen national candidates. But the miners gave him four hundred out of their six hundred votes and we made friends with the Durham Executive. When he spoke for the Executive on Ireland he was listened to respectfully but without cordiality. He cannot be said to be a popular figure. But he seems to have no desire to be so. Life to him is not "one d—d" but one pleasant job "after another"—and his attitude is one of continuous gratitude for his good luck. He is ridiculously happy.

We have a busy four weeks before we leave for Geneva and I am half-heartedly at work revising and adding to the supplement on the Co-operative Movement so as to transform it into a book to be published by the Research Department. The task bores me but I struggle to persist against the distraction of seeing all sorts and kinds of Americans, Japanese and other visitors.

I am keen to know what will be thought of our new book which appears in a week or so and of which we have already advance copies. Sidney warns me against being disappointed at its reception and tells me it will have a very bad press. I agree. "The Minority Report," I remind him, "had an unexpectedly poor reception—and I was disappointed. I am not going to be disappointed again! For, after all, the Minority Report won in the end, and to-day everyone accepts the 'Break up of the Poor Law' as inevitable—in course of being done." All the same, I shall not be exactly happy if the book is ignored alike by the capitalist and the Labour press. It is a nice question whether its parentage is for or against the scheme—our authorship gives weight but creates prejudice.

* * * * *

The Labour-Socialist delegates from Russia have brought over many diverse impressions of Russia. All agreed on the wicked policy of intervention. By a large majority they condemn the Soviet form of government for Great Britain. Some of them have seen a horrible spectre of Socialism in the Soviet despotism—a new creed autocracy—more terrible than any theocracy. The conclusion to which Sidney and I had come from a distance—that the Soviet Government had changed its basic ideal from workers' control and general anarchic freedom to rigid consumers' collectivism—seems to be true. The Soviet Government is the "servile state" in being—the very thought of which was denounced by the rebels of 1910–14. But it is a servile state run by fanatics who refuse any compromise with the "bourgeois fetish" of personal freedom. It is only fair to add that the fanaticism in question is the faith in the common good as interpreted by the Communists.

July 11th.—Sidney was unanimously chosen yesterday by the Seaham Divisional Labour Party to fight the next election. There is a strange irony in these simple-minded miners, living in a remote backwater, seeking out and persistently pressing into their service the most astute and subtle—and, be it added, the least popular leader of the Labour and Socialist Movement. The explanation is that these leading men in these isolated pit villages are readers of books and not hearers of revivalist speeches and propagandist lectures. And now we have got to win the seat from an astute Liberal solicitor who votes always with the Parliamentary Labour Party and who had a three thousand majority over the miners' candidate at the 1918 election.

*   *   *   *   *

July 20th.—Tagore, whom we met at lunch yesterday at Kate Courtney's, is in no doubt about the purpose of life—it is divine love working through the direct communion of individual minds with God —the Immanence of God, as he terms it. But he ignores science—or the knowledge of God working through nature, ascertained by the physical senses, and he unhesitatingly condemns any application of science to human relations—any deliberate ordering of these relations by the light of knowledge of results. Hence, whilst he resents any criticism of Hindu tradition or of Hindu rites, still more of Hindu mysticism, he is a bitter and uninformed critic of western government, of western industrial organisation and of western nationalism, of western science. "All governments are evil," he dogmatically asserts: "The intellect solves no problems" is his constant implication. He is not content to be the seer and the poet—the man who attains wisdom through intellect; he must needs condemn the man of action, the lawyer, the administrator and the politician, and even the scientific worker. This quite unconscious and spiritual insolence, this all-embracing consciousness of his own supreme righteousness (compared to men of action) is due, I think, to the atmosphere of adulation in which the mystic genius lives and has his being. The administrator, the man of science, the lawgiver, the engineer, exists and functions in an environment of mental and physical friction—he cannot succeed unless he adjusts and verifies—adjusts his own acts to other men's acts and verifies his own discoveries by other men's discoveries. The practical man is always being opposed and criticised; and he has to live with his critics and often actually to work with them. This tends to make him humble and tolerant, especially in a democratic country in which he cannot use force to compel his fellows to agree with him in word and act. The man of action may become cynical; he may become pessimistic; he may even take to violent courses. But he seldom becomes—at least, within a western democracy—insolently contemptuous of all other types of men. He may dislike the artist, the poet and the mystic. But he does not condemn them; he often values and adores them.

In this digression—a digression due to a latent feeling of anger at Tagore's quite obvious dislike of all that the Webbs stand for—I fail to do justice to Tagore as a unique person. He has perfect manners and he is a person of great intellect, distinction, and outstanding personal charm. He is beautiful to look at: he clothes himself exquisitely: the rich, soft grey ribbed silk wrap, in which his tall and graceful figure is enveloped, tones into his iron-grey hair and beard; a finely wrought, thick gold chain, winding in and out of the grey garment, tones into the rich brown hue of his skin. His speech has the perfect intonation and slow chantlike moderation of the dramatic saint. He is indeed an almost too perfect personification of his part in the world's history. Unwittingly one's practical imagination sees a great pageant, staged without limit of cost at Delhi, with Tagore the magnificent saint, standing in the centre in statuesque stillness, personifying Immortal India, and poor little ugly Lloyd George in shabby khaki furtively shifting about in a far off corner, representing dethroned western civilisation. Tagore may abuse western patriotism, but in his heart there is the pride of race as well as the pride of the man of God. He is not the perfect saint—he is far too conscious of his own personality. Perhaps one likes him the better when one discovers that after all he is an imperfect and limited human being, and, like the rest of us, far too conscious of his own excellence and of other men's failings.

August 20th. 41, Grosvenor Road.—Our week at the Second International in Geneva, in brilliant sun and seething heat, left on my mind a mixed impression of apparent futility and real usefulness. "All that is senile in the Labour and Socialist Movements" was the verdict of the Rebels, at home and abroad. "A first-rate conference— one of the most practically useful we have ever had," asserted the accomplished Camille Huysmans. "Dull and depressing," remarked the admirable C. R. Buxton,[1] fresh from investigating Soviet Russia. "It thrills me," whispered his no less admirable brother Noel,[1] "makes me more convinced than ever that I was right to leave the Liberals and come over to Labour."

Depressed and disheartened the conference undoubtedly was. To me there was a living tragedy in the German delegation. Some dozen persons, including three women (two of them members of the Reichs-

[1] Charles Roden Buxton (1875–1942) and Noel Edward, Lord Noel-Buxton (1869–1948). Charles Buxton, Liberal pacifist who joined the Labour Party, married Dorothy Frances Jebb, founder of the Save-the-Children Fund. Noel-Buxton, Minister of Agriculture in the first two Labour Governments, married Lucy Edith Pelham-Burn, M.P. for Norwich from 1945–50.

tag) headed by Scheidemann and Bernstein,[1] sat dignified and silent, and, with a grim realisation of their position as a beaten people and a beaten political party, accepted all the arrangements proposed by the British Chairman of the conference and agreed to everything passed by the majority of the British delegates. Three or four of them looked like corpses—so emaciated and bloodless they were—and few of them ever smiled. The blank and sullen despair written large on the face of one or two still haunts me. The three women, and one or two of the men, were eager to be friendly with the British delegation, and all the British delegation went out of their way to ask them to lunch and dinner and to single them out from among all the delegates for frequent consultation. There was, in fact more comradeship between the Germans and the British than between any other nationalities. Dear old Bernstein, now a frail and saintly old man, beamed goodwill to everyone. Adolf Braun[2]—a learned person—was almost too flattering to one's racial pride. "Lloyd George is the only big man who has emerged from the war," he suggests. But the main impression left by the German delegation was that of members of a vanquished and embittered people and of individuals who had been a Government and had found the task too hard.

On the other hand, the Swedish, the Danish and the Belgian delegations—being either Governments or parts of Governments—were self-complacent; the Dutch were chiefly engaged in assuring us that their leader Tröelstra,[3] with his vanity and impracticable proposals, did not represent them. There were the usual delegations from little states like Georgia, a few émigrés from Russia, representatives of minorities in the Socialist Movements of France and Italy, and a tragic little group of woe-begone Hungarians with the look of hunted animals. The British delegation, out for a holiday trip with their wives, dominated the conference—and some of them thought it necessary, in true English fashion, to provide "His Majesty's Opposition" to their own delegation. Tom Shaw presided and Sidney was Chairman of the British Section and of the Commission for the Political Systems of Socialism and Socialisation; whilst I was on the sub-commission on Socialisation. Fabianism [was] in fact dominating the Second International through the medium of British trade unionism. Business done: complete reconciliation of the Germans with the Belgians and the minority section of French Socialists—the only French delegates who were present—and the Webbs' resolution on the political

[1] Eduard Bernstein (1850–1932). Leader of the Revisionist wing of the German Social-Democratic Party.

[2] Leading German Social-Democrat, supporter of the German Socialisation Commission.

[3] Peter Jelles Tröelstra (1860–1930). Leader of the Dutch Socialist Party from 1894.

system and socialisation passed unanimously except for the aforementioned British "H.M. Opposition". Beyond this, there was a defiant repudiation of the Russian Soviet system and the dictatorship of the Communist Party. The conference, I gather, had a bad press because of the absence of revolutionary fervour.

* * * * *

Our sojourn for ten days' rest in the High Alps at Argentière led to our being absent from London in the critical days when Henderson and Bowerman, instigated by Bevin, called together the great conference of T.U. Executives and formed the Council of Action[1] against war with Russia on behalf of Poland. Crossing from Boulogne to Folkestone we ran across Adamson and Gosling on their expulsion from France after their interviews with the C.G.T. and the French Socialist M.P.s. From Gosling, and afterwards from Arnot and others, we had an enthusiastic account of the dignity and unanimity of the conference and the startling effect of the threat of "direct action" against war with Russia. Without doubt many non-Labour elements— all the middle-class pacifists and many middle-class taxpayers—were grateful for the Labour Party's intervention—believed that, whatever Lloyd George might say, it did stem the British Government drift towards war with Russia. But threats are one thing: performance is another. And I very much doubt whether "direct action", unless it proved to be a symptom of public opinion among all classes, would have been sufficiently universal to be effective. . . .

On the top of this colossal foreign turmoil comes the ballot for the miners' strike.[2] The miners have a strong case—but it is not a case that justifies—from a national point of view—direct action of the magnitude intended. The miners are among the best paid of manual workers—they are earning, as a matter of fact, as much money as they

[1] In July the Trades Union Congress had voted in favour of a general strike to end both the war in Russia and the war in Ireland. Almost immediately afterwards the Red Army rallied and drove back the Poles almost to Warsaw. The British and French Governments reacted with an ultimatum to Russia and threats of large-scale assistance to the Poles; but when the T.U.C. and the Labour Party summoned a Council of Action of their constituents to make immediate preparation for strike action Lloyd George retreated, and no troops were sent.

[2] The miners had voted in favour of a strike for increasing wages and lowering the price of coal, claiming that the industry could well afford both. Having tried without success to get the other partners in the Triple Alliance to come out in support, they struck by themselves; but dropped the demand for lower prices owing to lack of public support. The strike ended in a few weeks on the terms of a wage increase dependent upon output; it had shown the weakness of the Triple Alliance as a force and presaged the Labour disaster of Black Friday in the following year. (See p. 207). Another result of this strike was the passing of the Emergency Powers Act, which gave the Government extensive powers to deal with strikes in "essential industries".

can spend in their comparatively low state of civilisation. Their contention that the price of coal ought to be lowered is a matter for the organisation of the citizen consumers in Parliament, and, though here they are on stronger ground, so is the cognate question of nationalisation. On the other hand, the Miners' Federation, as a legal contracting body, has been swindled by the Government. The Cabinet promised to carry out the first Sankey Report and have failed to do so, and it was on that promise that the miners gave up their strike when all circumstances were in their favour. Further, if the country is to be run on the basis of the scramble for the product, direct action is always legitimate. The worst of the position is that, whether the miners lose or win, whether there is a strike or whether a compromise is patched up at the last moment, the present position of universal slacking in the mining industry, alike by capitalists and by manual workers, will be continued. The battle over nationalisation will not be avoided; it will merely be delayed or dragged out through a transitional period of under-production and the demoralisation which under-production entails. The spirit of service among the workers and the application of science to industry are, each one of them, threatened so long as the capitalist profitmaking continues. With disuse, human faculty gradually withers up, and when we do get nationalisation we shall have lost heavily in morality and in knowledge. It is on the heightening of morality and the spread of knowledge that the equalitarian community depends for its immediate and ultimate success. The outlook at home is as gloomy as the outlook abroad. Sidney, fortunately, refuses to be gloomy and laughs at my pessimism which, he declares, is utterly futile even if it were not unfounded. He goes on steadily, in the best of physical health and mental sanity, day in and day out, at his work for the world he lives in.

September 4th.—A week at the Fabian Summer School, Priorsfield, Godalming. Last spring the Fabian Executive determined to set apart a week for the entertainment of foreign Socialists in order to promote reconciliation and mutual consultation. We sent out about one hundred and twenty invitations to men and women of all schools of thought, from the leaders of the Co-operative and Trade Union Movements of various countries to the representatives of the Third International in France, Holland, Norway and Italy. The invitation was enthusiastically received and about forty or fifty Socialists, co-operators and trade unionists accepted it—among them some Communists. But as the day drew near, the great majority either withdrew for one reason or another, or were refused their passports by their own Governments or visas from the British Consuls. The French Government was especially obdurate: all the dozen French guests, even the leader of the co-operators, Poisson,[1] and the Secretary of a technical society affiliated to the C.G.T., being refused passports. Renaudel was the only Frenchman, and he got over by special arrangement with the British Embassy before his Government had realised the occasion. Our Belgian comrades, Huysmans and de Brouckère[2] and some others, were diverted from fulfilling their engagement by the invitation of the Georgian Government to visit the new Georgian Socialist Republic (an invitation which had been pressed on us at Geneva) with MacDonald, Mrs. Snowden, and other foreigners: Vandervelde could not leave owing to a Belgian Cabinet crisis, and the two Secretaries of the International Trade Union organisation at Amsterdam were prevented from coming by the boycott of munitions for Poland. Hence our guests were limited to Wauters,[3] the Socialist Minister for Labour, representing Belgium; Vibaut [Wibaut],[4] the Vice-President of the Amsterdam Municipality (a full-time salaried post); and Kupers,[5] the Secretary of the General Federation of the Dutch Trade Unions, representing Holland; Renaudel representing France; Frau Bang,[6] a member of the Danish Upper House and of the Executive of the Socialist Party, representing Denmark; whilst the German Majority Socialists sent Adolf Braun, a learned publicist and member of the Reichstag. There were some half-dozen other foreigners of sorts, and another half-dozen Americans, the remainder of the eighty guests being British. When we arrived as joint Directors of the School on Saturday 28th, I felt that our plan had failed and that the failure would be a disappointment to all the English and American frequenters of the School who had come specially to meet the Continental foreigners.

But the week turned out to be a brilliant success. Renaudel, Wauters, Wibaut, Kupers and Frau Bang, feeling themselves without critics from their own country, and being persons of considerable intelligence and experience, gave us frank and enlightening accounts of the Labour and Socialist Movement and its difficulties in France, Belgium, Holland and Denmark. Adolf Braun, in an address of one and a half hours (which Sidney had to translate as he did the others) achieved his purpose of harrowing the feelings and rousing the sympathies of the audience by a vivid account of the desperate material and moral condi-

[1] Ernest Poisson, leading French Co-operator, whose book on *The Co-operative Republic* appeared in English in 1925.
[2] Louis de Brouckère (1870–1951). Belgian Socialist professor and Chairman of the Labour and Socialist International.
[3] Arthur Wauters (b. 1890). Belgian Socialist who in 1929 became editor of *Le Peuple*: between 1919 and 1921 he was *chef de cabinet* to the Ministry of Labour.
[4] F. M. Wibaut, leading Dutch Socialist M.P.
[5] Evert Kupers (b. 1885), became Secretary of the Dutch Federation of Trade Unions in 1919 and its Chairman in 1928.
[6] Nina Henrietta Wendeline Bang (1866–1928). Danish Social-Democrat and economist, wife of Gustav Bang. The first woman Cabinet Minister in Denmark.

tion of the German people. Socialisation, he declared, was impracticable when there was nothing to socialise but internal debts and external liabilities which could not be met. Whether taxes could be levied best by capitalists or by state officials on persons who were incapable of paying them was a purely academic problem. In any case, there was nothing but financial and moral disaster in front of the German people. So convincing was his discourse that Wauters asked him to come back with him to Belgium so as to put the case before the Belgian Government. We had an interesting discussion on the future of the International and another on the relation of Socialism to religion. But the crowning success was the lightning visit of Kameneff and Krassin[1] on the Thursday afternoon. On the previous Sunday morning, when we were all discussing the programme for the week, I suggested that our Russian comrades should be invited to visit the School. The suggestion was received by all the English (except Haden Guest[2] and Aylmer Maude)[3] with the enthusiasm of a holiday party anxious for a sensation. Our foreign guests looked serious and evidently had some misgivings. We gathered that this and other incidents bewildered Wauters, Wibaut and Kupers as an amazing example of an almost anarchic tolerance on the part of the Fabians of hostile schools of Socialist thought. It was strange enough, they explained, to see Guild Socialists and members of the new English Communist Party on terms of intimate comradeship with Fabians, but to invite the official representatives of Lenin, who had expressly denounced all Fabians as traitors, and the Webbs as particularly pernicious ones, was really carrying the principle of tolerance too far! Moreover, Wauters and Adolf Braun, and even Wibaut, showed distinct shyness at being compromised by friendly association with such notable representatives of the Third International, and were nervous about the probable disapproval of their own parties at home.

After mysterious comings and goings of messengers and messages, and much uncertainty as to what would happen, two private motor cars, owned and driven by two naval officers, accompanied by General Thomson[4]—all members of the Fabian Society—were despatched on Thursday morning to 128 Bond Street, and at four o'clock that afternoon these representatives of H.M. naval and military forces returned with the Soviet emissaries.

[1] Leonid Borissovich Krassin (1870–1926). Russian revolutionary who negotiated Brest-Litovsk Treaty; in 1920–1 he was in London endeavouring to conclude a commercial treaty with Britain.

[2] Leslie Haden Guest (b. 1877), now Lord Haden Guest, doctor and Fabian of many years' standing.

[3] Aylmer Maude (1858–1938), the translator of Tolstoy, and an old Fabian.

[4] Christopher Birdwood Thomson, Lord Thomson (1875–1930). Soldier, joined Labour Party on his retirement in 1919. Secretary for Air in 1924 Labour Government; perished in the wreck of R 101.

Kameneff, a short, thick-set man with blunt features and a shifty eye, has changed considerably in appearance and manner since the evening, three years ago, when he was brought to Grosvenor Road by Litvinoff to complain of the insulting behaviour of Scotland Yard in its seizure of his "diplomatic valise" and to threaten us with reprisals on the English in Petrograd. He has grown stouter and far more self-important. Instead of the disagreeable combination of whines and threats of three years ago, he has developed the self-assured manner and easy address of one accustomed to exercise power over masses of men; moreover, it was clear from his private talk and clever speech that he had trained himself in the arts of diplomacy as these arts would be conceived by a common but shrewd journalist. Without intellectual distinction, moral refinement or personal charm, he is still a somewhat unpleasant personage.

Krassin, with his tall lithe figure, his head perfectly set on his shoulders, with his finely chiselled features, simple manner and keen direct glance, looks, every inch of him, the highly bred and highly trained human being, a veritable aristocrat of intellect and bearing. So far as one can gather from listening to him he is a curious combination of the practical expert and the convinced adherent of a dogmatic creed. But one is tempted to wonder whether this creed does not consist almost entirely in an insistent demand for the subordination of each individual to the working plan of the scientifically trained mind; though, of course, the plan is assumed to be devised in the interests of the community as a whole. Whether, for instance, he altogether believes in the Communist ideal of equality among men, in culture, personal freedom and the means of livelihood.

It remains to be added that from the way in which the two men looked at each other, or rather the way in which Kameneff observed Krassin, I gathered that there was no love lost between them, though they play up to one another with skill. Kameneff is clearly the master, the political boss; Krassin, the scientific and refined expert who has, at any rate ostensibly, to obey the boss.

Sidney and I received our visitors in a private sitting room and gave them tea and cigarettes. I laughingly told them that they would find themselves among members of the Second International but that we had two or three adherents of the Moscow International among our guests, and I introduced Dutt[1] and Arnot to them as samples. We brought into the private sitting room Wauters, Wibaut, Adolf Braun and one or two others to join us in the private talk. Wauters, who is a dominating personality, a ci-devant professor of physics, an admirably

---

[1] Rajani Palme Dutt (b. 1896). Leading Communist and editor of the *Labour Monthly*; in 1920 he was Secretary to the International Section of the Labour Research Department.

clear and humorous speaker and evidently an accomplished administrator, carried on a lively conversation with Krassin, interspersed with
sly criticisms of Krassin's administrative expedients and their relation
to democratic theory: Wibaut showed fatherly friendliness in his
curiosity, whilst the gloomy Adolf Braun kept carefully in the background, obviously disinclined for any personal intercourse with the
Bolsheviks. Presently it became clear that our Russian comrades were
not only willing, but anxious, to address the whole of the guests. So
we ushered them into the drawing room in which some seventy or
eighty persons were closely packed on sofa, chair and floor, eager to
see and listen to these mysterious visitors from the mythical Bolshevik
Heaven or the mythical Bolshevik Hell. Sidney devoted himself to
taking notes of the speeches for the translation, and I acted as informal
Chairman of the meeting.

Kameneff spoke for an hour in ugly but fluent French, giving a
journalistic account of the situation within Russia, and of her external
relations; the dominant refrains being the paramount need for peace
and the pacifist tendencies of the Soviet Government. The address
was plausible and diplomatic: it left little impression on my mind
because every word of it was devised to produce a given effect, and
quite obviously so devised. All that one gathered from it was that the
speaker was a competent person carrying out his instructions with quite
commendable skill, but lacking in the note of conviction. Directly he
had finished I suggested that the translation should be deferred until
our Russian comrades had left us (as they had to do at nine o'clock
that evening), and called on Krassin to address us. He spoke in German,
with the clear enunciation and the limited vocabulary of an accomplished linguist speaking in a foreign tongue so that even I could
understand every word of it. It was a remarkable address: admirably
conceived and delivered with a cold intensity of conviction which made
it extraordinarily impressive. Especially skilful was his statement of
general principles, combined with a wealth and variety of illustrative
fact and picturesque anecdote. The greater part of the speech was a
detailed account of the industrial administration he had actually set
up or hoped to introduce into Russia. *Working to a plan*, elaborated
by scientific experts, under the instructions of the Communist Party,
was the central idea of this industrial organisation. Russia's needs,
external and internal, were to be discovered and measured up and
everything was to be sacrificed to fulfilling them. All the workers by
hand and by brain were to accept this plan, and their one obligation
as members of the Soviet Republic was to carry it out with zeal and
exactitude. There were, he implied, two great sources of power in
Soviet Russia which would lead to its redemption and its complete
independence of the hostile world by which it was surrounded: the

*Beatrice and Sidney
Webb in the living
room at Passfield
Corner*

From the painting by
William Nicholson

Sidney Webb and Noel Buxton arriving at a Cabinet Meeting of the First Labour Government

fervour of the Faithful organised in the Communist Party; and the scientific knowledge of the experts specially trained to serve that Party in all departments of social and industrial life. Every expedient of modern industrialism designed to increase the output of the individual worker, whether new mechanical inventions, new forms of power, new methods of remuneration—piecework, premium bonus, the concentration of business in the best equipped factories—were to be introduced in order to achieve the working out of this plan. Even consumption was to be organised. Payment in kind, with a small balance of money for "supplementary needs", was to supersede the ordinary wage system so that the consumption of commodities by individuals might lead to the maximum mental and physical development of the race. He explained at length and justified the proposal of the Soviet Government to give terminable concessions to foreign capitalists in order to raise money for further developments. The peasants, comprising as they did the vast majority of the population, were, he admitted, the difficulty (on this point a lively repartee arose between him and Wauters). The Bolshevik Government had been compelled to accept individual production on the land. But land could not be sold in the market: if the peasant who worked it threw it up, the commune would allot it to someone else. Krassin, however, affirmed his faith that eventually the peasants would be converted to Communism and gave us a glowing description of what might be done by introducing scientific agriculture on a great scale and sweeping away individual production in favour of communal production according to a plan worked out by scientific agriculturalists. Finally, in a splendid peroration, which excited the most enthusiastic applause from all those assembled Fabians who understood German, he asserted that Soviet Russia alone among nations had discovered the "philosopher's stone" of increased productivity in the consciousness, on the part of each individual Communist, that he was serving the whole community of the Russian people—a consciousness which would transform toil into the only true religion—the service of mankind.

It is difficult in any summary to give the effect of Krassin's speech, because of its wealth of illustration and the eloquence of his voice and bearing, and his constant appeal on behalf of the heroic Russian soldiers fighting on a dozen fronts against capitalist imperialism, and the equally heroic workers in factories and mines struggling to increase their output whilst in a state of semi-starvation due to the blockade. The ovation from the audience when he sat down was far greater than that accorded to Kameneff. "Do all Fabians know German as well as French?" he asked me as we trooped into dinner.

As there was still one hour after dinner before the Russians departed in a taxi we had hired from Godalming to take them back to London, they good-naturedly submitted themselves to questions carried out in French. The company was exhausted and not inclined to be very serious. Aylmer Maude and Haden Guest enquired in acid tones about the fate of certain individual Russians they happened to know: Wauters continued his ironical questions about the peasants and their hypothetical conversion to Communism, and I attempted to discover, without much success, how far the teachers had to submit to tests of Communist faith and how far the normal schools were carried on under Communist discipline. But there was a general inclination to be polite among the questioners and to be diplomatic on the part of the lecturers. Krassin ended up his answers by definitely stating that the distinction between the Second and the Third International was the distinction between words and deeds. The Third International had established Socialism, the Second International only talked about it: Branting, he declared, "waited for Socialism to come down from Heaven with the permission of Lloyd George." This answer aroused the retort—which we were too polite to utter—that in western democracy we had far more Socialism in fact than there existed in Russia. When the time had come for departure Kameneff and Krassin were surrounded by a crowd of persons wanting their autographs, and the farewell was uproariously enthusiastic. If the Fabian Summer School had consisted of nothing but members of the Third International it could not have been more effusive.

Our foreign friends differed in their impressions. "Children in the task of administration" was Wauters' summing up of the rulers of Russia. "There are, of course, many things one dislikes in the Soviet Government," remarked the benevolent and open-minded Wibaut to me the next morning. "All the same," he added, almost under his breath, "we may be on the eve of great things in their experiment." Krassin's principle of working to a plan devised by experts clearly had its attraction to the most distinctively collectivist among Socialist administrators. Adolf Braun remained imperturbable in his gloom.

We learned little that was unknown about the Soviet Government from Kameneff's plausible and Krassin's eloquent address. In the masses of Soviet documents collected by journalists and delegates, and the recorded observations of the enemies and friends of Soviet Russia, can be found almost every fact and principle, every fear and hope, embodied in Kameneff's and Krassin's speeches. But certain points stood out in clear relief: first and foremost, the pessimism of Litvinoff and Kameneff, recorded in my diary of three years ago, with regard to the future of the Soviet system surrounded by capitalist states, had been replaced by confidence—or assumed confidence—in the ability of Soviet Russia to survive and even in her capacity to compete success-fully with capitalist states. This optimism was especially marked in

Krassin's speech—he had an ardent faith in the motive of service of the whole community and of the ability of the Communist workers to carry out the centrally devised plan. Both speakers admitted that Russia must be ruled by the Congregation of the Faithful, i.e. by the Communist Party—at any rate so long as she was surrounded by a world in arms against her. They did not claim that the peasants were convinced Communists. "The peasants will give us passive consent," said Kameneff, "not because they are Communists, but because the dictatorship of the town workmen has given them the land, whereas the dictatorship of the Czar and his bureaucracy meant the domination of the landlord." This realisation that the Soviet Government was in fact an oligarchy made up of the hired workmen of the towns governing a nation of peasant proprietors was certainly unexpected, at any rate to me. Finally, Krassin in his constant insistence on the need for working to a plan devised by experts admitted that all authority must be centred in one authority and one organ of government only, and that obedience to this one supreme authority must be considered a religious duty. Personal freedom, whether in the production or the consumption of commodities, had to be suspended until Russia had conquered her enemies and reconstructed her economic life. In the minds of many of the audience the question arose "How would it be possible to depose from power these three castes—the elders, and leaders of the Communist faith, the scientific experts and the town workmen, not to mention the two castes which were not referred to —the Red Army and the Secret Police—when the need for this autocratic government had disappeared with Russia's enemies?" "The re-establishment of a caste system—a very natural impulse in an Asiatic race," remarked the Belgian Socialist Minister with a grin and a shrug of his broad shoulders.

*　　*　　*　　*　　*

September 17th.—As I near the end of life I become more contemptuous of cynicism, more convinced that what we know as "goodness" is in accordance with "the nature of things". Looking back on my own failures and humiliations, they nearly all arose from a strain of worldliness or cynicism, a lack of scrupulousness in my manner of life, a giving way to personal vanity and vulgar egotism and all the petty lying that this vanity and egotism entails. The great sources of my happiness, my work and my marriage to Sidney, sprang straight out of a religious purpose, an ideal end, not for myself but for the world of men. And my faith in the scientific method and my delight in pursuing it, is not mere intellectual curiosity—the sport of discovery—though the sporting instinct—the chase of the investigator —adds zest to scientific work. But deep down in one's heart is a realisation that the discovery of the laws of nature in order that men may become creators of a better world, is an act of piety, one of the ways that we can bring about the Kingdom of God. The scientific temperament, the desire to measure, to record, to test, and to explain correctly what has happened or is happening in order to predict what will happen is a moral as well as an intellectual process. In its most perfect form it involves courage, honesty, good comradeship, an absence of vanity and spite—frequently the sacrifice of ambition, ease, health, and sometimes life itself. And though it is true that the scientific method may be used for damnable ends, it is seldom the discoverer himself who is impelled by hatred or greed to misuse his discoveries. Is it not usually, if not always, persons who appropriate and *exploit* the results obtained by the man of science, thus bringing the scientific faculty into disrepute?

*   *   *   *   *

October 21*st*, 1920.—Sidney off to Seaham to talk to miners who have nothing to do but to listen to the Gospel.

The long dragged out negotiations, nearing three months from the miners' initial demand of 2/- a shift increase and a reduction of 14/- in the price of coal, have at last ended in a national strike beginning last Saturday. That the miners' case has been wisely handled is emphatically denied by Labour leaders who feel they could have done it better themselves. It opened on the bigger issue of nationalisation and workers' control—the 14/- reduction in price being a symbol, involving continuance of state control and pooling of profits—which it was said would lead to nationalisation—whilst the very raising of the question of price was in itself an assertion of the right of the miners to concern themselves with trade policy not directly affecting the conditions of employment. But during the negotiations this wider issue was dropped, the miners' leaders being apparently unequal to withstanding the newspaper refrain that this issue was "political" and therefore not one that could be settled by a fiat of the workers concerned. Moreover, when the time approached for actually calling the men out, there was a fear that the country might hold that a lowering of price did not come within the definition of the Trade Disputes Act and would therefore render the miners' unions liable for damages to trade interests due to the strike. The negotiations were conducted on such a high plane of polite reasonableness on the part of the miners' leaders, the Government and the colliery owners that the whole Press assumed that there would be no strike. Great was the disappointment when the Government proposal to give the advance conditionally on an increase in the national output calculated on a datum line (supported by Smillie and other leaders) was decisively, almost contemptuously, rejected by an increased majority in a ballot of all the coalfields. Clearly it was not the leaders but the mass of the men who had gone "red".

Why did Robert Smillie, who opened the campaign at the end of July by declaring that the miners were out for nationalisation and nationalisation by direct action, crumble up so completely when confronted with the fact of a general strike? Last year when the moderate leaders of the miners attempted to convert the country to nationalisation, Smillie sulked in his tent declaring that Parliament was a futile institution and that the miners must take their fate into their own hands and force the position. And yet he promptly gave up the demand for the 14/- off the price when the Government declared that this very limited assertion of the right of control was "political". At the very end of the negotiations he implored the miners to accept the Government terms of wages determined by output rather than resort to direct action. The answer is, I think, that Smillie, who is governed, not by reason, not by any calculation of what will happen if a certain course of action is pursued, but by the "inner light", by the value he attaches to a big and righteous emotion, wanted direct action for its own sake, for the self-sacrifice and solidarity it involved quite apart from its probable success or failure. But directly this direct action was seen to involve increased hunger and cold, not only to the British workers, but also to the famine-and-disease-stricken peoples of Central Europe, Smillie's moral emotion swung violently back against such cruel consequences. To harden your heart to all this suffering in order to get 2/- a day more became to him an intolerable callousness, degrading the miners' cause. The reduction of the miners' claim to an increase in wages had in fact taken everything out of the claim that Smillie cared for whilst he had only just realised the cost in pain, to other peoples, of a cessation of work. Decidedly Robert Smillie is not fit to lead a revolution!

Of course the massive destructiveness of the instrument of a miners' strike is hugely out of proportion to the occasion for its use. When Ireland is being treated with savage brutality, when Central Europe is slowly dying, both catastrophes being deliberately brought about by the Lloyd George Government, it is tragically absurd to be destroying the national wealth for the sake of a 2/- increase per day in the wages of one of the best paid sections of British labour. And yet the strike is bigger than the occasion for it: the huge vote and hasty temper in the coalfields are in a sense a vote against the Government on all issues. What is still more apparent is that, if the strike spreads to the railwaymen and transport workers, it will not be in order to get the 2/- for the miners, but in order to defeat a detested Government. And the biggest causes of this active hatred of the Government on the part of the militants of the manual working class is a feeling of shame for the Irish outrages and a feeling of indignation at the continuous increase alike of unemployment and of the indecent overcrowding of working-class homes.

Henderson, the Clynes and the Noel Buxtons had arrived to lunch here before Sidney knew he would be away. The two Labour leaders thought that the Government would give way on the 2/-: if they did not there would be grave doings. But, having given way, the Government might appeal to the country to enable them to penalise general strikes which held the nation to ransom. And they would get a big victory at the polls. After lunch Mrs. Clynes and I, with Mrs. Buxton's help, fixed up my scheme for a social club of Labour members' wives to meet every month or so here or at some other house in the neighbourhood.

About five o'clock Mary Macarthur came to tell me that Bland Sutton[1] gave her only a few months to live; but that she had determined to undergo another operation by a young woman surgeon against the advice of this elderly specialist—just on the bare chance of survival and cure. She is magnificently brave and sat on the Hendon Bench of magistrates that very morning to hear a case of child murder. It is a tragedy to think of W. C. Anderson's death two years ago, and now *she* is leaving us in the prime of her powers. But I refused to be tragic: she had told me in Switzerland that she could not stand poor Susan Lawrence's[2] despairing misery. We talked about her spiritualistic experiences, the chances of survival, the meaning of life and the career of her little daughter and the last scenes of her husband's illness. But all the same I felt that I was a callous brute in refusing to reflect in my words and manner the awfulness of imminent death to one who feels the full force of mental vitality. It is this continued vitality—this ability to go on with work and pleasure, up to the last fatal diagnosis of certain death—that makes cancer seem almost to be capital punishment. "There can be but one end, and that in a month or two," Bland Sutton had said that morning, standing with his back to the fire. "I felt he was rather brutal, and I don't believe that the disease *is* malignant," she added defiantly. "I believe I shall survive and go on with my work." "It is curious for me to remember," she observed, as she got up to go, "that the last time Will and I dined here we said to each other as we walked away how terrible the survivor of the Webbs would feel life to be. Little we thought that the Webbs would survive

[1] Sir John Bland-Sutton (1855–1936). President of the Royal College of Surgeons, 1923–6.

[2] Arabella Susan Lawrence (1871–1947). The woman trade union organiser who became Parliamentary Secretary to the Ministry of Health in the 1929 Labour Government. A leading Fabian for many years and a devoted disciple of Mary Macarthur.

when both of us—satisfied that we had our career before us—had dropped out of the race for good and all." "I have been packing up for some time," I replied. "My one terror is the fear of losing my mind before I have lost my body. That fate, at any rate, you and your husband have been spared. Every hour of your life has been worth while, and the glorious courage with which you have both faced death may be the hour of your highest vitality." We embraced as warm friends and promised that I should come and see her after the operation—if she survived it. She has a wonderfully rich nature, exuberant in its enjoyment of personal life, and yet how persistent in its social purpose. A rare combination.

October 23rd.—After Mary Macarthur comes Margaret Hobhouse. She and I had spent three days at Margate a few weeks ago: she had seemed depressed and wanted a change of air, so I agreed to go down with her. We had long talks together about life and death and our old comradeship as girls before the lines of our lives diverged—hers into the county magnate's wife and mother of six children, and I into the professional publicist with a "socialist agitator" as husband and comrade. But throughout these intimate talks she had never hinted at the imminence of death. Yesterday she told me that she had undergone two operations for cancer of the breast, the last as recently as July, a bad operation involving the nerves of the neck. She is now suffering from a chronic cough and breathlessness—a bad symptom. She has told her husband, and after the second operation in July she told her children, but no one else knows. And she has evidently provided herself with the means of a voluntary and easy transit from this life. Her spiritualistic experiences—her certainty that, at any rate, there is proof of telepathy—of a sort of universal consciousness underlying individual life—is a great comfort to her. Poor human beings! How deep is the craving for extended personality beyond the limits of the thoughts, the feelings, the sensations of a mere life-time on earth. The young and the vigorous can ignore this craving, a life that is always unfolding seems to the liver eternal. When the inevitable shrinkage begins "which can have but one end" and one sees the blank wall of death close in front of one's dwindling stream of energy; then, not even the kindliest interest in the rising generation nor the most peacefully stoic philosophy suffices to still the grim irony of the unintelligible tragedy of the self-consciousness of human beings. The senseless cruelty of men and races of men, one towards the other, to-day vividly exposed in Russia, Central Europe, and Ireland, the millions who are being tortured by cold, famine and disease—quite unnecessarily and quite deliberately by dominant classes and dominant races—forms a dark background to the shortness and ineffectiveness of one's own life and the lives of those one loves. Ten years ago one would have left the world feeling that human society was getting steadily more loving and more enlightened. To-day it needs a robust "Will to believe" to avoid the fear that we are sinking back into a barbarism as dark as any endured since the times deemed "civilised". One dreads that human life is becoming worse and not better while one is finishing one's brief spell of work.

November 29th.—The autumn is over: Sidney left yesterday for Seaham and I follow him the end of this week, the two of us giving a course of some thirty or forty lectures in miners' villages.

For us these three months have passed away in health and personal happiness and quiet and successful work. The course of lectures at King's Hall in explanation of the proposals in our new book went off well. About these lectures we had had many misgivings, and I had even had sleepless nights with visions of an empty hall and a large deficit for the Fabian Society. The subject was a stiff one; we had to cram the lectures into two a week (not being able to get the hall for the same night in successive weeks)—there was reported to be a slump in suchlike instructive entertainments, and, most annoying of all, both the I.L.P. and the National Guilds League had paid the Fabian Society the compliment of imitation, and had arranged and advertised rival courses for the very same weeks and in some cases on the same subjects. . . . We filled the hall with course tickets and made a profit of £180 and sold some £30 of literature on the five nights of Webb lectures—not so bad for the poor old Fabian Society and the "Obsolescent Webbs". G.B.S. gives his last lecture on Friday, a criticism "on the Webb Constitution" and the place will be packed. The audience has been mainly non-Socialist; there were even two Rothschilds, peers and princes and a minor Royalty. But the two lectures I gave cost me a month's agitated existence and some work, and were not much of a success. Sidney's three were unusually good; he is in great form just at present.

But these lectures have been a diversion—our main task has been re-writing and extending the MS. supplement on the Consumer's Co-operative Movement into a book, now in the press, awaiting completion when we return from Seaham. A side show has been starting a social club for the wives of Labour M.P.s and T.U. officials about which more anon.[1]

In spite of all this peaceful and successful activity I am continually oppressed by the increasing gloom of the world's affairs. There must

---

[1] This was the beginning of the Half-Circle Club, so named because it catered for one sex only, in which Mrs. Webb endeavoured to "groom" Labour women and the wives of Labour men to hold their own in political society.

have been many happy hardworking and successful Roman administrators when the Roman Empire was breaking up and when all that these men valued—intellectual enlightenment, good manners, the reign of law, the enjoyment of art and literature and cosmopolitan intercourse, not to mention the amenities of social and domestic life —were about to disappear in the dark ages of brutal disorder, universal poverty, chronic war and creed persecutions.

One absorbing pre-occupation during the last few weeks—alas! a symbol of what is happening—have been public funerals! The public pageant of the "Unknown Warrior" symbolising the ten million white men killed in the war, the funeral of the martyred Lord Mayor of Cork,[1] and, as a reprisal, the military parade through London of the corpses of the English officers murdered in Dublin. Yesterday Downing Street was barricaded lest there should be yet another and still more impressive public ceremony—the funeral of an assassinated Prime Minister! It is said that he lives in fear of the Green Terror and is looking for a compromise with Sinn Fein.

A trifle to note. We are reconciled to H. G. Wells. He sent me his *History* with an inscription; I wrote a friendly acknowledgment; which he bettered in reply. And after he returned from Russia I asked him and his wife to dinner to meet Haldane and Krassin, Cole and the Shaws. He came: Mrs. Wells was otherwise engaged. He is fat and prosperous and immensely self-congratulatory; towards us he was affable; but suspicion lurked in his eye and I doubt whether he is really friendly. Nor do I desire any renewal of friendship. But I am too near to the end of life to care to keep up a vendetta with any human being. Also I have never ceased to respect his work, and his *History* is a gallant achievement. . . .

December 21st. Roker Hotel, Sunderland.—Clearing up papers, packing books and our scanty wardrobe; a last walk on the sands: Sidney off to give his last lecture. Depressed tiredness is the sensation left by my ten lectures to Durham miners. The campaign has been remarkably successful—Sidney has lectured in every pit village. Only one evening since he began on November 29th has he been free and that he spent accompanying me on one of my lectures. The Haldane address to a select but somewhat small audience in Seaham Harbour Theatre, and Robert Smillie's two packed meetings at Wheatley Hill and Dawdon collieries have been an admirable climax. If an election came now Sidney would be returned with a four figure majority over either or both Liberal or Conservative candidates.

But it has been an exhausting experience for me. I am not facile at

---

[1] Terence Joseph MacSwiney (1880–1920). Lord Mayor of Cork from 1918–20; he starved himself to death in Brixton gaol during the Irish war.

lecturing—I have no natural gift for it. Giving decidedly stiff discourses on difficult subjects to little meetings from 40 to 150 miners, in bitterly cold miners' halls—starting off at 6 o'clock and getting home at 10, is rather an ordeal for a woman over sixty. I was dead tired after the first five consecutive evening lectures, but recovered with two days' rest sufficiently to take four more consecutive meetings and one odd one yesterday. All the same, I shall not do it again—it takes too much out of me. Part of my nervous exhaustion was, however, due to the shock of hearing from dear sister Maggie that the radiograph showed her lungs covered with cancer spots and that the end could not long be delayed. She is brave and I try to help her by taking an equally philosophical attitude—treating death as the last adventure in life. All the same, the thought that she also will have gone in a few months—the seventh and best beloved sister—the oldest of my living friends—is gloomy for the survivor. And feeling so near the end, it seems almost absurd to be starting on the new life of having Sidney in Parliament. I console myself with the thought that if anything should happen to me I should like to leave him in a new mental environment and with engrossing calls upon his time and thought—it would be the only distraction for the first months and years of supreme loneliness. And he remains brilliantly well and happy —ridiculously young for his age. . . .

JANUARY 1921—DECEMBER 1921

January 1st. 41 Grosvenor Road.—The wicked 1920 dead: but judged by British doings in Ireland and French doings in Germany the child will be as wicked as the parent.

So far as we personally are concerned, the last year has been happy and successful with a distinct dash of adventure. The publication of the Socialist Constitution was an event in our lives—the summing up of our observation and reasoning about political and industrial organisation—and on the whole the book has been well, though hardly enthusiastically received. It is far too full of new ideas and detailed application to be a popular work, and we are taking no steps to popularise it as we did with the Minority Report. Then there has been the Seaham adventure with a new outlook for Sidney; the growing success of the London School of Economics (a solid satisfaction to us); and the progress of the Labour Party as the only possible alternative Government to the Coalition. Also all our personal relations are of the pleasantest: we are at peace with everyone we have to work with: and all the dissidence of dissent and personal jealousies within the Labour Movement seem to leave us comfortably on our eminence of old age and respected service. Very different from that uncomfortable unpopularity which overtook us between 1912 and 1917, when all sorts of little cliques seemed to mark us down for abuse or avoidance. Personal popularity is a strangely capricious goddess: almost occult in its changefulness. One seems to become the victim of malign influences, and then, almost suddenly, the malign influence passes on to other quarry and an almost undue appreciation follows. Old age is a great protection from abuse if one "has the courage of one's obsolescence," as Cole was kind enough to say of us. The dark features of the year have been Robert Morant's and Mary Macarthur's deaths and Margaret Hobhouse's mortal illness. Outside one's own immediate concerns one's state of mind is one of a tragic bewilderment—races and classes seem everywhere intent on mutual destruction and no one now talks of progress: we ask each other—Is it unmistakable decadence—is there any hope for a new social order?

January 29th. Leeds.—Ten days investigating the Co-operative Movement in Manchester and five days here in getting new lights on an old subject.

At Manchester Ivy Schmidt and I stayed with a bevy of students at a university hostel, going in to Manchester to interview Co-operators from 10 to 5 o'clock every day. It was amusing to go back to my old haunt of more than thirty years ago—the C.W.S. central office. I think it was in the spring of 1889 that I settled down in little lodgings in Manchester for some two or three months and attended the weekly meetings of the Directors, or rather their midday meal after the Board Meeting. I remember well the long talk and rough food—I had always to do the carving for the men. To-day there is an elegant and sumptuous club with the best of cooking and service to which I and my secretary are admitted free to regale our-selves whenever we feel inclined, with comfortable committee room in which to interview officials and Directors. They do themselves well, those 32 Directors, and half-dozen Managers of the main departments, quite regally; the comfort and quiet dignity of the place is conducive to good comradeship and effective work. My special Director was a forceful man in the prime of life, W. Blair.[1] He had been General Secretary of the Liverpool Society which he had com-pletely reorganised on the most up-to-date principles and which is now the largest and most successful retail business in the City. He is an ardent Labour man of the moderate I.L.P. type; his views gradually drifting from the standpoint of the producer to that of the consumer. Recently he has been to the U.S.A. enquiring into the latest develop-ments in business management, and is full of new ideas. The Directors are for the most part "relics of the past"—elderly men of cautious temperament, some of them able and shrewd, others almost senile, with a sprinkling of younger men who have graduated in the Co-operative civil services as secretaries or managers of successful stores. They have usually taken part in the work of the Co-operative Union and the quarterly meetings of the C.W.S. and in the course of a few years felt themselves to be sufficiently well known in the Co-operative Movement to contest a vacancy on the C.W.S. Directorate. It is in these men that lies the hope of the Movement. They are always idealists—in words at any rate—usually in disinterestedness of life; they have had experience of administration; they are not well educated but they are capable of learning. Where they fail is in the capacity for group work; they are jealous of each other and of the leading heads of departments, given to a mild form of democratic intrigue to get and keep their position; they tend to get "declassés". But on the whole they compare very favourably with a middle class Directorate in desire for knowledge and an appreciation of their own limitations. That amazing insolence, taking the form of abject ignorance of all

---

[1] William Richard Blair (1873–1932). Co-operator and member of I.L.P. Became Secretary to Liverpool Co-operative Society in 1905, and a director of the C.W.S. in 1919.

industrial organisations save capitalism, which one finds in the wealthy entrepreneur, would be inconceivable in the Co-operative official or Director. The stupid Co-operator is more inclined to depreciate co-operative organisation than to be intoxicated by its success. The clever ones are always alive to the superiorities of their main enemy—the picked capitalist captain of industry. What the C.W.S. needs is a strong General Manager, younger Directors, a strong Chairman, and more freedom to dislodge worn-out or incapable heads of departments. And like all the rest of the Co-operative Movement, there is complete chaos in the levels of salaries and wages. At the X Soap Works seedy young men were earning £9 a week at machine work, whilst responsible Assistant Managers were getting £400 a year or less. This is partly due to war conditions. But no brains have been put into methods and amounts of remunerations: only a sullen obstinacy, tempered by panic at the pressure brought by A.U.C.E.[1] However, I will not run on with these casual observations.

Ivy Schmidt and I have investigated the constitution of some six or seven Yorkshire societies, the results of which will be embodied in the forthcoming book. Going up and down the country I have met many interesting, public-spirited young men, and I go back far more hopeful about the advance in the Co-operative Movement and its possible developments. What is most promising is the drawing together of the three working class movements—the Co-operative and Trade Union Movements and the Labour Party.

February 8th.—The growing unemployment has added to the ferment of rebellious discontent. The wonder is that there is not more outward sign of angry resentment. Perhaps it is due to the fact that for the first time some sort of weekly allowance is being received without the stigma of pauperism and that even the Boards of Guardians dare not refuse unconditional outdoor relief to those without it. The *principle* of deterrence is completely discarded: no one suggests that unemployment is to be "punished"—everyone accepts the "innocence" of the unemployed person and admits that he ought to be maintained either by his own industry or by the community. But "at what rate?" and is he to be allowed to refuse work except at the high standard rates brought about by the rise of prices and the shortage of workers during the war? There are vague schemes, none of them immediately practicable, of industrial maintenance; there are the echoes of the Minority Report proposals to equalise employment. But this last proposal is obviously inconsistent with the present anti-

---

[1] Amalgamated Union of Co-operative Employees; later, by extending its range of membership, it became the National Union of Distributors and Allied Workers, and still later amalgamated with the Shop Assistants' Union.

government and anti-municipal capitalistic crusade, and whilst the Cabinet doles out a few millions to help L.A.'s to make roads they are stopping L.A.'s going on with urgent schemes of repairs and extensions of municipal enterprise. The Government have no plan of dealing with unemployment nor have the Asquithian Liberals. The Labour Party alone has had its enquiry and report. What with the Report on Ireland followed by the Report on Unemployment—both written by Sidney and Arthur Greenwood—the Labour Party is more and more taking the position of the only alternative Government to Lloyd George.

*   *   *   *   *

March 16th.—Margaret Hobhouse died early this morning: I saw her every two or three days and longed that she might sink swiftly. But in spite of all the discomfort and weariness she seemed to cling to the miracle of recovery. The last time we talked together she suggested that we should go to Eastbourne when she was better, though she was quite obviously dying. How difficult is the art of dying. I often wonder whether one will be able to "live up" to death so that one's last act shall be good: a help and an inspiration to others. Unfortunately I am constitutionally a coward: whether I could master cowardice by will and philosophy and a certain subconscious religious feeling I do not know. But when the time comes I will try to. . . .

April 14th. Roker Hotel, Sunderland.—I was exhausted with the winter's work on the book and with sorrow, and I was glad to escape with Sidney to this quiet little place with the North Sea to look at, sometimes in dead calm and sometimes surging in on a north east gale. The sea is always to me at once a tonic and a sedative, inspiring with new energy and calming down earthly fears. For the last week has been one of panics, foolish panics, fears now for Sidney's safety in Herron's[1] side-car, then of some quite imaginary ailment of my own. But the sight of the sea, and the bracing walks along the strip of sand and rock, have swept the panics away by sheer shame at my own weakness. I while away the day browsing over newspapers and a few books we have brought with us or recalling scenes of childhood and girlhood and memories of the sisters and friends on the other side. Old age makes vivid these memories.

The Labour storm which has been beating up for the last two years has at last burst. I do not know whether other people are as tired as I am of these storms; but though this one is catastrophic in its bigness I am merely bored by it. We tell each other that it means a good deal: the miners have a splendid case; there was never so great a solidarity of

---

[1] Rev. J. D. Herron, then Secretary of the Seaham Divisional Labour Party.

working class feeling and action. With so much fervour and determination, *something must happen.* And yet it all seems to be a futility—a wasteful futility which has little constructive element in it. Of course there will be another compromise; one side or the other will get scared and temporarily give way. But no progress will be made towards a better state of things. The capitalists, the Government and the Labour Movement will all come out of this big clash of arms rather more angry and rather more obstinately set on not playing the other's game; determined to manoeuvre for a better vantage ground from which to deliver yet another battle. It brings nearer a general election on a purely class basis—that is all. And in that election the present wicked Government will win the odd trick and Sidney will find himself in Parliament. The prospect is not pleasing.

April 16th.—"The strike cancelled": was the staggering news line of yesterday's evening paper.[1] A catastrophic anti-climax (if such a term be permissible); my forebodings were justified. "A wasteful futility" has been this aspiration towards decisive solidarity. We know nothing of what has happened except what is in the newspaper. But the leaders clearly funked it: Thomas, Bevin, and even Williams[2] and a majority of the Executives of the N.U.R. and Transport Workers rode off on the refusal by the Miners' Executive to ratify Hodges's unauthorised offer to give up temporarily the national pool and national rate and discuss the district rates offered by the employers. Hodges is paying the penalty of his swelled-headedness of the last years, as leading tenor of the Labour chorus. Considering that the miners habitually refuse to their officials and M.P.s any liberty of action, Hodges's insistence on ploughing a lonely furrow in negotiations is really amazing; more especially as the ballot was taken on exactly this proposal to negotiate district rates and decisively turned down. There is also something strangely ludicrous in these unauthorised friendly talks with the capitalist Government and the capitalist M.P.s after all the tall talk about "the enemy". These Labour leaders are really the limit of inconsequence: ready to be hail-fellow-well-met at one moment with any casual minister or M.P.—

---

[1] This was "Black Friday". The miners having rejected the large wage-cuts which the owners proposed on the return of the mines to private ownership, their partners in the Triple Alliance (the N.U.R. and the Transport Workers' Federation) voted to strike within a week's time. On the evening before the notices expired, however, Frank Hodges, the miners' General Secretary, at a meeting in the House of Commons made a speech which suggested willingness to compromise. The miners' Executive repudiated the interpretation; but the leaders of the other Unions called off their strike by telegraph. This was recognised, whatever the reasons, as a disastrous defeat and blow to morale in the Trade Union Movement.

[2] Robert Williams (1881–1936). Coal-trimmer and journalist; General Secretary of Transport Workers' Federation, 1912–23.

not omitting the Prime Minister—and at another time denouncing these same men as the mammon of unrighteousness whom they are out to destroy. As for Thomas, he feels himself at home in Downing Street, and among noxious competitors in a Trade Union conference. The manual workers, organised as producers, cannot find men of sufficient character and intellect to lead them in the higher ranges of statesmanship. That is the plain truth. The Trade Union officials are not "fit to govern": they are not even equal to their own extremely limited business of collective bargaining with the strike as the sanction.

This cancelling of the strike may produce an internal turmoil that will destroy any semblance of unity in the Labour and Socialist Movement. Of course it will play into the hands of the Communist Party and stimulate and justify its disruptive policy. And that makes for reaction. There must be a gay party at Downing Street or Chequers to-night! It may have been unwise to proclaim a strike: but it was one of those decisions which had to be carried through if it was once begun even at the risk of failure. If the men, in spite of their seeming unanimity, had refused to come out or had dribbled back again in a few days, then direct action would have proved to have failed. Now all those who believe the strike would have succeeded will go on working for it: whilst the public at large will think these perpetual threats, without action, are at once ruinous and futile; a Government run on these lines would be disastrous. Imagine foreign policy guided by the Executive of the Triple Alliance. We should have declared war on Germany and withdrawn our army after Germany declared that she would respect "the independence of Belgium" when she had beaten France!

April 24th. 41, Grosvenor Road.—I came away from Roker four days before Sidney could leave in order to be present at a gathering of the Half-Circle Club and their male friends to be held, by invitation from John Hodge, at the Steel Smelters' office. It was typical of the paralysing indecision and inconsiderateness of the T.U. official that three days before the event they informed my secretary that the gathering must be cancelled owing to office exigencies. As these office requirements had been known for some few weeks and had been acute for at least ten days, the announcement was an unnecessary inconvenience. "Damn," said I, as I read the telegram. "A miniature reflection of the cancelling of the general strike," I remarked to Sidney. Ivy Schmidt meanwhile hurried ahead, called an Executive and, reinforced by an urgent telegram from me, got the gathering transferred to this house. Over 100 persons turned up and we had a rollicking evening; with friendly chatter and a vivid entertainment by

Ellis Roberts[1]—recitals from Vachel Lindsay's negro poems; the company who could not get seats squatting on the floor, all of us trying to sing the boisterous choruses. Henderson acted as Chairman, introduced Ellis Roberts and was in his most beneficent mood and delighted with the entertainment. At the end of the evening he talked quite seriously with me about developing the Half-Circle Club by a grant from the Labour Party Executive so that we might entertain on a bigger scale. What interests me is the unusual friendliness, the absence of any constraint between the different sections of women who have joined; the wives of the Labour M.P.s and Trade Union organisers, the professional Labour women like Susan Lawrence and Margaret Bondfield, the wives of the well-to-do Labour Party candidates like Mrs. Noel Buxton and Mrs. Trevelyan. I am aiming at bringing into the workaday Labour world an element of intellectual distinction. We have to remodel official society on the basis of the simple hardworking life tempered by fastidiously chosen recreation and the good manners inherent in equality between man and man.

The gossip of Eccleston Square throws no further light on the great strike fiasco. Thomas and Bevin had from the first objected to the Triple Alliance strike and Thomas had been intriguing with other parties to prevent it. Hodges knew on the Thursday night that Thomas & Co. intended to call off the strike and therefore was more inclined to find a way out for the miners or, by being reasonable, to compel the Alliance to keep their word. He made no *offer*: he merely answered a question put to him. It was Thomas who clinched the proposal by accepting it on behalf of the Alliance. One of the worst features of this ludicrous and tragic business has been the failure in loyalty of these men to each other; even poor Clynes, the leader of the Parliamentary Labour Party, being left to make his speech on Friday afternoon in total ignorance of the cancelling of the strike when the Front Bench had been informed of it by Thomas. I wonder when these men will learn the elements of good comradeship. According to Cole, the Cabinet had decided to climb down when they were told that the strike was cancelled.[2]

Apart from all these petty personal jealousies it is as clear as noonday that a general strike on such a narrow issue as whether you are to decrease rates of wages first or insist on a national pool before you decrease wages is an absurdity which could not be carried through. So far Thomas was justified. But he manoeuvred to get *this issue substituted for the broad one of supporting the miners in their fight against impossible wages*. But the very fact that these changes in issues can

---

[1] Richard Ellis Roberts (b. 1879). Literary editor of the *New Statesman*, 1930–2; pen-name "Richard Sunne".

[2] G. D. H. Cole has no recollection of making this statement: the fact may have been correct, but it was probably merely a rumour passed on.

always be brought about by a new offer from the employers or the Government and that you cannot be perpetually putting off general strikes in order to consider a new offer, really destroys the instrument. The general strike will only be successful to resist some revolutionary action on the part of the Government, like an unpopular war or a change in the constitution not sanctioned by public opinion, or the imprisonment or execution of some person or persons. Intense suffering by the strikers, overwhelming loss and inconvenience to the community will never be endured in order to improve the terms of employment of some other sections of the community. A general strike must, in fact, be political in the largest sense of the word: otherwise it won't happen or will peter out before its effect is felt.

* * * * *

June 19*th. Brighton Labour Party Conference.*—After a refreshing three weeks at Dunford, the country house of the London School of Economics, in glorious sunshine and without other work but a little proof correcting, we find ourselves once again at the Labour Party Conference. Clynes brought down the news, told him by Lord Robert Cecil, that Lloyd George was considering resigning, and, after the King had sent for other leaders and failed to get a Government, he would advise the King to dissolve Parliament. Supposing that he, Clynes, was sent for was he to accept office and form a government, and go to the country as a government? The little sub-committee—Henderson, MacDonald, Clynes and Sidney—decided that he must accept and go to the country as a government. However absurd and unexpected such an acceptance would seem to all the other politicians, it would give status to the Labour Party and improve their chances at the polls. In forming such a government, outsiders will have to be invited to join; Haldane as Lord Chancellor, possibly Parmoor, and some Liberals—but they were to join *not as Liberals but as "nonparty" Labour sympathisers*: it was also taken for granted that Labour Party candidates would be included in such a Cabinet: MacDonald and Sidney, for instance. (From what Henderson said to me S. was to be Chancellor of the Exchequer!) However, I very much doubt whether anything so dramatic will come to pass: it would be a phantom Cabinet and would disappear at the Election. It is inconceivable that Labour should come back a majority with only some 300 candidates in the field. One satisfactory feature of the present situation is the completely friendly partnership between Clynes and Henderson.

June 27*th.*—The Conference was a gloomy gathering with the imminence of the miners' defeat, with the funds of every Trade Union fast disappearing, some of the wealthiest Unions—e.g. the Steel

Smelters—being bankrupt, not through any strike or lock-out, but merely because of unemployment benefit; whilst other Unions are not only denuded of money but are engaged in or on the eve of a strike or lock-out. But though the delegates were depressed, they were not exasperated or revolutionary. Quite the contrary: the trend of opinion was towards the Right, the pendulum was once more swinging back to political action. It was a "Clynes-Henderson conference"; the I.L.P. being in abeyance and the Communists a despised minority. And outwardly there was no sign of impending disaster to the manual working class. The leading Trade Union officials and Labour M.P.s were there with their wives, living at expensive hotels, and enjoying the brilliant sunshine at a fashionable seaside [resort], without any consciousness of the disparity between their lives and the circumstances of their members. It is difficult to criticise their conduct in this respect; though my instinct is against the extreme comfort, not to say luxury, in which the Labour Party and T.U. Congress Executive Committees live and have their being at these annual conferences. *We* find ourselves, for instance, living far more sumptuously when we go on Labour Party business than we should do if we were "on our own". But who would suggest that it would pay the Labour world for their Executives to be quartered at hotels where they could not get the necessary facilities for committee meetings? All the same, *I think the standard ought to be a simpler one.*

One of the pleasantest functions was an "at home" of the Half-Circle Club, attended by some 170 women and their husbands and the officials of the Labour Party office and the organisers. Mrs. Clynes was a dignified hostess: a graceful speech by Clynes and a boisterous one by me as Secretary of the Club were the features of the gathering. The Half-Circle Club, if it has done nothing else, has led to something like personal friendship between the little group of women who form the Executive and to friendliness among some hundred others.

The last evening of the Conference Henderson told us that Herbert Smith[1] had asked him to bring about renewed negotiations, with a view to the settlement of the strike on the best terms they could get. Despite the huge ballot vote for continuance on the part of the rank and file, he and Hodges had settled that the men were beaten and that the Executive had to take the responsibility for climbing down. Hodges in a dignified and sombre address to the Conference had openly said as much. It is significant that after this speech he was elected at the head of the poll for the Labour Party Executive. There was a curious sentence in his speech in which he blamed the *occupational* basis of the Trade Unions for the lack of solidarity shown in the action of the

---

[1] Herbert Smith (1863–1938). Yorkshire miner; became President of Miners' Federation of Great Britain in 1921.

Triple Alliance. Hodges is apparently no longer Guild Socialist, nor does he any longer believe in direct action. He now looks to Parliament as the appropriate place for him to fight the miners' battle and he is considering giving up his General Secretaryship and becoming a candidate for a mining constituency. The see-saw in the trade union world is disheartening.

When the Trade Unions are strong they rush from one extravagant idealism to another and miss the opportunity of their strength: it is only when they are too weak to act that they become sane: and then their sanity cannot be used! To-day the manual working class is descending rapidly into destitution: not far off, relatively to the standard they attained during the war, from the destitution they suffered in 1840-50. What the reaction from this misery will be now they have the vote we none of us know. But if the Labour Party had £100,000 they could win the next election however soon it came. The universal lowering of wages of the factory operative and the mechanic and the sweeping away of the Agricultural Wages Board has completed the disillusionment; and the miners are now proved to have been right when they told the other trade unionists that if they were beaten it would be a rout for the whole working class.

But the Labour Party has *not got* £100,000, and there are only 320 candidates in the field; the Trade Unions being no longer able to finance them are withdrawing one candidate after another, so that as things stand at present the Party could not win a majority however much the constituencies desired it.

July 12*th*.—There is a strange feverishness in London to-day, a physical feverishness brought on by the amazing light and heat of the drought; a mental feverishness arising from the truce in Ireland and the peace conference at Downing Street. We are all of us restlessly hopeful that there is to be at last an end to the infamous tragedy of a peculiarly bestial civil war, for which we, the British democracy, are responsible. It is a blow to the Government of Great Britain that it is the Premier of South Africa,[1] backed up by those of Australasia and Canada and the foreign power of the U.S.A., to whom Ireland will owe her liberty of self-government, a sign that power to rule is passing from England to other English-speaking communities.

There remains the black fever of unemployment. The Embankment at night is once again the resort of tired and hopeless men and women. This rising tide of destitution is still inarticulate and orderly. But will it remain so? And if the "miserables" of Great Britain take to direct action like the "miserables" of Ireland, will there be yet another civil war, more chaotic and disastrous because it concerns a greater mass of

[1] Field-Marshal Smuts.

human beings? "The manual workers are not going to settle down again under capitalism; they are not going to produce as they have done in the past," said the staid Hutchinson to me the other day. "And if they are punished by low wages and unemployment, without unemployment pay, we shall have revolution." I wonder!

* * * * *

July 16th.—Whilst I was at Dunford I read with delight William James's Letters, giving, in an intimate and conversational manner, his outlook on the universe. It is strange to recall that we stayed a couple of nights with him at Brynmawr, U.S.A., in 1898 and that he made so little impression on me that I did not even note the meeting in my elaborate traveller's notes. I remember listening to his address to the girls with full appreciation of its literary form and with amused observation of the discontent of his audience who felt that they were being "talked down to" (he notices this fact in a letter about this particular address and visit to Brynmawr, without of course mentioning that he had met the Webbs). Otherwise I regarded him as one American professor like another; except that I was prejudiced against him as the brother of Henry James whom I had known in London Society and heartily disliked, a dislike which was reciprocated.

To-day, and ever since I first began to read William James's works, I find him the truest to me of all metaphysicians. I am exactly at his stage of thought; I doubt where he doubted, I believe where he believed. I "take the risk" of faith in a spiritual force which makes for righteousness, seeing that risk of error must be taken on whichever side you finally come down. Whatever we believe about man's relation to the unknown we are certain to be in error, regarded from any other standpoint than that of the human being at its present stage of development. James, in fact, was a firm believer in the relativity of all truth and on that fundamental conception he based his pragmatism. (It is interesting to note that Einstein announced himself, in an interview with the *Times* the other day, as a disciple of William James in metaphysics.) And like James I am more deeply convinced every day of my life that human beings, whether as individuals or in relation to one another in a community, are only admirable so long as their emotions and their thoughts are suffused with faith in a spirit of righteousness, so long as their conduct is guided by the ever-present desire to become part of the manifestation of this spirit of righteousness in the world. And when I am asked "What is righteousness?" I can only answer the morality which has been associated with the great religions of the world, which seems to spring from the mystical consciousness of man, that he is in communion with a spiritual force outside him. And yet how miserably ineffective are these stilted words.

213

Faith transcends expression. It is thought and felt but it cannot be spoken.

Our personal life flows smoothly to its end with a settled conviction, on my part, that for me the end is not far off. Every night when I embrace my boy and give him my blessing before I retire to my room there is sadness in my heart at the thought that some day—and a day that cannot be far off it will be our last embrace and that one or other of us will have to live for days, months, possibly a decade of years, alone, bereft of our comrade in work, thought and happiness. But with this sadness there is always present a warmth of gratitude for our past and present happiness. For happy our life undoubtedly is, and that is exactly why I hate the thought of leaving it! In some ways Sidney and I have never been so happy in our personal lives. Welded by common work and experience into a complete harmony of thought and action, we are also in harmony with those with whom we work and have our being. Our servants and secretary are devoted to us: with our relatives we are on the best of terms. In our inconspicuous way we are successful: our books sell better than ever before, the London School of Economics (Sidney's favourite child) is brilliantly developing under the able direction of Beveridge, whom Sidney selected; *The New Statesman*, though still losing money, is not losing our money (!) and is daily gaining credit under Clifford Sharp's editorship and is now independent of our helping hand. And Sidney's work in the Labour Party, whether at Eccleston Square or in the constituency he is contesting, brings with it no personal friction and a good deal of pleasurable comradeship with men who respect and trust him. With Henderson, the officials at Eccleston Square, and with the leading Trade Union Secretaries, he is on the best of terms, and by rank and file he is respected more universally, I think, than any other intellectual. Witness his high place in the vote for the Labour Party Executive. Of course J.R.M., whilst outwardly friendly, is always trying to injure him. But then J.R.M. is equally bitterly malicious to the younger intellectuals of the Labour Movement, to Cole and Arnot and Tawney. So his malice is now universally discounted, and outside I.L.P. ex-Liberal circles he does not count.

For myself, I have not done badly these last nine months. I have carried out all the investigation into the Consumers' Co-operative Movement; I have planned the new sections of the book and helped Sidney with the actual composition of them. I have set going the Half-Circle Club; helped with Stephen Hobhouse's prison enquiry, and corrected the larger part of the MSS. of Stephen's chapters. And last and least, I have revised the diary of our first tour round the world and got the whole typewritten by Miss Schmidt. And though I suffer now and again from insomnia and indigestion and aches and pains

here and there and occasionally have a panic about a mortal complaint
—usually cancer—which turns out to be wholly imaginary, I enjoy
good health, if health be measured by capacity to walk eight or ten
miles, to concentrate very rapidly on investigation of fresh subjects,
and to do all the lecturing and entertaining that is required of me as
Sidney's wife. So far, so good. What gives rise to fear is the thought of
Sidney in Parliament, still more in a Government. He is young
enough for such a change of life: I am not. However, the chances are
that the political turnover will not come in my life time, and probably
not in his working life. And if I were gone, the transformation of his
activities might be wholly beneficial to his health of body and mind,
might just save him from sinking into a dull and grey old age.

One of the new interests of my life, but one that gives me some extra
work, is the running of the Half-Circle Club. We have had some half-
dozen gatherings, either of the women themselves or of members and
guests—Labour Party candidates, officials of Trade Unions, etc. On
the whole I have succeeded better than I hoped in welding together in
friendly intercourse the wives of Labour men, women organisers and
the wives of the intellectuals who have formed the Labour Party. The
idea arose in my mind in a long talk I had with Mrs. Frank Hodges
steaming up the Lake of Geneva at the International Socialist Conference last August. . . . After some shyness, she let herself go about the
loneliness of her life in London. In Wales she and her husband had
their own set, their relatives and childhood friends, they had a common
life together. But since she came to London she lived in complete
isolation. She knew no one in her immediate neighbourhood; Frank
was always away and was making his own friends. . . . When he came
home he was too dead tired to talk about his work or about public
affairs. "I can talk politics as well as anyone else, and the wives of other
Labour Party and Trade Union officials feel just the same as I do.
Some of them are becoming hostile to the whole Labour Movement in
consequence." So I got hold of Mrs. Henderson and Mrs. Thomas,
who happened to be at Geneva, and opened up communication with
Mrs. Clynes when I got back to London and induced them to issue a
private letter asking other Labour women to meet at my house. Hence
the Half-Circle Club. At first the menkind were hostile: Henderson
was sceptical: Egerton Wake declared that "Not even your genius for
organising, Mrs. Webb, will make the wives of Labour men come out
of their homes and hob-nob with the women organisers and the well-
to-do women." Now Henderson and Clynes are the keenest supporters of the Club, and Egerton Wake is more than satisfied, whilst
most of the women members are enthusiastic and every day brings
new applicants for membership. Only J. R. MacDonald remains
actively hostile. George Lansbury is suspicious, and some others jeer.

But Bramley told me that it had completely revolutionised the life of some of the wives; they now felt that they were for the first time part and parcel of the Labour Movement.

What has interested me is getting intimate with some of these women. Mrs. Clynes, for instance, turns out to be a woman of strong character and good intelligence. She dresses immaculately: looks a Duchess! She reads G.B.S. with appreciation and delights in good music. She is a gracious hostess and though she may have social ambition she is extraordinarily free from any desire to separate herself off from the other wives of the Labour men. . . . Working in a cotton factory from ten years old to twenty (when she married another cotton operative in Clynes) she has adjusted her life skilfully but unpretentiously to her new circumstances. (Has she not stayed at Balmoral and Windsor though she never mentions it, which is characteristic of her social good sense.) And she is a woman of strong will. Brought up a Catholic, she refused to send her children to the Catholic school and quarrelled with her confessor over her freedom to attend Socialist and Labour meetings. And yet she has no bitterness against the Catholic Church. When one priest refused to baptise her fourth child, unless she promised to withdraw her other children from the Council schools and send them to a far off inferior Catholic school, she marched out of church and succeeded in getting her child baptised by another priest, and actually got the obstructive priest reprimanded! Always direct of speech and unaffected, with neither self-assertiveness nor undue humility, broadminded and uniformly charitable, she makes an ideal mate for the Labour leader who may easily be the first Labour Premier. . . . Altogether the 150 women of the Half-Circle Club would compare well, alike in character and intelligence and even in personal charm, with the 150 principal ladies of the Coalition or Free Liberals. There is not the remotest reason why they should not become real leaders of society under a Labour Government. The society led by this group would not only have a higher standard of personal conduct and better manners but also just as good an appreciation of public affairs. Where the group might fall short is in brilliancy of repartee and in criticism of the newest fashion in art and poetry. . . .

*　　*　　*　　*　　*

August 24th.—I have lectured at three Summer Schools this August: the Fabian at Priorsfield, the West Riding County Council teachers' school at Bingley, and this morning at the Summer School of the L.R.D. at Herne Bay. These Summer Schools are the most typical development of social life of these days: a school of manners, without class distinctions, with definite subjects to discuss—the discussions being led by experts. It is a far higher form of social intercourse alike in manners and in thought, than the social intercourse of the aristocracy and plutocracy; it is an invention of the intellectual proletariat, whether these earn their livelihood by their hands or their brains. Old and learned persons like ourselves are treated with great kindness and with some deference, even by Rebels. But the community life, the perpetual talking, lecturing and being lectured to, is a physical ordeal, which Sidney and I do not care to endure for more than a night or two. G.B.S., in his wonderful good nature, stays for weeks where we stay days. He certainly is a perfect marvel of kindness, a faithful friend to his comrades in the Labour and Socialist Movement whom he perplexes and enlightens by his perverse and stimulating genius.

August 28th.—This August we have completed two new books— a large one on the Consumers' Co-operative Movement and a smaller one on the History of Prisons under Local Government, 1689–1894. The first of these has been my special job during the last year—heavy and at first dull task work. But it had to be done, and though I began by loathing the subject because it was stale to me, I ended by getting genuinely interested in the new developments, and Sidney and I when we got to work together managed to enjoy ourselves. The book is dull reading, I think; it bears the marks of task work undertaken from the sense of duty and not for the love of it. The other book is a fragment of our completed but unpublished local government series. In order to bring it up to date and carry the narrative down to the period dealt with by Stephen Hobhouse and Fenner Brockway,[1] Sidney had to put in six weeks' drudgery, using up the material collected two years ago by Felix Crosse and supplementing it by reading at the British Museum. Meanwhile he was deputed by the Labour Party Executive to get the Agricultural Unions and Labour candidates from agricultural constituencies to agree to an agricultural programme which he of course, had to draft—another job he dislikes because he has no interest in agriculture and knows nothing about it. But he is "the man of all work" of Eccleston Square and accepts his position with almost excessive good nature. When no one else likes doing a necessary job, he brings it home and sits down resignedly to do it until it is done. Very naturally he is much beloved at the office.

Meanwhile I have struck against turning on to another big book of fresh investigations until I have tried my hand at a labour of love. For many years I have wanted to give my personal philosophy of life —the underlying intellectual principles and emotional impulses out of which has grown the conduct of my daily life. And so for the last

[1] Archibald Fenner Brockway (b. 1888). Member of I.L.P. and conscientious objector. Associated with Stephen Hobhouse in the Fabian enquiry into the prison system.

fortnight or so I have been attempting to formulate on the one hand my faith in the scientific method as applied to social institutions, and on the other my realisation that, without the religious impulse directing the purpose of life, science is bankrupt or may lead as well to the decay and death of civilisation as to its life and ennoblement. Whether I shall succeed in writing anything that is worthy of publication remains to be seen.

* * * * *

October 16th. Roker.—Before we left London Sidney, MacDonald, Henderson, representing the Labour Party, and three others representing the General Council, interviewed the Prime Minister and the Cabinet Committee on unemployment. To Sidney fell the task of dealing with foreign relations and export credits, Russia and other destitute countries, and I gather from his colleagues and also from Maurice Hankey (whom we met the next day at lunch at H. G. Wells's) that he distinguished himself in lucidity and persuasiveness of his exposition. The Prime Minister and his colleagues were negative and implied that nothing could be done except keep the unemployed from starving. Their coldness about Russia was marked. We travelled up here to-day with Henderson and Egerton Wake on their way to Scottish conferences. They were both very severe on J.R.M. and his aloofness from, almost hostility to, the Labour Party. Henderson told us that MacDonald (about 1910–11) proposed to enter a coalition Cabinet with Lloyd George and Balfour (to oust Asquith) and offered him (Henderson) an Under-Secretaryship! Henderson refused decisively and declared that any such action would destroy the Labour Party and that he would not consent to it. J.R.M. tried to get George Roberts, who also refused. No more was heard of it. Henderson believes, or says he believes, that if only J.R.M. could get into Parliament he would become a useful member of the Labour Party, either in Opposition or in the Government. Egerton Wake is not so complimentary. . . .

October 28th. Roker.—The sixteen days at Roker have passed energetically for Sidney and slackly for me. For on only two of Sidney's nineteen meetings have I accompanied him. I came here ill at ease with rheumatism and bad sleeping, and though I have got through three heavy volumes since I have been here, and marked for extracting by Miss Schmidt, I have done no more to my book. The plain truth is that I am a little depressed: wondering whether what I have to say is really worth the toil of saying it. I know I can do useful work in descriptive sociology—and there are four or five books nearly completed which await me. However, having settled to do this job I will do it. But it is futile to worry over the length of time it takes to collect and express my thoughts and feelings. My trouble is that I cannot decide how far to limit myself to my own hoard of ideas and experiences or how far to supplement these ideas and improve their literary expression by extensive reading.

Meanwhile Sidney's little meetings have gone off successfully: not a ripple of discontent in these audiences of 100 to 400 miners. At Wingate when all the miners were under notice of the closing of the pit, the miners' hall was packed and men and boys were standing outside. There was something infinitely pathetic in the dead silence and intense interest with which they listened to his long and carefully phrased description of the causes of paralysed trade. There were no questions; but considerable enthusiasm for him personally. But the dominant note was depression—puzzled depression. "What next?" seemed to be in their hearts: but their wills were too numbed to express it.

The net impression left on my mind from all Sidney and others have told me is that there are two distinct currents of feeling passing through the minds of the miners and shipbuilders of the N.E. coast. They are disgusted with the Government and have forgotten all their patriotic emotions about "winning the war". The war was lost by the peace so far as they and their families are concerned. But they are also disillusioned about their leaders; and the bulk of them are reverting to acquiescence in the existing order of society lest worse befall them. The failure of the strike and the increasing suspicion that strikes "don't pay" and have increased unemployment, a growing doubt in their own and their fellow workers' capacity to govern—all this reinforced by the famine following on Bolshevik Government has tended to set up in their minds a counter-revolutionary current. Whether these mixed emotions will lead the workmen to vote massively Labour at the general election, or whether it will be general apathy and a casting of votes according to some local or personal circumstance it is impossible to say. I am inclined to think that on balance it makes for the Labour Party; but for a very unrevolutionary Labour Party. It will lead the Seaham miner to vote for Sidney: it is very doubtful whether they would have voted for one of their own officials. If I had to put a figure, I should say that Sidney will get 14,000 and the other two candidates some 7,000 apiece. Herron thinks that Hayward will get 10,000—Bradford 4,000: Sidney is inclined to reverse these figures. But there are some prophets who believe that Labour will not win Seaham. In that case there will be little increase in the numbers of the present Parliamentary Labour Party! And in that case Liberalism may rise up again as the only alternative Government, possibly with Lloyd George as leader. But we do not agree with this pessimism.

December 7th.—The Irish Treaty is the big event since the Great War and its warlike peace. The amazing skill with which Lloyd George has carried through the negotiations with his own Cabinet and with Sinn Fein has revolutionised the political situation. Whether or not it be true, few enlightened persons, even among Liberals and Labour men, believe that any other man could have got this peace by understanding; no other leader could have whipped the Tories to heel and compelled them to recognise the inevitability of Irish independence. Moreover, the peace puts us right with the world, at any rate until Indian troubles bring up the same question of racial self-determination in a far larger and more complicated way. The other great event (at any rate in appearance)—again redounding to the credit of the present Government and the present governing class in Great Britain and U.S.A.—is the Washington Conference. The virtual repudiation of Communism by Lenin, the readiness of the Bolshevik Government to come to terms with capitalist governments is another blow to international socialism and to the revolutionary movements in all countries. On the other hand, the economic disasters brought about by the peace have discredited Capitalism—more perhaps the motives which lie at the base of Capitalism than its actual administration of industry. The British working class is worse off now than before the war, and whole sections are sinking into chronic poverty made worse by compulsory idleness. Whether the Government's success in external affairs will counterbalance the growing gloom in home affairs is the electoral problem that must now be agitating Downing Street in deciding whether or not to have a general election after the Irish Treaty has been endorsed by the British Parliament.

These great events taking place above and beyond our own activities have had little or no effect on our daily existence. Except for Sidney's Labour Party business and my smaller doings in connection with the Half-Circle Club and the Fabian Society we have been hard at work on our books—Sidney finishing up the prison book and I at work on the "Social Investigation" as I intend to call it. After the drudgery of last winter on a task which had to be completed but which bored me, this labour of love is thoroughly enjoyable. Now I have to turn away from it to read up all our eighteenth and nineteenth century material so as to sketch out the final chapter of the volume on *Statutory Bodies for Special Purposes*, a chapter which is intended to sum up our conclusions about the transformation of local government between 1787 and 1834. . . .

JANUARY 1922—DECEMBER 1922

February 7th.—A question of conscience has been agitating my mind these many days. I read those gruesome accounts of the Russian famine and wonder whether we are not brutes in failing to give all our available income, over and above the bare requirements for our own work, to the Russian Famine Fund? It is futile to salve one's conscience by giving a few guineas: *if it be right to give anything at all it would be right to make a big sacrifice.* Hitherto Sidney and I have refused to be moved: and for good or for evil I think we shall stand by this heartless decision. If we are to depart from our settled policy of expenditure, I would rather do so to save the family of a German professor or Austrian official from semi-starvation. Russia to me is not much better than China, and who ever suggested, outside the official British-China trading and financial firms, subscribing to save a Chinaman from death by famine? The always-present doubt whether, by saving a Chinese or Russian child from dying this year, you will prevent it from dying the next year, together with the larger question of whether those races are desirable inhabitants, compared to other races, paralyses the charitable impulse. Have we not English children dying from lack of milk? Obviously one would not spend one's available income in saving a Central African negro from starving or dying from disease; I am not certain that I would deny myself to save a Frenchman! If I decided to reconsider our personal expenditure I should reconsider it in order to provide more scientific research for the world. Meanwhile we go on with our customary standard of life: I am comforted by the thought that our critics always abuse us as penurious and over-economical in our personal expenditure and our clothes and in our *way* of entertaining our friends. We keep open house: but the food and appointments are of the barest. Where I am extravagant is in resolutely refusing to use my scanty brains in *thinking out economies*: I either refuse to have the service or commodity or I afford it without wasting temper and thought on how to get it in the cheapest way. I might, of course, personally give up the daily stint of tobacco, the tea and coffee and the occasional whisky at the evening meal: I suppose I ought to do so *if I really followed the inner call of a scrupulous conscience.* But it would mean the perpetual friction of resisting constantly recurring temptation, and I am not certain that there would not be loss as well as gain. I should not advise another old person to do it; which is a sort of test of what is permissible. The perfect puritan is not lovable: or rather is there not some secret reaction that is the flaw in the crystal of a meticulous abstinence? All the same, I wish I had been brought up with physical habits *ideally healthy for the brainworker*, which is of course a different aim from ideally healthy habits. If maximising intellectual output is inconsistent with the most perfect health—then I would deliberately choose a lower level of health and a shorter life, measured in the time spent in living as distinguished from the task accomplished.

*   *   *   *   *

May 2nd. Dunford.—Early in February I expected to finish the last chapter of our new volume of English Local Government History —now developed into two chapters running into 140 pages—in six weeks' time! After ten weeks' persistent and concentrated toil on my part and a good three weeks' work on Sidney's part we got it off to the printer last week on the eve of coming down here for our delayed Easter holiday. Towards the latter end I got weary and overstrained and am suffering now from a reaction with nerveless inertia, insomnia and indigestion. Also I have been anxious about dear old Kate, who has been suffering for a couple of months from persistent headache which may or may not be the beginning of more serious trouble. It was a shock to find myself as her nearest and most responsible relation —practically her only sister. . . .

This place would be an ideal rest house if it were not for the screeching of the peacock and his wives, who annoy me by their noise and the housekeeper by eating the vegetables, imposed on the establishment by the donors of Dunford—the Fisher Unwins. I curb my irritation by remembering that unless Mrs. Fisher Unwin (née Cobden) had been a sentimentalist she would not have given her father's old home to the School of Economics. To-day, the poor lady, because she cannot insure that the use of the place corresponds to her dreams, is regretting the gift and makes fretful complaints if a single bush is cut down or a stone shifted, whilst she vehemently resents the high spirits of the students and their extremely moderate use of alcohol, not to mention the opinions of some of the lecturers. Old people are horribly troublesome when they lay their trembling old hands on the ways of the young: it is a chronic fear with me that Sidney and I may be doing it without knowing it, in one or other of our activities. To some of the younger intellectuals our persistence as publicists, using up one subject after another, must be a cause of annoyance—an annoyance which Mrs. Cole freely expressed in her description in *The Guild Socialist* of Sidney Webb and his irritating "permanence" as a leader of Socialist thought. To a whole bevy of younger Socialists our energetic survival must be as tiresome as the presence of the Fisher Unwins at the gate is to the administrators and guests of Dunford. So I end on a note of genuine sympathy with the Unwins in spite of the screeching of the peacocks.

May 14th. Dunford.—The eve of our departure. The two last week-ends the house has been filled with congenial guests who have timed their visit to be with us. Last week-end the Laskis brought down Finer[1] and Smellie[2] (the two youngest lecturers, with Labour and Socialist sympathies), and we had the Tawneys to meet them: this week-end the Director[3] and Mrs. Mair, her husband and daughter, and the Gregory Fosters[4] (University College) joined us. From all these separate persons we heard a good deal about the School and its internal life. . . .

May 25th. Llandrindod.—Again in London, I found dear old Kate better, but longing to get out of town: no one to go with her, so S. and I decided that I had to take her here until her companion friend could join her.

After an interval of five months I am back again at my little book with the summer before me to be broken by one visit to Seaham and Edinburgh with incidental lectures, my secretary's absence on her honeymoon—all of which stops any continuous concentrated work. I mean to finish this book before taking up any other work, and I mean to write it according to my conscience and not shamefacedly in fear of scoffing remarks. The difficulty is to tell the truth without being self-conscious in the telling of it. For the purpose of the book I have been reading through my diaries and dictating extracts so as to base my autobiographical element in it not on memories but on contemporary evidence exactly as if it were about somebody else. It is amazing how one forgets what one thought and felt in the past, and even what one did and with whom one was intimate. Reading of all our intrigues over the Education Bill was a shock to me, not so much the intrigues themselves as our evident pleasure in them! How far is intrigue permissible?

* * * * *

August 9th. Bryan's Ground.—About a fortnight ago we started from London, taking Longfords on our way, with a great kitbag of work which we proposed to do down here during our six weeks' stay. We find ourselves in the hands of the local doctor, Sidney for severe

[1] Herman Finer (b. 1898). Reader in Public Administration, London School of Economics, 1920–42.
[2] K. B. Smellie, now Professor of Political Science, London School of Economics.
[3] The present Lord Beveridge (b. 1879). Mrs. Mair became Lady Beveridge in 1942.
[4] Sir T. Gregory Foster (d. 1931). Provost of University College, London, from 1904 to 1929; his wife was Fanny Maud Sledge (d. 1931).

nervous breakdown and I for equally severe colitis—living the life of invalids anxious about each other and unpleasantly doubtful about the future of "the Webbs". Sidney's breakdown is the most disconcerting. He seemed right through the last year, up to and over the Labour Party Conference, in the best of health, working easily and steadily. One little episode made me anxious. When we were at Hastings in the winter he and I went out immediately after lunch and walked quickly up a steep hill, the sun hot and he with a heavy overcoat. Quite suddenly his face became purple and he became faint—with cold perspiration—and I had to put him on the ground for two or three minutes before he recovered full consciousness. But he was quite well the next day and walked some nine miles in a bitter wind to Winchelsea. The present breakdown started off suddenly with an attack of vertigo in the night, followed by occasional dizziness. When we got here, having to call in the local medical man for my own complaint, I asked him to examine Sidney. Every organ was found to be healthy—no blood pressure and arteries very young for his age —the only apparent cause of the vertigo and dizziness being a pad of wax in the ear, which was removed. But the dizziness and weakness and uncertainty in walking continued and even got worse, and the doctor became seriously concerned. "Must stop work for three or four months" was the verdict.[1] Meanwhile I was feeling horribly unwell with bowel and back ache and losing weight. I am now undergoing treatment and slowly, I think, improving. What troubles me is not my own health; I don't believe my life is a good one, and I don't much want to drift into a long senility. But what would Sidney do without me if he became an invalid? I have always contemplated leaving him still vigorous with Parliament as a new career to interest and absorb him. There is no one to look after him, and he is so absurdly dependent on me. However, the Lord will provide! We have had a good life together; we leave finished work; and the one who is left behind for a few years more life will have, as consolation, the memory of a perfect marriage. What more can a human being expect or demand? One of us *must* go before the other. It is for the one who is left to rise to the height of the gratitude due for our superlative good fortune.

*   *   *   *   *

October 17th.—The political world is tumultuous, but we hear little of its tumult, though it may whirl us among a multitude of other folk into the rapids of a general election.

When we returned to London six weeks ago we found our MS. on the *Capitalist System*—written some three years ago—approved by

---

[1] As later passages show, this attack was much less serious than the doctors anticipated. Mr. Webb recovered completely, and it was many years before he had a real stroke.

Laski, Pease and Galton for publication by the Fabian Society and we had to set to to prepare it for the printer. This took me the better part of a month or six weeks and occupied Sidney's time spared from more pressing business. Now the first proof is in G.B.S.'s hands being pointed and perfected. He has been incredibly generous over this little book, giving up days to going through it, first three years ago when he was staying with us and this autumn on the first proof. We shall get it off for final revise before the general election starts—presumably in a few days' time. Meanwhile I have been brooding over my own little book, deciding to recast the first chapter in a more autobiographical form. In order to make up my own mind I experimented on the mind of Professor Wolf[1]—the logic lecturer at the School of Economics—who had offered to read anything I wrote on methods of investigation. It was easy to see that whilst he was not much impressed with the *Treatise* he was delighted with the *autobiography*—and if that is so with him it will be so with other people. Moreover, I prefer giving my own experience—it interests me more —than summarising and analysing the net result of experience plus reading. So when once I am free again I shall describe my apprenticeship to social investigation instead of the more impersonal "How to approach the Science of Society".

Absorbed in our own work we have only heard the echoes of the battles of Downing Street and the Carlton Club and the fall of Lloyd George brought about by the Newport victory of the Diehard.[2] "Except that one does not like to lose a single election," said Henderson yesterday, "the Newport defeat is a fine piece of luck for us." All the same, the omen is unpleasant: Eccleston Square was quite confident of victory at Newport.

Sidney and I are becoming every day more philosophical. We do not want a Labour Government before the Labour Movement has found its soul. . . .

October 24th.—"A melancholy lunch," remarked Sidney when our six guests departed to-day—Henderson, Lansbury, Hamilton Fyfe,[3] Noel Buxton, Emil Davies[4] and Colonel Williams.[5] The causes of

[1] Abraham Wolf (b. 1876). Now Professor Emeritus of Logic and Scientific Method, University of London.

[2] R. G. Clarry, a vehement Tory, won the seat at Newport previously held by a Coalition-Liberal, beating Labour by 3,000. The Liberal was far at the bottom of the poll.

[3] Harry Hamilton Fyfe (1869–1951). Editor of the *Daily Herald*, 1922–6.

[4] Albert Emil Davies (1875–1950). London County Councillor and writer on nationalisation, a Fabian of many years' standing, and Honorary Treasurer to the Society from 1936–47.

[5] Thomas Samuel Beauchamp Williams (1877–1927). Lieutenant-Colonel in the Indian Medical Service, joined Labour Party and was elected to Parliament for Kennington, 1923.

depression were various. The editor and general manager of the *Daily Herald* thought the paper could only go on until the election day. The circulation, in spite of the drop to a penny, remained stationary, and the £20,000 voted by the T.U.C. would presently be exhausted. Also there was a general uneasiness that the splitting of the Coalition would strengthen the position of the Tories on the one hand and the Liberals on the other: both parties being now liberated from the incubus of past misdeeds and failure. No money and therefore no publicity for leaders, and no more candidates for constituencies— that was the plaint of Eccleston Square. Was the workman sufficiently intelligent to vote Labour without it being suggested to him by the newspaper he reads? Would he vote dead against all the suggestions of the united capitalist press? Also the workmen's clubs were on the war-path in favour of cheap liquor, free from any kind of control, a policy which the Tories were surreptitiously pushing. "What the ordinary workman wants is to be able to sit and booze at his club any day, and at any time during the twenty-four hours," remarked Lansbury bitter-ly. There was every kind of misrepresentation of the policy of the Labour Party. The ordinary Labour M.P. put the Labour members in the new House of Commons at 150: though Henderson sticks to his 200, Sidney to his 160. But there are many Labour men who will welcome 100; some say they will actually lose seats!

Sidney goes to Seaham on Friday and I follow the next week with Mrs. Bolton.[1] Sidney believes he will win, though less confidently (because of the general depression) than six months ago. If a Tory stands I think it is a certainty, and even with one candidate a proba-bility. But there is one consolation. If Sidney fails to win Seaham the Parliamentary Labour Party will not increase its numbers to one hundred. And with less than a hundred members the House of Commons would be a waste of his time. I have grave doubts whether either he or I will stand the additional strain. But I am satisfied that he could not have failed the Labour Party: he had to stand at this election, and if he had not accepted Seaham he would have stood elsewhere at the last moment with less chance of winning a seat for Labour. And if he could not win Seaham, no one but Frank Hodges could. He could not stand out. So I don't fret about it one way or the other. We have done the right thing according to our lights. Hender-son offered to send one of his paid agents into Seaham, but we felt it was selfish to take the offer when others need help more than we do.

Meanwhile we have applied for permission to build a cottage[2] at

---

[1] Her secretary, previously Miss Schmidt.
[2] This project did not materialise; instead, the Webbs bought the house at Passfield Corner near Liphook.

Dunford with right of exclusive possession during our lifetime but to fall in to the School with its equipment and a £1,000 endowment for rates and taxes at our death. We felt that we must make some provision for retirement and relaxation and that it was now or never! If Sidney gets into Parliament, we can't go on working through every week-end; if Sidney is rejected, continued residence in London in the spring and summer is a futile waste of diminishing strength. The countryside of Dunford is enchanting and we shall build and equip with far greater zest if we know that our home will fall into the School of Economics—our most successful child. Also the neighbourhood of Dunford with its relays of lecturers and students will provide us with companionship in our old age; with young people to be interested in and perhaps to help. Insignificant students welcome converse with master craftsmen, even aged craftsmen, and are inclined to repay sympathy with some affection based on reverence for good work done. I spend this week-end, before going to Seaham, at Dunford, consulting with the Director and Mrs. Mair about a site.

October 28th.—Depressed at the prospect of the larger life of Sidney in Parliament. I shall hate him to be beaten—I should thoroughly enjoy a rattling big majority on the day of the count and a few days after—but if he were beaten, through no fault of our own, there would be a subsconscious sigh of relief when I had got over the first shock. We should then settle down to a half-retirement—both of us doing our best to help the Labour Party in a quiet way behind the scenes—but making our literary work our predominant concern and feeling free to be at leisure during long months in the country. The life of learned leisure is what we both best enjoy; at work every morning, and walking and browsing over books and seeing a few intimates in the afternoon and evening. And especially now that I have this little book of my own—which is a big book in its high endeavour really to explain my craft and my creed—I long for leisure and a quiet mind. During the last year I have been perpetually called off, not only for the two books we have had printed but also for miscellaneous activities connected with Seaham and Eccleston Square. However, the two books are a solid achievement. The last volume on local government[1] promises to be a *succès d'estime* among the few who are capable of reading it. *The Decay of Capitalist Civilisation* will, I think, be a big piece of propaganda and give a lift to the Fabian Society and its doctrines. About this latter book we have been very much touched with G.B.S.'s gallant generosity in devoting days of his time to our proofs—pointing and repairing our style and adding one or two para-

---

[1] *Statutory Authorities for Special Purposes* (1922). An extremely interesting and informative book, notwithstanding its forbidding title.

graphs of his own where he thought we have not made our meaning clear. He has also played up about the Fabian course of lectures at King's Hall, agreeing to take the place of Hugh Dalton as well as give his own lectures. He is a real dear of a friend and comrade—he becomes less of a mocking self-asserter as he grows old: more serious in his concern for the world. He is really frightened that civilisation, as we know it, is going bankrupt and not so sure that he knows how to prevent it, even if the stupid fools and naughty children would take his advice. "Can Anyone Govern?" (the title of his Fabian Lecture) is a quite genuine question on his part.

I called this morning on Haldane to ask him to speak for Bertrand Russell who is standing for the Labour Party at Chelsea. He has courageously come out for the Labour Party. But he was contemptuous of the political folly of the manifesto, wanted the Party to restrict itself to "Ideals" and not to touch such thorny problems as the capital levy and nationalisation. "Well; I believe in telling the electors what you actually propose to do quite honestly. We don't want to get votes on false pretences: we want to build up a Party on common ideals and common ways of reaching those ideals honestly and explicitly stated so that there can be no misunderstanding." "Then, Mrs. Webb, you will never get to Downing Street." "We personally don't want to, Lord Haldane," I retorted; "that is exactly our strength." And there we left it.

And now to Seaham for a fortnight's speaking and talking, as much of it as I am capable of; whether Sidney is in or out we shall say "content".

November 9th.—Sidney is thoroughly enjoying himself in this election: six meetings he is taking to-day, morning, afternoon and four "appearances" in the evening. He is remarkably fit—all his giddiness has ceased; he sleeps well and eats sufficiently. In the intervals between the meetings he writes letters and articles. His enjoyment is partly due to the nature of the constituency. The thirteen miners' lodges stand solidly behind him, acting as committee rooms and placing their "halls" at his disposal. These simple-minded miners listen to his words, as the words not of a politician but of a teacher. In spite of their present poverty the lodges send up cheques towards his electoral expenses: and the officials act as his local agents. Their naïveté is amusing. When the two other candidates apply for some hall, they are far too honest to put up the price; but they solemnly reply that "when they know Mr. Webb's dates they will let them have it for any other night," a reply which infuriates the Conservative and Liberal agents. His return seems certain, but whether he is a majority or a minority member remains doubtful. . . .

C. P. Trevelyan came to speak for Sidney, and S. returned the service yesterday. C.P. was full of confidence: he has proved himself to be the "popular" candidate at Newcastle; and he is certainly an efficient and carefully trained speaker. He also is enjoying himself. "For the first time in an election I am saying what I really think." . . . He is certain that Labour will pull off many victories on the N.E. coast, his own included. With the Bear Garden on the other side— every leader of the propertied class abusing the other leaders—Labour ought to do well. The Labour Party might even do too well! We don't want to go to Downing Street either alone or with the Liberals. But, says Sidney, "there is not the remotest chance of our being tempted." He still thinks 120 is the minimum and 200 the maximum Labour members.

November 15*th. Polling Day. Seaham Harbour.*—Spent this morning touring the miners' villages; received everywhere by a little band of enthusiasts. In the pit villages Webb is strong—those who oppose him are lying low and seem about equally divided between Bradford and Hayward. In Seaham Harbour itself the Bradford cars, scores of them, are whizzing around conveying women to the poll. If we lose, it will be the women who will have done it. Sidney keeps cool: he feels he is doing what he had to do; even at considerable cost in money and effort. I have been living in an unpleasant dream: feeling ill and old and not suited to the talk of a candidate's wife; hating the thought that he should be beaten and yet disliking the prospect of a change in our daily life. I do not like the speaking involved in an election: one has to think too much of pleasing one's audience and too little of expressing the faith that is in one. As one approaches the end of life one longs for a period of peaceful recollection and disinterested contemplation of the problem of human life. And that book: shall I get the restful leisure necessary to finish it?

November 17*th.*—The long day at the count—from ten o'clock to six—was an exciting, tiring but triumphant experience. We knew we were winning after the first box had been opened; and after the first two hours it became apparent that S. would have a great vote and a great majority.[1] There was a little patch of Bradfords (Conservative) in Seaham Harbour and a thinner patch of Haywards (Liberal) in the remoter pit villages. But the larger collieries were solid for Webb; the ballot papers [which] were counted in lots of five and twenties looked almost as if they had been marked by a machine with here and there a fault in the working of it.

[1] The poll was: Webb (Labour), 20,203; Bradford (Unionist), 8,315; Hayward (Liberal and sitting member), 5,247.

Sidney continued his almost boyish pleasure in the adventure to the very end. I really believe he is going to enjoy Parliament. He is amazingly young for his age. The miners from the first treated him as their "property": the serious ones regarded him as their local preacher and the younger ones as their "professional" football player whom they had acquired at a high price and had to look after. I gather the Seaham miners had betted heavily on him in Sunderland: the odds were quoted two or three days before the poll as 7 to 3 on Webb. A miners' constituency, if you are the miners' candidate, is the pleasantest to work: we had fourteen [sic] halls, committee rooms, and bands of voluntary workers, at appropriate intervals throughout the constituency placed at our disposal, free of cost or trouble. The lodges were apologetic about not paying his expenses and sent up little cheques in spite of their present poverty. Altogether we were a happy family party. Our great pleasure was the satisfaction of the Herrons—for it was Herron who brought Sidney to Seaham and it was he who organised the victory.

November 23rd. 41 Grosvenor Road. Sidney in Parliament.—To enter Parliament for the first time at sixty-three years of age is a risky adventure from the standpoint alike of health and reputation. It would be a foolhardy risk if the need within the Parliamentary Labour Party for steady-going intellectuals were not so great and Sidney's training in government departments, L.C.C. administration and sociological research did not fit him in a peculiar way for the task. Also his very age—the fact that he can hardly look forward to being in any Labour Government or even to becoming an outstanding popular leader in the country—makes his presence as a detached and disinterested counsellor of special value to a party. Even more than the older parties the Labour Party is broken up into circles within circles of slightly different economic creeds, and of clashing temperaments, and of separately organised occupations.

The story of the Parliamentary Party of 1922 opened yesterday with what might have been a discreditable struggle for leadership. It was generally assumed that Clynes would be re-elected Chairman for the first year and J.R.M. Deputy Chairman. But the I.L.P. members, reinforced by the Scottish group of extremists, had determined to give that pride of place straight away to their chief man. Whilst more than twenty Trade Union members failed to attend the Party Meeting, the I.L.P. and Scottish groups had already met and decided to carry J.R.M. by bringing up their full contingent and outvoting the Right Wing. Clynes behaved with admirable manners: he accepted the position of Deputy Chairman without demur and appealed for unity under MacDonald. He even took J.R.M.'s place (absent through illness) at

the I.L.P. victory meeting last night, again appealing for an absence
of the spirit of rivalry and the presence of team work. And looked at
impartially and without considering the way it was done, MacDonald's
chairmanship has much to recommend it. He is abler than Clynes: he is
free to devote his whole energy to being Parliamentary leader; he has
a greater hold over the Scottish contingent, and his chairmanship
prevents him from depreciating the Parliamentary Party in the
country which he would have done if he had been passed over. If he
is not the best man for the post, he is at any rate the worst and most
dangerous man out of it! He has now the opportunity of his life, and
it remains to be seen whether he is a big enough man to rise superior
to his personal hatreds and personal vanities and sectarian prejudices
and do what is wisest for the cause in its largest aspects.

We are rapidly settling down to the new life. So far as I can foresee, I shall have a quiet time of it. Except for little dinners and lunches
of Labour M.P.s during the session and the monthly gatherings of the
Half-Circle Club, I shall avoid all social functions—excusing myself
on grounds of age and health and pressure of work. There will be
some preoccupation with Seaham—I feel that now we are in we must
do something to rouse the miners and their wives to be interested in
public affairs. So I am planning a monthly letter to the women's
sections, and I shall have to lecture there twice a year and do odds and
ends of letter writing in the intervals between our regular visits in the
spring and autumn. I am haunted by the vision of those pit villages
and those strained faces of the miners—their wives listening to our
words. Can we get into an intimate and sincere relation to them, so
that we may understand their lives? For the rest, I can get back to
my little book: Sidney's absorption in his new life will leave me free
to become absorbed in this curiously personal task—and yet a task
which cannot be well fulfilled without an almost unnatural detach-
ment from one's own personality and complete freedom from the
challenge of personal vanity. . . .

New Year's Eve.—The short session proved that the new Parliamentary Labour Party is exactly opposite to the old one in its obvious
characteristics. The Scottish contingent reinforced by the new intellectuals were always in attendance; they spoke incessantly, with ease
and without any concern for the opinions of the "gentlemen of
England"; they are intensely aggressive without being disorderly.
Altogether they made the rest of the House "sit up" and the Press
became attentive. Sidney has not yet spoken: he has been an amused
and interested spectator; but he has not yet found either a fixed seat
or his footing in the Party. J.R.M. sent for him and told him that he
intended asking him to sit on the Front Bench: but the intention has

not yet been carried out, and Sidney wanders about the House a little disconsolately. The I.L.P. is very much in the ascendant, and the non-I.L.P. section is discouraged and feeling itself at a disadvantage. If Henderson is returned at the forthcoming by-election in N.E. Newcastle,[1] it will redress the balance and certainly make it pleasanter for Sidney and some others. Meanwhile S. finds that he can do little else but his correspondence and current Labour Party work while the House is in session; and I discourage him from taking up any big literary job—like the Poor Law book—at any rate not until the autumn recess. I want him to give his Parliamentary activities a good chance of development by concentrating all his energy on the House of Commons work and going slack when the House is not sitting. Now he is in, he might as well try to make a success of this phase of his life. If after a year or two it becomes clear that he is not really needed and cannot be effectively used, he can hand over a safe seat to a younger man and we can spend the rest of our lives getting out more books. Anyhow he will be able to study Parliament from the inside. Meanwhile I can get on with "*My Craft and Creed*". If I keep my health the book ought to be largely written by the next New Year's Eve. But I doubt whether it will be ready for publication before the winter of 1924–5. I am quite prepared to spend two years on it: I have done so much drudgery that I think I have a right to let myself go in a work of art! But have I the capacity—at sixty-five years of age—of anything approaching a work of art?

[1] He was, by a majority of 4,384. The vacancy was due to the death of the sitting Labour member, J. N. Bell.

The results of the election as a whole were: Conservative and Unionists, 347; Labour, 142; Independent Liberal, 64; National Liberal, 53; Others, 9.

FEBRUARY 1923—JANUARY 1924

February 9th. Lyme Regis.—We came here a week ago for a spell of rest and walking and Sidney has returned to London to-day and I follow on Sunday evening. A happy time—wandering together six or seven miles over the cliffs and hills every morning; reading and talking over our bedroom fire in the afternoon and evening, with another little stroll for me on the Cobb while Sidney stuck to the twenty books we accumulated here for this week's reading—too many for even *him* to get through! He starts next Tuesday on his Parliamentary work in good spirits: J.R.M. has repeated his invitation to sit on the Front Bench—given also to Snowden and Patrick Hastings[1]—and treats him in all ways as a principal colleague—the party has had two electoral successes during the recess—Newcastle and Whitechapel, and the Liberals have had two heavy defeats, which is even better, in view of their stampede back into extreme individualism. But except for this mere party advantage public affairs look more and more gloomy. Our book, largely on account of its title—who can dispute that civilisation is decaying and who can deny that it is capitalist?—is selling at a great rate and the edition of 3,500 will be exhausted before a month is out. All the better, as there are some bad misprints and unchecked quotations to correct.

My life will now be divided into quite unconnected strands. My first duty is co-operating with Sidney's parliamentary work: the monthly letter to the Seaham women: the spell of meetings in Easter week: entertaining Labour men and running the Half-Circle Club: and I assume a certain amount of dining out which I shall limit to the least amount consistently with Sidney seeing the persons he ought to see—foreign diplomatists for instance. The other strand is getting on with the little book—a delicate and exciting task to which I should like to devote myself wholly buried in the country where I could brood and meditate. But that cannot be done and the book must be written on those mornings when I am free and fit for work. Fortunately Sidney's parliamentary life will leave me a good deal alone, and I have hopes that he will be asked out without me—already, I am glad to say, that is happening. Then there are the Fabians and the students and lecturers of the London School of Economics, and Kate

[1] Sir Patrick Hastings, K.C. (b. 1880), Attorney-General in 1924 Labour Government.

233

Courtney and Mary Playne and the few nephews and nieces who affect us, and Rosy Dobbs and her children, all of which sops up the energy of an old woman of sixty-five. The plain truth is that the life I have got necessarily to lead is far more suited to a woman of thirty-five, and strong at that.

There is a certain morbid tendency in writing this book—it is practically an autobiography with the love affairs left out—the constantly recurring decision of what degree of self-revelation is permissible and desirable. The ideal conduct would be to treat the diaries exactly as I should treat them if they were someone else's—of course a contemporary person—with the same objective requirements about other people's feelings. But it is almost impracticable to get into that frame of mind—one's "self esteem" is too deeply concerned—also Sidney's feelings have to be considered. On the other hand, many personal traits and experiences may seem significant to the auto-biographer which are really uninteresting—mere flashes of personal vanity. For that reason it is perhaps just as well that I have another life to lead which is purely objective and one in which my personality is subordinate to other people's interests and aims. But how short is the time before Sidney and I will be nothing more than names on the title pages of some thirty books! I suppose all old persons are haunted by the nearness of death? In our case this consciousness is saddened by the practical certainty of separation for one of us, before death. We sometimes agree that the ideal ending would be for both of us to be simultaneously shot dead by an anarchist on the day of our golden wedding, July 23rd, 1942. Another twenty years in which to write books and to infuriate the younger publicists by our "permanence", already objected to by the Coles.

* * * * *

February 13th. Session of 1923.—Sidney is like a boy going for his first term to a public school! This light-heartedness, odd for a man of sixty-three, is due to the youthfulness of the party, as individuals and as an organisation, and to being elected on the Executive Committee of the Parliamentary Party and also to being asked by J.R.M. to sit on the Front Bench. How long this phase of youthful keenness will continue, when exactly it will give way to physical fatigue and mental nausea, it is difficult to foresee. He used to be intolerant of the public sittings of the L.C.C., and his enjoyment of the work was limited to administration on Committees over which he presided. To be happy in Parliament he has got to be successful as a debater. In debate he excelled on the L.C.C.—he has still to make his maiden speech at Westminster.

The Party meeting yesterday was reported by him as foolishly fractious and suspicious. The officers of the Party wanted to have monthly rather than weekly meetings of the whole of the members and to distribute these into subject groups. After a long wrangle a fortnightly meeting was agreed to and the grouping by subjects was held over. The meeting wanted to see the draft amendment to the Address; they objected to the Privy Councillors being invited to the Executive; they were nervously suspicious of any assumption of authority by the officers. On the other hand, Wedgwood[1] was delighted with the meeting—so were the other old Liberals—they enjoyed the free atmosphere, the individualism of the rank and file compared to the conventional "follow my leader" of the old political parties. Some of the Scottish stalwarts whom I met last week at the great reception —3,000 strong—were suspicious of J.R.M.'s tactics in having a composite resolution on the Labour amendment to the Address covering foreign policy and unemployment in order to keep out the Liberals from having the monopoly of our questions. "Dishing the Liberals," I call it; "always objectionable to sacrifice the policy of 'thorough' to the policy of dishing another party" said R. Nichol,[2] one of the youngest of the Glasgow contingent. . . .

March 6th. 41 Grosvenor Road.—My old friend, Alice Green, staying here for a week's respite from a Senator's life in Dublin; with an armed guard always in her house, the armed guard being almost as dangerous as the I.R.A.! She is now an old woman of 76 who has been living an heroic existence doing her little best—and alas! it is little she can do—to save Ireland—her romantically loved country. She is desperately pessimistic. "All the idealism is dead; the people have become thoroughly demoralised; they no longer care about Ireland; all they care about is living to indulge fanatical passions or mere lawless crime or to avoid the results to themselves of fanatical passion and lawless crime in other people. Every man's hand is against his neighbour either in offence or defence. Religion is dead; Irish tradition is dead; co-operation is dead; decent methods of trading and agriculture are dead; there are a few heroes and many martyrs, but the bulk of the people have no notion of being citizens." She is querulous, poor dear, with old age and loneliness; but she has kept her wits and has developed her wisdom. And she is only too grateful for affection. She thinks she sees in her old friends, the Webbs, an amazingly fortunate couple living an ideal existence of successful citizenship. And it is true that Sidney is enjoying himself in Parliament. He likes being on the Front Opposition Bench. His first speech in the dinner

[1] Josiah Clement Wedgwood (1872–1943). "Jos" Wedgwood, Liberal Single-Taxer who joined the Labour Party, and was Chancellor of the Duchy in the 1924 Labour Government.

[2] Robert Nichol (1890–1925). Glasgow teacher and Labour M.P. for East Renfrew.

hour on pensions was a success. But his more prepared speech, when he was appointed by the Party to wind up the debate on Unemployment Insurance, was half and half—first part success and last part failure. He was nervous, and the jeers of the Tory back benches, infuriated by the defeats of Willesden and Mitcham,[1] threw him off his subject— he repeated himself and failed to make all his points; and sat down without making his last words intelligible to the reporter for Hansard. But it was a sincere utterance and based on thought and knowledge, and he was simple and humble in his recognition of partial failure. I think he will pull through all right as a Front Bencher, and the rank and file of the Party are genuinely and affectionately appreciative of him. J.R.M. of course does not like him, though he has behaved very well and even generously since he has been the Leader of the Party.

* * * * *

April 11th.—An odd and not altogether pleasing episode in the social life of the Labour Party. Early in the year the Countess of Warwick,[2] who has been a member of the Labour Party for nearly twenty years, made an attractive and discreetly worded and generous offer to the Executive of the Labour Party: she put at their disposal Easton Lodge[3] as a week-end resort for small conferences and intimate consultations. There would be little more to pay than the railway tickets. The number of guests were to be notified to the housekeeper —it being left uncertain whether or not she herself would be present. The offer was so unexceptionable that the Executive decided to accept it and a small party consisting of the Hendersons, MacDonald, Egerton Wake, the Frank Hodges, Ammon[4] and Mrs. Clynes and ourselves were deputed to go over and prospect. Unfortunately Lady Warwick unwittingly published the fact, and from the beginning to the end of the episode we were pestered with photographers and film producers. As our hostess obviously desired these attentions, the rest of the party had to submit, and we appeared in groups not only in the newspapers but also on the movies. Coming directly on the top of the row over the Astor dinner, the impressions left on the minds of the more austere members of the Labour Party have been unfortunate.

[1] Two by-elections fought at the beginning of March. East Willesden was won by an Independent Liberal, H. Johnstone, over Oliver Stanley; Mitcham by Chuter Ede for Labour.

[2] Frances, Countess of Warwick (1861–1938). Reformer, Socialist, and authoress; friend of Edward VII, Joseph Arch, George Lansbury, H. G. Wells, etc.

[3] Several attempts were made, without success, to make Easton Lodge a permanent residence for some part of the Labour Movement; but it was an inconvenient building not very conveniently situated. It was, however, the scene of the inauguration of the New Fabian Research Bureau which resulted in the 1939 revival of the Fabian Society.

[4] Charles George Ammon, Lord Ammon (b. 1873). Parliamentary Secretary to Admiralty in 1924 Labour Government.

"Can the Party touch the pitch of luxurious living without being defiled?" many of the Left ask. And, personally, though I agreed to the acceptance of the offer, I am in two minds as to the wisdom of this acquiescence. In principle there is nothing wrong in it: Lady Warwick cannot help being a Countess, and the best use she can make of her trust property is to lend it for co-operative entertainments. The Labour Party does not preach or practise a fanatical carrying out of the "simple life": the middle class members of it have always lived according to the simpler canons of expenditure current in their own class—and that is exactly what Lady Warwick is doing. . . .

Lady Warwick herself, whom I had not seen for twelve years—ever since I stayed at Warwick Castle for a Minority Report meeting —has become an old woman like myself—a benign and hard-working old woman who has gained the respect of her neighbours by a sterling public spirit—supporting a secondary school—by turning a mediaeval barn into a fine hall for plays and meetings, by promoting the local Labour Party, and by opening her park to all sorts of festivals and jaunts for the common people. Of course H. G. Wells says she is a spoilt child and that she is moved by a desire for notoriety—but I am convinced that there is also an element of genuine conviction and sincere reforming zeal—otherwise she would not have persisted in her good intention. I should think it probable that the Easton Lodge arrangement will break down; there are too many weak links in the chain, and she is giving too much—it would be wholesomer if the Labour Party paid more so that the tax on her should not be so heavy. But something will survive—at any rate, the habit of meeting together.

* * * * *

May 11th.—Now that I have this autobiographical book on hand I have not the energy to write up current events. And yet Sidney's life in the Parliamentary Labour Party is full of interest. The Parliamentary Labour Party is unlike either of the other political parties as I knew them through my brothers-in-law and friendly M.P.s: it is a closely knit organisation with a vivid internal life of its own. The leaders do not dominate; and in so far as they lead, they lead by perpetual consultation with the rank and file members. There is the Parliamentary Labour Party Executive, of some 20 members, meeting two or three times a week in J.R.M.'s room: there is also the full Party meeting which controls all published declarations of policy, which meets every fortnight and is a very real body. The Whips are distinctly the servants and not the bosses of the Party; and there are eight of them, each having his own quota of M.P.s. Sidney is in Robertson's[1] division—an able outspoken Scottish miner. It is charac-

[1] John Robertson (1867-1926). Scottish miner; M.P. for Bothwell, and Scottish Whip to the Parliamentary Labour Party.

teristic of the atmosphere of complete and easy-going intimacy that Robertson gave Sidney some hints about his speaking. "Speak out; and speak more slowly: you are too accustomed to talk to small classes of persons who *want* to listen to you". The Tories are of course very hostile to Sidney, as they are to Hastings, K.C.—they resent these two newcomers being on the Front Opposition Bench; they want to run them down as leaders. So whenever either of them gets up, especially to wind up a debate for the Party, the crowded Tory benches, hilarious from dinner, amuse themselves and vent their spite by talking audibly, and then when they have made the speaker inaudible, crying out "Speak up". When Sidney wound up the debate on the Housing Bill (I was in the Ladies' Gallery) the Tories kept up a continuous hum broken by interjections, and when he rose to correct a statement by the Minister which referred to him, a young "Gentleman of England" shouted "Sit down, Nannie". Whereupon Kirkwood[1] protested furiously and the row ended in the Minister not being able to complete his speech. Patrick Hastings resents this hostility bitterly: but he has scored off the Government by getting a decision against them in the Court of Appeal on the Irish Deportation case.[2] "Does your husband mind?" he asked me yesterday when he dined with me. "No, I don't think he bothers," I answered quite sincerely. "You see he has his career behind him. It lies in his books", I explain—an explanation which is always accepted with alacrity!

But Sidney is very happy in Parliament and they all say he looks more vigorous and younger than he has done for years. "Getting quite combative;" one of the I.L.P. members said. As a Parliamentarian he is not yet a success: but as a member of the Party he is very useful.

This week all my energy has been taken up with political work. On Monday I travelled up to York to the conference of women's sections; spent the whole day in conference; entertained the four Seaham delegates to lunch and left York 6.20, arriving in London 10.30. Yesterday I had an M.P.s dinner with Lord Acton[3] thrown in as a possible Labour peer: to-day a lunch of 12 Labour M.P.s to meet Shaw and Henderson: to-morrow I must draft the monthly letter to the Seaham women; in the evening I have 130 Fabians coming here for a reception: on Saturday I shall have to finish the monthly letter and I have a Half-Circle entertainment all the afternoon. Not a stroke of work done at the book! The end of next week

---

[1] David Kirkwood, Lord Kirkwood (b. 1872). Engineer, leader of the Clydeside shop stewards during the first world war; M.P. for Dumbarton Burghs.

[2] The British Government, under the Restoration of Order in Ireland Regulations, had deported over a hundred persons to the Irish Free State. The House of Lords finally decided that this was illegal, and an Indemnity Act had to be hurriedly passed.

[3] Richard Maximilian Dahlberg Acton (1870–1924). Second Lord Acton, son of the historian.

we are off to the Hamburg Socialist Congress. It is a good thing I have cut off all other social intercourse. For the next few years Labour Party business will take up a good part of my strength. But then I have always had some such double life to lead—literary work on the one hand, and some cause to advance by social intercourse. Fortunately I have ideal servants and no friction: if it had not been for the admirable running of my housekeeping, it could not have been done.

May 30th.—We have just spent ten days with the British delegation at Hamburg attending the International Congress which has united in one body the Second International with the $2\frac{1}{2}$ or Vienna Union—it would be more correct to say that it has merged the latter in the former. The leading elements in the Vienna International (created during the war out of the pacifist groups in all countries) were the Independent Socialists of Germany, the Minority Socialists of France, and the I.L.P. of England. The position of the I.L.P. was anomalous; it belonged to the older body as a member of the British Labour Party, and MacDonald was for some time serving as Secretary of the Second International and yet had joined the other organisation. Continuance of this combination of fractions became ridiculous directly they had antagonised the Communists in each of the separate countries, in some cases to a greater extent than the pro-war Socialists.

The British contingent, twenty-five strong, including the British members of the Executive of the International representing the Labour Party (4), the General Council of the Trades Union Congress (4), the I.L.P. (4), and one each from the Fabian Society (B.W.) and the S.D.F. (Kennedy),[1] and they were by far the most powerful of the countries represented. The Germans as the hosts and with 50 delegates were at a disadvantage (as they were at Geneva) in being the representatives of a defeated race, hanging on to the British in what was called, by the rest of the Congress, "the Anglo-German *Bloc*". The French were few in number and belonged to a discredited and insignificant fraction in their own country, which is also a country detested by the Germans and disapproved of by the British delegates; whilst the Belgians, represented by the accomplished Vandervelde, De Brouckère and Camille Huysmans, were the representatives of a country in league with the French and in opposition to Germany. But the French and the Belgian delegates are not Germany's enemies in the Congress; they are cancelled by the fact that they do not agree with the Governments of their own country. Germany's enemies, who organised the group hostile to the Anglo-

[1] Thomas Kennedy (b. 1876). M.P. for Kirkcaldy Burghs, and a Whip in the 1924 Labour Government.

German *Bloc*, were the Czechs—by far the ablest of all the Succession States who have gained at the expense of Germany. The Congress became a battle-ground between the Czechs and the Poles on the one hand and, on the other, the Germans. Tom Shaw, the Secretary of the International, was at work for the three days before the meeting of the Congress trying to prevent an openly displayed hostility between these two great European factions. In vivid phrases he described his long negotiations—"My sympathies are ninety per cent with the Germans, but the Czechs are the abler men, most of them lawyers. They have given themselves away, however, by holding a preliminary meeting of the delegates of the Succession States at the Czech Embassy in Berlin; thereby proving that they are in league with their Government."

The net result of Hamburg is one Labour and Socialist International, confronting the Communist International, based on uncompromising acceptance of political and industrial democracy in the western sense. Tom Shaw and Felix Adler[1] were appointed Joint Secretaries, and an Executive was made up out of the leading men of all the countries.

The interest of the Congress to me arose from experiences and impressions of these ten days: first about Germany and the Germans; secondly about the meetings of the Congress and its Commission; and lastly, about my fellow delegates from Great Britain.

The countryside through which we passed to and from Hamburg looked the picture of prosperity; well cultivated and well stocked, substantial peasants' houses, some of them obviously newly built and painted; altogether there is apparently no dearth among the peasants. But Hamburg struck me as strangely empty of traffic, scarcely any private motor-cars, few taxis and no rush of trading cars or lorries. "The port," said the experienced Gosling, who knows Hamburg well and who chartered a small tug to make a tour of the docks, "is as on a Sunday." The crowds of pedestrians in the streets on Whit Monday and attending the demonstration in the park were neatly clothed, the women's and children's hair was carefully and even elaborately dressed, the boots were good, but the clothes were shoddy in material and much mended, hats were cheap and often absent. What was painful to see was the pallor and the apathy of the faces, the lack of joy and laughter, the "oldness" of the quite little children, above all the suppressed anger in some faces as they stared silently at us. Our French and Belgian comrades were frequently insulted in the streets; the British and Americans were treated with effusive politeness, especially by

---

[1] This is a mistake for Friedrich Wolfgang Adler (b. 1879), the Secretary of the Austrian Social-Democratic Party from 1911 to 1924, and of the Labour and Socialist International from 1923 to 1940. In 1934 he was exiled, and thereafter went to the U.S.A.

officials, everything being done for our comfort. For the rest, the population was dignified; but there was silence—dark brooding silence.

The Congress opened crowded and confused. Characteristically our German hosts had provided 2½ hours of fine music: the orchestra of the State Theatre and a choir of a hundred males as well as a lady elocutionist to recite an anti-war poem. And this in spite of the over-full agenda and the shortness of the time with all the problems of Europe to settle in three days. As a matter of fact, we got through the whole business, it being done in the four Commissions, within the allotted time. But then the big delegations—German and British reinforced by the Scandinavian *Bloc*—always voted together and could carry anything by their national vote. The one big antagonism was German versus Czech—a bitter feud between the only able Succession State and the former German Empire. Being two highly civilised and organised communities, they may eventually agree as against the in-capables. The other controversy which raged in my Commission was the European [political] reaction, keeping us sitting till twelve at night because of the attitude to be adopted towards Soviet Russia. The British contingent with Lord Carson's ultimatum hanging over the Soviet Government were naturally enough against any pronounce-ment against Russian Communism. The Russian *émigré* Socialists, backed by Poland and other hostile neighbours, framed and carried a resolution, the British contingent abstaining, and the Germans voting perfunctory approval. But hatred, intense and bitter, of the French overwhelmed all other feelings on the part of the Germans.

The British delegation was singularly harmonious among them-selves. The I.L.P. delegates were in the ascendant; but they were well-mannered and anxious not to be cliquey, Brailsford,[1] Clifford Allen and Ben Riley[2] being especially cordial to the trade unionists and Labour Party group in general, and to us in particular.

One scene on our return journey remains in my mind. Most of us went back by Magdeburg and Flushing, changing at Magdeburg at 10 p.m. and taking the 12 o'clock express with a sleeper reserved for us from Berlin. We were a rollicking party, 6 Labour M.P.s of the trade union type headed by Henderson, big robust men with jolly faces and loud voices, with the tall spare C. Roden Buxton acting as interpreter. We woke up the Rathhouse Kelun,[3] the proprietors and visitors being only too anxious for pecuniary as well as political reasons to give us their best. At the station the group of fourteen prosperous and slightly elated Britishers, with their suitcases piled up, stood talk-

[1] Henry Noel Brailsford (b. 1873). Socialist journalist and war correspondent. Editor of the *New Leader* (I.L.P.) from 1922 to 1926.
[2] Ben Riley (d. 1946, aet. 81). Bookbinder; M.P. for Dewsbury. I.L.P. and strong pacifist.
[3] Original wording undecipherable: probably Rathhaus-Keller.

ing and laughing, awaiting the train. Presently I became aware of a stream of pale-faced silent Germans walking slowly round us, gazing at us neither in a friendly nor in an unfriendly way—an expression of indefinable *malaise*, mingled melancholy and curiosity. To break the weirdness of this silent perambulation of stricken spirits I ventured to remark to one of them that this was the British delegation to the Hamburg Socialist Congress—Labour members of the English Parliament: he merely bowed his head and continued his encircling movement with an even more set and enigmatical expression. "Pardon me, sir, but can you show me an American dollar?" asked one of the railway officials of Roden Buxton, whom he mistook for a Yankee. "I have never seen one," he added in a tone of reverence for an almighty power—the dollar being the standard by which the mark has fallen thousandfold during the last months.

During the last week or so, Sidney has much improved his position as a front bencher by a brilliant speech on the Labour Party Amendment for the rejection of the Rent Restriction Bill on second reading —the first really successful speech he has made. Hitherto, his speeches, though full of good matter, have not been successful; they have excited the more insolent Tories to jeer and have not altogether secured the attention of his own side. Now I think he has caught the right tone and has got command of his audience. His work becomes every day more exciting as the Parliamentary Party is making full use of his services. It is clear that with the prospect of an autumn session all joint work will be out of the question for another year or more; in the few months' holiday he must lie fallow so that he can bear the strain of close attendance at the House. He is enjoying the life: enjoying it far more than either he or I could have expected. And his relations with J.R.M. are certainly most unexpectedly cordial.

June 8th.—We have made the acquaintance of the most brilliant man in the House of Commons—Oswald Mosley.[1] "Here is the perfect politician who is also a perfect gentleman," said I to myself as he entered the room (Sidney having asked him to come back to dinner from the House). If there were a word for the direct opposite of a caricature, for something which is almost absurdly a *perfect type*, I should apply it to him. Tall and slim, his features not too handsome to be strikingly peculiar to himself; modest yet dignified in manner, with a pleasant voice and unegotistical conversation, this young person would make his way in the world without his adventitious advantages which are many—birth, wealth, and a beautiful aristocratic wife. He is also an accomplished orator in the old grand style; and assiduous

[1] Sir Oswald Ernald Mosley (b. 1896), the founder of British Fascism Joined Labour Party in 1924 and left it in 1930.

worker in the modern manner—keeps two secretaries at work supplying him with information but realises that he himself has to do the thinking! So much perfection argues rottenness somewhere. . . . Is there in him some weak spot which will be revealed in a time of stress —exactly at the very time when you need support—by letting you or your cause down or sweeping it out of the way? And what about his wife, the daughter of Lord Curzon?

This question is a pertinent one, as it seems likely that he will either now or in the near future join the Parliamentary Labour Party. J.R.M. is much taken with him, and he with J.R.M. Even the Clyde contingent have been fascinated by his personal charm and the wit and wisdom of his speeches. It is, by the way, interesting to note that the Scottish Covenanters are prejudiced in favour of anyone who is particularly hated by the other side. "There are three men in the House who are detested and reviled by the Tories," says Johnston,[1] the editor of *Forward*, who is himself in the House—"Sidney Webb, Patrick Hastings and Oswald Mosley"—a remark that accounts for the growing popularity among the extremists of the two very "bourgeois" figures and the one super-aristocrat. "Why are they so hated?" asks *Forward*; "because they are traitors to their class," he answers triumphantly, as if he were canonising them!

Sidney is completely absorbed in his Parliamentary work and it is clear there will be no time for the writing of books. During the session the work is continuous. For four days he is at the House from 2.30 to 11 or 12 o'clock at night, coming home for 1½ or 2 hours' dinner hour. On Friday he is there from 11 in the morning till 4 in the afternoon. The habit of a cup of coffee and a piece of bread and butter at 8 o'clock survives, and the morning is spent on correspondence with the constituency, drafting reports and resolutions for the Party in Parliament and the country, and, once a week or so, some Parliamentary committee. Now he is on the Standing Committee on the Rent Restriction Bill which will meet in the morning. Saturday and Sunday I try to get away if only for one night; but my attempts have not been very successful, as he prefers to remain in London to clear up correspondence and to see foreigners and students on Sunday afternoons. Parliament in fact is not a half-time job as the L.C.C. was: it is a full-time job. And moreover, the long hours and continuous work of the sessions make a complete holiday afterwards imperative. And I have refused to let him take down the Poor Law book to finish up in the August holiday.

I watch his career in Parliament with a sort of motherly interest. He is singularly simple about it; just does what the Party tells him to

[1] Thomas Johnston (b. 1882). Founder of *Forward* and its editor for 27 years. M.P. for various Scottish constituencies, and Secretary for Scotland, 1941-5.

do, to the best of his ability, enjoying the life and interested not only in all the questions which come up but also in the ups and downs of Party organisation. He does not seem in the least to resent J.R.M.'s leadership, always treats him as his leader, with no reserves, and with no desire to "manipulate". Partly I think he feels that he is himself too old for leadership except the indirect leadership of disinterested counsel when appealed to—neither does he seem to wish to lead. In one word, the desire to serve, to do any job that no one else wants to do and which the Party wants to get done, seems to be his only guiding motive. He has lost his will to *power*—even to hidden and unrecognised power. Here again the disinterestedness of old age comes in. "I am no longer quite so certain that I am right" he says; "in any case, it will be younger men who will settle the matter." What adds, I think, considerably to his light-heartedness is the attitude of the Party to him—they are not suspicious or resentful as the Progressives on the L.C.C. were; they are affectionate—call him "Sidney"; push him to the front in spite of his protests; the "Whip" who looks after him—Robertson—gave him some advice about his speaking a month ago and was delighted when Sidney did so well on the Rent Restriction Bill. The Parliamentary Labour Party is in fact very much a family party living on terms of frank intimacy—some of the members are young and disorderly, though the majority are austere in their habits; others are past work; one or two get on occasions a little the worse for liquor. But on the whole they stick by each other and work loyally together. Undisciplined in appearance, they are in effect the most highly disciplined political party that have ever existed in England—a discipline which has perhaps more solidarity than discipline brought about by the perpetual mutual consultation that goes on in the Party meetings, the large Party Executive, and through the eight Party Whips, each Whip looking after his own batch of members. There is a similar compactness in the organisation in the Committees—the trade union basis giving the Party an organic form, and its creed endowing it with little groups of enthusiastic revivalists. What it lacks is the convinced adherence of the average sensual man. The British people are *not* Socialists: only a minority believe in equality of opportunity for the children of the race, and a still smaller fraction in the substitution of service for self-seeking in the conduct of men. The growth of the Labour Party and its present position as the alternative Government does not represent a movement of thought among the whole population; it is largely, if not mainly, the result of the striking capacity for organisation of the British working man inspired by the fervent nonconformist spirit, which no longer finds an outlet in religion and has found it in social reconstruction.

* * * * *

June 28*th.*—Sidney is presiding over the Labour Party Conference for five days this week and doing it very successfully. His opening address, *Labour on the Threshold*, has been well received and considerably reported. But even he is no longer fit for day and night work, and I persuaded him to "shut off" Parliament for these five days. As for doing *more* than Parliament, plus Labour Party business, every day shows it to be an absurd expectation. For the next few years—perhaps for the remainder of our working life—there will not be any further joint research and joint publications. We shall help one another, but the work itself will be separate and individual—he in Parliament and on platform and in the Press, I on some book, written slowly and with spells of effort between blank days of entertaining, constituency organisation and sheer incapacity for any kind of effort. And I am not going to worry over my decline of strength. After all, sixty-five is the recognised age for retirement, and it is doubtful whether any books one writes after that age are of much value to the world.

The last three weeks I have been trying to describe Herbert Spencer as an influence in my life. It is difficult to sum up in one short paragraph the greatness of his purpose and the nobility of his self-sacrifice and the pettiness of some of his little ways and the mean misery of those last years of declining strength. How much of this misery was due to a poisoned body, to unhealthy living: how much to loss of faith in the beneficent course of evolution and to the adoption of an impossible rule of conduct, it is difficult to say. Alike in physical and mental behaviour he went down the wrong turning and ended in long-drawn-out disaster. He began life as a mystical optimist; he ended it as a pessimistic materialist; the cause of this transformation being that he allowed his creed to be determined by the findings of his reason working on fanciful data—he practised neither the scientific method in the ascertainment of fact nor the *will to believe* in what is essential to the salvation of man. Human life is intolerable without Faith. Alas! these words mean something to me, but little or nothing to other people.

* * * * *

August 11*th. Longfords, Minchinhampton.*—The fortnight here, looking after Mary while the faithful Bice takes her holiday, has passed happily enough with Sidney down here for a week of the time and the old schoolroom for our sanctum. I have actually written, or rather "put together" out of my diary some dozen or more pages of the second chapter of my little work; Sidney meanwhile lazing by my side, finishing up Parliamentary correspondence, writing an article for the *Labour Magazine* and discussing with me the offers of cottages and sites, arriving, by every post, owing to the gratuitous repetition of our *New Statesman* advertisement in a dozen papers, some of them with leaderettes on our dislike of dogs and cocks.[1] Such are the pecuniary benefits arising out of a little fame. . . .

August 31*st*.—After Longfords we went for four days to the *Radnorshire Arms* at Presteign. Then back to London and from thence in search of our proposed country home. This was a tiresome but, thank heaven! a quickly successful venture—lasting only four days in all. After seeing two or three other impossible places we plunged on 8½ acres with a habitable cottage two miles from Liphook and four miles from Hindhead—costing £1,750 for the freehold, a sum well within our means. With the addition of a third sitting room for our sanctum and three more bedrooms it will be a home we can retire to in case either of us breaks down, and it can meanwhile be used as a holiday residence. Enclosed in the estate of a wealthy bachelor it seems free of "barking dogs and crowing cocks"; it has a sufficiently pretty view and includes a delightful corner of woodland with big forest trees and some acres of hay field. I mean to plant the garden with heather, broom and gorse and bushes of lavender, sweeping away all the ugly patches of cabbage and potatoes and silly little beds of formal flowers, so as to dispense with a gardener. Happy hours Sidney and I spend in discussing alterations and possible extensions, and if we keep our health and strength we can hope for a happy old age under our own oak tree—with intervals of creative work and friendly inter-course. If *one* goes and the other is left, the unlucky one will still be conscious of the presence of the other if only in the choice of the home chosen for our last years together. And after our death it will go, with adequate endowment, for the use of students of narrow means—not so privileged as we have been.[2]

* * * * *

October 27*th*. 41 *Grosvenor Road*.—Ten days with Sidney at Sea-ham Harbour in our comfortable lodgings with the peaceful view of the dale and, at night, the twinkling lights of the collieries on the horizon of the hills surrounding us. After eight meetings in ten days of my womenfolk with the charming and eloquent little Mrs. Anderson Fenn (Labour Party organiser for the north-east coast) to help me, and the devoted Herrons to back us up, I return here

[1] 'Mr. and Mrs. Sidney Webb require a building site of an acre or more within radius of 50 (or 75) miles of London in any direction (south preferred); preferably with a habitable cottage which could be developed. It must be relatively high, with pretty view; and above all completely isolated from houses harbouring cocks or dogs. Anyone knowing of such a site for sale is begged to inform Mr. Webb, 41 Grosvenor Road, Westminster.' B.W.

[2] Passfield Corner was bequeathed to the London School of Economics, which, however, was unable to make use of it; and it was sold after Lord Passfield's death.

exhausted but satisfied with our position at Seaham. There is something very touching in these few hundred miners' wives, with here
and there a professional woman, gathering round me with a sort of
hero worship. Of course I see only the best side of them—I am too far
away to know or bother about the endless little jealousies which mar
this still feeble organisation. The monthly letter I started last spring
has been a great success. This time I have begun another experiment
—a free circulating library of some 150 or 200 books distributed in
dozens among the 11 sections; each local secretary having a complete
descriptive card catalogue of all the books. Whether the books will get
read except by the select few remains to be seen—probably the plan will
break down in some places. One feels the whole initiative comes from
above and the execution depends on a very few of the women. The
little group in each pit village waxes and wanes; springs up and flickers
out according to the presence or absence of this or that woman. When
Mrs. Herron goes in July the whole thing may die down. Meanwhile Sidney has been holding one or two meetings every day and
remains up there for another week to complete the tour round the
constituency, all the keener because it seems probable that we shall
have another election this spring, or even earlier.

Two big events happened while we were at Seaham: General
Smuts's speech on the European situation, which was broadcast as
he spoke it—asides and interruptions included—and Baldwin's declaration in favour of protection with its intimation of a general election
to secure a national mandate for protection as a cure for unemployment. Of these two events General Smuts's speech was incomparably
the most important. This is the second time that Smuts, the Prime
Minister of the youngest member of the British Commonwealth, has
intervened and has seemed to speak as the recognised leader of the
British people. It is an amazing testimony to the elasticity of the *ci-
devant* British Empire, the transformation of the British Constitution by universal consent without any "sanctions", and it is still more
startling that not even the Conservatives protest against this assumption of leadership of the British Commonwealth of Nations by a Boer
General whom we defeated in the Boer War. General Smuts declared
that the Treaty of Versailles was an unjust treaty which he signed
under protest; that the British and American representatives knew
that it was unjust. Moreover, that France has broken even this treaty
in her own favour; that she is now acting more criminally than Germany acted before and during the war; that the march through
Belgium by the Germans is as nothing compared to the illegal occupation of the Ruhr and the deliberate attempt to break up the unity of
Germany, and that a conference of all the nations must be called to
determine exactly the position of Germany, whether as debtor or as a

nation whose sovereign rights, even under the Treaty of Versailles, have been infringed. This speech is not repudiated by the British Cabinet: quite the contrary—Baldwin and other British Ministers say that they agree with it substantially. But they come limping after Smuts—sheltering behind his skirts as if they had not had the courage to say anything until he had said it. He might, except for the name, be the Prime Minister of the Commonwealth of Nations.

The other event, which affects us more nearly, as it means a general election, if it means anything, is the capture of the Prime Minister by the Tory machine and the younger members of the Cabinet. Apparently a full-blooded protectionist policy is to be put before the country in the near future and a verdict taken. But it is not merely protectionist. It is openly said that two other reforms are to be carried if the Conservative Government gets this blank cheque from the constituencies—the re-establishment of the veto of the House of Lords and its extension to finance, and the cutting off of the political activities of the Trade Unions: in short, the destruction of the present Labour Party based as it is on Trade Union funds. This is reaction with a vengeance! So we are in for a hot fight and the expenditure of some six hundred pounds on Seaham. We shall hold our seat—perhaps with a big majority—but it is a poor prospect for the Labour Party as a whole, exhausted as it is in funds by unemployment and short of candidates who can pay their own expenses. Henderson believes the Parliamentary Labour Party will come back 200 strong: Sidney doubts it: more likely 170 or 180. If we had £100,000 to spend on the general election we would come back with a majority. With no press, no money for literature or motor-cars in the constituencies we contest, and unable to contest more than 350 seats, the outlook is not promising. However, enthusiasm is growing and wonders may occur, as they did on the Clyde last year—or they may not; we may even lose Scottish seats.

Meanwhile I have to set about furnishing the cottage so that we occupy it in December and decide on the extensions to be made early in the year. The book has again to be put on one side while more pressing jobs are done. And then, in all probability, an election and three weeks of exhausting turmoil at Seaham, with a new Parliamentary Party to cater for during the session. . . .

November 5th.—Went yesterday to the luncheon of J.R.M.: some 100 Labour M.P.s and candidates and the General Council of the Trade Unions. The leader was looking fit and well, courteous and conciliatory in his manner to everyone, and especially civil and friendly to me. He delivered a clever and, in places, eloquent speech—not the oration of a *great* leader of men—but certainly of an *accomplished* leader of a Labour Party. There were few mistakes, sufficient and not too much definiteness—some very clever hits at Baldwin and his sudden adoption of protection as a cure for unemployment; but the speech lacked intellectual and emotional grip and utter sincerity. J.R.M. is certainly more than a passable leader; he is an extremely *accomplished* leader—nothing ragged or obviously defective in him— but he is not more than that except perhaps in the tenacity of his purpose, and it is certainly marvellous how the achievement of his ambition has improved his manners and swept away his rancours. The company was enthusiastic; the tone was not *very* confident, and though Henderson talks of 200 coming back from a general election, there are some who doubt whether the Labour Party will not lose seats on balance. The municipal elections this morning, however, look far more hopeful for Labour—and may even frighten the Tory Government sufficiently to make them doubt the wisdom of an appeal to the country with the present unemployment. Especially significant is the defeat of the Liberals. Until they are out of the way we cannot hope for any considerable success.

November 19*th*.—Sidney off this morning for Seaham in first-rate form with no anxiety about his own seat, merely a question of whether the majority is less or more than last year, a matter of immediate prestige but of little consequence. With his record of service to the constituency and status within the Parliamentary Labour Party, he is a far better candidate than he was last year; he is the sitting member; the Conservative candidate is a carpet-bagger, and, if the Liberals dare to run their own man, they will only get a hireling to hurl in at the last minute.

Hence our whole concern this time is: What will happen in the country? One result is practically certain: on the referendum demanded by Baldwin, protection will be beaten; probably conclusively beaten. The unfortunate Premier has, by his method of approach, fore-doomed protection. He tells the country that he cannot introduce protective tariffs as a fiscal principle, to cure unemployment and raise revenue(!), unless he has a clear mandate from the country. This is taken to mean a majority vote for protection of the total voting electorate. Now as the Government at present is a minority Government ($5\frac{1}{2}$ million out of 11 million voters) that eventuality is ruled out, for it is inconceivable that the Government candidates will do *better* than last year. Indeed the Conservatives themselves admit that they will lose seats on balance, though not enough, they say, to put them out of office. But all signs point to a considerable loss of seats either to Liberals or to Labour—one Conservative Cabinet minister

(Joynson-Hicks)[1] whom Sidney saw last week, put their losses at 20. Thus, whether or not the Conservatives return a Parliamentary majority, it will have to be a free trade Government—and probably some of the die-hard protectionists with their unlucky hesitating leader will retire into the background, possibly from the Front Bench. The real and significant issue before the country is Liberalism v. Labour—there is no other issue of any importance. That issue *is* of importance: if Liberalism were to secure the first place as His Majesty's Opposition, Labour would be set back for a decade or more.

The Liberals, reunited under the ostensible leadership of Asquith, but really under the leadership of Lloyd George and Winston (Simon having faded into the background), supplied with both oratory and money by the Lloyd George faction, seem to be in a first-rate position to win in the fight with Labour. Through Lloyd George's brilliant performance in U.S.A.; through the return of much of the old glamour of a great Liberal Party; through the cry of Free Trade v. Protection; through the support, not only of powerful Liberal newspapers but indirectly of the anti-Government Tory Press, the Liberal Party has suddenly blazed out again into a possible, some would say probable, *alternative government*. To read the capitalist press, whether Tory or Liberal, the Labour Party barely exists as a political party: it is a mere group of disorderly extremists without brains or money—of course they don't say this in so many words; they only imply it by refusing steadfastly to report anything about the Labour Party. With the exception of an occasional paragraph about J.R.M. (never more than a paragraph) they report no speeches—the last few days Henderson and Clynes have been boycotted. Lloyd George and Winston, and less usually Asquith, are given verbatim reports—they are treated as His Majesty's Opposition. As for the Liberals themselves, we are told they are already making up their Cabinet—or rather, Lloyd George and Winston are—whilst the Asquith group try to look sly and say "Wait and see".

On our side there is complete confidence that we shall retain the great industrial centres and hold them by bigger majorities: there is a certain confidence that on balance we shall win seats; but there is no confidence that we shall retain the first place, though we think so. When Massingham dined with us on Saturday Sidney wrote out his forecast: Government 280–290, Labour 170–180, Liberals 140–150. Massingham thought Labour would do better than that, and Liberals worse: Henderson sticks to his 200. Sydney Arnold[2], who prophesied

---

[1] William Joynson-Hicks, afterwards Lord Brentford (1865–1932). Held various ministries in Conservative Governments; notable chiefly as the very anti-Labour Home Secretary of 1924–9.

[2] Sydney Arnold, Lord Arnold (1878–1945). Liberal M.P. who joined the Labour Party in 1922. Under-Secretary for Colonies in the 1924 Government.

correctly at the last election, gives Labour another 15 to 20, and Liberals 20 to 30—leaving Labour just in front of Liberals. If any of these estimates are correct the position will be just saved. There will have to be a coalition between the free trade Conservatives and Liberals: an anti-Labour Government with Labour and disgruntled Liberals as His Majesty's Opposition. With this result we should be satisfied—amply satisfied. A strong anti-Labour but virtually Liberal Government that could make friends with U.S.A., settle with France; with one Opposition, and one Opposition only—Labour Party— would be the ideal solution alike for us and for the community at large. For my part, I should like to see Lloyd George back as Premier: he would be most likely to get an agreement with the U.S.A., and he knows his Poincaré and his French people. But more likely it would be some great figure like Balfour, or some dark horse put forward as a stop-gap. Not poor Mr. Baldwin; who is now regarded, alike in his dealings with Poincaré and in his surrender to his Under-Secretaries, as a—politically speaking—"Natural". To-day the poor man is perpetually saying that he is stupid, and everyone, whether Conservative, Liberal or Labour, now believes it! I am glad that idol—the honest but stupid man—is discredited. It takes a big intelligence to be honest in politics; there is no meaning in an honesty that does not know its own mind from one day to another—any more than you can give financial security to your creditors without knowing whether or not you have an income! Honesty *is* security for other people's warranted expectations—that is the test of honest behaviour between man and man.

I dropped in to the Fabian Society and found Sanders (home from Geneva) and Galton lugubrious as to the practical certainty of Liberalism beating Labour. "I shall be satisfied if Labour comes back 120 strong," says Sanders, and Galton agrees with him. Ben Spoor takes this line and is despondent. And this opinion is representative of an undercurrent of pessimism among Labour sympathisers. There are quite a number of old observers who have been active political workers in many general elections who believe that a Lloyd George-Winston Churchill-Asquith combination will be irresistible as against *Labour* —not necessarily against the Tories. Labour succeeded last year because Liberals were quarrelling among themselves, the advance from 70 to 140 was fallacious; we did *too* well last time; we ought to have risen to 100, then 120 this time would look good. Money, brains and a great tradition are now united in the Liberal Party and the old followers will rally to the standard. That is the case of the pessimists.

At Eccleston Square all was buzzing; candidates plentiful; money slowly but surely trickling in—sufficient to enable candidates to take the field; and constituencies were being fitted with candidates every hour of the day. There will be 400 by nomination day, it is thought. But the wisest heads say the least: no one at H.Q. has the remotest idea what will happen except that Baldwin will not retain his present majority and that Liberalism will better its present position. Whether it is old age I do not know, but I am singularly indifferent. With Germany slowly drowning and those damned French knocking her on the head whenever she tries to save herself, what does it matter who wins this election—it is too late for Great Britain to save Europe from chaos and another war. The only hope is U.S.A., and here a Liberal Government might possibly do most to persuade U.S.A. to act decisively. . . .

To sum up my own opinion. Unless Labour can retain its present position and even better it when Conservatives and Liberals are fighting each other with their gloves off, its present position as His Majesty's Opposition has not been warranted by the state of mind of the bulk of Englishmen. In that case it is better that the Labour Movement should be referred to its studies. It would be bad for Labour and bad for the community if Labour was to get into the position of an alternative Government by some fluke—some exceptionally advantageous combination of circumstances. I have no desire for a fallacious and insincere acquiescence in Socialist doctrine—a mere revolt against the two capitalist parties because leaders were disliked or because the state of the world was uncomfortable. Leaders will be incompetent and the state of the world after the catastrophe of the great war *must* be uncomfortable. This would be so under a Labour Government. We must have the same widespread faith in social democracy that we had in political democracy before the world will be ready for a deliberate transformation from self-seeking to public service as the leading motive at work in society. So if Labour is beaten by Liberalism I shall not regret it—except as a symptom that we are not yet fit for a higher stage in social evolution. . . .

November 22nd. Passfield.—Entered with furniture and Jessie yesterday according to plans made before general election; stay here five nights, lock cottage up and go to Seaham. Impression of our new home not altogether favourable in this dank weather. Silence absolute —no crowing cocks or barking dogs—not even the hoot of the motor. Cottage comfortable with distinct charm: country beautiful for walking and dry under foot on commons. But dankly cold after sundown owing to prevalence of water—near to river, and series of ponds. Also cottage arrangements about water, relying on pump which is tedious to work, and troublesome after the modern conveniences. Not a possible all-round-the-year place because of the ground mist.

But is this not true of all country places that are below the highest hill in the neighbourhood: and even high places like The Argoed were sometimes enveloped in bitterly cold mist in the winter months—ditto Beachy Head! It is only paved ground which is free of ground mist, and pavement usually means streets. We shall come here for a fortnight at Christmas and then see whether we like it sufficiently to plunge into extensive building and expensive upkeep—the latter would involve Kate Courtney joining us. We might decide to keep it as week-end and summer cottage and not retire here for old age or illness. Put off Kate Courtney coming here as I felt that neither Jessie nor I were sufficiently sure of our strength to risk it. Certainly the silence is weirdly attractive.

November 25th. Passfield.—Feel ever so much better for the complete rest and silence of this place in spite of a cold north-east mist—not without its beauty with the hoar frost on the forest trees, the warm tints of heather and the golden leaves of the birch trees and the russet-coloured bracken. I think I shall get very fond of this place: it is sympathetic to me even in these days of dank darkness—pierced now and again by feeble gleams of moonlight or sunlight—silence, stillness and mysterious indistinctness in form and colour. I shall be happy here if I keep my health and can get on with the work with its memories of the past and its hope and faith in the future.

December 3rd.—The Sunday before an election is always a day of rest in your *own* constituency as it is bad form for the candidate not to seem to go to church or chapel, or at any rate to refrain from speaking to his own electors; Sidney spoke for Whiteley[1] this morning (Whiteley himself was taking Sunday school) and is speaking to-night for Lawther[2] (South Shields): our agent, Herron, is busy with his services, and Molly Bolton and I are doing nothing. This afternoon S. and I started to go through every constituency and forecast results—mine appeared first, 276 Conservative, 206 Labour, 118 Liberals. Whereupon S. protested that I was far too optimistic, especially about nonsuccess of Liberals. So he started out to canvass each constituency by the light of 1922 results—and came out at 300, 176, 114 respectively (returns not complete), giving Liberals rather less than I did but Conservatives more. That shows how one is biased by one's desire and by the atmosphere in which one personally lives. Up here on the north-east coast Liberalism has disappeared—the turnover of the miners being complete, and the disaffected trade unionist of the

[1] William Whiteley (b. 1882). Durham miner; elected M.P. for Blaydon, 1922. Now Chief Labour Whip.
[2] Sir William Lawther (b. 1889). Durham miner, now President of National Union of Mineworkers.

Party being Conservative when he is not Liberal. But clearly *we must be wrong*: we always forget the lower middle class who really do believe in the old Liberal doctrine of *laissez-faire*. Also it is quite inconceivable that with money, oratory and practically the whole Press working directly or indirectly for them, the Liberals should not pull off a great triumph, though not so great a triumph as they think. The results will probably be like a year ago in that the enthusiasts of the Labour Party will be heavily disappointed and the other two parties astonished at Labour success. The *Observer* to-day puts the Labour Party at not less than 130 and the Liberal Party at not less than 150.

So far as we ourselves are concerned we are on velvet in this ideal constituency. There is far more enthusiasm than a year ago—far more voluntary work. The miners have become genuinely attached to their member: they are proud of him; they trust him and they feel that he is "their man"—that they have put him into Parliament; that he sits on the Front Opposition Bench; that he has proved himself to be, even in the eyes of many Conservatives, the best member Seaham has ever had for local purposes. And the miners' wives are fond of me; I have raised their status with their husbands and neighbours; they regard me as *their representative* and they are delighted with the monthly letter giving them special news from London. There is a certain charm in the packed little meetings at the pit villages and the atmosphere of intimate comradeship within the Labour Party— all of us on terms of social equality. There is not the relationship of angling for votes in order to win the seat, as at Deptford L.C.C. elections; far more the relationship of teacher and student—quick questions and answer—the answer taking the form of exposition, quite frank exposition of difficult or intricate subjects. After an hour's address the other night I found myself being asked a series of questions which seemed to be about every department of foreign and home affairs—our present relations to Russia, the character of the Soviet Government, the capital levy, the Treaty of Versailles, the cure for unemployment, the possibilities of protective tariffs, the state of education. I answered to the best of my ability—exactly as I should have done at the School of Economics. I discovered afterwards that these were the questions with which they had been plying the unfortunate Tory candidate, who tried to evade them and ended by flatly refusing to answer. "Even our candidate's wife can answer our questions— leave alone our candidate," shouted one miner at the Tory candidate to the delight of the hostile audience. "We hear so much at your meetings—it is as good or better than a tutorial class," said one of the leaders to me. The miners like the pedagogue! And what surprises me is the number of quite young men who come and listen intently in silence, leaving it to a few older men to ask questions. Also this time there are always a group of women, sometimes 60 or 70, at the meetings. Last year if there were two or three women one was agreeably surprised. Of course in the Herrons we have ideal agents. And the Herrons we shall lose this summer. But they will leave some of their spirit behind them.

December 12*th*.—These are the hectic days of victory tempered by the cold feet of the leaders at the consequences of victory![1] On the Saturday—the day of our return—Massingham appeared in the evening to implore us *not* to allow the Labour Party to enter into any relations with the Liberal Party—even with regard to conditional support of a Labour Government by the Liberals or *vice versa* (we did not remind him that it is barely a year ago that he was denouncing Sidney in the *Nation* for being the main obstacle to such an understanding)! On Sunday Henderson lunched here; and after lunch, talking alone with Sidney, he pressed for taking office at once if J.R.M. was sent for by the King (as seemed likely then); bringing in a moderate programme and continuing in office, with support of Liberals. Sidney agreed to taking office but demurred to "moderateness"—if it was moderateness in order to get Liberal support and not a moderateness synonymous with administrative practicability. He was definitely against governing with consent of Liberals to a specific policy. Far better be defeated early in the day, perhaps on the King's Speech. At first I was against taking office, instinctively fearing the "John Burns" attitude on the part of the Labour leaders when once they are face to face with officials. In the afternoon Clifford Sharp appeared and showed Sidney the silly article he was publishing over his own name in the *Daily News* advocating a coalition Liberal-Labour Government, in the interest of his hero Asquith! But on Tuesday at lunch he said that he retracted his proposal as even the Liberals were against it! We laughed at him, but were unconcernedly friendly. On Monday we had a dinner here of leaders; J.R.M., Henderson, Clynes, Thomas and Snowden—to discuss taking office and what exactly they would do if they did. Sidney reports that they have all, except Henderson, "cold feet" at the thought of office, though all of them believe that J.R.M. ought not to refuse. Henderson wants to take office—to concentrate on unemployment—to set up committees to enquire *how* capital levy and nationalisation can best be carried out. Sidney sticks to a bold declaration of policy with the probability of being beaten on the Budget or before. What came out was that Snowden, who thinks he has a right to be Chancellor of the Exchequer, is chicken-hearted and will try to cut down expenditure—he even

[1] Election result : Seaham ; Webb (Labour), 21,281; Ross (Unionist), 8,546. General; Conservative, 258; Labour, 191; Liberal, 158; Others, 8.

demurred to a programme of public works for the unemployed. Where was the money to come from? he asked, with a Treasury Clerk's intonation. "Far better to have Clynes as Chancellor of the Exchequer," said I to Sidney afterwards, with Pethick-Lawrence[1] as Financial Secretary and a good Cabinet Committee on the Budget. The leading propagandist Socialists like Snowden and even J.R.M. are Utopians who start back from every step towards their Utopia. If Sidney and I were not philosophers we should be disheartened. But what happens to the first Labour Cabinet? Acting merely as a stop-gap Government is not really of much importance. If they can get over their teething troubles before they have a majority in the House of Commons, J.R.M. may consider himself uncommonly fortunate. And these few weeks or months of office, if it comes off, is like a scouting expedition in the world of administration—a testing of men and measures before they are actually called to exercise majority power.

The meetings of the various Executives—Labour Party, Trades Union Congress, Parliamentary Labour Party—have all shown the most exemplary unity of front and atmosphere of mutual congratulations. "Mac has forty offices in his pocket and there are about forty people present," whispered the somewhat cynical Gillies to Sidney at the first meeting of the Labour Party Executive and General Council. But certainly I have noticed among the leading people very little of the office-seeking business: Henderson is amazingly disinterested—so appears Clynes—Snowden is the only one of them who has been busy making out his claim to the Exchequer; partly perhaps he feels himself increasingly isolated. It is possible that the great "Jimmy"[2] with the record of the £10,000 from the N.U.R. in the acute crisis of the empty coffers of Eccleston Square, confronted with a general election, has been bargaining for a big office—some say the Foreign Office—but there is no proof of this. Certainly at the little dinner here on Monday no one mentioned men and offices. Sidney himself seems absolutely unconcerned—regards being a Cabinet Minister as rather a joke—and says he would be immensely interested in almost any one of the offices. "Between ourselves," he said in a moment of self-confidence, "I think *I* could manage those Treasury officials better than any other of the Front Bench, but I neither desire nor expect J.R.M. to ask me to be Chancellor of the Exchequer: the best choice for them to make would be Clynes with a strong Cabinet Committee. But J.R.M. may feel that Snowden has a claim.". . . .

---

[1] Frederick William Pethick-Lawrence, Lord Pethick-Lawrence (b. 1871). Militant suffragist and Socialist. M.P. for West Leicester, 1923–31. Later Financial Secretary to the Treasury and the last Secretary of State for India.
[2] J. H. Thomas.

The reception, on the Wednesday after the poll, to the Half-Circle Club and "the victors and non-victors in the battle for Labour" was a great success and certainly justifies the starting of the Half-Circle Club three years ago. Our little house was crowded with over 200 chattering men and women—some 20 or 30 M.P.s; another 20 defeated candidates, all in a state of emotional strain and physical and mental fatigue, eager to congratulate and console. J.R.M., Henderson, Egerton Wake, Frank Hodges, Fred Bramley and their womenkind came—the two leaders, the Parliamentary agent, and Sidney making little speeches. It was a funny thought, this first gathering of the victorious Labour Party, at the house of Altiora and Oscar Bailey[1]—H. G. Wells ought to have been here to describe it! Funniest of all is the cordial relationship between J.R.M. and ourselves—all the more cordial because there is no pretence of personal intimacy or friendship. We have learnt not only to accept each other but to respect and value our respective qualities. J.R.M. is apparently not capable of personal intimacy: he never had "loves" among his colleagues. What has happened to him in the blaze of success is that he has lost his hatreds. All men and women are to him just circumstances —an attitude in a leader which I can readily understand and do not altogether disapprove! It is not unlikely that J.R.M. and Sidney will end in a sort of intimacy based on the common task of discovering the great measure of administrative and political efficiency. It will be interesting to watch the development of this relationship of mutual confidence and helpfulness without personal friendship.

January 3rd, 1924. *Passfield Corner.*—This time last year Sidney was on the threshold of his Parliamentary career; to-day he is on the threshold of the Cabinet! So far as I know, no member of the Labour Party, certainly not any Front Bench man, foresaw the possibility of a Labour Government arising out of the election. We all imagined that if the Conservatives were defeated, it would be by a narrow majority and that there would emerge a Conservative-Liberal or Liberal-Conservative Government. And I still think that would have been the logical result of the election and would in fact have best represented the opinions of the majority of the electorate. The British constitution, however, has a certain wisdom in it. From the standpoint of eventual stability the constitutional custom that His Majesty's Opposition is the only alternative to His Majesty's Government has the advantage that it gives to a young party, presumably representing a new movement of thought or emotion, a chance to go in and learn the business of government. Among wise Conservatives and Liberals, among the great mass of non-political but sensible citizens, there is a

---

[1] The names under which Wells satirised the Webbs in *The New Machiavelli*.

half-conscious opinion that there is virtue in giving the new team a chance of playing the game of government under conditions in which *they can be controlled* by the general will of the whole community. The team of course starts for some purposes heavily handicapped; it cannot play up to its own followers—it cannot indulge in reckless hitting—it may not even be able to play a sufficiently bold game to win any kind of approval. For Labour to accept the responsibilities of government is a big risk: it may lead to immediate disaster. But its leaders will become educated in the realities of *political* life and in the work of administration; and even their future behaviour as His Majesty's Opposition will become more responsible, more intelligently courteous and bold.

Meanwhile Sidney and I have had a peaceful Xmas in our dear little cottage, though, in his case, there has been considerable suppressed excitement owing to his immediate destiny. He has felt certain of Cabinet office—but which office? "It is disturbing not to know," he has said more than once: "I could be preparing myself for the particular job: there will be precious little time to do so if we are to do anything for our brief spell as heads of departments."

On New Year's Eve came a letter[1] from J.R.M. offering him the Ministry of Labour. "He has learnt the manner," says Sidney in a contemplative tone; "he tells me that it is the post of greatest difficulty! Anyway, it just suits me—it is an unpretentious office with a low salary and no social duties." And then he starts off to discuss the various departments of the work, and during the following hours we consider all the different moves that could be made. "You had better go up on Thursday and leave me to follow on Saturday," say I; and after a demur about leaving me alone he becomes eager to get to work. He is still in the humour of a schoolboy: last year it was before his first term at a public school: to-day it is looking forward to acting for the first time as "prefect". He is excited, naïvely excited, really enjoying his life hugely in a simple sort of way, but he has no kind of self-importance or self-consciousness, and very little anxiety or diffidence. "What a joke, what an unexpected and slightly ludicrous adventure," said he to me as we smoked the after-lunch cigarette, "for a man of sixty-four to become, first, a member of Parliament, and, within a year, a Cabinet Minister; and that with colleagues none of whom have held Cabinet office before; whilst only three of them have been in the Government—and these three do not include the Premier! If anyone had prophesied ten years ago that J.R.M. would be Prime Minister and would invite me to be in his Cabinet, I should have thought the first extraordinarily unlikely, but the two combined a sheer impossibility."

[1] See next page.

Very confidential.   *The Hillocks,*
                                                               Lossiemouth.

My dear Webb,

Would you take the Ministry of Labour and shoulder the unemployment difficulties? I suggest Miss Bondfield as your Parliamentary Secretary. It strikes me that you two would make a strong combination, and I have a Board of Trade head in my mind, and shall soon be in a position to sound him, with whom you could work with enthusiasm. If you consent, please say nothing to a living soul—not even to Miss Bondfield, whom I have not yet sounded. You might do that when the time comes, if you agree. *But* if you agree, go ahead with your plans. As little legislation as you can do with, please, though you will need some. Think over your staff and get everything ready to put into operation *at once*. If you care to see Sir Allan Smith and get a programme from him you can say that the interview has my approval. I leave this to your discretion. You might let me have reports from time to time, and let me have your first impressions without delay. I should in the ordinary way be inclined to offer you another office, but Labour and the Foreign Office are the two arduous and most important jobs we have to face. I pray of you to consent.

Yours very sincerely,
J. Ramsay MacDonald

During the first week down here before the arrival of J.R.M.'s letter I worked at my book and he copied out and slightly amended what I wrote. But for these four days I have been companionising him, discussing his plans for the Cabinet and for his own office, and settling with the architect and builder for the additions to the cottage. Also, though we came down to what we thought would be complete solitude, thirteen separate persons have come here to see us ("we should have had thirty in London," Sidney remarked), among them the Noel Buxtons (probable Minister for Agriculture), Arthur Ponsonby and Susan Lawrence, probable Under-Secretaries. As J.R.M. had expressly asked Sidney not to speak of his office it was impossible to ask either Ponsonby or Noel Buxton whether they had had any intimation from the coming Prime Minister—our impression from their respective manners being that Buxton had, and Ponsonby had not. It will be amusing to watch the secrecy breaking down between persons who believe that they are to be colleagues. How, for instance, can Sidney refrain from discussing it with Henderson? So far as Sidney's office is concerned, the President of the Board of Trade and the Minister of Health, and of course the Chancellor of the Exchequer, are the crucial colleagues on whose co-operation, initiative and commonsense his own success depends.

And what about my own life this coming year? We are agreed that it would be undesirable for me to take any active part in his administration. If I had been ten years younger I might have thrown my energies into helping him with his plans—more especially if there had seemed to be a long spell of administration in front of him. But I am no longer so energetic or so capable of mastering a new technique. A wife intervening would, in any case, upset official decorum, and there will probably not be time for the officials to get used to it. The most I can do for him is to undertake that part of his ordinary correspondence and interviewing, now likely to be increased, with strangers, acquaintances and friends, who want, for one reason or another, to see and talk to him. He will need protection from these intruders so as to save his time and energy for his Parliamentary work. He is far too long-suffering with these intruders. I shall pursue my intimacy with the women of Seaham; I shall take part in the social life of the Labour Party and be an active hostess to the Parliamentary Labour Party, to his departmental officials and others connected with the Ministry of Labour. But beyond that I shall not go. I intend to refuse all invitations to dinner—to keep out of London society and court functions, on the plea of age and delicate health. One might as well make the fullest use of the disability of "old age" in avoiding useless dissipation of time and energy. Also I want to give a lead against participation in London society, as a desirable part of the routine of a Cabinet Minister and his family. My lead will not be followed by those with social ambition, but it will strengthen those whose instinct is against it. For the rest, I shall go on, as steadily as I can, with my book—alas! poor book, you will not be finished this coming year—and I shall make our country home fit to retire to, if one or both of us breaks down.

This last year has not been ill-spent: one chapter of the book has been completed; another, a long one, is almost finished; and a good deal of the others thought out, in spite of all my preoccupation with Sidney's new career.

This volume of the diary began in February of last year; it gives a fairly detailed account of Sidney's first year in Parliament. The next volume will open with his first days as a Cabinet Minister. And there remains in the next four pages just enough space to describe the Party meetings next week before the debate on the Address decides the fate of the Labour Party. Meanwhile there is Sidney's account of affairs at Eccleston Square.

January 15th.—"The blank page between the old and the new Testament," Sidney calls this last week before the opening of Parliament to-day. To me it has been distracting—seeing one person after another mainly on the personnel of the Labour Party Government. This "inner circle" of possible Cabinet Ministers has been a monument of discretion and apparent disinterestedness—not a single word having been said at the various party meetings about men and offices. Whether other members of the inner circle know their own fate as Sidney does, it is impossible to find out seeing that they all pretend not to know, like S. does. When Sidney saw Henderson privately the other day the only office he, Henderson, knew for certain was Sidney's appointment to the Ministry of Labour. J.R.M. had offered Henderson the chairmanship of Committees—rather an insult as if Henderson were in the House[1] or could get into the House early enough to take up that post, he would have an undoubted claim to high Cabinet office. He was also doubtful whether such appointments as were likely to be made by J.R.M. were wise: "the Trade Unions were being too much ignored," he said. The only light on MacDonald's intentions have come characteristically through the two outsiders who are joining the Government—Haldane and Parmoor. On Saturday we dined with the former—one of those little confabs we have had now for over thirty years with this fellow conspirator. J.R.M. had consulted him about appointments and had persuaded him to become Lord Chancellor and Leader of the House of Lords. We talked to him freely about all the possible persons for all the possible posts; and he was to pass these suggestions on as his own to J.R.M. before MacDonald's dinner on Monday night at Haldane's house to the Front Bench of the Labour Party. We deprecated Snowden as Chancellor of the Exchequer—preferring Clynes; we pleaded for Frank Hodges as head of the transport department, owing to his general capacity and interest in electricity; we suggested that Henderson might be made Privy Seal which would free him from Eccleston Square—all of which Haldane wrote down. Then on Monday morning Parmoor came in to tell us that he had consented to be Lord President of the Council and act as J.R.M.'s Deputy on Foreign Affairs in the House of Lords. So there will be two "R.P." husbands in the Labour Government—the Tory and the Socialist! He did so, he said, because he had faith in J.R.M. and had worked with him through the war and since.

To end the tale: there was the secret dinner at Haldane's last night, to which Sidney and others had been invited by J.R.M. to discuss the King's speech and procedure. Sidney sat between Ben Spoor and Snowden. "I'm Labour," said Sidney, hoping that confidence would bring out confidence. "I have not the remotest notion what I am going to be," said Snowden in evident bewilderment. "Mac tells me not to expect to be more than 'Chief Whip,'" said Ben Spoor disconsolately.

[1] Henderson, always unlucky in general elections, had lost his seat at Newcastle; a vacancy was found for him at Burnley on the death of Dan Irving.

"Thomas is to be Colonies," said Henderson to Sidney, "and he is quite pleased with himself." As Sidney walked away with General Thomson they exchanged confidences: Thomson is to be Air Force and in the Lords. So there will be three peers at any rate in the Cabinet. There were 17 present at the dinner: J.R.M., Haldane, Parmoor, Henderson, Thomas, Clynes, Hastings, Spoor, Greenwood, Trevelyan, Buxton, Webb, General Thomson, Snowden, Adamson, Walsh, Wedgwood. J.R.M. was careful to explain that it was not a meeting of the future Cabinet, but only of the Front Bench to discuss the King's Speech. The dinner seems to have been a model of good humour, joint discussion and dignified self-restraint, "the best Cabinet meeting I have ever attended," said Haldane to Sidney, which was of course mere "preliminary compliments" on the part of our old diplomatist.

The main business which I have been doing has concerned the social life of the Labour Party. We started our weekly lunch last Wednesday—ten of the new members to meet J.R.M. and Henderson; to-morrow we have eleven new members to meet G.B.S. and Henderson. Last week we had a gathering of 700 Half-Circle Club and Parliamentary Labour Party at the University of London; on the following Friday there was a fancy dress dance which I did not attend. The women are delighted with the Half-Circle Club and the Press is beginning to say that "the Labour Party with its usual foresight has organised its own London society"! It is precious lucky we have done so, as it is clear we shall need all our sense of solidarity and puritanism to keep some of the frailer vessels upstanding against the onslaughts of duchesses and millionaires against their integrity. "Are Labour Privy Councillors to appear at court in uniform?" is one of the questions—"Are Cabinet Ministers' wives to attend evening courts?" is another. And then there is that mark of servility—the curtsey! It is all very ludicrous; though not altogether unimportant. Altering the form may easily transform the substance!

January 18th.—I add a few words to this MS. book to end the "making of the Cabinet" business. J.R.M. sent for Sidney on Thursday and Friday to consult him alike about his own post and also about others. Apparently some of the inner circle had objected to S. being relegated to so small a post as the Ministry of Labour, and J.R.M. said that he had not realised that the Ministry of Labour was so much the "Cinderella of the Government offices", and pressed S. to take the Board of Trade. Sidney replied that the lowly status of the Ministry of Labour did not concern him—he would prefer to remain there especially as Wedgwood, he understood, wanted the Board of Trade and would not be content with Labour. "If they were all as considerate as you have been," remarked J.R.M., "there would not be any difficulty in making a Cabinet." And then he explained how Lansbury had insisted on Cabinet rank which he, J.R.M., would not give him: how this man or that had held out for a superior office, and so on. And he said that he would consider it but that he wanted S. to be Chairman of the group of Ministers dealing with unemployment, and that would hardly be possible if he were head of the least important and most recently created department. Sidney left it in his hands, and they discussed other affairs. Sidney came away feeling that the Cabinet would err on the side of *respectability*—too many outsiders and too many peers. J.R.M. oddly enough does not like the plebeian element and chooses as his more intimate associates not the workman but the lawyer or big administrator, with the manner and attitude of the ruling and "thoroughly comfortable" class. If S. had had the making of the Cabinet it would have been far more working class and more to the "left" of the Labour Party. For instance, he would have taken Lansbury, and if possible Wheatley,[1] into the Cabinet, and would not have had so many peers, nor would he have asked Chelmsford[2] to come in—a good fellow but a timid Conservative. Henderson, we are glad to find, is to be Home Secretary—a post which is sufficiently impressive. Yesterday Bruce, the Prime Minister of Australia, an English public school and university man, just an upper middle class Englishman, came to lunch with us, to talk over the Economic Conference and Preferential Tariff; this morning Sanders arrived from Geneva to press the I.L.O. scheme on Sidney; then we lunched with the Parmoors—Marion in great state of excitement and very anxious to be introduced to the Half-Circle Club and make friends with her husband's colleagues' wives. Haldane arrived for a chat at six o'clock. To-night we have a big permanent official coming to dine with us to talk about unemployment and what can be done by this department. . . . . .

To return to the last days of Cabinet making. The "Inner Cabinet" —J.R.M., Clynes, Snowden, Thomas, Webb, Henderson, and Ben Spoor as Chief Whip—met this morning in J.R.M.'s room to hear final list of Cabinet and discuss Under-Secretaries. As S. expected, the Cabinet, which J.R.M. had decided to limit to 14, was now 20— various important persons having refused to take office, *unless in Cabinet*. S. is to take Board of Trade, on ground that he is to preside over unemployment: Tom Shaw is to be Labour: Wheatley, Minister of Health—both excellent appointments from Trade Union and Left

[1] John Wheatley (1869–1930). By origin a miner. M.P. for Shettleston, and Minister of Health in 1924 Government.

[2] Frederick John Napier Thesiger, Viscount Chelmsford (1868–1933). Member of London County Council; a Conservative who agreed to be First Lord of the Admiralty in the 1924 Government.

sections standpoints; Sidney is to have Alexander,[1] the Co-operator, a first-rate man, as Parliamentary Secretary. The T.C. accepted Haldane and Parmoor gladly, demurred slightly to Chelmsford, welcomed Olivier and Thomson and new peers; Sydney Arnold is to be added as an Under-Secretary in the Lords; other Under-Secretaries are more from I.L.P. section—Arthur Greenwood is out of the Cabinet but is Under-Secretary for Trevelyan in Board of Education. "Much better balanced than I feared," reported Sidney. He is still in high spirits, thoroughly looking forward to presenting himself at the Board of Trade on Friday, and he is chuckling over his prospective encounter with the redoubtable Llewellyn Smith, marooned by Lloyd George as Economic Adviser to the Board of Trade.

"And what do *you* feel about the change in *your* life?" asked Kate, somewhat perturbed at my detached and unexcited attitude. "Personally, I prefer a quiet student's life, but of course I am glad for Sidney's sake," I replied. "I believe you long to settle down to write at Passfield," she remonstrated. "Well, yes; personally, I should prefer it—but Sidney as Cabinet Minister is one job like another—I shall chime in with it," I concluded.

Here ends the Old Testament.

[1] Albert Victor Alexander, now Lord Alexander (b. 1885).

INDEX

INDEX